Border Country

Raymond Williams in Adult Education

Edited by
John McIlroy
(University of Manchester)
and Sallie Westwood
(University of Leicester)

National Institute of Adult Continuing Education

First published 1993 by the National Institute of Adult Continuing Education
(England and Wales), 19B De Montfort Street, Leicester LE1 7GE

British Library Cataloguing in Publication Data
A CIP record for this book is available from the British Library

ISBN 1 872941 28 1

Cover design Prestige Filmsetters, Leicester
Cover photograph The Hulton Deutsch Collection
Typeset in Sabon by The Midlands Book Typesetting Co., Loughborough
Printed and bound in Great Britain by The Cromwell Press, Melksham, Wilts

Contents

Acknowledgements

The publishers are grateful to the following for permission to reproduce copyright material as follows:

Essays in Criticism for 'The idea of culture'; 'The new party line?'; 'Fiction and the writing public'.
McGibbon and Kee, an imprint of HarperCollins Publishers Limited for 'Culture is ordinary'.
Blackwell Publishers for 'Our debt to Dr. Leavis'.
New Left Review for 'Working class attitudes'.
Partisan Review for 'The new British left'.
Frederick Muller for extracts from *Reading and Criticism.*
The English Association for 'Books for teaching culture and environment'.
New Statesman and Society for 'Going on learning' and 'Sensible people'.
Tribune Publications Ltd for 'Voices of Socialism: R. H. Tawney'.
Verso/NLB, London and New York for extracts from Raymond Williams, *Politics and Letters: Interviews with New Left Review.*

Extracts from *Rewley House Papers* are reproduced with the permission of the Workers' Educational Association and the University of Oxford Department for Continuing Education.
　We are also grateful to the Workers' Educational Association for permission to reproduce extracts from *The Highway*, Williams's Open Letter to WEA Tutors and the extract from *Adult Education and Social Change.*

We are indebted to the late Joy Williams and the estate of Raymond Williams for supporting this project.

If there are any copyright holders who have not been credited, we will be happy to rectify such omissions.

Acknowledgements

The publisher is grateful to the following for permission to reproduce copyright material as follows:

Introduction

Raymond Williams was a towering figure within left culture and beyond it. He was revered, celebrated and debated in Britain and across the world for the contribution he made to the generation and sustenance of socialist thought and to the cause of innovative scholarship in literature, cultural studies, politics and sociology. Despite this, his work in adult education, the forcing house of his interdisciplinary approach, has received scant attention from the left, from academic interrogators of his achievement and, surprisingly, from within adult education itself. We can only speculate on the reasons for this. Perhaps for the left neglect was conditioned by the fact that his adult education work pre-dated his renewed activism in the sixties and his second and major encounter with Marxism. Within adult education it is possible that relative silence has stemmed from the fact that his world-wide reputation burgeoned later and was perceived as based upon his renewed radicalism. Whatever the reasons we take issue with these silences. They deny a specific and, we would argue, an important part of the personal and intellectual biography of Raymond Williams. This collection is our attempt to draw attention to Williams's life and his preoccupations in the immediate post-war period and to place on record his early writings.

Much of Raymond Williams's early work has long been inaccessible. The articles written during his years in adult education were scattered in small journals, sometimes long defunct, buried in the reserve stack or available to the student only through inter-library loans. More extended essays such as *Reading and Criticism* remain much-cited but out of print. This volume gathers together for the first time most of Williams's short pieces, the majority of them out of print for 20 years, together with extracts from longer work. Our hope is that a new generation may discover at first hand the quality of Williams's writing in this period and its relationship to the development of his classic texts *Culture and Society* and *The Long Revolution*.

The book opens with a brief account of Williams's involvement in teaching adults, his intellectual influences in the forties and fifties and the relationship of his educational and intellectual life to his personal experience and political concerns. This is a precursor to an extensive selection of Williams's published work. The second section of the book documents in some detail his pressing intellectual concerns during these years. We reproduce a range of writing from pieces in the shortlived journals *Politics and Letters* and *The Critic*, through early essays on the theme of culture and society to Williams's first engagement with other students of cultural change, his review of *The Uses of Literacy*, an extended conversation with Richard Hoggart and a contemporary evaluation of

1

the New Left. The third section, Teaching and Learning, demonstrates just how seriously Williams took his work as a teacher. It illustrates the changing curriculum and methods of literature teaching in university adult education and illuminates in fascinating articles on teaching culture and environment, public expression and film criticism, the beginnings of today's well-established 'cultural studies'.

We return in the next section, Adult Education, to a series of essays in which Williams addresses his own environment and analyses contemporary controversies and concerns in adult education. This section also includes later reflections by Williams on the philosophy and purpose of adult education. The last part of the book, Retrospect and Prospect, contains a long essay seeking to situate and integrate Williams's intellectual production of this period in his role as a tutor in adult education. Adopting Williams's approach of these years we place it after his own texts, which first speak for themselves. This essay provides important detail on the landscape in which he worked, essential to his development. Finally having looked back we look forward, using a discussion of Williams's later book *Towards 2000* as a timely and appropriate conclusion to this collection.

John McIlroy would like to thank all those who assisted him in his attempts to reconstruct post-war university adult education and Raymond Williams's role in it, particularly: Simon Bailey, Andy Croft, Pat Hurst, Barbara Littler, Stephanie Jackson, Keith Sagar, Bruce Spencer, Derek Tatton, Richard Taylor, Geoffrey Thomas, and the late Joy Williams; the Universities Funding Council, which provided a grant which funded some of this research; and all those involved in adult education after the war who took the time to answer queries by interview and correspondence: Fred Bayliss, Ron Bellamy, Eric Bellchambers, Lalage Bown, Cecil Davies, Lionel Elvin, Jim Fyrth, Constance Grover, Douglas Hewitt, Bridget Hill, Richard Hoggart, John Levitt, Alethea Lyall, Wolf Mankowitz, Arthur Marsh, Lionel Munby, Michael Orrom, Patrick Roberts, Cecil Scrimgeour, Sir Roy Shaw, Geoffrey Stuttard, Graham Taylor, Gerry Bowen Thomas, Edward Thompson, Mary Visick, the late Charles Wenden and Jack Woolford.

Sallie Westwood owes special thanks to Ali Rattansi, Bill Forster, John Cunningham and members of the University of Leicester Adult Education Department for their unerring support and generosity.

Both of us remain indebted to Alan O'Connor's pioneering bibliography in his *Raymond Williams: Writing, culture, politics*, Blackwell, 1989. Our particular gratitude goes to Christopher Feeney, who has been involved with this book from start to finish and whose passionate advocacy of adult education is bearing fruit in the increasingly impressive publications list of the National Institute of Adult Continuing Education. Without the support and hard work of Christopher and his indefatigable Editorial Assistant Susan Flude this book would not have been possible.

JOHN McILROY
SALLIE WESTWOOD
November 1992

Section 1:
The Unknown Raymond Williams

John McIlroy

Another addition to the proliferating collections of writing by Raymond Williams might seem to require some justification. The response is simple. The flood of literature published since his untimely death on 26 January 1988 has had very little to say about Williams's life and work during the immediate post-war years when he was a tutor in adult education. Yet in important ways these years were the making of Raymond Williams as a socialist intellectual whose influence stretched far beyond his political allegiance to the left.

For many of the hundreds of students Williams taught, women and men whose further education was snatched in the hours free from work, the experience stayed with them for life. That in itself is important. Williams's mature achievement commenced with the publication in 1958 of *Culture and Society*. We should not underestimate the work of 1958–61 – or what went before. I find a tendency amongst some who admire the later Williams to downgrade the earlier work as a series of incidents, even detours, along the path towards *Marxism and Literature* and beyond. Reading backwards was advocated at times by Williams; it is not the best way to understand him.

Few now consult *Reading and Criticism* or *Drama in Performance*. Yet they are very much part of his work, to be considered in themselves as well as contributions to its ultimate formation. The same goes for many of Williams's shorter pieces from this period. Any other emphasis is ahistorical and runs the risk of failing to understand the detailed, concrete unfolding of Williams's work in its actuality and the scope of his overall achievement by inadequately allowing the autonomy and importance of the past. Williams began writing *Culture and Society* around 1950 and pondering its ideas long before that. Together with *The Long Revolution* it represented the culmination of his early intellectual struggles and like them was strongly influenced by his role between 1946 and 1961 as a Staff Tutor for the Oxford Delegacy for Extra-Mural Studies, organising and teaching classes in collaboration with the Workers' Educational Association.

It seems vital that we should examine Raymond Williams not as an isolated individual but as part of the world in which he worked. Recreating Williams means recreating post-war adult education. The first point I want to make is how important adult education was to Williams's work and to

3

the important current of social thinking in the late fifties and early sixties
to which that work was central. As early as 1950 in his first important
work he noted:

> The method and order of the book are based in part on experience
> in tutorial and other adult classes. For the opportunity to experiment
> in this work I am grateful to the Oxford University Tutorial Classes
> Committee.[1]

Two years later, in his second book, he again paid graceful tribute
to the influence of his colleagues and students. In 1954 the dustjacket of
Drama in Performance hoped that it would:

> be found particularly useful by students and tutors of the extra-
> mural departments of the universities, of the local authorities' further
> education schemes, of such voluntary bodies as the Workers' Educa-
> tional Association and Adult Education Centres and in technical
> colleges.[2]

Similar statements are scattered through many of the books he wrote.
All the 10 people Williams thanks in the Foreword to *Culture and Society*
had been involved in adult education; it was the full-time occupation of
five of them. Yet in most accounts of his work the role of adult education
is only briefly mentioned. One version even goes so far as to suggest 'The
Uses of Literacy and Culture and Society were both produced by critics
working in university English Departments'.[3] This at least gets to the heart
of the matter. *Had* Richard Hoggart and Raymond Williams been working
in most English departments they may well have been simply literary critics.
They would as junior lecturers have been teaching subjects designated by
others. Even later their curriculum would have been subject to the policy
of departments in which theirs would probably have been minority voices.
They would, as many contemporaries with experience of adult education
and internal teaching attest, have lacked a great deal of the autonomy and
freedom to range widely across disciplines, benefiting from the impetus to
innovative thinking such travel can stimulate.

When I made this point in an earlier paper one distinguished teacher
of literature wrote:

> I don't think you make quite enough of the advantages to Williams of
> being in adult education. 1: The freedom to choose one's own syllabus
> and gear this to whatever one happens to be researching or writing on.
> 2: The opportunity to study literary texts and topics at much greater
> depth than the pressures of time and crowded survey syllabuses in
> English departments allowed for. 3: The opportunity to teach beyond
> the usual frontiers of English, not only into cultural studies but into,
> for example, European and American drama.[4]

We must not forget about the students in this. Although their freedom to choose or at least influence the subjects of study was on the wane, it was still a factor. And of course it would be wrong to conceive of tutorial classes as operating at too elevated or intensive a level. Williams found many of them were fertile and productive: 'The general level of discussion remains high . . . reading is sustained, able, written work is improving'.[5] In considering another year's work in Bexhill he felt satisfaction with 'a marked increase in capacity and assurance in the students' reading of literature. This has been reflected in the improving quality of discussion'.[6] But sometimes: 'the class has not yet succeeded in finding a common educational level – some members are very good students, others attend for entertainment'.[7] The experience was variable. The going was sometimes good, sometimes heavy. But almost always it was possible to learn – from the difficult classes as well as the good.

One small example of how the interaction between student and tutor could relate to the genesis or reinforcement of Williams's thinking relates to his famous dictum: 'Masses are other people . . . There are in fact no masses, only ways of seeing people as masses'. In 1953 a student in one of his classes wrote an essay on *The Secret Agent*. She described a scene whilst waiting for her husband at Brighton station: '. . . a train came in and disgorged, yes disgorged, like some giant whale with a distaste for fish that day – masses of men on the way to football . . . Not one of them looked "handsome, good and clever". . . the overall colour of their dirty, dingy mass was depressing and dead'. The essay goes on to relate these feelings to disassociation from awareness of individual humanity and the ability to kill men in the mass in wartime. In a characteristically restrained written comment Williams observed that 'the "man in the street" (I don't only mean "the average" but any man there) is always less than himself – the man back home is more real'. In conversation with the student, however, he pointed out that he himself had arrived on a train during that period; he himself, an individual known and respected by the student, had been disgorged dirty and dead along with the rest. This suggested to both of them the distortion of vision and humanity such formulaic seeing entails and the utility, in breaking this sterile, routine thinking, of applying the formula to include oneself. These ideas were then developed by Williams in his review of Colin Wilson's *The Outsider* and later at length in the 'Conclusion' to *Culture and Society* and, of course, in *Keywords*.[8]

As an internal lecturer Williams would not usually have been confronted with the same necessity for activity and dialogue in the classroom. Or confronted daily with the valuable collision between the urgently articulated needs and experience of part-time adult students from all walks of life, voluntarily sacrificing their own time for education, and the concerns of a developing intellectual. The results of solitary interrogation sometimes had to be quickly tested in practice. Williams had to wrestle with his ideas and wrestle on their behalf with students whose learning from life was often greater than their formal education. It was important for a thinker who placed such importance on experience.

In the classroom he was usually a close listener, courteous and re-strained, suggestive, reflective, undogmatic: 'The objection as a matter of fact is not to telling anyone anything. It is a question of how one tells them, and how one would expect to be told oneself'. Williams saw teaching as the guiding of discovery; if possible, collective discovery. His later writings are freighted with the lessons he learned in the classroom. Pedagogy was organic to philosophy. The failures of communication that he acknowledged in his own early teaching and in other areas of education he came to see as characteristic of industrial society itself. It was far from an accident:

> *The failure is due to an arrogant preoccupation with transmission which rests on the assumption that the common answers have been found and need only to be applied. But people will (damn them do you say?) learn only by experience and this normally is uneven and slow.*[9]

Active reception, the living response which real communication elicited, in adult education as in life, depended on creating 'a community of experience' and human and intellectual equality. It was this aim Williams set himself. In this context the students, it must be remembered, were often far from the proletarian cadres some fondly imagine and whom Williams originally wanted to teach. Williams was not preaching to the converted; he had to argue through fundamentals. Indeed the link between his teaching and his published work is demonstrated by the way his books influenced many of those whose concerns were not bounded by academic discourse or a shared left culture. Perhaps centrally for the making of Williams:

> *It is probably easier to grasp and sustain the notion of culture as a collective social activity and as a material process of production, in the context of a continual engagement with thinking and learning adult students than in any other space of the educational system.*[10]

Williams's position on the edge of, but not in the academy, employed to spend his time, rather, taking it into the world, is important for an understanding of how his work was made and what it means for us. It has been suggested that the absence of this dynamic after his move to Cambridge in 1961 contributed to a change of focus in his concerns and the growing complexity of his writing.[11]

Certainly Williams himself always emphasised the importance of the work we are paid to do to our development. He conceived of work as 'a crucial experience', a central means of 'getting in touch with ourselves and with others in new ways'.[12] Unlike many university teachers, he did not distinguish between 'work' and 'work'. For Williams teaching, researching, writing and actively contributing to social change through political initiatives was all of one piece. And he often remarked how important the adult education threads were to the seamless robe of his working life.

Intellectual Influences

The second point I want to emphasise is that Williams creatively utilised adult education; but he was not confined by it or within it. It would be simplistic and one-sided to argue that his writing sprang simply and directly from his teaching. A range of intellectual resources was available to him. In one sense Terry Eagleton is right to evoke his isolation and the individualism of Williams's early achievement: 'What he did then, he did almost single-handedly, working from his personal resources without significant collaboration or institutional support'.[13] His colleagues in the Oxford Delegacy were scattered across the country. He encountered the majority on only a handful of occasions each year, usually working closely with three or four. But in addition to the stimulus his teaching provided in testing ideas and provoking response Williams was also in contact with a galaxy of gifted thinkers in and beyond adult education which often provided a meeting place. The extent of the fertilisation which flows from formal and informal, extended and casual encounters, is always difficult to gauge. But as Williams put it in 1954: 'No writer is ever alone; and no man can ever trace the sources of all that he has taken into his own substance'.[14] He himself considered he had incurred a variety of debts. In this sense his isolation was limited, although in the end it was Williams, nobody else, who did the thinking and the writing.

It is usual – partly because of his centrality and power, partly as shorthand – to point to Leavis as the prime intellectual ancestor.[15] But Williams, writing in 1948, cited as well as Leavis, Eliot,[16] Middleton Murry,[17] Richards,[18] Empson[19] and Knights.[20] In terms of direct comment on his work he was particularly grateful to Denys Thompson.[21] The strength of the *Scrutiny* tradition and its influence on Williams cannot be overstated. He was, moreover, in the late 1940s, apprentice to an adult education already marked by Leavis and Thompson as a key site and already colonised by tutors who paid broad tribute to Cambridge – although from that viewpoint a lot still remained to be done. Thompson's *Reading and Discrimination* (1934), for example, had already gone through seven impressions by 1951 and was revised in 1954. Like *Culture and Environment*, which was specifically aimed at WEA classes, it was influential on a whole generation of adult education tutors.[22]

Reading and Criticism was far from a bolt from the blue. Contemporary with the early work of Leavis and Thompson, the use of close reading and criticism in enriching and empowering the individual and providing him or her with the tools to control their environment and re-establish an organic community had been advocated in adult education by E.G. Biaggini. His work was based on his teaching with the Australian WEA and the University of Adelaide and had received the imprimatur of Leavis himself. Biaggini's handbook *The Reading and Writing of English*, published in 1935, sold widely, was influential in Britain and was made available in a revised edition in 1946. A further volume of exercises in reading was, like its predecessor, enthusiastically reviewed in *Scrutiny*. The reviewer felt it would be 'especially welcomed in WEA classes'. When Williams began teaching adults many tutors were already using the practical criticism approach which Williams embraced with such enthusiasm.[23] And Williams had a personal link with earlier attempts to introduce the new approach into the adult classroom through his discussions with Edmund Poole, who worked at the WEA Head Office.[24]

Clifford Collins and Wolf Mankowitz, Williams's fellow editors of *Politics and Letters,* provided a direct link with *Scrutiny*. Both had been recently taught by Leavis, Mankowitz was a contributor. Both were involved in adult education and discussions with them affected his thinking. Over a long period Williams particularly singled out the influence on his thinking of Collins, with whom he taught classes and who regularly stayed over at his house.[25]

However, his intellectual world was not bounded by 'literary studies'. Attempts to work at the frontiers between Leavis and Marxism were far from novel. Francis Mulhern has suggested a genealogy for attempts to integrate *Scrutiny*'s investment of literary studies with a social warrant into socialist politics, running from A.L. Morton, in the early thirties, through Williams and Hoggart to the Centre for Contemporary Cultural Studies.[26] Williams was linked into a broad, left, literary culture in which Douglas Garman, poet, critic, publisher and in the forties Education Officer of the Communist Party, a friend of Thomas Hodgkin, Secretary at the Oxford Delegacy, had himself contributed to *Scrutiny* before the war and 'surrendered to the Marxist conclusion', together with his fellow poet and critic Edgell Rickword, whose work Williams used in his classes. Williams later looked back with admiration at the work of *Left Review*, which was published by the Communist Party as a Popular Front journal between 1934 and 1938, a project to which Rickword, Garman and Hodgkin were all deeply committed. Williams was impressed by *Left Review*'s attempt to build a more democratic culture. It was, he observed, 'a necessary landmark of a brave, urgent and humane struggle', but also, he felt, 'at the same time of a substantial confusion and failure'.[27] In the immediate aftermath of this failure, the forties were, as Williams often remarked, the last time that the study of literature was to play such a central role in intellectual life in England. In his work and on its frontiers he was able to take advantage of a political, historical, literary tradition – declining, though not foredoomed then, perhaps a hangover from the thirties, certainly a casualty of 'affluence' – through intersecting networks of intellectual acquaintances and occasional collaborators.

In view of its chronic inferiority complex and the view of many that university adult education was second-rate, the calibre of many of the colleagues who had an impact on Williams is worth noting. In Oxford Hodgkin, even to his political antagonists 'an intellectual of the first rank, by today's standards, a bit of a polymath', immediately incarnated the Marxist influence. From a famous academic, Quaker family Hodgkin was converted to Communism by his experiences as a civil servant in pre-war Palestine. After leaving the Delegacy in the wake of the controversy about Communist activities he became a distinguished African scholar. He was heavily involved in the Algerian war – and continued to teach philosophy in adult classes when available. Hodgkin took a very keen interest in literature and its role in adult education. In the thirties he had reviewed novels for *Left Review*, which its most effective editor Rickword saw as aimed at adult education and which was widely read within it. In the late forties and early fifties he discussed Williams's work with him, insisted on its importance and sought to find him a publisher in the difficulties he had over what was to become *Culture and Society*.[28]

Williams also benefited from discussion with H.P. Smith, a veteran of the adult education movement. As organising secretary of the Tutorial Classes Committee, Smith's responsibilities were essentially administrative but he also wrote on economics and adult education. He was interested in the development of popular culture, the history of workers' reading habits and the problems of teaching literature in adult classes. Williams appreciated his help with both *Culture and Society* and *The Long Revolution*. Smith in his turn acknowledged Williams's help with his own writing.[29]

There were several teachers within the university with whom Williams established fertile relationships.[30] Humphrey House, 'a splendid, Rabelaisian character', was a Fellow of Wadham College, a distinguished Dickens scholar and a regular broadcaster. Williams organised a number of interdisciplinary conferences on the teaching of history and literature in which House and Asa Briggs played leading roles.[31] F.W. [Freddy] Bateson, university lecturer in English and a Fellow of Corpus Christi College between 1946 and 1961, helped Williams with his books and as founder and editor of *Essays in Criticism*. Doubling as agricultural correspondent of the *New Statesman* and an active socialist, Bateson epitomised the rebellion against received, imposed, categories that stamped Williams. He was 'one of the born heretics, the dissidents, the enemies of all establishments' and '. . . a man to whom the standard academic opener, "What is your field?" would have made little sense'.[32]

In Sussex, where Williams did most of his teaching, his close friend Tony McLean was moving from teaching politics to developing his interest in art history. McLean, who had fought in Spain, remained in the Communist Party until the late forties. He was singled out by Williams for the help he gave him in developing the concerns that informed his work then and later.[33] The literature tutors with whom he worked at various times were not amongst his closest intimates, but fellow tutors such as Patrick Roberts, Douglas Hewitt, Graham Taylor and John Levitt were men of intellectual substance and broad interests, whose insights were valuable. Williams also discussed his writing with and received assistance from part-time tutors, notably the voluble A.K. Hudson.[34] He was also involved in helping the well-known adult education enthusiast, Marxist philosopher and Buddhist scholar Eberhardt (Edward) Conze in the difficulties he experienced with the Delegacy.[35]

Williams acknowledged his debt to the WEA District Secretary Eric Bellchambers, an Oxford literature graduate who was himself a product of the tutorial classes, awarded a Delegacy scholarship in 1939. 'Shunted into administration', he kept up his scholarly interests and 'taught as well as wrought'.[36] Another colleague, Jack Woolford – who like Bellchambers was far from being a Marxist – was briefly a prolific contributor to *Scrutiny*.[37] Michael Carritt, appointed in 1949 to organise classes for trade unionists in Brighton, was another CP member and former full-timer who had spied for the Indian Communist Party whilst a civil servant in India. Williams collaborated with him on classes which dealt with both philosophy and literature and felt that the experience had informed his work in *The Long Revolution*.[38] Another party member whose comments on his work Williams appreciated was Henry Collins, a historian with whom he kept in touch whilst Collins worked for the Delegacy in Staffordshire; they enjoyed closer contact when the latter moved to work with Williams in Sussex in the late fifties.[39]

Through such contacts Williams was open to wider influences. In July 1954 he attended, together with other outsiders such as the Africanist Basil Davidson, a week-long school organised by the Communist Party Historians group at Netherwood House, Hastings.[40] A member of the group particularly influential on Williams was the economist and historian F.W. Klingender, whose work on agriculture, white collar workers and the commercial organisation of the film industry was well known. A Party member since the early thirties and a regular contributor to *Left Review*, his most influential work, developed outside the structures of the university, was in art history, notably the seminal text *Art and the Industrial Revolution*. In this period the German-born Klingender was a lecturer in sociology at Hull, and Williams knew him through his work with WEA classes.[41] By the late fifties Williams was on the editorial board of *New Left Review* and was benefiting, through the New Left, from the committed writing of an emerging group of socialist intellectuals, from the anthropologist Peter Worsley and the economist Michael Barratt Brown to the philosophers Alasdair McIntyre and Charles Taylor. He particularly acknowledged the influence of Edward Thompson, who worked in adult education slightly longer than Williams – in the Leeds Extra-Mural Department from 1947–65 – and Stuart Hall, who also taught at weekends with Williams.[42] And in, as it were, another sector of his intellectual endeavour, Williams enjoyed until the mid-fifties close collaboration with Michael Orrom: 'Raymond and I were working closely together in another field altogether, trying to analyse the technique of film and drama to lead to creative production'.[43] This work produced *Preface to Film* and the script for the expressionist film *Legend* (1956), which they hoped would bring alive the ideas outlined in the book.

Williams was always ready to draw, energetically and imaginatively, upon wider work and upon experts outside his immediate circle. While he was writing *Drama From Ibsen to Eliot*, in 1947–48, he extensively used the work of the scholar of ancient Greek drama Sir Arthur Pickard-Cambridge, whom he was to meet later in a very different capacity as the chair of the London Tribunal of Conscientious Objectors which heard his refusal to serve in the Korean War. He acknowledged the assistance of Dorothea Krook, a Cambridge academic with a deep knowledge of the historical development of tragedy and a specialist on the work of Henry James.[44] Another help-mate who commented on his writing was Bertram Joseph, whose work on the Elizabethan theatre was to attract attention in the 1950s. Joseph, a lecturer at Bristol University, was a friend of the actor and producer Bernard Miles, who used many of Joseph's suggestions in his productions at the Mermaid.[45] Williams corresponded with Miles about his account of contemporary acting in his manuscript, as he did with Nevil Coghill, a don who produced work on the commercial stage in this period.[46] The book's attempt to relate text to production, melding analysis of language with analysis of performance, was helped by discussion, particularly for the chapter on Eliot, with E. Martin Browne. The latter had himself been involved in adult education and worked with Eliot from 1933 to 1958, directing the first productions of all his plays during that period, as well as several by Christopher Fry. Williams watched Browne's productions, discussed them with him and comments on them in the book.[47] Williams talked to a variety of actors. Colleagues who taught with him were also pressed into service. One recalls in relation to *Drama in Performance*:

> *I was going to Greece at that time on a holiday and I was deputed to take photographs of the Greek theatres, all the Greek theatres I visited. Not the general photographs you usually get of the seats which were of course of no great interest to Raymond but the photographs were of the connection between the orchestra, the circle of the orchestra and the actual stage. Because his argument, if you remember in that book, was that in the early theatres the orchestra is completely round and the dancing is therefore of great importance and the chorus of great importance. And the protagonists, the actors, were of less importance up on the stage and as time went on the stage became more and more important and began to obtrude on the orchestra which gets smaller and smaller.*[48]

In work on the drama which he characterised, in contrast with his other work developed 'outside the university', as a continuation of an academic project begun at Cambridge, Williams still rigorously drew on both scholarship and experience.[49]

Last, but not least, there was his wife Joy, with whom he shared all his ideas and who, in at least one case, 'argued the manuscript with me line by line to an extent which, in certain chapters makes her virtually the joint author'.[50] And the security his family gave him:

> *You must always put into the centre I'm sure of Raymond's life his marriage. His absolutely amazing glorious marriage. Now I know that you cannot tell very much about a marriage from the outside in any way – it is like E.M. Forster used to say 'It is behind a plate glass*

window'. But his devotion to Joy and her's to him and his family life
was quite, quite clearly central to him all his life. They were as in love
by the end as they were in the beginning.[51]

We can, therefore, whilst granting the importance of his lonely
professional regime, make too much of his intellectual isolation. If this is
taken to suggest the non-availability to Williams of work that later excited
him, the later Lukacs, Goldmann, this was a general condition for British
intellectuals and we can have no idea of its impact on Williams had he read
it earlier. If his isolation is understood as relating to his non-membership of
the Communist Party then all we know about Williams suggests that this
was a wholly healthy thing. It is difficult to see how he could by 1956
have worked through the problems he did as a follower, no matter how
disenchanted, of Stalinism. It was a time when Fadayev was still lecturing
communist intellectuals: 'if hyenas could use fountain pens and jackals
typewriters, they would write like T.S. Eliot'; and when debates inside
the British Party on matters of literary criticism and cultural theory were
carefully orchestrated by the leadership.[52]

He was intellectually distanced from the Party but he was, it appears,
in touch with its thinking. He recalls meeting 'often' with Communist Party
members in Hastings to drink and discuss. He states he took *The Daily
Worker* during this entire period, except for a break between 1948 and
1952. He tells us that he 'followed very carefully in the later forties and
early fifties' the argument about Caudwell which was conducted in *The
Modern Quarterly*, and we can see the evidence in *Culture and Society*.[53]

His engagement with the intellectual mainstream was, surely, more
fecund than the dangers of marginality Communist Party membership
would have entailed. Williams was by 1949 well known enough to be
broadcasting on the BBC and writing in *The Listener*.[54] He was in contact
with and in dialogue with leading scholars, and in the first dozen post-
war years was editor of three important journals. He later recalled the
intellectual value of this in relation to *Essays in Criticism* and its socialist
editor:

> *The corrections he offered me I could not deny ... his literary*
> *scholarship was continually finding me out in ignorance. Bateson,*
> *even more than Tillyard had done, used to say to me 'you simply*
> *are wrong, you have misunderstood this, you have not read that, you*
> *have used these technical terms inaccurately'. I think this is a very*
> *difficult moment for anybody trying to develop a new intellectual*
> *project, because you have to be able professionally to take on people*
> *who have a different perspective ... I felt at the time that association*
> *with a professional organ was necessary for me and that I had to be*
> *able to produce work that was valid in its terms.*[55]

Williams had an inheritance which he chose himself. In investing in
it he certainly lacked the daily interaction a more conventional academic
existence might have offered. What is remarkable is the extent to which

his range of contacts intersected with, though remaining outside the formal structures of the academy. But he was not alone. A variety of influences operated on his thinking through overlapping circuits of adventurous, iconoclastic, generally left-leaning intellectuals, working in a range of fields. How the alchemy of intellectual exchange and development ignites is elusive. But Williams himself paid tribute to the different influences on his work and it can be discerned in his writing. His books benefited. They were made, however, by Williams working long solitary hours at a last which was distinctively his own.

Adult Education and the Working Class

In all this, adult education was the ballast. Williams's interest and induction began early. The first tutor to teach the 18-year-old Williams in the Cambridge of 1939 was Lionel Elvin, the son and brother of trade union leaders, who took a keen interest in the WEA and who in 1944 became Principal of Ruskin College.[56] Williams was still an undergraduate when his first WEA class was arranged and he proved to be what old WEA hands termed 'a natural', especially 'interesting all his students and gaining their confidence and affection'.[57] His first mentor, Bill Baker, was for more than a decade a fellow social historian of E.P. Thompson's in the Extra-Mural Department of the University of Leeds.[58] The following year saw Williams, still barely 25 but with the forced maturity that came from the experience of four years of war and two years as an officer in the Guards Armoured Division (and with the experience of both the fighting in Normandy and organising army education classes), launched on a full-time career in adult education, following the path blazed by contributors to *Scrutiny* in the 1930s.

Williams wanted to bring literature and drama into closer relationship with everyday life. He was imbued with the concerns of Leavis, with the conception of the central importance of the critic and the power of practical criticism to cultivate responsiveness and discrimination. He talked the language of Cambridge and soon too did his students. He put before them the theory of culture which saw a rich, rural organic community disrupted by machine civilisation and high culture alienated from the masses. But as a socialist he pursued in his classes on 'Culture and Environment' other analyses of the ills of mid-century society, particularly Marxist analyses. He was uneasy about the ideas of a golden age, a great fall, a cultural decline. It was growing dissatisfaction with this which prompted him to start thinking about the history of cultural response, to examine in more detail how important social thinkers had responded to the industrial revolution, and begin 'the almost constant redefinition and reformulation'[59] which provided *Culture and Society*.

But he was also very unhappy with the lack of any clear social response from the *Scrutiny* school in terms of understanding the necessity for a radically different kind of society to nurture true community or appreciating the need for political action to achieve it. Fundamentally he was dissatisfied with the view that only the 'chosen', the worthy minority, were capable of the fully articulated response and that the preservation of the human inheritance fell to this educated and class-related élite. Williams came from a strongly socialist family. His father was a Labour Party branch secretary and active in his union. All of his early experience in Wales had nurtured a deep, abiding faith in democracy and the human potential to communicate, control and create; this had been strengthened by his experience at Cambridge and in the army. Williams believed in the majority. He wanted to write novels and pursue these problems. He felt a political class allegiance but did not wish to formally enter politics. The expanding field of adult education, which was attracting so many of his generation and inclination, was bound to fall for consideration as the next stage in his future.

The factors which led Williams into adult education ran back far further than his literary-political concerns in 1945 or even his immensely valuable, if brief, encounter with the structure of feeling of the 1930s in his first period at Cambridge. The third point I want to make centres on Williams's lifelong commitment to the working class, its values and its institutions, its collective democracy, its solidarity, its potential for making a better society. For Williams, involvement in adult education was first and foremost about the working class, his own relationship with the class he came from and the collective emancipation of that class. Both directly, in terms of how adult education could help provide workers with emancipatory knowledge for the extension of working-class democracy and the best of working-class culture and, indirectly, by providing a site for his own work which would, he believed, ultimately serve the interests of those workers. The complex interrelations between education and class were to haunt his work for the rest of his life.

Despite his extraordinary self-confidence and the evidence that he had negotiated the path of the scholarship boy with minimal loss, he was Jim in Pandy and Raymond in his new life in Cambridge, Oxford and Sussex.[60] Despite the surety of his identification and his commitment to his memory of his home community, by 1950, Williams, who in his periods at Cambridge had felt 'no sense of being cut-off', was aware of the reality of separation.[61]

The experience of crossing the frontier, moving out of the working class was vital to his development, if far less painful than it was for many in the post-war years.[62] For Williams:

> . . . *learning was ordinary; we learned where we could. Always from those scattered white houses it made sense to go out and become a scholar or a poet or a teacher.*[63]

Left at that, the transition was unacceptable. At the end of the journey the scholarship boy or girl became a sort of superior servant of the establishment. The individual escape did not help to solve the problem of class relations in capitalism. It provided a substitute, serving to maintain a *status quo* which:

in practice was a denial of equity to the men and women amongst whom I had grown up, the lower servants whose lives were governed by the existing distributions of property, remuneration, education and respect.[64]

The freedom of the minority was purchased at the price of injustice, of feeding the feeling of failure to the majority; the sense of injustice of the majority was fully justified.

It made sense to leave. But for the socialist it also made sense to return – in as many ways as possible – to 'your own people, whom you could not if you tried desert'.[65] The minimal validation for leaving was continued solidarity. Solidarity involved bringing back home the best of the new world to limit the damage done to 'the principle of common betterment which ought to be an absolute value' by the facts of division, betrayal and failure that the ladder spoke of, by the fact that many had 'scrambled up and gone off to play for the other side; many have tried to climb and failed'.[66]

For some Williams had an idealised view of the working class and of adult education in 1946.[67] No doubt. The integrated Welsh community he knew so well could hardly of itself suggest the complex variations and disunities of the British working class. A few years later others contrasted him with Hodgkin:

> ... he had an almost romantic view of working class people, did Tommy, and his duties to them, but then, of course, Raymond was working class so he wouldn't have that attitude anyway. He hadn't got what I would call the narodnik attitude, the 'truth is in the working classes' attitude, not at all.[68]

Certainly the critical awareness which came with prolonged experience of teaching and political difficulties failed to erode his essential commitment to class politics or adult education. Perhaps some element of idealism is as essential for those who seriously wish to continue their affiliation to the class they have left as a dose of cynicism is to those who wish to make good their getaway with a quiet mind. In 1946, and later, there was a real relationship between adult education and working-class institutions – although only 'the earnest minority' of workers was directly involved – which was declining then and has atrophied today. In the 1940s making oneself an educator of adults meant keeping the connections open and contributing towards the making of a common education. For the young Raymond Williams it was an act of identification, a declaration of continuing allegiance. His labours in adult education, as well as his journeys to Pandy, kept him in touch, kept up his affiliation. Adult education provided on the whole an excellent site for his intellectual struggles against the stream of social thinking in the 1940s and 1950s.

I say 'on the whole' because I do not wish to idealise adult education or Williams's view of it. And I do not believe it met in any full sense the hopes many of the 1945 generation, affirmed by the experience of the Army

Bureau of Current Affairs and army education and the Labour victory, had for it. Adult education in 1945 was contested territory. But in retrospect its commanding heights were already commandeered by officers who were far from radical. The tensions between facilitating the release of working class potential for a radical transformation of society and moulding it to play a subaltern role in the maintenance of a reformed *status quo* were soon to be resolved in the latter direction. In itself adult education was an imperfect instrument for redress of the inequity and waste of the mainstream education system.

It was far from providing a vehicle by which the working class could rise *together*, a serious alternative to the system through which individuals rise *from* their class. Only in certain areas of work in the community or based on the trade unions did it provide even the makings of a solidaristic answer. But here, too, the ladder applied; individuals scaled its rungs to service in the labour movement or the institutions of the welfare state – or slipped away to re-appear in the colours of the other side. The practice of adult education was increasingly, as the post-war years went by, the practice of individual development and individual mobility. Its tendency was to become a spare ladder, a second chance, as far as working-class students went, a means of keeping intellectually fit, up-to-date and career mobile for the already educated middle-class elements who became the majority. But for Williams and for his fellow socialists adult education was a good place to be, a better workplace for learning their craft than most others available. It was a well-equipped site for endeavour which bore important fruit. It was not to be the cockpit which could begin to remake the rest of the education system or rescue higher education from its crippling élitism.

Williams himself was a critical believer in the organisations for which he worked. He showed impatience with the emphasis on numbers, more courses, feeding the machine, respectability, safety. He had no time for petty bureaucracy. He found it difficult to accept the replacement of Hodgkin by Frank Jessup in 1952. This was adult education as a collective, intellectual, political endeavour making concessions to adult education as book-keeping.[69] He observed with distaste those who used adult education for their own ends. His efforts 'to attempt (as one strand of his work) to develop a popular working-class education'[70] can be exaggerated. At times the pressures of work, money and family got too much for him. At least once he wrote in a depression: 'I am in fact nearer the edge as far as carrying on satisfactorily goes than might be expected'.[71] He sometimes felt the tensions between his teaching and his research. But he did carry on. And the experience was crucial to his development.

One cannot understand Williams's youthful love affair with practical criticism, his 'very strong sense as in everything else, that working people needed to command all the tools with which social transactions are conducted',[72] without understanding the conditions in which he taught and the people with whom he learned. The strengths of the mature work of the early Williams, his deepening of our understanding of culture, bear the mark of the strengths of the university–WEA alliance. His writings resonate with the belief in the power of education and the centrality of communication in the making of a new 'knowable' community. They are impregnated with the values of spontaneity, voluntarism, democracy, the self-governing community. The emphasis on the political importance of the personal, the ordinary, the woof and warp of people's lives, the quality of life in a society, informed both his work and the politics of the New Left – many of whose leading protagonists were involved in adult education.

His work and his politics in these years also carry the limitations of the social democratic ethos of adult education. Knowledge is not in itself power and it can only help those who possess power to pretend it is. Communication is a problem but not, in itself, the major problem. 'Explanation' of the right path, 'extension' of the whole true way of life is far more problematic than it appears in some of Williams's work. Whether we like it or not the New Left and its attempt to mobilise the people over the quality of the lives they lived was not successful. In these years Williams passes too easily over too many harsh barriers – the realities in capitalist societies of power, domination and subordination, of the conflicts of interest which undercut communication. He takes far from adequate stock of the fractures of working-class community, of the barriers to a common culture and the difficulties inherent in its creation, of Edward Thompson's counterposing to Williams's 'culture as a whole way of life', 'culture as a whole way of struggle'.[73]

Later, of course, Williams thought again. But an inheritance of his formative years as an intellectual was a continuing belief in adult education and a continuing commitment to the working class, remarkable in its intensity. Whilst he welcomed the new movements of women and black people and the new stress on the environment he never sought to substitute them for the working class as the central potential agent for social transformation. He questioned Thompson's suggestion that the nuclear threat transcended socialist politics. As Williams grew older he stuck doggedly to the values of his youth. He supported the miners' strike, deserted by so many left intellectuals, despite his anxieties at the immobility and opportunism of the labour movement. He was critical of the proponents of 'New Times' and tenaciously asserted the continuing reality of class and class politics in the Britain of the 1980s.[74] And he saw that Britain as requiring the best adult education, the real adult education in which he had been involved as a young man, more than ever before.[75] There are many versions of Raymond Williams but this is central to them all.

Williams Today

In the way of the world and the way of Britain we can, no doubt, shortly expect a counter-attack, a re-assessment of Williams's reputation. His values are not the ruling values of the present period. Already we can find him dismissed as 'rhetorical, evasive and vacuous'.[76] Yet as an assessment of Williams, that offered by E.P. Thompson two decades ago, in the days before inflation set in, still seems a sure one:

> *. . . if his material is largely national, the moral inquiry which informs his books is not. It remains part of that stubborn, uncompromising clarification of socialist thought which historians will come to see as more important and more lasting in influence than better advertised products. There is something in the unruffled stamina of this man which suggests a major thinker. The very awkwardness of his style is that of a mind which must always find its own way . . .* [77]

Williams did not only live through his writing. I would like to set beside this the view of a colleague of Williams from 1946 who was far from sympathetic to all his ideas but who found in him, in 1961, 'the personality and purpose of an inspired educator'.[78] The unknown Raymond Williams, the educator of the post-war years, is vital to an overall understanding and assessment. He must not elude our attention. Our attention is insufficient.

The fourth point I want to make is that we must not make Williams an icon of past success, a house god of adult education. We have enough of those. The work and example of Raymond Williams is, if it is for real, for now. The task is not to venerate his work but to test its values in the world we face today, where culture is branded by intellectuals as a word most people cannot abide. Williams's dense, corporate, collective, working-class culture was always less homogeneous, less sealed off, more subordinate to bourgeois culture, more fractured by fissures of gender, ethnicity and localism; vitally, far less socially assertive than *Culture and Society* allowed. Today it is more under threat than ever from the neo-conservative mobilisation of its real inherent deficiencies and the worst of bourgeois culture to drive out 'service' in favour of a narrow and selfish individualism. Williams wanted to redefine politics. Politicians of all hues, and, it must be said, many educators, demonstrate little interest in deepening the quality of life, in extending democracy through enlarging our capacities for thinking, criticising, creating and controlling. Even on the left we have seen a surrender to individualism, consumerism and the celebration of shopping. Literature seems to have abandoned its social warrant. Far from a Ministry of Culture we have a Ministry of National Heritage whose conception of cultural extension is to talk in terms of 'the leisure industry' and 'the Ministry of Fun'. The quality of the popular media and the critical response to it, the educational deficit Williams spoke of, is wider than ever; the reassimilation of the educational system to the ladder is far gone.

How have the weapons of critical awareness been developed and utilised to subordinate social processes to the control of a revitalised majority; how has the strategy for communications Williams put forward in the early 1960s been implemented; how has the common culture he cherished advanced; how distinctive today is the basic collective idea? What progress has it made in our society during the last three decades? These questions, unfortunately, answer themselves. What is most disheartening is how little progress has been made through the years in a range of different historical conditions: the capitalist stability to which Williams's work was a response, the disintegration of that stability between 1968 and 1979 and the re-emergence of conditions reminiscent of – but different from

– the 1930s over the last decade. Anybody from the tradition embodied in different ways by Raymond Williams, Edward Thompson and Richard Hoggart who did not feel some sense of defeat would possess little purchase on the deadening terrain of the 1990s. The hopes of *Culture and Society, The Long Revolution* and *Communications* have not been fulfilled.

Precisely because of this the challenge facing adult educators has never been greater. Adult education, too, has felt the winds of privatisation, commercialisation and the market economy. The emphasis is not on the public education Williams espoused – despite the crying need for it – but on education seen as a consumption good or help up the vocational ladder. Courses about work proliferate, but are centred on professional techniques, not the social and personal meanings of work. Williams would have hated the way that education dealing with the rich, complex, painful experience of life suggests all problems can be solved by a speedy subjection to counselling technique. His 'Industrial Trainers' are in the saddle; his 'Old Humanists' and 'Public Educators' are embattled. But they are still battling; for a glance at the curriculum of adult education shows that the game is far from up. We are still in our teaching and research doing work that he would find admirable. He remains a good measuring rod for its quality and its extension. And an educational response to our present predicament is still important. So too is patience: 'But people will (damn them, do you say?) learn only by experience and this, normally, is uneven and slow'. But we do have to recognise that a purely educational response is too limited. That was Williams's own conclusion. As he said when talking about the quality of the press just months before his death:

> I don't see how the educational response can be adequate. The manipulative methods are too powerful, too below the belt for that. These people have to be driven out. We have to create a press owned by and responsible to its readers.[79]

Easier said than done. Strategy was not – and could not be expected to be – Williams's strong point. Yet it is only by keeping our bearings and engaging in the difficult work of developing strategies for deepening the best of adult education and ensuring that the democratic values which inform it are extended to our economic and social institutions that we shall successfully resist the new authoritarianism which is determined to stop people thinking for themselves. In this way we can redeem the faith and hope Raymond Williams always placed in the education of adults. We hope that what follows in the pages of this book will, as well as placing on the historical record Williams's neglected work, make a small contribution to that task.

Notes and References

1. R. Williams, *Reading and Criticism*, Frederick Muller, 1950, p ix.
2. R. Williams, *Drama From Ibsen to Eliot*, Chatto and Windus, 1952, p vi; R. Williams, *Drama in Performance*, Frederick Muller, 1954.
3. M. Poole, J. Wyver, *Power Plays*, British Film Institute, 1984, p 12.
4. Keith Sagar, Correspondence with author, 28 November 1990.

5. Oxford University Archives DES/RP/2/2/12, Tutorial Classes Committee, Class Reports, 1946–1954: 'Drama', Battle, 1952–3.
6. Oxford University: 'Victorian Literature and Society', Bexhill, 1950–1.
7. Oxford University: 'Literature', Eastbourne, 1952–3.
8. Student essays in author's possession. R. Williams, 'The New Party Line?' see pp 81–3. R. Williams, *Culture and Society*, Chatto and Windus, 1958, pp 287ff. R. Williams, *Keywords*, Fontana, 1976, pp 192–7.
9. R. Williams, *Culture and Society*, p 302.
10. Graham Holderness 'Introduction' to R. Williams, *Drama in Performance*, Open University Press, 1991.
11. S. Laing, *Representations of Working Class Life 1957–1964*, Macmillan, 1986, pp 216–7.
12. R. Williams, 'The meanings of work' in R. Fraser, ed., *Work: Twenty personal accounts*, Penguin Books, 1968, p 298.
13. Terry Eagleton, 'Criticism and politics: the work of Raymond Williams', *New Left Review*, 95, 1976, p 9.
14. R. Williams, *Drama in Performance*, p vi.
15. F.R. Leavis 1895–1978, Fellow of Downing College, Cambridge 1936–62. The power behind *Scrutiny*, he was a central and controversial figure in literary criticism. It will surely not do to overlook Q.D. Leavis 1906–81, his wife and close collaborator, whose *Fiction and the Reading Public* was very influential in this area.
16. T.S. Eliot 1888–1965, poet and essayist. Williams was particularly influenced by *Notes Towards the Definition of Culture*, 1948.
17. John Middleton Murry 1889–1957. Critic and novelist, edited the influential *Adelphi* as well as *Peace News*. Married to Katherine Masefield. His influence and those of the following critics is acknowledged in R. Williams, *Reading and Criticism*, Frederick Muller, 1950, p ix. But Leavis and *Scrutiny* are singled out as the most important influences.
18. I.A. Richards 1893–1979, pioneered Cambridge English and fathered practical criticism. He was a university lecturer in English and Fellow of Magdalene College in the pre-war period.
19. Sir William Empson 1906–, a pupil of Richards who enjoyed wide influence through *Seven Types of Ambiguity*.
20. L.C. Knights 1906–, founding editor of *Scrutiny* and important contributor. Professor at Sheffield, Bristol, Cambridge. Advocate of literature teaching in WEA classes.
21. Denys Thompson 1907–, editor of *Scrutiny*. A schoolteacher who collaborated with Leavis on *Culture and Environment*. See Williams's comments in *Reading and Criticism*, p x.
22. I am grateful to Keith Sagar for strongly emphasising some of these points to me.
23. Biaggini's *English in Australia: Taste and training in a modern community*, Education Research, 1933, had an introduction by Leavis. See also E.G. Biaggini, *Education and Society*, Hutchinson, 1939; E.G. Biaggini, *Progressive Exercises in Reading*, Hutchinson, 1947; Frank Chapman, review of *The Reading and Writing of English*, *Scrutiny*, vol. 3, 1936, pp 334–5; T.A. Birrell, review of *Progressive Exercises . . .*, *Scrutiny*, xvi, 1, 1947, pp 160–1.
24. Williams first discussed the idea of *Reading and Criticism* with Poole, *loc. cit.*, p x. See also H.E. Poole, *The Teaching of Literature in the WEA*, British Institute of Adult Education, 1938.

25. Wolf Mankowitz 1924– went on to become a popular novelist, playwright, screenwriter and producer. For his first steps in this direction after *Politics and Letters* see Ken Worpole, *Dockers and Detectives*, Verso, 1983, p 114. See also *The Penguin Wolf Mankowitz*, Penguin Books, 1967. W. Mankowitz, 'Dylan Thomas', *Scrutiny*, xiv, 1, 1946, pp 62–7. Williams mentions his help in *Reading and Criticism*, p ix, *Drama From Ibsen to Eliot* 'Foreword' and *Culture and Society*, p 11. Collins was unable to obtain the full-time post in adult education he wanted, had serious personal difficulties and gradually drifted away. Williams thanked Collins for help with *Reading and Criticism*, *Drama From Ibsen to Eliot*, *Drama in Performance* and *Culture and Society* and retrospectively honoured his role. See, for example, R. Williams, *Politics and Letters*, New Left Books, 1979, p 74: 'Probably Collins held us together and it's worth saying as Mankowitz and I have published so much since, that Collins at the time was the clearest of us about the need for *Politics and Letters*'.
26. Francis Mulhern, *The Moment of Scrutiny*, New Left Books, 1979, p 329, note 47. A.L. Morton, 1903–87, was a Communist Party historian and author of *A People's History of England*, 1938. He had polemicised with Leavis in the early 1930s, assuring him that his hostility to Marxism was misplaced. Communists, too, he argued, desired the remaking of an organic community; their strategy to that end was more realistic than that of Leavis. A.L. Morton, 'Culture and leisure', *Scrutiny*, 1, 4, 1933, pp 324–6.
27. R. Williams, 'The Left in the Thirties', *The Guardian*, 22 March 1968. F. Mulhern, pp 17–18, 70–71. Edgell Rickword 1898–1982 was editor of *The Calendar of Modern Letters*. He contributed to *Scrutiny* and, after joining the CP, edited their cultural journals *Left Review* and *Our Time*. See Charles Hobday, *Edgell Rickword, A Poet at War*, Carcanet Press, 1989. For Douglas Garman see *ibid.* and Andy Croft, *Red Letter Days: British fiction in the 1930s*, Lawrence and Wishart, 1990.
28. Hodgkin 1910–82 after periods of work and travel in Africa took up a lectureship in the Government of New States at Oxford in 1965. Among his works were *Nigerian Perspectives*, Oxford University Press, 1960; *African Political Parties*, Pelican, 1961; *Vietnam: The revolutionary pathway*, Macmillan, 1981. Interview with Charles Wenden. Oxford DES F/10/3. Various correspondence between Hodgkin, Dan Davin, Oxford University Press publisher and Williams, February 1946–February 1951. T.L. Hodgkin, 'New Novels', *Left Review*, September 1937; 'The Individual and the Group', *Left Review*, November 1937; 'Novels and Social Change', *Left Review*, December 1937. Information from Eric Bellchambers. Lucy Sutherland, 'Thomas Hodgkin', *Rewley House Papers*, 3, 1953, pp 13–15. R.W. Johnson, 'Thomas Hodgkin: A biographical note', in Christopher Allen, R.W. Johnson, eds, *African Perspectives: Papers presented to Thomas Hodgkin*, Cambridge University Press, 1970. Helen Callaway, 'A conversation with Thomas Hodgkin', *Convergence*, 11, 1978, pp 18–26.
29. H.P. Smith, *Labour and Learning: Oxford and the WEA*, Blackwell, 1956, p 5. R. Williams, *Culture and Society 1780–1950*, Chatto and Windus, 1958, p 11; R. Williams, *The Long Revolution*, Chatto and Windus, 1961, 'Foreword'. H.P. Smith, *Literature and Adult Education a Century Ago*, Oxford, published by the author, 1960.
30. Oxford University: R. Williams to F. Pickstock, 17 November, 1950.
31. Humphrey House 1908–55 was the author of, *inter alia*, *The Dickens World*, *Coleridge*, *Aristotle's Poetics* and *All in Due Time: The collected*

essays and broadcast talks of Humphrey House; John Saville, 'A red in the Raj', *The Guardian*, February 6 1990; *Culture and Society*, p 11.

32. F.W. Bateson 1901–78 was a prolific critic. He also published *Mixed Farming and Muddled Thinking – An analysis of current agricultural policy*, 1946 and *Brill: A short history*, 1966. W.W. Robson, 'F.W. Bateson', *Essays in Criticism*, xxix, 1979, p 2; S. Wall, 'Editorial commentary', *Essays in Criticism*, xxix, 1979, p 108; *Culture and Society*, p 11. *Politics and Letters*, pp 84ff.

33. Jack Woolford, 'Tony McLean: A memoir', WEA South Eastern District, *Adult Education and Social Change: Lectures and reminiscences in honour of Tony McLean*, n.d., probably 1983, pp 1–7. For McLean, 1911–82, see *Culture and Society*, p 11.

34. Work by Williams's full-time literature colleagues included Douglas Hewitt, *Conrad: A reassessment*, Bowes and Bowes, 1952; Douglas Hewitt, *The Approach to Fiction*, Longman, 1972; Patrick Roberts, *The Psychology of the Drama*, Routledge, 1975. The publications of part-time staff included A.K. Hudson, *Shakespeare in the Classroom*, 1954 reprinted Heinemann, 1963; H. Peschman, ed., *The Voice of Poetry*, Evans, 1950. For Hudson see *Reading and Criticism*, p x. In later years he worked for the BBC and the universities of Bristol and Bath, publishing prolifically in the fields of social history, archaeology and public relations. Some of his later work reflected his early concerns – see Kenneth Hudson, *The Dictionary of Diseased English*, Macmillan, 1977, with an introduction by Richard Hoggart.

35. Edward Conze 1904– was, like Klingender, educated in Germany. In the 1930s he worked for the National Council of Labour Colleges as well as taking university extra-mural classes. His work on philosophy prompted controversy in left-wing circles. See E. Conze, *An Introduction to Dialectical Materialism*, NCLC Publishing Society, n.d.; Eden Paul, Cedar Paul and Edward Conze *An Outline of Psychology*, NCLC, n.d.; Ellen Wilkinson and Edward Conze, *Why War? A handbook for those who will take part in the Second World War*, NCLC, 1939; see also Jonathan Rée, *Proletarian Philosophers*, Clarendon Press, 1984. Conze wrote prolifically on Buddhism, on which he became a world acclaimed authority, into the 1980s. See E. Conze, *Buddhism: Its essence and development*, Hutchinson, 1951; Ian Oliver, *Buddhism in Britain*, Rider and Co., 1979, pp 45–8.

36. Interview with A.J. Woolford, 1990. See Eric Bellchambers, *Both Sides of the Wall*, People's Press, 1988; E. Bellchambers, correspondence with author; *Culture and Society*, p 11.

37. A.J. Woolford, 'The interpretation of history', *Scrutiny*, xiii, 1, 1945, pp 2–11; 'Non-sequitur', *Scrutiny*, xiii, 2, 1945, pp 153–9; 'Clio elevated', *Scrutiny*, xiv, 1, 1945, pp 51–3.

38. Michael Carritt 1906–90 privately published his memoirs *A Mole in the Crown* in 1985. See also John Saville, 'A red in the Raj'; *The Long Revolution*, 'Foreword'. Carritt was a close friend of Humphrey House. Williams also recorded a debt to John Coleman who together with his wife R.V. 'Vi' Coleman worked for the Delegacy in the immediate post-war years: 'Foreword' *Culture and Society*.

39. Henry Collins 1917–69 wrote widely and contributed to *Politics and Letters*. H. Collins, *Trade Unions Today*, Frederick Muller, 1950; H. Collins and H.J. Fyrth, *The Foundry Workers: A trade union history*, Amalgamated Union of Foundry Workers, 1959; H. Collins and C.

Abramsky, *Karl Marx and The British Labour Movement*, Macmillan, 1965. He also translated Julius Braunthal's *History of the International* into English. H.J. Fyrth, 'Dr. Henry Collins' *Bulletin of the Society for the Study of Labour History*, 20, 1970, pp 9–10; *Culture and Society*, p 11; *Politics and Letters*, p 70.

40. Eric Hobsbawm, 'The historian's group of the Communist Party', in Maurice Cornforth, ed., *Rebels and Their Causes*, Lawrence and Wishart, 1978, p 37.

41. The major concerns of F.W. Klingender 1907–55 were summed up in the two books he published in 1942, *Russia – Britain's Ally* and *Marxism and Modern Art*. Herbert Read called his *Goya in the Democratic Tradition*, reissued in 1968, 'a classic of art criticism'; See F.W. Klingender *Art and the Industrial Revolution*, Paladin, 1972, edited and revised by A. Elton. *Culture and Society*, p 11.

42. Foreword, *The Long Revolution*. Thompson 1924– and Hall 1932–, who succeeded Hoggart as Director of the Centre for Contemporary Cultural Studies and is now Professor of Sociology at the Open University, were continuing mutual influences in relation to Williams.

43. Michael Orrom 1920–, correspondence with author. Williams remained in close contact with Orrom, whom he met at Cambridge in 1939, until the mid-fifties. They wrote *Preface to Film* (1954) together and Williams acknowledged Orrom's help with *Drama in Performance*, see *ibid.*, p vi.

44. Sir Arthur Pickard-Cambridge 1873–1952, was a former Fellow of Balliol College, Oxford and Professor of Greek at the University of Edinburgh. He was the author of, *inter alia*, *Dithyramb, Tragedy and Comedy*, Clarendon Press, 1927; *The Theatre of Dionysus at Athens*, Clarendon Press, 1946; *The Dramatic Festivals at Athens*, Clarendon Press, 1953. R. Williams, *Drama in Performance*, p 192; R. Williams, *Politics and Letters*, p 88. Among Krook's works were *The Ordeal of Consciousness in Henry James*, Cambridge University Press, 1962 and *Elements of Tragedy*, Yale University Press, 1969. See Brian Cox, *The Great Betrayal. Memoirs of a Life in Education*, Chapmans, 1992, p 102.

45. B.L. Joseph was the author of *Elizabethan Acting*, Oxford University Press, 1951; *Conscience and the King: A study of Hamlet*, Chatto and Windus, 1953; and *Acting Shakespeare*, Routledge and Kegan Paul, 1960. R. Williams, *Drama in Performance*, 'Foreword'. Orrom made award-winning documentaries in this period with Paul Rotha and was later a successful film-maker for television.

46. Later Lord Miles 1907–, a famous theatrical all-rounder. Nevil Coghill 1899–1980, Fellow of Exeter College, Oxford 1925–57, later Professor of English Literature. *Drama From Ibsen to Eliot*, 'Foreword'.

47. E. Martin Browne 1900–80 wrote 'The poet and the stage' in John Lehmann, ed., *The Penguin New Writing*, 31, 1947, pp 81–92 and 'The dramatic verse of T.S. Eliot' in Richard Marsh and Tambimuttu, eds, *T.S. Eliot: A symposium*, Editions Poetry, 1948, pp 196–207; both of these were of interest to Williams. See also E. Martin Browne, *The Making of T.S. Eliot's Plays*, Cambridge University Press, 1969. *Drama From Ibsen to Eliot*, 'Foreword'.

48. Alethea Lyall, tape, May, 1991.

49. *Politics and Letters*, p 189.

50. *Culture and Society*, p 11.

51. Alethea Lyall, tape.

52. E.P. Thompson, 'Caudwell', in Ralph Miliband and John Saville, eds, *The Socialist Register*, 1977, pp 228–76.
53. *Politics and Letters*, p 90, 92; R. Williams, *Marxism and Literature*, Oxford University Press, 1977, p 3. *Culture and Society*, pp 268–70.
54. *Drama From Ibsen to Eliot*, 'Foreword'.
55. *Politics and Letters*, p 86. E.M. Tillyard 1889–1962 was associated, together with Richards, in the reform of Cambridge English. He was Williams's tutor in the second year of his first period at Cambridge.
56. *The Story of Ruskin College*, Oxford University Press, 1968, p 23. R. Williams, *Politics and Letters*, 1979, p 50. Lionel Elvin 1905–, a Fellow of Trinity Hall 1930–44, later contributed to *Politics and Letters* and wrote on literature and education, particularly after becoming Professor at the Institute of Education, University of London, in 1956. See, for example, his *Introduction to the Study of Literature*, Sylvan Press, 1949; *Education and the Contemporary Society*, Watts, 1965; *The Place of Commonsense in Educational Thought*, Allen and Unwin, 1977. Lionel Elvin, correspondence with author, 1992.
57. W.P. Baker to H.P. Smith, July 13 1946.
58. Baker, who died in 1961, may be taken as typical of many adult educators of his generation: 'he devoted his life to adult education ... He is a scholar of distinction whose love of learning combines perfectly with his love of people to make him an outstanding teacher ... His contribution is recognised by his students, who have learned from him the relevance of history, the value of careful study, the joy of discovery and both the rewards and limitations of knowledge'. G.F. Sedgewick *Fifteenth Annual Report*, University of Leeds Department of Adult Education and Extra-Mural Studies, 1961, p 8. See W.P. Baker, *The English Village*, Oxford University Press, 1953.
59. *Politics and Letters*, p 97.
60. *Politics and Letters*, p 283.
61. 'In the late 1940s I knew that I was separated from the village in which I had grown up', R. Williams, 'The city and the world', in R. Williams, *What I Came To Say*, Hutchinson Radius, 1989, p 82.
62. For an angry description of the experience of the working-class boy at Oxford in the years Williams worked for the Delegacy, written by a New Left supporter, later a prominent playwright, see Dennis Potter, *The Glittering Coffin*, Gollancz, 1960.
63. R. Williams, 'Culture is ordinary' in N. McKenzie, ed., *Conviction*, McGibbon and Kee, 1958, p 76; see pp 89–102 this volume.
64. *Culture and Society*, p 316.
65. R. Williams, 'Fiction and the writing public', *Essays in Criticism*, 7, 1957, p 425, reprinted in this volume pp 106–10; *Culture and Society*, p 317–18.
66. For an interesting comment by Williams on why he and other leading members of the New Left entered adult education see R. Williams, 'The uses of cultural theory', *New Left Review*, 158, 1986, p 25.
67. Wolf Mankowitz, conversation with author.
68. Alethea Lyall, tape, May, 1991.
69. E. Bellchambers and F. Bayliss, correspondence with author. F.W. Jessup 1909–90 was heartily disliked by Williams and there was talk of Williams himself applying for the position of secretary to the Delegacy on Hodgkin's resignation. Jessup was the author of *Problems of Local Government*, 1949, and *A History of Kent*, 1958. Jessup's succession strengthened

the cordial relations Williams enjoyed with Frank Pickstock 1910–85, organising secretary of the TCC and a former station master on the London and Midland.

70. S. Laing, *op. cit.*, p 80.
71. Oxford University: R. Williams to F. Pickstock, November 17 1950.
72. *Politics and Letters*, p 179.
73. E.P. Thompson, 'The long revolution', *New Left Review*, 9, 1961, pp 24–33; 10, 1961, pp 34–9.
74. R. Williams, *Towards 2000*, 1983, Penguin Books 1983, particularly pp 152ff, pp 243ff; 'The politics of nuclear disarmament', *New Left Review*, 124, 1980, pp 25–42; 'Mining the meaning: key words in the miners' strike', *New Socialist*, 25, 1985, pp 6–9; 'Splits, pacts and coalitions', *New Socialist*, 16, 1984, pp 31–5.
75. R. Williams, 'Adult education and social change', reprinted in this book pp 255–64.
76. Noel Annan, *Our Age*, 1990, Fontana 1991, p 360.
77. E.P. Thompson, review of R. Williams 'The Country and the City' in *New York Review of Books*, 6, February 1975, p 37.
78. Oxford University: F. Pickstock to W. Styler, 8 January 1962.
79. R. Williams and T. Eagleton, 'The politics of hope: an interview', in T. Eagleton, ed., *Raymond Williams: Critical perspectives*, Polity Press, 1989, p 181.

Section 2:
Cultural Politics

The first pieces in this section are from the journal *Politics and Letters*, which Williams edited between 1947 and 1948 with Wolf Mankowitz and Clifford Collins. The purpose of the journal and its even more short-lived companion *The Critic* was to attempt to relate the struggle for a new popular culture to socialist politics and to education, specifically adult education. '*Politics and Letters*, I am sorry to say, has disappeared', wrote George Orwell in the autumn of 1948. Its disappearance was a loss to those forces hoping for a more radical continuing education. If there was a group to which *Politics and Letters* referred, Williams recalled three decades later, it was tutors and students in adult education.[1]

The project of the journals has to be understood in the context of the years 1945–48, as the hopes of the left for a radical post-war reconstruction collapsed into the cold war. The problem was particularly sharp for Williams. He was not prepared to choose politically between what, increasingly disillusioned with the Labour government, he saw as right-wing Fabianism and a mechanical Stalinism at a conjuncture where phobias about the destructive levelling of state planning, the spectre of the concentration camp and assimilation of Labour's policies to the situation in the Soviet Union were provoking a discernible right-wing shift amongst artists and intellectuals.

In this situation Williams sought to develop the work of Richards, Leavis and Thompson and interrogate Marxism. Leavis's project aimed at the regeneration of a past organic culture or at least the maintenance of its high culture remnant through the training of a cadre in discrimination and sensibility. It privileged literary criticism. It refused politics but countenanced educational work which some saw as democratising an élitism: a good culture had to be a minority culture. Hence the challenge to *Scrutiny* in the manifesto in the masthead, *Politics and Letters*, directed simultaneously against reductionist, philistine Marxism. In practice the politics were muted and the journal was far from explicitly socialist. The concerns of Williams and his colleagues are set out in the editorial of the first issue, **For Continuity in Change**. The Journal is to be exploratory not partisan. It will seek to develop not reject 'the best that is thought and known in the world' and bring the criteria of literary criticism to bear on the new popular culture. Note the range of contributors from Communist Party members such as Christopher Hill and Henry Collins to F.R. Leavis and Professor Rostow.

Orwell, then reaching the peak of his fame, also contributed two pieces, 'Writers and Leviathan' and 'George Gissing' – the journal went down before the latter could be published.

The major debate in the journal involved an exchange between R.O. Winkler, Leavis and Christopher Hill, who criticised the critics, arguing that the cultural malaise was a *capitalist* malaise and required socialist organisation and action to create a new culture and a new civilisation.[2] **Culture and Crisis** gives the views of the editors in a tentative expression. Note the stress on Lawrence. Williams's attitudes in this period seem summed up by the confidence expressed by the editors in their powers as literary critics, 'while in politics we are undoubtedly naive'.

Politics and Letters did not stand alone. In spring 1947 Collins, Mankowitz and Williams published the first issue of a companion journal. *The Critic* was published first from Mankowitz's home in Essex and then from an office in Noel Street, Soho. It was intended to mine and develop the pre-war criticism of Eliot, Leavis and Middleton Murry. It would focus on art and criticism, while its sister journal would relate art and criticism to society. As with *Politics and Letters* (which managed only four issues) the journal's life was brief: its second issue in autumn 1947 was its last. **The Reading Public and the Critical Reader** sets out the editors' determination to enter the long-standing debate about the relation of art and the critic to the reading public and the urgency of 'creating again an intelligent reading public'.[3]

Soviet Literary Controversy in Retrospect (published in *Politics and Letters*) is Williams's first extended published piece.[4] It again demonstrates his dilemmas. He was convinced that art and literature were not the unproblematic children of the material base, simply requiring analysis of how they reflected economic change – with such analysis controlled by a dictator or bureaucracy. Literature was not economics and politics, as John Lewis, editor of the *Modern Quarterly* supposed. Williams is impatient with 'socialist literature', whether Priestley's Utopian *They Came to a City* or the Communist Montagu Slater's documentary *A Century for George*. Nor, alternatively, could it be severed from politics and left to patronage and capitalist economics, as Cyril Connolly, editor of *Horizon*, a flagship of Americanism in the cold war, advocated. For the market was corroding the values of minority culture whilst providing the majority with packaged pap. The problem in capitalist societies was not the growing power of the state but the conditions on which it could succour the regeneration and extension of a healthy culture.

As Williams, writing under his Cambridge pseudonym Michael Pope, notes in **The State and Popular Culture**, the Labour government was in practice doing little to mobilise support for popular education and culture. With a nod towards the educational work he was doing he concludes:

> *Democracy does not demand a cultural levelling down and the*
> *general record of the Labour movement with the example of the*

Workers' Educational Association before them ought to lead to sensible discriminating aid. But so far there has been too much evidence of a stand on the untenable principles of cultural demagogy, the indeterminacy of taste, the proof of value in commercial success and the shaky populism which was given title by Mr Priestley's Let the People Sing.[5]

As *Politics and Letters* and *The Critic* collapsed and the post-war recovery set in, Williams continued to grapple with the problem of culture. He had used articles from the journal in his classes on 'Culture and Environment' from 1947. The problems thrown up led him to explore theories of culture. **The Idea of Culture** demonstrates the unfinished state of his analysis in 1952. Many of the ideas of *Culture and Society* are rehearsed; many of the key thinkers he later addressed and the powerful concluding synthesis relating his historical analysis to contemporary society are absent. With *Culture and Society* completed by 1956, Williams took up some of its concerns in shorter pieces. **The New Party Line?** strongly demonstrates his sense for the counterfeit and refusal to follow fashion. He is critical of Wilson's fascination with individualism and private escapes from what are social dilemmas. The vogue for Colin Wilson's *The Outsider* soon faded. By the time the review came out Wilson was attempting to found a neo-fascist party and meeting with Sir Oswald Mosley. Today he writes science fiction.

A Kind of Gresham's Law is, in contrast, part of Williams's settling of accounts with the élitism of Leavis. He affirms his belief in progress. Bad culture does not necessarily drive out good. The evidence from the press, cinema and television seem to show there is 'no simple opposition of bad and good but a great variety of levels, the majority of which are accepted as good at the cultural level at which they are received. All criticism now is social criticism and it is vitally important which way criticism goes: either to the assertion of cultural class distinctions or to the direction of an expanding common culture'. **Culture is Ordinary** is one of Williams's best pieces of writing, a simple and clear statement of his current concerns, integrating experience and analysis.

Much of Williams's intellectual energy in the forties and fifties had been devoted to an attempt to emancipate himself from the limits of 'left-Leavisism'. Williams honours the critic's engagement, intelligence and sensibility in **Our Debt to Dr. Leavis**. His doubts about Leavis's critical method, which once seemed to him 'the central point', are related to the broadening of his own approach in these years.

Williams's fellow adult educator Richard Hoggart shared many of his concerns, and despite important differences between them the two were often bracketed as examples of the new culturalist working-class intellectual. The proximity of publication of *The Uses of Literacy* and *Culture and Society* meant that, as Williams remarked, Hoggart and Williams came to be coupled like the name of a firm.[6] **Fiction and the Writing Public** outlines Williams's view of Hoggart's pioneering work. He praises the quality of observation as superior to Orwell: 'he writes not as a visitor but as a native'; but wonders whether autobiography or the novel might not be a better form of articulation. He is concerned at Hoggart's assimilation of popular culture to working-class culture and what he sees as his too easy acceptance of the decay of working-class politics.

Although Williams had briefly responded to Hoggart's writing on adult education a decade earlier,[7] Hoggart and Williams had never met. **Working Class Attitudes** is an invaluable record of a unique conversation. It provides fascinating information on the differing backgrounds of two working-class intellectuals and how this background influenced them and their work. The way in which Williams's childhood remained very much part of him, integral to his everyday reality, comes through very strongly. The conversation demonstrates his powers of self analysis and self situation. Note too Williams's explicit eschewing of nostalgia in relation to his project for the recreation of working-class community in a common culture, 'we're not interested in the business of reproduction: it's the principle that's important'; his commitment to 'the fact that communication is the basic problem of our society', criticised at the time for ignoring the configurations of interest and power; and his comments on the general political situation and the conservatism of the Labour Party – observations which appear far-seeing and pertinent today. The depth of his continuing interest in working-class politics is also clear: 'I watch every strike for evidence on this question: whether the practice of solidarity is really weakening or has been really learned'.

The Press and Popular Education from 1959 takes up some of the major concerns examined in detail two years later in *The Long Revolution*. By 1959 Williams was very involved in the New Left. The final piece here, **The New British Left**, traces its development. The initial comments on the Labour Party are somewhat puzzling as he was shortly to rejoin it. His views on the breadth of the Broad Left are perhaps exaggerated. His overall assessment – unless the movement made sense to industrial workers its potential would be limited – was, however, prophetic. At the heart of his approach is the argument central to *Culture and Society*: the need for a new common culture which would not take as its starting point 'the old working-class community feeling', as opposed to the new mass culture, but, rather, 'the democratic institutions which however tarnished still comprise the British Labour movement'.

Notes and References

1. Orwell to Julian Symons, 29 October 1948, *The Collected Essays, Journalism and Letters of George Orwell, Vol. IV*, ed. Sonia Orwell and Ian Angus, Secker and Warburg, 1968, p 449. Raymond Williams, *Politics and Letters*, New Left Books, 1979, p 69.
2. See also, Lionel Elvin 'David and Goliath', *Politics and Letters*, 2/3, 1947–8, pp 61–5. W.W. Rostow 1916–, the American economist and later Presidential Adviser, was Professor of American History at Oxford in 1946–7. Raymond Winkler d. 1962 was a civil servant who had been involved in Army education. Of the other contributors to the first issue of *Politics and Letters* Grattan Freyer, an Irish academic, later published *W.B. Yeats and the Anti-Democratic Tradition*, Gill and McMillan, 1987.

Hemming was an educationalist who later wrote books on philosophy. For John Wisdom, a Fellow of Trinity College Cambridge who became a leading philosopher, see I. Dilman, ed., *Philosophy and Life: Essays on John Wisdom*, Nijhoff, 1984. Of Orwell's contributions 'Writers and Leviathan' is in vol. IV of the *Collected Essays*, pp 407–14. The Gissing piece is in the same volume, pp 428–36.

3. D.J. Enright 1920–, critic, novelist and poet, was a prolific literary reviewer of the period. Anabel Farjeon 1919– was a niece of Eleanor Farjeon, later author of *Morning Has Broken: A biography of Eleanor Farjeon* (1985).

4. Anna Akhmatova 1889–1966 was a famous visionary poet victimised by Stalin and characterized by Zhdanov as 'half nun, half whore'. Mikhail Zoshchenko 1895–1958 was the greatest Russian humorist of the period. Cyril Connolly 1903–74 was a novelist and journalist who edited *Horizon* 1939–50. Connolly published Auden, Orwell and Dylan Thomas but for Williams he 'symbolised a self-indulgent decadence', *Politics and Letters*, 1974, p 72. John Lewis 1889–1976 was a well-known member of the Communist Party. A former clergyman, lecturer at the Cambridge University Extra-Mural Delegacy and organiser of the Left Book Club, he was later to incur the antagonism of Louis Althusser. Cecil Rickword 1900–31 was a critic whose work was praised by Leavis.

5. J.B. Priestley 1894–1984 was a famous novelist, playwright and critic who epitomised for Williams a certain cheap populism and who was at this time an admirer of the Soviet Union. Priestley had supported the Popular Front and his novel *Let the People Sing* (1939) captured its ethos for many.

6. Hoggart 1918– was Staff Tutor in English Literature at the University of Hull Extra-Mural Department for 13 years from 1946. At the time of the conversation he had recently moved to the University of Leicester as an internal lecturer. Subsequently, in 1964, as Professor of Modern English Literature, he established the Centre for Contemporary Cultural Studies at the University of Birmingham. His recollections of the period are in R. Hoggart, *A Sort of Clowning – Life and Times: 1940–59*, Chatto and Windus, 1990. Asa Briggs 1921– was known to both Williams and Hoggart through involvement in Oxford adult education and the WEA, of which he was later President. At the time he was Professor of Modern History at Leeds, later Vice-Chancellor of the University of Sussex, Provost of Worcester College Oxford, Chancellor of the Open University and Baron Briggs.

7. See pp 143–5.

8. Balachandra Rajan 1920–, referred to in *The State and Popular Culture*, was a Fellow of Trinity College Cambridge, (later) a noted Milton scholar and Professor at the University of Western Ontario.

For Continuity in Change

From: *Politics and Letters*, 1, 1, 1947, pp 3–5

If a formal position were implied in the phrase *Politics and Letters* it would, necessarily, be a complex one. But our function is exploratory rather than partisan. It is not that we undervalue social action, but rather that we are convinced that in the crucial problem of the synthesis of human and material richness, the first essential is a greater awareness, a more complete consciousness; and that in the exploration towards such awareness, any settled preconceptions or alignments would act only as limiting factors.

There exists, it would be widely agreed, a dichotomy between politics and letters; between, that is, the direct tackling of the objective and impersonal problems of our society, and that realization of the deepest levels of personality which is traditionally associated with literature and the arts. In our generation this problem has been stated at every possible level, and with the aid of every possible subterfuge. Its most familiar statement expresses a belief in the incompatibility of planned government with individual freedom. But too often, in this context, the affirmation of human values has served as nothing more than a protective screen to industrial and economic irresponsibility. Another statement of the problem, which has greatly occupied the periodical press, sets down 'morals' and 'politics' as if they were opposition. One review, in particular, has confidently stated that its values of 'kindness, objectivity, and moral courage' cannot be exchanged for the offerings of 'social responsibility, efficiency, and discipline', which are the criteria of its opponents. In our opinion, both sides in this debate neglect evidence which is important in resolving the essential difficulty. On the one hand, the 'moralists' too often rest their case on a parade of abstract values which they rarely seem concerned to relate to any detailed experience of living. Morality, in such cases, is merely a theoretical, at times a personal, indulgence. Yet, on the other hand, the 'political' group, which centres around the English Marxists, rarely misses an opportunity to attack, often gratuitously, a position (under the heading of 'literary decadence', 'idealism', 'absolutism', etc.) of the real nature of which they are demonstrably unaware.

The case which those whose concern is for morals might have made, and which the Marxists throughout the thirties tried to find room for, seems to us to rest upon experience of literature and the arts. For in these the values which we must be concerned to preserve find their most actual and complete expression. Opposition to evolutionary social change (in the widest sense of 'evolutionary') has for us no secure foothold in moral argument, unless the most permanent and profound qualities of human experience (as seen, for example, in the writings of Yeats and Lawrence) are acutely known and personally known. In social life it is not abstractions that we have to deal with; nor is any opposition of 'personality' to rational change rightly based on them. What is valid, and in our opinion supremely important, is that the structure of society, its institutions and directions, should be constantly assessed by standards resting on certain immediate qualities of living, qualities which social history scarcely records, but which, 'for continuity', our cultural tradition embodies.

It is hardly realistic to assume that such ways of living will be automatically carried over to a new social order. New social forms, as they develop, must be adaptable to the fullest expression of human personality: in their development those who are aware of the kind of experience described must make their influence felt. But again, the risk of losing such experience in the mechanism of social change is not a valid ground for opposing change which both social science and common sense diagnose to be necessary.

In short, we must ensure that critical activity continually draws attention to 'the best that is thought and known in the world', while at the same time we must recognise that the mechanisms of society, acting by their own laws, must also be examined and reckoned with. No backwater social group can hope to preserve the human values of the arts merely by concentrating on personal cultivation and personal communication. But, on the other hand, the usual 'progressive, scientific' assessment leaves no room for anything but the satisfaction of routine appetites in group activity. It is not sufficient to label the significance attached to inwardness as 'morbid introspection'. Nor, on the other hand, can active social participation be dismissed as a mere escape from the deeper problems of personality and tradition. There is a 'self' to be reckoned with at the level at which it finally comes to rest, a level which can have the sanction of our main literary tradition. But at the same time this self remains not only impotent but unexpressed unless it continually interacts with the group. For the survival of the group, diagnosis at every level is needed.

Politics and Letters. There exists not only the dichotomy suggested, but cross-currents, most of which have yet to be plotted. And levels of social planning and personal value are so widely separate that it is not possible to trace the connection with the convenience and simplicity of an equation. Much of the necessary work in researching the ground has hardly been attempted. First: the division must be explored, and its real nature disclosed. Second: the criteria of literary criticism must be brought to bear on social art forms – such as the cinema, and popular literature – in which the absence of the qualities that go to make a civilization is now obvious. Third: the continuity of standards in all fields of education must be examined, and ensured. Fourth: though it seems to be impossible directly to relate the highly specific experiences of a work of art to any more general qualities of living in the society in which it is provided, we must attempt to plot the social and intellectual background of the present time. And to this end, the most satisfactory means (failing the direct relation of literature and social events) would seem to be the enlistment of specialists to assess evidence provided by their own fields of enquiry, and to revalue the conclusions arrived at by other disciplines.

In this issue, the articles on Yeats and Lawrence attempt an application of literary critical method to Yeats's politics and to Lawrence's 'philosophy'. The article reviewing the Soviet literary controversy brings our outlined preoccupation to bear on a current disagreement in this country, as well as in the Soviet Union. James Hemming attempts the application of psychology to the group force in politics. R.O.C. Winkler initiates a discussion on the relationship of politics and the arts; Christopher Hill provides a Marxist comment. (This discussion will be continued in future issues. In our second number there will be a comment by Dr F.R. Leavis. To this discussion, we particularly invite contributions from our readers.) Professor Rostow contributes the first article in a series on American politics and letters. In addition there are two specialist review articles: John Wisdom on Bertrand Russell and modern philosophy; and Henry Collins on K.R. Popper's thesis of the Open Society.

Finally, we would wish to draw attention to the special editorial relationship between this review and *The Critic*, a quarterly of criticism. The reviews were planned to be complementary: *The Critic* tackling the direct valuation of contemporary and traditional work in the arts, by publishing and encouraging criticism based on close, textual analysis; and *Politics and Letters* attempting to place such value-judgments in their social context, and to assess social development in the light of the gained literary experience.

Culture and Crisis

From: *Politics and Letters*, 1, 2/3, 1947, pp 5–8

'This is not merely a battle for material things, for food and raw materials; it is a struggle to prove to the world the value of our democratic way of life, it is a call to reinvigorate the spirit of our nation. There is not one of us who does not realize in our heart of hearts that there are greater values in our lives than the mere material things of which we may now have to go short. The love of our families, the friendship of our comrades, our attachment to our home and our countryside, our passionate loyalty to the welfare of our country, all these prove to us day by day that our strength and happiness reside largely in the things of the spirit. Strong in that spirit we have the power to overcome all difficulties that confront us. Faith in the divine purpose and guidance which comes to us through the things of the spirit can, as has been said, move mountains, mountains of material difficulties'. Sir Stafford Cripps.

'Plenty of people will try to give the masses, as they call them, an intellectual food prepared and adapted in the way they think proper for the actual condition of the masses. Plenty of people will try to indoctrinate the masses with the set of ideas and judgements constituting the creed of their own profession or party. Our religious and political organizations give an example of this way of working on the masses. I condemn neither way; but culture works differently. It does not try to teach down to the level of inferior classes; it does not try to win them to this or that sect of its own, with ready made judgements and watchwords.' Matthew Arnold

If a critic of literature is genuinely interested in the contemporary and traditional work which he criticises, then he cannot fail to be concerned about much more than literature itself. He is obliged to enquire particularly into what modern literature reflects of contemporary social experience and into the way in which social life influences the subject, form and language of literature. But beyond these researches, he must accept responsibility for whatever it is that literature *represents* in society. In these concerns he must certainly not forget that he is primarily a literary critic, whose first function is to know for himself, intuitively and directly, with control, what a work of literature *is*. His second function, we are suggesting, is that of a self-elected literary representative. Now if a reader of the above were to ask, what is it that literature represents in society? Our reply would probably sound vague and inconclusive, and would in any case need to be qualified on the grounds of ignorance. We can indicate a direction for social enquiry into the place of literary experience – taking into account its level and intensity – in the family, school, and church. We can remark its general absence in the cultural life of the majority of the people – people whose culture can be defined as little more than leisure-time activity (or, even more frequently passivity). We can attempt to do as much as a critic can do to remedy this life-wasting deficiency by offering what instruction we are able to in literary responsiveness and literary meaning. But we cannot give an answer which would satisfy the social scientist, because the final statement cannot be given in terms of science. It is a literary statement.

Perhaps we could put the question of what literature represents in another way. We can ask – what forms of human organisation are compatible with our experience of literature? Among modern writers, it is D.H. Lawrence who has most to say on this question, whose writings are of central importance in the work which *Politics and Letters* will undertake on culture and environment. He represents the achievement in human relationship of the double meaning which Dr. Martin Buber has attached to the word *responsibility*. It is a noun signifying obligation but it also denotes the capacity to respond. The primary human obligation is towards responsive relationship, and relationship for which one is responsible in society. D.H. Lawrence realized in his work that deepest and innate responsiveness which is life, and defined the failure in *responsibility*, the absence or destruction of response, which is not life. He saw that responsibility for life in the present cannot be abandoned while planning for life in the future. His morality consisted in carrying forward into social terms – in his criticisms of popular literature and of architecture, above all in his novels – the meaning of relationship. It was a meaning which could be realized only by the loosening and dying away of obligation for other things than itself. D.H. Lawrence would not dilute the significance of his experience by reconciling it with its opposite, the *knowledge* of obligation, the biological economic or political estimate; the survival value denied the meaning of survival.

Literary experience, we may say, is a complex development, refined and enriched, of innate human responsiveness. So far the issue is clear: the forms of human organizations which are compatible with this, are those which are compatible with the principle of the *responsibility* – the school, and university, insofar as these institutions can offer training in relationship and in community fostered by training in literature as the central humane study; and where attempts are made to integrate participation in a literary and social tradition with the study of society. So the critic to-day almost inevitably sees educational reform as an interest kindred to his literary activities. Beyond the educational sphere, with lessening competence, there are not many positive measures he can recommend. But he can interest himself in conditions in industry, and in the relation between mechanical work and mechanical leisure; he can diagnose the destructive effects that work in offices and factories, which, concerned with simple repetitive tasks making no demands on skill, rule out as a result any positive role which the family might be expected to play in promoting *responsibility*; though there are, in this case, many reservations to be made, he can draw attention to books like *Democracy and Industry*, which document some of the effects of industrial competition. He can enlist the aid of architects, who are aware of the nature of this problem, to undertake field-work attempting to relate the absence of *responsibility* and particular and local housing conditions. In doing all these things the critic risks a good deal. The worst risk is that of distraction. He may come to place continually lessening emphasis on his acute and concrete perception of *responsibility* informed by literary tradition. He may cease, in Matthew Arnold's sense, to be 'disinterested', cease to be the representative of literature.

So when we come to the present crisis in production, we have, it will be seen, already weighted the scale. There exists another and related crisis in international relations from which recovery is problematical. The critic stands subject to two autonomies; that of planning for material survival and prosperity (it is an estimate which we must make objectively and with the methods of science); and that of allowing for and fostering *responsibility* in society, an effort in which we are supported by what evidence there is of human maturity, by tradition evidenced by literature and social history, by experience. We have at present to make separate estimates of these problems remembering that as literary critics we have training to aid us in the latter, while in politics we are undoubtedly naive. But because the present crises only negatively involve culture – because those whose business it is to remedy the former are largely unaware of the latter, because where the objective estimate conflicts with the cultural one it is always the interests of culture which are suspended – it is the present need for *responsibility* upon which we must primarily insist. The juxtaposition of quotations from Matthew Arnold and Sir Stafford Cripps at the beginning of this editorial makes further comment unnecessary.

The extremely varied contributions that are made to *Politics and Letters* make it necessary for the editors to stress connections and continuities. In this issue the variety has, in part, been forced upon us by the amalgamation of our two reviews – by the paper shortage, and by difficulties of printing and publication. Variety also plays an acknowledged part in achieving an influence through circulation. But the direction of our efforts, our stated and differentiating policy, is that of *social integration* – of connecting private meaning with public fact, of making meaning responsible for fact. We attempt to establish connections, which have been little sought after before, particularly in the sociology of literature and with those values we abstract from literature and confirm in it. Yet our readers must know that a repetitive statement of the contemporary best in literature, the exploration and definition of what constitutes the best, only goes a little way towards the *achievement* of our policy. It is a difficult and indispensable preliminary, but it is not the whole. There remain other approaches from scholars and critics not immediately in contact with the P. & L. line which, though they do not directly reinforce policy, offer material which extends our enquiry. The relevance of this material depends upon the use we make of it – by selection, and by later attempts to align directly with the needs of social integration. The material is often, as in this issue, miscellaneous. It is the editorial function to make its relevance explicit.

We can start by saying that the English language as it was used by Blake is a fact of social importance, an importance which is extended when we observe that Blake's language is available to us to-day solely in literature. The importance is inseparable from Blake's pre-occupation with the *essential* life and death. As in Lawrence, Blake's literary statement is urgent and contemporary because of present deprivation, and because in literature itself it constitutes a living principle. The present issue commences with a statement on two aspects of Blake's work. In *The Sculptures of Lippy Lipschitz* attention is drawn to the achievement of this principle in another equally important field. In *Matthew Arnold To-day*, R.C. Churchill draws attention to those qualities in a critic of literature and society which are directly related to the function of P. & L., and which in *The Function of Criticism* and *Culture and Anarchy* were the beginning of the study of Culture and Environment, and still serve as models for it.

In this journal's first editorial statement, we singled out sociology as of primary concern to the critic in his work of integration. It is the means of assessing those trends in society with which literature might ally itself, and through which its educative influence must percolate. Further, its given aim is that of correlation. Professor Ginsberg's distinction in this field will be known to our readers. His disinterested assessment of Freud's social theories puts into perspective a study which is responsible for many contemporary assumptions about psychology, assumptions which have found place in both creative and critical equipment. Professor Cole's essay has obvious relevance to our insistence on those aspects of social education which must accompany and be guided by education in literature.

Following the amalgamation we will in future have less space in which to carry further these purposes, though a certain gain in force may result from the appearance of the literary and the social statement under one cover. As soon as conditions permit P. & L. will be published bi-monthly. In the senses we have stressed above it will be an all round cultural review; and it will be the only such review whose primary concern is with criticism.

The T.L.S. reviewer of the first issue of P. & L. remarked that though the editors conjoin Politics and Letters in their title 'they find no such connection in the *larger* world' (our italics). This reviewer managed to suggest that such a correlation was of very minor importance. We must reject this suggestion. The integration of what literature *is*, and what society, if it is to remain alive, must *become*, is the major problem for both reviewers and editors to face.

The Editors

The Reading Public and the Critical Reader

From: *The Critic*, 1, 2, 1947, pp 5–6

If the purpose of criticism is to cultivate an intelligent reading public then the function of THE CRITIC may be understood without strong underlining from a manifesto. For whilst no one denies that intelligent people still exist, no one suggests that they exist as an *intelligent reading public* with the organic unity which that phrase suggests. The situation is one which will be examined closely in POLITICS & LETTERS, the companion quarterly to THE CRITIC.

There is, however, one fact concerning the immediate importance of an intelligent reading public which a generous reviewer of the first issue of THE CRITIC raised. The reviewer of TIME & TIDE remarks apropos of Mr Enright's article in our first number:

> *Mr Enright seems to believe that good constructive criticism has the power to create good artists. . . . I think he has seriously over-rated the actual influence of criticism. . . . Good criticism has small ability to reform the artist by its direct impact, but only the public, the backwash of whose responding taste will ultimately, but more circuitously affect trends in the artist.*

How criticism affects the artist directly will always remain an individual question, but the question of public good taste and public bad taste is one which we can discuss with more certainty and to a more practical purpose.

The absence of taste in the general reading public is something which we can assume as proven. The dominance of that public's standards is something else which we can assume, and which the economics of publishing support more strongly than any theoretical argument. Against this domination minority standards and minority magazines assert themselves only with great difficulty. And then it is hardly possible for the assertion to be anything but sporadic and unmaintained. Nevertheless, as TIME & TIDE's reviewer knows, the quality of art is to some extent determined by the quality of the public taste. So that if we are interested in the standards which many works of art embody, and if we wish to see those standards preserved and extended, and if we do not wish to dictate terms to the individual artist, we had better concentrate our powers upon the cultivation of public taste; we had better concern ourselves with the problem of creating again an intelligent reading public.

Whilst THE CRITIC is first of all addressing itself to the reading public, it is also concerned directly with the practitioner in the arts. No one who is interested in art can fail to be interested in artists. But the interest of THE CRITIC follows directly from its interest in the artistic work itself; it follows from that work and moves towards it. It is always concerned with the painting, or the film, or the words on the page. The personality of the artist it does not take to be a critical concern.

The reviewer in TIME & TIDE makes a remark which sufficiently indicates the situation against which the preceding paragraph is aimed. She says:

> . . . *what minute percentage of artists are able to take anything but praise seriously – except from adherents to their own opinion or attitude?*

Now surely the most surprising thing about this remark is that the writer does not expect to be contradicted. The situation which the question implies, the absence of criteria, of critical training and method, the warfare between cliques and the battles between personalities, the sheer egocentric blindness of the majority of artists 'who can only take praise seriously', all of these the writer assumes to be natural phenomena. And Miss Annabel Farjeon (from whose review we have been quoting) is not ignorant of the artists she has been discussing. We may take her implication to be a fair comment on the situation as it is.

At the risk of unsatisfactorily re-stating what Mr Eliot has already said, it seems necessary to assert again that the mechanisms of criticism are not wholly distinct from those of art. Intelligence is not opposed to the creative processes, nor is the intellect antipathetic towards, and destructive of, the finest which has been thought and said in our history. In fact, it is only by the free and honest functioning of intelligence and sensibility that the finest may be experienced again, and may be concretely realized in the life of an individual. And this must be particularly true in an age in which one half of the world is dominated by the standards of Hollywood, whilst the other half is so concerned with adjusting itself to the newest social developments that it is forced to revise its artistic criteria every five minutes.

The first number of THE CRITIC did not contain a manifesto because it seemed more reasonable to await a re-action than to anticipate one. Yet we never intended announcing that a new time had come or was imminent; it has always been more likely that the present time, with its particular complexities will continue. Instead of a manifesto, then, we can only say that there is a great deal in criticism which has not been done. There is a great deal in the early work of Mr Middleton Murry, in the criticism of Mr Eliot, in the writings of Dr Leavis which has not been adequately followed up. The critical outburst of some years ago seems to have lost a great deal of its energy, has no doubt become tired because of that very energy, and whilst the vitality waned the old, dead ideas which were threatened have crept back in different disguises to a new dominance. THE CRITIC will attempt to assert the values which the criticism associated with the above names re-discovered, and it will open its pages to all writing which operates from an honesty and with a strength similar to that which initiated criticism in this century. So that THE CRITIC is, so far as methods are concerned, partisan rather than polemical, direct rather than oblique, in taste, puritan rather than catholic. But we should prefer the reader to discover what THE CRITIC is by reading the articles and reviews which it contains, for what THE CRITIC is can only be defined in that way.

The relationship which exists between THE CRITIC and the quarterly review of intellectual background, POLITICS & LETTERS, is something to which the reader's attention can be profitably drawn. Clearly there is a danger that criticism which is concerned pre-eminently with the thing itself may lose sight of the context of the thing, of the environment of the man who made the thing and that of the man who looks at it. POLITICS & LETTERS will concern itself with the relationships between works of art and the artists who create them, between the artist and his society, between art and the society in which it occurs. Complementary to THE CRITIC it will be concerned to see that we do not make a game of criticism in which other aspects of experience become neglected, and all becomes devitalized.

The Editors

Soviet Literary Controversy in Retrospect

From: *Politics and Letters*, 1, 1, 1947, pp 21–31

I

The press in England is rarely concerned with literature, or with news about literature. In the popular dailies literature is relegated to reviews which approximate to library lists, except on certain rare and sensational occasions. Three such occasions which spring to mind from recent months are the legal action which followed publication of an alleged imitation of 'Lady Chatterley's Lover'; the reception, on the monarchic or stellar pattern, of Mr John Steinbeck in Copenhagen; and the succession of events, centring around the Russian writers Zoschenko and Akhmatova, which have come to be known as the Soviet literary controversy. The conjunction is sufficient to indicate the value of the Soviet literary controversy at the popular level. Sex, Glamour, War – the staple of acceptable news: it is only as related to war, or potential war, that the Soviet literary disturbance has been retailed to the British general public. Motives were mixed, but probably weighted on the side of malice.

At a different level, in the periodical press, these events in Russia have been widely discussed, with varying degrees of seriousness, but as a rule in the context of their bearing on literature, and on the twin topical problem of the place of literature in the modern, centralised state, and of the obligation of such a state towards literature. And yet no very adequate comment has appeared, which is perhaps symptomatic of our prevailing muddle about the relation of politics and letters.

From the most complete surveys that have appeared, in the October *Horizon* and the Winter and Spring issues of *Modern Quarterly*, the facts at least can be ascertained. Briefly, they are: the periodicals *Zvezda* and *Leningrad*, on one of which the humorist best-seller Zoschenko was a member of the editorial board, and in both of which his work (short stories) and the verse of the elderly Mme Akhmatova had appeared, were publicly criticised in August 1946 by the Central Committee of the Soviet Communist Party. Publication and approval of such work, it was said, were symptoms of a general loss of contact with Soviet life, and of a neglect for the positive educational role of Soviet literature. The reviews had shown decadent foreign influence, had put personal friendship before literary standards, and had been irresponsible. The Executive of

41

the Union of Soviet writers, especially its president Tikhonov,[1] and the Communist Party authorities in Leningrad, where both reviews were published, were criticised for allowing this degeneration. The Central Committee recommended that the level of work in the periodicals be raised, and that in present difficulties, said to be technical, only one of the reviews, *Zvezda*, should continue publication; and it named for this a fully responsible editor-in-chief, A.M. Yegolina, who was also to continue as acting-chief of the Central Committee's Propaganda Administration. Zdhanov, Central Committee secretary, reported these criticisms to a meeting of Leningrad writers, who thereafter passed a report endorsing the criticisms, confirming the decisions, and proclaiming the functions of literature as defined by the Central Committee as a militant programme. Subsequently the Presidium of the Soviet Writers' Union further endorsed the criticisms, criticised other recent literary work on similar grounds, made provision for the training of writers and critics, and excluded Zoschenko and Mme Akhmatova from membership of the Writers' Union.

That, in summary, is the core of the controversy. A first, elementary point is inescapable: to call the actual events in Russia a controversy is misleading. The Editor of the *Modern Quarterly* tells us that 'the whole Soviet Union is arguing about this issue'.[2] If this is not just another argument of the '180-million-Russians-can't-be-wrong' type, we are surely entitled to comment that it is, at the very least, careless, that not a single attitude which at all varies from the official one has been reported. If, as would appear from the striking unanimity of the published reports and speeches, the whole Soviet Union is not arguing but agreeing about the literary habits of Leningrad, then, after a deep breath, we may be disposed to accept the affair as a proof of Soviet unity. But it can't be had both ways; on the evidence there is no controversy, in the normal sense, at all.

But in this country the events have provoked controversy: comment has ranged from *Horizon*'s attack on the principle and practice of state interference in cultural affairs to *Modern Quarterly*'s defence of the affair as an example, not of interference, but of healthy self-criticism, which might be expected to arise in a country where human values are assured by a rational social organization. These contrasted attitudes represent their respective bodies of opinion well enough, and their arguments are worth examination in a little detail.

II

Dr. John Lewis's editorial in the Winter *Modern Quarterly* is typical of the popular marxist writing on culture to which we are by now well accustomed. Its tone may be judged from the following:

---

[1] Tikhonov may be known in this country as the author of an interesting story, 'The Teakhan', which appeared in *New Writing One*.
[2] M.Q., Winter., p 4.

Dr. Lewis attacking:

*'That inward-turning, utterly corrupt, and anti-social literary tendency
which . . . has been characteristic of our dying culture';*
*'many writers here are reduced to morbid introspection, bitter cynicism
and dreary lamenting';*
*'the completely nonsensical pose of the independence of art from
politics and ideas';*
'fuel to the fire' [twice] 'of anti-Soviet propaganda';
'well-meaning liberals';
'cynical hypocrisy';
'carrying on the work of Goebbels';
'sordid muck-raking'; etc.

Dr. Lewis defending:

'the whole Soviet Union is arguing about this issue';
'tough, able and independent-minded literary men';
'a good healthy downright discussion';

and so on.

One's estimate, that the sensibility which permits such writing is
inadequate to its subject, is soon confirmed. The basis of his argument
is that this is not state interference but self-criticism. He instances the
self-criticism which has been the practice in other fields. Now obviously,
this feature of Soviet life, which incorporates their attempt to solve a
universal problem – of providing a channel for popular opinion within a
mass-democracy and a necessarily centralised state – is valuable. Certainly
no state has anything much better to show, either in theory or practice. But
that this controversy may be so classed is open to objection on two grounds.
First, it seems surprising that the widespread and apparently deeply-felt
concern of the leading Soviet writers at what they held to be degenerate
tendencies in their literature should not have been publicly expressed, in a
country which preaches self-criticism, until after a strong statement by an
official, highly-placed, non-literary central authority. It is no good saying
that the initiative is to the Central Committee's credit, and that the party's
closeness to the masses is proved by the width of popular response. To most
people the order of events is bound to appear suspect. Criticism from below
is the essence of the democratic safeguard in Soviet society. The way this
business has gone does nothing, in itself, to disprove allegations that Soviet
government is based on decision from the top, followed by organized and
manipulated public approval.

But the more serious objection to Lewis's argument is that the practice
of literary criticism, and of creative literature, is bound to be different
from the administrative self-criticism to which he has attempted to relate it.
The exposure of bureaucratic abuses is surely far removed from questions
affecting value in literature. It may be argued that this was not a literary
upheaval, but essentially an organisational one, that it was, in effect, a

removal of an incompetent bureaucracy in Leningrad's literary affairs. But a full reading of the documents must show that although the superstructure of the controversy is organisational, the foundation is literary, a question of value, method and purpose.

Important literature will often, of course, contain social criticism either implicitly or explicitly. Literature, naturally, cannot be independent of politics and ideas in all its ranges. But the point which the literary marxists will not grasp is that (to adapt a phrase of Mr C.H. Rickword's about plot and character in the novel) ideas, or social criticism, or philosophy are only accessible in literature as a precipitant, but are only valid in solution. 'Poets', as the younger Mr Middleton Murry wrote,[3] 'are not tragic philosophers; if they were they would have written tragic philosophies'. It is failure to understand this which leads Lewis, and others like him, not only to go hopelessly wrong about the question of belief, or doctrinal orthodoxy, in literature, but also to misunderstand the nature of literature itself. The most vital philosophy of his time is not necessarily any more important to a writer than its most mediocre individual, or a succession of inanimates; any one of these may be his raw material; none of them can be his literary product. The function of literature in keeping society healthy (the function is by no means always conscious) is that it injects realised immediate experience, personal and traditional, into the abstractions which inevitably form the body of social thinking. And 'Extension, co-ordination, and refinement of experience; that is the business of reading'; – literary criticism is reading of that order in its most conscious, stated, form.

Now surely it is pointless to compare literature and criticism, as here conceived (the conception will be developed below on the basis of the Soviet documents) with the habits and terminology of administrative democracy. And the question of relative value need not here enter; the essential point is to realise the difference.

Dr. Lewis, in fact, makes the most damaging of all criticisms of the present cultural situation in the Soviet Union if he insists on the identity of Bolshevik self-criticism with criticism in literature. For many critics the most serious reservation to be made about Soviet culture is that it has, consciously and deliberately, narrowed the function of the latter to that of the former. But it will be better to consider this on the basis of the Soviet material itself, without Dr. Lewis in the way.[4]

---

[3] In 'The Problem of Style'.

[4] The Spring issue of 'Modern Quarterly' appeared, with some fresh material, after this essay was in type. Dr Lewis's renewed editorial does not seem to me to add anything of importance; the deeper discussion of the principles involved seems mainly illusion. A.A. Zdhanov's speech to the Leningrad writers is on the expected lines. The points he makes are, already, I think, discussed in Section 3 below. The only fresh comment to which one is impelled is the now characteristic Bolshevik slang. (Cf: 'swamp of mysticism and pornography'; 'swamp of ideological sterility and vulgarity'; 'reactionary literary swamp'; 'hideous slanders'; etc.) It is surely time that an Anglo-Russian linguist established for us whether this recurring tone is due to translation difficulties (we should all like to know if in Russian it is usual to have a '*swamp* of *sterility*') or whether precision in language is just a casualty of the new society.

It is necessary first, however, to consider Mr Cyril Connolly's remarks on the controversy, as they provide the basis for a vital reservation in this critique of literary marxism and Soviet culture.

Mr Connolly is breezy. He takes us over to the 'Fifth Form at St. Joe's'. He rehearses the documents, and presents a manifesto. His second point is central to an understanding of his position:

> *'There is only one judge of books . . . the Reading Public. A Buy-More-Books campaign with writers and publishers touring the country in a ballyhoo travelling circus is safer than the best-intentioned crumb of State patronage.'*

In the mechanical age, we may observe, touring isn't necessary; ballyhoo starts at home. In this century we have seen in our own society the invasion of publishing by mass advertising with all its vicious exploitation of human irrationality, ignorance and weakness. We have seen fiction develop into a business, and popular literature become the stale copy, instead of the mentor, of popular journalism and entertainment. We have seen consumer demand surveyed, manipulated, and standardized by the institution of book societies, fiction guilds, and readers' unions. We have seen critics selling out to commercial literary standards. And, most important because least easily recognized, we have seen a dereliction of duty by those who have assumed cultural responsibility, the participation of most of the surviving cultural reviews either in the new commercialism, or in an assertion of minority social standards which have been assumed to be identical with the standards of our literary tradition, but which, on the evidence of their practice, are as destructive of the tradition as their grosser neighbours. In their practice; and, too, in the fact, which cannot be ignored, that the kind of living which we can class as the product of commercial sensibility has been fostered by the growth of a society in which commercial profit has been the only acceptable social aim; on the profits of that commerce the mechanics of culture have hitherto alone been possible. To take refuge in the value of the by-product – minority culture – and to ignore the commercial process which has sustained it amounts to sanctioning the commercial process

---

A supplementary article by A. Cornu on literary decadence is remarkably hollow: it dismisses modern literary criticism without a mention of the practice of textual criticism, and its own positives seem to neglect actual work altogether in the exhilaration of the game of 'hunt-the-message'. It discusses themes in modern literature (at least the sub-heading says so), without reference to a single literary work (some philosophical works are discussed – the usual inability to discriminate); and it abuses Rilke for three pages with hardly a hint of demonstration. (M. Cornu, we notice, is 'in charge of research at the French National Centre of Scientific Research'. Other jobs; other habits.)

An interesting article by Mr Chen shows that informally Soviet pictorial artists make rather more humane and intelligent remarks about their work than do the Soviet writers, formally, about theirs. This is refreshing, but the fact of the difference between the levels of intelligence displayed in formal and informal discussions cuts boths ways.

which, grown sick, is destroying the living values by which minority culture survives.

The travelling circus exists, and *Horizon*, an impartial observer might comment, is one of its most valuable caravans, different from the rest only by a certain refinement of decoration.

What we are faced with at home is not so much a monopoly of opinion, as a monopoly of standards, of assumptions. Art generally has either been standardized for easy commerce, or reduced to an undifferentiated place among the essentially social pleasures of privileged living. It would, I think, be easy to show (though this is not the place for it) that a review like *Horizon*, which may show the antithesis of commercialism, is in fact its passive ally; certainly, when art is reduced to a social pleasure consonant with travel, gossip, or a long-range interest in delinquency, it has left none of the vitality with which mass-produced existence can alone be successfully combated. But the relevance here of this general point is that it invalidates Mr Connolly's criticism of the recent events in Russia. It is no use saying that state interference with art, or the suppression of nonconforming writers which may be involved in state patronage, is worse than the effects of commercialism or of advertising manipulation. Both are bad; neither is admissible. An attack on all external forces which work to destroy culture and the personal and social living which sustain it would be valid, whatever political motives were ascribed to it. But to ignore the destructive elements in our own society, and to concentrate on them in another (a society moreover which can hardly be criticised without large political repercussions) – surely that is not defence of culture but rather political opportunism in the real sense of that abused term.

Ten years ago, Mr Connolly tells us (ten is an interesting estimate) we went into action against the '*nascent* totalitarianism of the Nazis' (my italics) in defence of our liberal beliefs. Now he raises the cry 'Once more into the breach'; (and, presumably, he to-day who sheds his blood with Mr Connolly may call him brother, if that is any recompense). As the manifesto stands we can hardly assent to that.

III

The Zoschenko story, 'Adventures of an Ape', which was at least the occasion for the disturbance we are considering, is a very slight affair. Even in the rather arbitrary literary situation of this country it would find its natural level in the commercial fiction packet. In the December issue of *Lilliput*, where it appears in translation between one of Mr David Langdon's cartoons and an artistic nude, it seemed completely in place.

A tale of a monkey which escaped from a Russian zoo during an air-raid, which was adopted by a soldier and then by a boy, which stole carrots from a co-operative store and bit an invalid's finger in a communal bath-house, which was chased by a dog and nearly sold in a market, and which finally learned to wipe its nose with a handkerchief and eat rice gruel from a teaspoon, is quite new as a centre for literary controversy. But Mr

Kingsley Martin, and others whose literary qualifications are obvious, have 'interpreted' it: the monkey stands for a 'recalcitrant, discipline-disliking' soldier or fighting citizen. Dr Lewis writes: 'a literary man in a "safe hotel" tells the people of Leningrad that they were stupid to fight on and get bombed; any monkey in the zoo knows better than that'.[5]

Most of this sort of thing is quite gratuitous. Because of the notoriety which the story gained as the spark of the fire which consumed the review *Leningrad*, it has suffered accretions which a return to the text do not justify. Before I had read the story I had heard how mordant a picture was given of the Soviet citizens in the bath-house, how sharply the behaviour of Russians under bombardment was observed, and so on. I found none of all this in the story.

It is a children's story to which a moral has been added – the custom with children's stories.

The monkey does not pay for carrots: 'what do you expect of an ape? It has no grasp of the scheme of things'.

It steals an old woman's half-eaten cake: 'Well, what can you expect from an ape? It's not a human. Humans, when it comes to pinching anything, will never do it straight in Grannie's face'. It runs away from the bombed town: 'It has no idea of the general scheme of things'.

But, when it has learned human manners, *and stopped stealing and running away*, 'all the children and even some of the grown-ups may take it as an example'.

There is, obviously, an undercurrent of lack of respect for certain contemporary social habits. When the monkey's cage was blasted open by a bomb,

> *'it did not remain still after the fashion of humans used to military exercises.'*

But such criticism is essentially trivial; its level, a curiously exact parallel, is precisely that of the well-worn story which relates the comments of the monkeys inside a cage on the humans who stare at them, who are themselves seen through bars. To call this sort of thing social criticism is as realistic as to call the cartoon in the same issue of *Lilliput* (which shows a schoolgirl sulking because she has discovered that James Mason is married) criticism of the commercial cinema. And to react at all violently to it is surely no sign of maturity.

More important documents are the critical ones. One random comment may first be made. In a review of Zoschenko's 'Before Sunrise' in the magazine *Bolshevik*, the following quaint piece appears:

> *'It is not possible in the Soviet Press to tell the contents of such a vile story as "An Old Man Dies", the theme of which is a description of*

---

5 Lewis, Martin quoted, M.Q., Winter, p 7. See also quotation from Alexander Werth, same page.

the lechery of a dying man. Not to weary our readers with examples
of unmentionable vulgarity, suffice it to say that in this book we are
confronted with a sea of vulgarity and filth.'[6]

On this one might at first cry Bowdler, or perhaps, on the other hand,
acclaim it as an example of a regard for health, such as D.H. Lawrence
preserved: 'What an evil thing . . . is . . . all sex palaver.' But, on reflection,
the relevant comparison seems to be with the following:

'If you want to be a successful writer for American publications, for
which high prices are paid for really first-class matter, bear in mind
that American fiction, in the main, is not pessimistic, nor is it lewd or
irreverent, neither is it red nor un-American.
Avoid morbidity. The Americans don't want gloom, but something
that will brighten life. The sun must always be shining. Treat sex
reverently, and avoid its unsavoury aspects. Don't be vulgar'.[7]

The Russian

'all that is fine, all those things would have lifted any real person out
of his melancholy'

reinforces the comparison, and we are left to wonder about the curious
spectacle of seemingly similar qualities of living in what we are normally
given to understand as diametrically opposed societies – commercial,
monopoly-capitalist USA, and socialist-communist USSR.

The large point in the documents, of course, is the very clear definition
of the purpose of Soviet literature:

'The task of Soviet literature, therefore, is to aid in the education of the
people, especially the youth, to answer their questions, inspire people
with courage, faith in their cause, and the determination to overcome
all obstacles';[8]
'to turn . . . attention . . . to themes of the heroic labour of our people
in the restoration and development of Socialist economy and the
representation of the finest aspects and qualities of Soviet humanity';[9]
'this meeting demands of every Leningrad writer that he devote all
his creative power to the production of works of the highest purpose
and literary value, reflecting the greatness of our victory, the moving
inspiration of restoration and Socialist construction, the heroic deeds
of Soviet people.'[10]

---

[6] Bolshevik, 2, Jan. 44.
[7] From circular of Anglo-American Manuscript Service. Quoted in *Fiction and the Reading*
     Public by Q.D. Leavis.
[8] Central Committee Resolution.
[9] Resolution of Presidium of Union of Soviet Writers.
[10] Resolution of meeting of Leningrad writers.

From the beginning the importance of art in the modern state has been very clearly realized by the Soviet leaders. In the positive educational (not propagandist) sense the role is partially valid. (Cf. Strindberg's 'Biblia Pauperum'.) The disturbing thing, however, is the exclusiveness, the narrowness, of the role which literature is called upon to play.

'The function of literature in keeping society healthy is that it injects realized immediate experience, personal and traditional, into the abstractions which inevitably form the body of our social thinking.' The point made above needs development. Writers and critics who accept, who expand, the literary tradition of their country and their language are keeping alive the most exact record of experience, and so necessarily of wisdom, which the history of their people provides. In a period when economic crisis has enforced large social changes, and when inevitably a great deal of social experience based on different economic conditions is becoming obsolete, it is all the more important to preserve the individual experience, the wisdom of ages of living, which is most immediately accessible in literature. And this cannot be done by a mere genuflection to the prestige of the past; it is in new, valid work, the tradition become a living and growing organism, that we rediscover, in immediate experience, the value of the best that has been lived and written

Some practices of the writer as social critic may be quickly distinguished. He may, as in some senses Dickens did, accurately describe and analyse conditions of his society; (and sometimes with the non-literary result of arousing his readers to necessary change). Only this kind of social writing is normally recognized by political critics. True, a great deal of important literature may be so placed, but certain elementary distinctions have to be made and insisted upon.

Art, we may say, cannot exist without a moral centre; by which we do not mean the parading of a set of philosophical or ethical abstractions as a background to the immediate experience, but a full and constant consciousness, an access to the deepest seams of personality, through which *fact* becomes *pattern*, and *event* is assessed by (while at the same time making a new gradation upon) the scale of the human limit. This degree of consciousness, of full human awareness, states the difference between on the one hand the Dickens of 'Hard Times', the George Eliot of 'Middlemarch', the Conrad of 'The Secret Agent', who are all in this sense social realists, and on the other the socialist realism of both Soviet and Western writers. The first kind of writing is anchored in certain moral ideas emerging out of concrete human experience, values which test, and are tested by, the newly experienced facts. In the second, emphasis is placed on an exclusively social remedy; the lack of any interest in *individual* morality and experience either tends towards a judgment of social events in the terms of a hypothetical, future, 'good society' (which as it cannot be experienced cannot serve as a criterion); or, alternatively, the work, making no judgment at all, exists only as rapportage. It is not surprising that so much socialist realism appears in literary terms to be on the one hand socialist fantasy, a cheap brand of vision literature, or on the other a bound volume of newspaper reports.[11]

Apparently closely allied to social realism as defined, but in fact something very different, is another distinct body of work. In this, the writer may use social facts, of his own or another society, for the realization of a particular experience. (This may in itself often be a problem of social-individual morality – such as that of order, or of responsibility.) The writer's experience may be projected, as it were, into a selected fragment of social history where it can be made immediate and tangible.[12] As such we might class the English and Roman history plays of Shakespeare (with a reservation on their different levels of maturity), the history plays of Strindberg, and many of the 'Social Plays' of Ibsen.

Again: social conditions may be seen by the writer as an extension (at times a projection) of individual conditions. Here the control is the experience, however symbolically expressed, of an individual man in contact with powers which are different in both space and kind from the normal facts and relationships of social living. Under such a description exists much valuable social criticism, of which the work of Lawrence, Dostoievsky, and Strindberg provides the readiest examples.

Similarly in allegorical writing the control is constant. Personal re-creation, it seems, may be achieved in terms of the response to a related social experience. When allegory comprises social criticism – as in Swift – it will usually be found to depend for its effect upon the existence of controls which are directly personal and not mechanically assumed. This determines the distinction between, on the one hand, literary allegory, and on the other, political fantasy or analogy. (Between, that is, 'The Trial' or 'Gulliver's Travels' on the one hand, and, on the other, Mr Warner's 'Wild Goose Chase' or Mr Orwell's 'Animal Farm'.)

In all forms the recurring test is depth of response. The existence of a basic ideology will not, of course, preclude this. But the essential is never the ideology, nor its 'correctness'; it is the width of exploration, the depth of response. And this width and depth, since they exist primarily in words, can only be measured by literary analysis. Language is the scale. Political or philosophical implications, which can only be an aspect of the total effect of the work on the reader, have to be assessed basically in literary terms.[13] In the functioning of intelligence or sensibility there is no orthodoxy.

These remarks cannot, of course, be represented as at all an adequate account of social criticism in literature. The problem is too many-sided for

---

[11] In current English terms, (a) 'They Came to a City'; (b) ' A Century for George'.

[12] Cf. Mr Eliot's well-known conception of the 'objective correlation'.

[13] After literary analysis, work on the *writer's* society is obviously important. But surely, even then, the achievement of exact detailed experience through analysis is more historically useful than the quotation-lifting (finding an apt illustration regardless of the total experience of the work) which now has both academic and marxist sanction. in the light of the re-created literacy experience the known social and economic facts can be re-surveyed, and surely that should be the basic method in this connection.

satisfactory treatment in summary. In any case, the distinction between social and individual themes, between 'the inner and the outer life', is usually an artificial one. To make the distinction, from either side of the literary fence, is usually to impose a fatal limitation upon the artist's status as a fully responsive individual. And where this imposition is made the problem of communication cannot be negotiated.

But the account given may serve to show three things. First, that valuable creative writing about society cannot without overwhelming loss be confined to the very limited field of naturalism. (And to attempt to call socialist realism – the work done, not the work imagined – something other than naturalism is just technical ineptitude. Naturalism is not merely a question of 'the fourth wall', or of the theatrical and fictional methods of neo-Ibsenism. It is art which has lost its moral centre and purpose, a simply zoological art.)

Second: that a defence[14] of social writing which relies on an undiscriminated list of writers under the single label of 'social authors' is so superficial, ignores so many elementary differences as to be meaningless.

And third, the vital point: that the place of literature in society (of past literature as the tradition of the best that has been lived and written; and of contemporary work as its re-creation and expansion) is one which the best-administered society will tamper with at its peril.

IV

We must, then, retain the right to judge a civilization by its culture. For culture is the embodiment of the quality of living of a society; it is this 'standard of living'[15] with which the critic is concerned. Assessment of it is the social function of the critic and the creative writer. And the function is surely so important that in its valid exercise the writer is entitled to practice in the teeth of economic crisis, and without being overawed by the claims of that narrower section of politics which is both the total preoccupation of the professionals and the average man's major intellectual distraction.

In the emergent Soviet civilization on all the accessible evidence, we see, certainly, socially desirable attributes of width. What as yet we cannot see is depth. Now it is of course habitual, among many of those who 'cry culture', to be intolerant of the immense difficulties of the Soviet Union: of their early struggle for life against armed Western intervention; of their efforts, in the disintegrated class society of Tsarism, to secure elementary material needs; of their very recent immense sacrifice and bloodletting in defence of their land against the fascist soldiers of half Europe; of their understandable

---

14 Langland? Chaucer? Milton? Dryden? Swift? Defoe? Dickens?' – letter from Douglas Garman, M.Q. cit., p 89.
'The Bible, Dante, Milton, Cervantes, Shakespeare, Dryden, Ben Johnson, Defoe, Swift, even Wordsworth and Shelley' – Dr. Lewis, M.Q. cit., p 10.

15 As insisted upon by F.R. Leavis and Denys Thompson in 'Culture and Environment'.

present fears for their security against the expressed desire of important sections of world opinion to destroy them, and their consequent labours for survival. Any assessment which ignores these factors cannot be tolerated. But still, on the kindest estimate, they serve only to explain the present lack of depth. What now we have a right to deplore is the active influence of the State – as shown in the actions we have been discussing – towards stabilising the quality of their civilization at its present level. To insist that the only task of Soviet writers is

> *'to reflect the image of soviet man, brought up by the Bolshevik party, tempered in the fire of patriotic war';*[16]
> *'to be the Party's assistant in the Communist education of the people';*[17]
> *'to treat themes of the present day, themes of the heroic labour of our people'*[18]

is, surely, to condemn Soviet literature to superficiality, to the replacement of the individual by the unreal composite 'Soviet Man'. So mechanical a figure is as far from any kind of realism as the 'Average Man', the 'Little Man', the 'Successful Man' which have been created by the press-peers and advertisers of the West. And the substance of this shadow – a decline in the quality of social living (the comparison made above to the American commercial ethos is relevant here) – is certain also under such conditions. Only a writer like Mr Priestley, whose literary productions display the same qualities, and who, significantly, appears to be highly esteemed in Russia, can feel happy about that.

We cannot tell if work which deals seriously with the deeper problems of human personality, or even which treats the problems of a real individual (and not a composite figure) in adjustment to a fast-changing society, is being widely written in the Soviet Union. It would be ludicrous, for want of a better, to elevate Zoschenko to such a position and such work. But if it is being written we can, it seems, feel only too certain that it will be exposed to the characteristic abuse of

> *'morbid introspection'; 'sickly admiration of suffering and misery'; 'pessimism and decadence, superficiality and mysticism'; 'tastes inclined towards allegory ... inflated complexity'; 'petty personal feelings ... rummagings in little souls';*[19]

and so on.

---

[16] Resolution of Leningrad writers.
[17] Resolution of Presidium of Union of Soviet Writers.
[18] see footnote 17.
[19] The real comparison with this gallery is Mr William Archer's collection of the abuse (by 'bourgeois critics', notably Mr Clement Scott of the *Daily Telegraph*) of Ibsen's plays when they were first performed in London. See 'The Mausoleum of Ibsen' – *Fortnightly Review*, August 1893.

'All that is fine, all those things which would have lifted any real person out of his melancholy'

may be trusted soon to dispose of it.

That, on the fairest reading, is the present tendency. And it is on that point, rather than the point of State patronage, that we must seize.[20] Instances are not lacking from the history of literature, painting, and so on, to show that in commissioned work, or in circumstances where explicit respect for established society, its leaders and kings, must be shown, an artist may satisfy both his patron (or society as his patron) and himself. This is not an argument for State patronage. Most writers would be better without it. But state patronage is not, in itself, the most serious tendency. The open and powerful campaign, by those who struggle for social development, against inwardness, against that quality by which the artist (and not the artist alone) must, as artist, live or die, is the major factor in the Soviet literary controversy, and in its echoes in this country, which we are left to deplore.

Our precept is clear: we must, negatively, by the application of the strictest critical standards, ensure that inwardness is neither abused (becoming 'profitable introspection') nor set up for sale in the commercial market; and positively, we must attempt, however often we fail, to ensure that in our own inevitable development towards a planned, rational, society, the distinctive values of living embodied in our literary tradition are preserved, re-created, expanded, so that ultimately with material may grow human richness.

---

[20] Obviously certain general political-philosophical questions arise at this point; the relations of the individual to planning and materialism; the relation of capitalist depersonalization to the problem of individual witness in a capitalist society; the conception of the impossibility of culture without religion. The questions cannot be disregarded, but they are obviously outside the scope of this essay.

The State and Popular Culture: A Note

From: *Politics and Letters*, 1, 4, 1948, pp 71–2

State policy towards certain institutions of popular culture is becoming clearer, and certain judgements may be made. The Royal Commission on the Press has been established for some time. It was obviously a desirable move, although its terms of reference were disappointingly limited. The demand came from the National Union of Journalists, and the whole tone of discussion of the issue has been, in the narrow sense, professional. It is right that journalists should work to improve (in the widest sense) their conditions of employment; but it might well be argued that the vital, and difficult, issue, which demands public discussion, is the state and tendency of the Press as a popular institution. There is much one might wish to see altered in the economic status of newspapers; but the importance of the popular newspaper in contemporary society is more determined by its standards, its contents, and its implicit or explicit values. The journalists might be happy if ownership were more widely spread; but if this happened, what present likelihood is there of newspapers ceasing to be the medleys of distraction, prejudice, and vulgarism which the majority now certainly are? The issue is being shirked because it involves a consideration of *value*; whereas all the politicians seem willing to tackle are issues of organisation.

In the theatre one would not say this, since the drama, whatever its present state, is a real art, and questions of value can only be negotiated within its own context. The recent legislation permitting local authorities to spend a 6d. rate on public entertainment, and the expressed desire that part of this should be used for cultural ends, ought certainly to be set to the Government's credit. Those proposals which arose from the recent Theatre conference, supporting a National Theatre and Civic Theatres, are being considered by the Government, and are projects which ought to be supported. The Theatre Conference, of course, was professional in the narrow sense, and the sense was theatrical rather than dramatic. As one expected, there was a resolution or so in favour of better plays, and the tone of the Conference, under Mr Priestley's chairmanship, was rather like that. But the material reforms suggested are valuable.

So far as books are concerned, the only policy is the restriction due to the paper shortage. The facts provided by Mr Rajan in our last issue demand some sane revision of policy, although Mr Rajan surely went too

54

far in putting all the blame on the present administration, overstating his case to the point of collapsing it. The general features of his argument remain valid, and there is no real excuse for inaction. Certain books *are* more valuable than others; and extra paper ought to be provided for those firms willing to publish them, being withdrawn from those purveyors of out-and-out trash (leaving elegant trash tactfully out of the question) who still clutter the bookstalls. Looking at a Smith's stall in any railway station, it is impossible to believe in the paper shortage. The quota system based on pre-war publishing is simply an organisational device to avoid the difficult question of value.

With films, the Government has made several moves. It has, as yet, done nothing to remedy the legal fiction of present A, U and H classifications, or to attend to the serious problem of children's Saturday morning clubs. But it has stood firm on the Hollywood tax, which is to its credit,[1] and the new arrangements for exhibition and distribution seem to offer a chance to many films – such as documentaries – which hitherto were inadequately circulated. The consideration of the establishment of a State Film Bank is also encouraging, since such a Bank could provide money, outside the present monopolies of the Rank Organisation and the COI, to experiments and those more serious workers in the medium. But it is no use Mr Harold Wilson intruding the old bogey of 'taste'. A State Film Bank ought to be prepared to lose money, as museums or libraries lose money. If producers who borrow from it are to be nagged about 'what the public wants', and made to balance their accounts in advance, the result will simply be a new series of perfectly ordinary commercial films. Any such organisation must take a chance with ideas that seem valuable, be prepared to stand the loss, and make suitable arrangements for tax discrimination against the usual hokum and in favour of serious or original films which might not otherwise pay their way.

The Government's worst record in this general field is in advertising. The general development of State advertising is a complex issue, and may be evaded here. The intrusion of cheap or catchpenny commercial techniques into every branch of community activity is something, however, that ought not to be ignored. One read with pleasure that a recent Public Committee had seriously criticised Government advertising, including the *Work or Want* series, but one read on with astonishment to the criticism that the advertising was 'too intellectual' and that what was wanted was 'more emotional pull'. At this rate, the export drive could succeed by Black Magic. But the main advertising point of administration has been the question of the proposed, and abandoned, tax. Such a tax, it may be said at once, would hit a journal like *Politics and Letters* severely, since its ability to pay its way depends entirely on its receiving a full quota of advertisements. Yet, clearly, the tax ought to have gone on, perhaps with certain modifications. The advertisers' own proposal, which is being given a year's run, to reduce expenditure by 15% is ludicrous. Instead of

---

[1] Written in February

twenty Black Magic chocolate girls in a week we shall get seventeen. But can the country afford the energy, money, or material for the vast amount of wasted persuasive mass advertising? The Government seems to think so, because the advertisers have told them how it is the thing which really makes the wheels go round, and in spite of all the serious evidence, they are believed.

It would be unwise to generalise about the Government's attitude to cultural issues. It has done little that is positively harmful, and some things which have been good. Its general record in educational matters encourages one to hope that the many outstanding cultural issues which legislation can aid will receive attention. Perhaps the key point is the tendency already isolated: the tendency to attend to matters of organisation, and to shirk issues of value or intelligent discrimination. Democracy does not demand a cultural levelling-down, and the general record of the Labour movement, with the example of the Workers' Educational Association before them, ought to lead to sensible, discriminating aid. But so far there has been too much evidence of a stand on the untenable principles of cultural demagogy: the indeterminacy of taste; the proof of value in commercial success; and the sticky populism which was given title by Mr Priestley's *Let the People Sing*.

The Idea of Culture

From: *Essays in Criticism*, 3, 3, July 1953, pp 239–66

(i) The Idea and the Word

1. The idea of Culture, in contemporary English thinking, is of considerable complexity. It is widely current in history, in criticism, and in sociology, yet often without definition, and obviously with a marked range of meaning. Its scientific uses, in agriculture and in bacteriology, are also widely current, but have a precise application which enables them to be readily distinguished. Its use in anthropology, however, belongs to the main complex, and must be discussed within the general field.

In history the term has two main uses, which it is necessary to distinguish. On the one hand, culture signifies 'the intellectual side of civilization' – a common dictionary definition; on the other, it frequently signifies a narrower field, 'the general body of the arts'. Under the former heading, culture includes the philosophy and thought of a period, its religious modes and beliefs, its scientific work and theories, its general scholarship, and its arts. 'Intellectual and spiritual activities' is a common paraphrase. But the narrower definition of culture, solely in terms of the arts, also holds. In general speech, indeed, this use is perhaps the more frequent.

The variation requires notice, although estimates of its significance will differ. It is the next major sense, however, which is more likely to cause confusion. For culture is used in sociology and social anthropology in the sense of 'a whole way of life', and the impact of these studies upon general thinking has led to similar uses in history and in criticism. In social anthropology the best use of culture as a social term is still a matter of dispute, but a common use has emerged, which is sufficient for recognition. Dewey, in *Freedom and Culture*, provides a text:

> The state of culture [he writes] is a state of interaction of many factors, the chief of which are law and politics, industry and commerce, science and technology, the arts of expression and communication and of morals, or the values men prize and the ways in which they evaluate them; and finally, though indirectly, the system of general ideas used by men to justify and to criticize the fundamental conditions under which they live, their social philosophy.

'This complex of conditions which taxes the terms upon which human beings associate and live together', he writes again, 'is summed up in the word *Culture*.'

This use of the term is growing, in spite of the range of fact which it attempts to include. The growth of comparative studies of society, and the strong tendency to wish to study societies as wholes, obviously require some such term. *Culture* is more neutral than *civilization*, and for this reason has been increasingly applied to our own kind of society, as well as to simpler kinds. And one might set it aside as a technical term for the study of society, without admitting it into general use, were it not that in other studies a similar shift is often apparent. In criticism, for example, the desire to relate works of art to the society in which they were produced has led to a very similar use. From Ruskin and Arnold to Eliot, Read and Leavis, this extension of a critic's activities in the judgment of works of art to the study and thence the judgment of 'a whole way of life', has been a marked element of the English tradition. These critics, and others like them, have certainly always been concerned with the arts, and beyond them with 'the intellectual side of civilization', but from Ruskin's ideas of wealth to Eliot's ideas of class there has been this distinctive tradition of influential social thinking, by men who took their experience of the arts as a starting point. And the key word in these inquiries, as a glance merely at titles will confirm, has been *Culture*.

From these two sources, then, the use of *culture* to indicate 'a way of life' is passing into ordinary speech. But there is yet another sense, of considerable historical importance, which is certainly still active in language. It is a sense more difficult to define than any other that has been noted, but it may be paraphrased as 'a standard of perfection', and classified as a description of an ideal state of mind. As such, it is perhaps necessarily vague, but it is much too important to be overlooked. It may be recognized by its normal association with 'perfection', and clearly owes much, for its currency, to Arnold. There is a quality of mind, an ideal of personality, which is by its nature not susceptible to definition, but which is claimed as of the highest value. 'Culture is what is left when all the facts you have learned have been forgotten'; it may perhaps be recognized there. *Culture* is undogmatic, seeketh not its own; is humane, tolerant, doth not behave itself unseemly. 'A man of culture', in this sense, is recognizable not by any specific attributes, but by certain qualities best perceived by others of the same kind. The use, that is to say, is difficult, but it cannot be left out of account. Sensibility, refinement, good taste, breeding: all are its adjutants. When one recalls the other uses in general currency, and their likely concomitance with this, the complexity of the general idea of Culture will perhaps be sufficiently apparent.

2. In attempting to define *culture* in its sense of 'a state of mind', one encountered immediately those cross-currents and deposits of emotional association which further complicate the use of the idea and the word. It is not only hostility, as expressed by many of the newspapers and by the classes which they represent. For these, culture is affected, pretentious, precious, highbrow – the flow of little expletives is familiar enough. The pursuit of so-called culture is mainly by so-called intellectuals; hothouse culture is at best a kind of old-fashioned and unsuccessful entertainment.

Nor is it only the stocktaking brevity of the word in political discussion, where culture appears in manifestoes as a paragraph at the end of the Social Services, or in military treaties as one of the saving clauses of the 'arts of peace'. In verbal routines of this kind, culture is normally a 'department' of what is known as 'leisure-time activity'; it is, undoubtedly, of the very greatest value – we will have some if we can afford it.

But the hostility and the indifference might be discounted (let the dead bury their dead, although it is worth seeing how the death came about). Yet even among those who practise in the arts or in education, the word, *culture*, has often a tone of embarrassed parody. Indeed, to use it seriously, in other than a professional context, is often to convict oneself of the enthusiasm of E.M. Forster's Leonard Bast, or to announce that one's culture is a matter of aspiration rather than of practice ('those who have it *do not* talk about it'). *A person of culture*, we say, is almost current, but is used only by the gently senile or the seedily genteel. *A cultured voice*, we recognize, is the desperate parenthesis of a tiring or tiro novelist. *A man of wide culture* is journalese for a public man who reads books.

Abstraction, snobbery and fear are facts, and it is not surprising that they have left their mark on this difficult idea and word. We note the marks, not to set them aside, but to assemble them, as active senses of *culture*, along with the more formal definitions. For every phase of the word is part of the history of the idea.

3. The history of a word is in the series of meanings which a dictionary defines; the relevance of a word is in common language. The dictionary indicates a contemporary scheme of the past; the active word, in speech or in writing, indicates all that has become present. To distinguish the interaction is to distinguish a tradition – a mode of history; and then in experience we set a value on the tradition – a mode of criticism. The continuing process, and the consequent decisions, are then the matter of action in society.

The history of the word *culture* is interesting. Its normal primary meaning, since medieval times, has been 'cultivation (of the land)', which was also the sense of its French and Latin antecedents. From about 1420, it was widely used in English in this direct sense. As early as 1483, however, it was being used, figuratively, to mean 'worship', a sense in which it was preceded by *cult*, which, in a weaker sense, we still have. From the early seventeenth century, *culture* was extended to the cultivation of both plants and animals, with something of the sense of 'breeding'. It was then further extended to the sphere of human development; Sir Thomas More has a phrase 'to the culture and profit of their mindes', and Hobbes, in *Leviathan* (II, xxxi, 189), writes of the education of children as 'a Culture of their minds'. Hobbes also used the word in the sense of 'physical culture', to describe the training of the body. These uses persisted, and *culture* was recognized as a figurative term for the 'refinement of mind, faculties and manners'. But the reference was always to a *process*, never to an achieved state. Culture was the act of training, and never an entity. Thus Johnson, in *Rasselas*, writes of a person that 'she neglected the culture of her understanding'; a century later he might

have written that 'she was deficient in culture'. The decisive change came
in the first half of the nineteenth century. Wordsworth, writing of popular
education in *The Excursion*, is still conscious of the figurative sense of
the word:

> . . . . *that none*
> *However destitute, be left to droop*
> *By timely culture unsustained* . . . .

But in *The Prelude* (XIII,193–9, *1850*; XII, 192–8, *1805*), while combating the
argument that 'love' depends on 'leisure' and its advantages, Wordsworth
writes:

> *Must live within the very light and air*
> *Of courteous usages refined by art*
> *(Of elegances that are made by man – 1805).*
> *True is it, where oppression worse than death*
> *Salutes the Being at his birth, where grace*
> *Of culture hath been utterly unknown,*
> *And poverty and labour in excess*
> *(And labour in excess and poverty – 1805)*
> *From day to day preoccupy* . . . .

This use of *culture*, it seems to me, is genuinely transitional. It has elements
of the old sense of *process*, but it can be read also in the developed
nineteenth-century sense of an *absolute*. However this may be (and I
think myself that it is the first significantly modern use), the development
of *culture* as a concept, the *idea* of culture, was thereafter rapid. At the
end of the development is Arnold, in *Culture and Anarchy* (1869): 'Culture,
disinterestedly seeking in its aim at perfection to see things as they really
are.' But already, before Arnold, the word was commonly used in this
sense. It is used in 1839, by Henry Nelson Coleridge, in his *Introduction*
to S.T. Coleridge's tract *On the Constitution of Church and State*; it is
frequently used by Newman in *The Idea of a University* (1852). Arnold,
one might say, performed the final act of abstraction; in earlier uses, *culture*
was commonly defined by an adjective, *moral*, for example, or *intellectual*;
Arnold offered the thing in itself. But whatever the exact provenance, the
decisive change is clear; in the nineteenth century the word had become
the Idea.

    4. The study of the development of a word is necessarily schematic,
but in the case of *culture* it provides evidence of a kind which indicates
the decisive point of entry for analysis. The word which had indicated a
process of training within a more assured society became in the nineteenth
century the focus of a deeply significant response to a society in the throes
of a radical and painful change. The idea of culture, it seems to me, is best
studied as a response of this kind; the response of certain men, attached to
certain values, in the face of change and the consequences of change. The
idea of Culture, in fact, is an aspect of that larger and more deeply

complex response which men of the nineteenth and twentieth centuries have made to the Industrial Revolution and its results.

The Industrial Revolution is a myth; that is why it is important. The economic and social changes which the phrase indicates are real enough, and I do not subscribe to the tendency to play down their importance which has been evident in the work of some recent historians. It is necessary, of course, to recognize the antecedents of the changes which we call the Industrial Revolution; necessary also, and particularly to the student of culture, to recognize the unevenness of the growth of industrialism and its consequences in the nation as a whole. But the Industrial Revolution is a myth, not in the sense that the process is historically untrue, nor in the sense that the process is not of the first importance, but in the sense that it is, in the general consciousness, 'a legend, magnified by tradition, and given out as historical, which affects the origin of a race'. The Industrial Revolution, that is to say, is a concept, a significant myth, in terms of which we have come to understand our origins as an industrial people.

In this understanding, the development of the idea of Culture has played a vitally important part. It is necessary to examine this development, for two reasons: first, because it is in itself a part of history, and as such needs constant reference to the facts of social development as a whole; and, second, because it has been and remains an important formative concept, yet one which has never been adequately traced or valued. We are looking back into history, observing tendencies and forces, discovering theses and categories. The process tends always to abstraction, and this, within its limits, is a proper procedure. But the history of ideas is only temporarily a special study; the danger, for the critic, is that he will fail to realize sufficiently the intimate and complex relations between ideas and the other products of man's life in society. An idea can be assigned to a man or to a book, and the history of ideas to a series of isolated men or groups. But we need a more than ordinary awareness of that pressure of active and general life which is misrepresented entirely by description as 'background'. There are no backgrounds in society; there are only relations of acts and forces. The idea of culture is not to be considered as a process of independent evolution; it is shaped and at times directed by the total environment to which it is one kind of response.

It is not enough, then, to note the first emphasis of the idea in Arnold; nor is it enough, although it is important, to go behind Arnold to his immediate precursors. The idea of culture is a focusing of a number of particular responses to change, and what is now required is an analysis of these responses, in terms of the changes which conditioned them. I propose, as a matter of working convenience, three heads under which this analysis may be begun. They are, first, the idea of a standard of perfection, ground for ultimate valuation; second, the new conceptions of art, and of the artist, and the consequent re-definition of their relation to the rest of society; and, third, the process of development of Cultivation into Culture, with reference to the changing relations between social classes. I propose to examine, under these three heads, what may properly be called the first phase: the emergence of these issues at the time of the Industrial Revolution and the first major impact of industrialism, and on into early Victorian England. This account should then provide the necessary ground for the subsequent analysis of more developed systems of ideas in this field.

(ii) The Standard of Perfection

5. One of the needs which the idea of Culture was to supply may be seen very well in this paragraph from the beginning of Newman's *Discourse V, On the Scope and Nature of University Education* (1852):

> *It were well if the English, like the Greek language, possessed some definite word to express, simply and generally, intellectual proficiency or perfection, such as 'health', as used with reference to the animal frame, and 'virtue', with reference to our moral nature. I am not able to find such a term; – talent, ability, genius, belong distinctly to the raw material, which is the subject-matter, not to that excellence which is the result of exercise and training. When we turn, indeed, to the particular kinds of intellectual perfection, words are forthcoming for our purpose, as, for instance, judgment, taste, and skill; yet even these belong, for the most part, to powers or habits bearing upon practice or upon art, and not to any perfect condition of the intellect, considered in itself. Wisdom, again, which is a more comprehensive word that any other, certainly has a direct relation to conduct and to human life. Knowledge, indeed, and Science express purely intellectual ideas, but still not a state or habit of the intellect; for knowledge, in its ordinary sense, is but one of its circumstances, denoting a possession or a faculty; and science has been appropriated to the subject-matter of the intellect, instead of belonging at present, as it ought to do, to the intellect itself. The consequence is that, on an occasion like this, many words are necessary, in order, first, to bring out and convey what surely is no difficult idea in itself – that of the cultivation of the intellect as an end; next, in order to recommend what surely is no unreasonable object; and lastly, to describe and make the mind realize the particular perfection in which that object exists.*

This is surely a remarkable paragraph; first, for the characteristic subtlety of Newman's analysis; second, for its clear insight into a growing need; and third, strangely, for the fact that Newman did not meet the want of the 'definite word' with *culture*, as a generation later, from a similar analysis, he would have seemed certain to do. It is the more remarkable, this final point, because in his writings on university education Newman is the first English writer to use the word *culture* with anything like its contemporary frequency. The word he actually suggests, with some hesitation, is *philosophy*; but this is less important than the cue he undoubtedly gave to Arnold.

In fact, however, Newman himself had been preceded. His analysis is in terms of 'a state or habit of the intellect', a 'particular perfection', and he makes the express analogy with 'health'. It is interesting to take his analysis back to a vital passage in Coleridge's fifth chapter in the tract *On the Constitution of Church and State* (1830):

> *The permanency of the nation . . . and its progressiveness and personal freedom . . . depend on a continuing and progressive civilization. But civilization is itself but a mixed good, if not far more a corrupting influence, the hectic of disease, not the bloom of health, and a nation so distinguished more fitly to be called a varnished than a polished people, where this civilization is not grounded in cultivation, in the harmonious development of those qualities and faculties that characterize our humanity.*

Here, quite obviously, Coleridge is attempting to set up a standard of 'health' to which a more certain appeal may be made than to the 'mixed good' of 'civilization'. He finds this standard in 'cultivation', and goes on to use 'cultivation' for the first time to denote an abstract condition, a 'state or habit'. He ends his discussion of the function of the National Church with these words:

> *And of especial importance is it to the objects here contemplated that only by the vital warmth diffused by these truths throughout the many, and by the guiding light from the philosophy, which is the basis of divinity, possessed by the few, can either the community or its rulers fully comprehend, or rightly appreciate,* the permanent distinction, and the occasional contrast between cultivation and civilization; *or be made to understand this most valuable of the lessons taught by history, and exemplified alike in her oldest and her most recent records – that a nation can never be a too cultivated, but may easily become an over-civilized, race.*

'The permanent distinction and the occasional contrast'; and Coleridge has already spoken of cultivation as 'the ground, the necessary antecedent condition, of both . . . permanency and progressiveness'.

His analysis, clearly, has wider implications than Newman's. In Newman, the idea is of 'a state or habit' which as a process of perfection is an end in itself. For Coleridge the process is certainly an end, but he is much more explicit about its relation to the rest of human activity. For he sees cultivation as the source of health in a community, the guarantee against 'corruption'.

This analysis of Coleridge's is the first Idea of Culture, in its modern sense. And in order to understand it, we need to consider the nature of the 'corruption' against which this specific was proposed. It is both Liberalism, in its sense of a habit of mind, and Industrialism, in its sense of the reshaping of values consequent upon economic and social change. On the one hand, the 'corruption' is conveniently symbolized by Bentham;

on the other, by the developments which prompted Coleridge's famous questions:

Has the national welfare, have the weal and happiness of the people, advanced with the increase of the circumstantial prosperity? Is the increasing number of wealthy individuals that which ought to be understood by the wealth of the nation? (On the Constitution of Church and State, *p 67*)

If the opposition to utilitarianism gave the lead to Arnold, it, and these more direct questions, also gave the lead to Ruskin. The similar questionings of Carlyle were yet to come.

The utilitarian calculus could only be set aside if a source of independent value could be affirmed. 'Man', wrote J.S. Mill, 'is never recognized by Bentham as a being capable of pursuing spiritual perfection as an end.' Man, was, of course, so recognized by many, but it was Coleridge who first attempted to define, in terms of his changing society, the *social* conditions of such a pursuit. His characteristic emphasis, as in all his social writings, is on instruction. For he might assign the promptings of perfection to 'the cultivated heart', and so apparently to man's inward consciousness, but his sense of society was such that he perceived the need for an agency of cultivation, in the form of a social institution. Cultivation, in fact, though an inward was never a merely individual process. And hence cultivation could not remain merely an ideal of personality, but must be re-defined as an activity on which society as a whole depended. In these circumstances, cultivation, or culture, became an explicit factor in society.

The vital new departure was the distinction between Cultivation and Civilization. Its immediate provenance was clearly a response similar to that of Wordsworth (in the *Preface* to the second edition of *Lyrical Ballads*, 1800):

A multitude of causes, unknown to former times, are now acting with a combined force to blunt the discriminating powers of the mind, and, unfitting it for all voluntary exertion, to reduce it to a state of almost savage torpor. The most effective of these causes are the great national events which are daily taking place, and the increasing accumulation of men in cities, where the uniformity of their occupations produces a craving for extraordinary incident which the rapid communication of intelligence hourly gratifies.

In such an environment, evidently, cultivation could not be taken for granted as a process, but must stated as an absolute, as an agreed centre for defence. Cultivation was isolated precisely because it had to be abstracted from one way of life, by way of preservation, and then transmitted and extended to another and (in the view of Coleridge and Wordsworth) inferior way. Against materialism, the amassing of fortunes, and the proposition of utility as the source of value, it offered a different and a superior order. It was, in the first place, an individual standard, but

Coleridge, as we have seen, extended it to a social ideal. In this, he was deeply affected by the ideas of Burke: the ideas of an 'organic society', of 'tradition', and of the determination of values 'in relation to the historical community'. These were the conditions of continuity in cultivation, the court of appeal by which a society construing its relationships in terms of the cash-nexus might be condemned. It was in terms of these values that cultivation might be taken as the highest observable condition of society, and its 'permanent distinction and occasional contrast' with civilization drawn. The process of cultivation of the individual was the process of perfection; and, as Burke had written, 'He who gave our nature to be perfected by our virtue willed also the necessary means of its perfection: He willed therefore the state'. And the state, historically considered, was 'a partnership in all science, a partnership in all art, a partnership in every virtue and in all perfection'. It was in this spirit that Coleridge examined the constitution of the state, and proposed the endowment within it of a class dedicated to the preservation and extension of cultivation. In the face of the disintegrating process of industrialism, cultivation had now more than ever to be socially assured.

We shall see how this worked itself out in terms of actual class relations, and the origin, in Coleridge, of the important idea of a minority dedicated to the service of culture. This idea was very closely linked, from the beginning, with the idea of education, and is to be considered in that context. The same link, of course, is implicit in Newman; it is in the writings on education that Newman finds the idea of culture so useful.

6. Newman's analysis of education is vitally important for an understanding of the nineteenth century, but I wish here to show only the explicit relation which he made between the idea of culture and the idea of perfection. Here is one of his central statements:

> *And so, as regards intellectual culture, I am far from denying utility in this large sense as the end of education, when I lay it down, that the culture of the intellect is a good in itself and its own end ... As the body may be sacrificed to some manual or other toil ... so may the intellect be devoted to some specific profession; and I do not call this the culture of the intellect. Again, as some member or organ of the body may be inordinately used and developed, so may memory or imagination or the reasoning faculty; and this again is not intellectual culture. On the other hand, as the body may be tended, cherished and exercised with a simple view to its general health, so may the intellect also be generally exercised in order to its perfect state; and this is its cultivation.* (The Scope and Nature of University Education p 58–9)

The assumption in arguments of this kind is, of course, that an ideal perfection exists, as an obvious end. Newman puts this quite clearly:

> *There is a physical beauty and a moral: there is a beauty of person, there is a beauty of our moral being, which is natural virtue; and in like*

manner there is a beauty, there is a perfection, of the intellect. There is an ideal perfection in these various subject-matters, towards which individual instances are seen to rise, and which are the standards for all instances whatever. (The Scope and Nature of University Education, p 113)

This metaphysical idea of the absolute standard cannot, of course, be explained as a simple reaction to a society in which values were being reconsidered on the new principle of utility. It is, rather, the assertion of a much older tradition against the challenge of the new. But what is important, historically, is that this ideal perfection is receiving a new foundation. Whereas its traditional sanction had been religious, its definition as the nineteenth century goes on is increasingly in terms of the new concept 'culture'. Arnold, later, was to make a fairly clear substitution of Culture for Religion; but the basis of the substitution had been laid earlier, and particularly by Coleridge. One would not expect such a substitution in Newman; indeed he denounces it quite plainly as a heresy, in terms which might well have been remembered at the end of the century:

Accordingly, virtue being only one kind of beauty, the principle which determines what is virtuous is, not conscience, but taste. (The Scope and Nature of University Education, p 192)

The whole of Discourse VII is the essential religious reply to the religion of Culture which later developed. Nevertheless, the tide was running against Newman's reservation. With the definition of culture in terms of perfection, and then with the development of culture from a process to an idea, from an act of training to an absolute and saving condition, the opportunity for the substitution was made. This development, to religious men, was the negative consequence of the new idea. Its positive consequence, in general history, was that an idea had been formulated which expressed value in terms independent of 'civilization', and hence, in a period of radical change, in terms independent of the progress of society. The standard of perfection was now available, not merely to influence society, but to judge it.

(iii) The New Concepts of Art, and the Artist, and of their Relation to Society

7. The idea of culture, at the stage which we have been considering, had not yet acquired that close association with the arts which has since been characteristic of it. Nevertheless, important changes had been taking place in the concept of art, and in the idea of the artist, which need to be understood if the significance of the later association is to be realized.[1]

The characteristic of these changes was an increasing consciousness of the special nature of art-activity, and the attribution to such activity of certain special qualities of mind. These developments may now be examined more directly.

8. Wordsworth, in the preface to the second edition of *Lyrical Ballads* (1800), marks a starting-point by contrast with subsequent ideas:

> *Among the qualities there enumerated, as principally conducing to form a Poet, is implied nothing differing in kind from other men, but only in degree.*

This moderate statement was to receive considerable amendment as the century progressed; indeed the conditions for its amendment were already laid down when Wordsworth wrote. What came to be stressed, in the new ethos, was precisely the difference of the artist, *in kind*, from other men.

This development has many sources, but the first that claims our attention is perhaps the most important. The artist's difference in kind could not have been stressed in the way it was if it had not rested on the doctrine of 'the superior reality of art'. It is customary to attribute this doctrine to the rise of Romanticism, but in fact it is as much a part of Classicism, as that category is normally defined. The confusion of the Romanticism–Classicism controversy rests largely upon a confusion about the nature of 'imitation'. It is easy to reject 'imitation' as the basis of art if it is understood as 'imitation of works already done', that is to say 'conformity to a set of rules'. This was the normal Romantic interpretation of Classicism, and was the basis of the opposition between 'genius' and 'study'. But where, as in many classicist writers, 'limitation' was defined as 'imitation of the universal reality', so that the artist's precepts are not so much previous works of art as the 'universals', or permanent realities, defined by Aristotle, the case is evidently altered. A 'romantic' critic like Ruskin, for example, bases his whole theory of art on just such a 'classicist' doctrine.

The tendency of Romanticism, it is true, is a vehement rejection of dogmas of method in art: 'modern writers have a choice to make . . . they may soar in the regions of liberty, or move in the soft fetters of easy imitation' (Young, *Conjectures on Original Composition*). But this rejection was accompanied by the claim that through the exercise of 'spontaneity' and 'natural genius', the artist would in fact 'read the open secret of the universe' (Carlyle), that is to say would be able to represent the 'superior reality'. The perception of ultimate truth which Plato had reserved to philosophers was thus extended to artists. This function was theirs by virtue of their 'master faculty', imagination. Thus the doctrines of 'the genius', the autonomous creative artist, and of 'the superior reality of art', the penetration to a sphere of 'universal truth', were in practice two sides of the same claim.

The claim was reinforced by the teachings of idealist philosophy. Coleridge's theory of Imagination is a special case, requiring specific study, but its nature is entirely consonant with the spirit of these claims for art. He had argued:

*the necessity of a general revolution in the modes of developing
and disciplining the human mind by the substitution of life and
intelligence . . . for the philosophy of mechanism which, in everything
that is the worthy of the human intellect, strikes Death. (Letters, II,
649)*

Artists, in this mood, came to see themselves as agents of the 'revolution for life', in their capacity as bearers of the 'creative imagination'. Here, again, is one of the principal sources of the idea of Culture; it was on this basis that the association of the idea with the practice of the arts was to be made. For here, in the work of the artist, was a practicable mode of access to that ideal of perfection which was to be the centre of defence against the disintegrating tendencies of the age.

The artist then, was a being devoted to the high calling of 'revelation'. He was a special *kind* of being; imagination was his genius. And it is worth noting that in the earliest formulations of this idea, 'genius' was often opposed to 'art'. Young, in the *Conjectures on Original Composition* (1759), wrote:

*An original may be said to be of a vegetable nature; it rises
spontaneously from the vital root of genius; it grows, it is not
made; imitations are often a sort of manufacture, wrought up by
those mechanics, art and labour, out of pre-existent materials not
their own.*

It is interesting to set this beside three lines of Wordsworth:

*And so the grandeur of the forest-tree
Comes not by casting in a formal mould
But from its own divine vitality.*

This is the typical rejection of 'the set of rules', but it is significant that the lines come from that sonnet to which he prefixed the sour note against 'artistical', which had better, he asserted, be written 'artificial'. *Art*, indeed, in the sense of a traditional skill, was generally rejected; it was a mere fetter on 'original genius'. The characteristic mode of operation of the latter was as 'artless spontaneity'.

Here is one of the crucial phases in the change in the concept of *art*. Art as a specific skill was being replaced by *Art* as the 'sphere of imaginative truth'. As Wordsworth again had written:

*High is our calling, Friend, Creative Art,
Demands the service of a mind and heart
Though sensitive, yet in their weakest part
Heroically fashioned – to infuse
Faith in the whispers of the lonely Muse
While the whole world seems adverse to desert.*

These are the lines to the painter Haydon, in March 1815. They are very significant, because they mark the fusing into the common 'sphere of imaginative truth' of the two separate *arts*, or skills, of poetry and painting.

It is evident how these various developments laid the basis for the increasing belief in the artist as a special kind of person. One can see the result in these lines of Shelley's:

> *On a Poet's lips I slept*
> *Dreaming like a love-adept*
> *In the sound his breathing kept;*
> *Nor seeks nor finds he mortal blisses*
> *But feeds on the aerial kisses*
> *Of shapes that haunt thought's wildernesses.*
> *He will watch from dawn to gloom*
> *The lake-reflected sun illume*
> *The yellow bees in the ivy bloom,*
> *Nor heed nor see*
> *What things they be,*
> *But from these create he can*
> *Forms more real than living man*
> *Nurslings of immortality. (*Prometheus Unbound*)*

What we have here is, first, the doctrine of the 'superior reality', and, second, the idea of the Poet in his characteristic degree of separation from 'mortal' concerns. We have also something else, which was present also in Wordsworth's lines to Haydon; the idea of the artist as a romantic figure, as hero. A comment of L.L. Schucking, in *The Sociology of Literary Taste*, is relevant here:

> *It is particularly instructive [he writes] to see how late the artist is in appearing in literature as an attractive figure. The hero in the romances of earlier centuries is a knight, a prince, a cavalier, an officer; sometimes in the eighteenth century a clergyman. A hundred years later all this was changed. Interest centred for the first time in the artist . . . He was almost a higher type of human being.*

However this may be historically, it is certain that since the nineteenth century the figure of the artist as hero has become commonplace (particularly in works of art). *Heroically fashioned . . . while the whole world seems adverse to desert.* Carlyle, when he came to number his heroes, wrote eloquently both of the poet and the man of letters as hero. And in Carlyle's account, as in Wordsworth's, we are reminded of yet another reason for the new attitude, the artist's intuition that in the newly evolving society he had no place:

> *Whence he came, whither he is bound, by what ways he arrived, by what he may be furthered on his course, no one asks. He is an accident*

in society. He wanders like a wild Ishmaelite, in a world of which he is as the spiritual light, either the guidance or the misguidance. (On Heroes, Hero-Worship and the Heroic in History; *Lecture V*, Everyman, *p 338*)

And so again, as one of the tributaries of the idea of Culture, we find this extended into a symptom of a more general disorder.

Complaint is often made, in these times, of what we call the disorganized condition of society: how ill many arranged forces of society fulfil their work; how many powerful forces are seen working in a wasteful, chaotic, altogether unarranged manner. It is too just a complaint, as we all know. But, perhaps, if we look at this of Books and the Writers of Books, we shall find here, as it were, the summary of all other disorganization; — a sort of heart, from which, and to which, all other confusion circulates in the world ... That a wise great Johnson, a Burns, a Rousseau, should be taken for some idle nondescript, extant in the world to amuse idleness, and have a few coins and applause thrown in, that he might live thereby; this *perhaps, as before hinted, will one day seem a still absurder phasis of things. Meanwhile, since it is the spiritual always that determines the material, this same Man-of-Letters Hero must be regarded as our most important modern person. He, such as he may be, is the soul of all. What he teaches, the whole world will do and make. The world's manner of dealing with him is the most significant feature of the world's general position.* (On Heroes, Hero-Worship and the Heroic in History; *Lecture V*, Everyman, *p 387*)

The artist, that is to say, was important because his genius gave access to the 'superior reality' and hence to 'spiritual light'. This was his heroic calling, but he was Hero because he was also victim; the nature of his genius, in the rapidly changing society, could not easily be found a place. He was the light by which men ordered their ways, the 'unacknowledged legislator', but he appeared as a mere 'accident in society'. Shelley spoke for others than himself when he wondered how 'one of so weak and sensitive a nature as mine can run further the gauntlet through this hellish society of men'. The height of the artist's claim was also the height of his despair. He had defined his calling, but even in his confidence he was conscious of the need for a new definition of his place in society.

9. The place of the artist in society was in fact at this time evidently changing. And one is faced with one of the recurrent problems of interpretation, whether the changes in society produced the new idea of the artist, or whether the idea forced the actual changes. Thus it is possible to relate the new ideas of art and the artist solely to a larger system of ideas — the general body of European Romanticism; to point out their relation to similar ideas in the writings of Goethe, of Schiller of Rousseau, and of Chateaubriand. The idea of the artist as a special kind of

person, and of the 'wild' genius, could be taken back as far as the Socratic definition of a poet in Plato's *Ion*. The idea of the 'superior reality' could also be taken back to Plato, and then, within the period, related to the philosophy of Kant and its English dilution through Coleridge and Carlyle. These relations are important, but they can never be made a substitute for an analysis of the conditions under which the ideas were applied, nor can the ideas alone explain the consequences of the new relations, which for our present purpose constitute their most important aspect.

The question of the relation of the artist to society is further complicated by the fact that, *as individuals*, the artists themselves, in different ways and degrees, responded directly to the general movement of society, and defined attitudes towards it which are not necessarily their attitudes *as artists*, but are primarily their attitudes as members of society. The responses are often closely linked. Young's definition of 'an original', for example, which has already been quoted, is certainly a statement of literary theory, but it is quite clearly made in terms of a general movement of feeling which is characteristic of the time. 'It grows, it is not made': is not this the whole tenour of Burke? And the definition of imitation as 'a sort of *manufacture*, wrought up by those *mechanics*, art and labour, *out of pre-existent materials not their own*': is not this, consciously or unconsciously, a statement in terms of the new processes of industrial production which were about to transform society? It was from this movement of feeling that the opposition between 'inward values' and the 'machinery' of society, first made explicit by Carlyle in 1829, and later widely publicized by Arnold, clearly stemmed. This is only to say what one should expect: that the movements in literary theory were part of the general movement of thought in the changing society.

Moreover, from Blake and Wordsworth to Shelley, Byron and Keats, the poets who lived through the Industrial Revolution registered on their senses 'the catastrophic dislocation of the lives of the common people'. Politically, they divided; but all were shaped by the impact of the general suffering of their times. It was not only artists who felt that 'man was no longer at home in the society he had shaped', and it was not only from their experience *as artists* that they drew the characteristic figures of the exile, the guilty wanderer, the solitary, and the remote, proud individual. In the years following the Napoleonic wars, one did not have to be an artist to feel that society was indifferent or hostile to individual desires.

The pattern of hunger and suffering was not background, but the mould in which general experience was cast. One does well to remember this in turning to consider those factors which affected artists in the actual exercise of their arts.

Artists had often expressed, before this time, a feeling of dissatisfaction with their 'public', but in the early nineteenth century this feeling became acute and general. One finds it in Keats: 'I have not the slightest feel of humility towards the Public'; in Shelley: 'Accept no counsel from the simple-minded. Time reverses the judgment of the foolish crowd. Contemporary criticism is no more than the sum of the folly with which genius has to wrestle'; in Wordsworth: 'Away then with the senseless iteration of the word *popular* applied to new works of poetry, as if there were no test of excellence in this first of the fine arts but that all men should run after its productions, as if urged by an appetite, or constrained by a spell'. These views were of course affected by the doctrine of the 'autonomous genius', but they were also affected by actual changes in the nature of 'the public'. The eighteenth century had brought about the growth of a large new middle-class reading public, and the system of patronage had passed into subscription-publishing and thence into general commercial publishing of the modern kind. These developments affected writers in several ways; first, in an advance in 'independence' and in social status; and second, in the institution of 'the market' as the type of a writer's actual relations with society. Under patronage, the artist had at least a direct relationship with an immediate circle of readers, from whom, whether prudentially or willingly, as mark or as matter of respect, he was accustomed to accept and at times to act on criticism. It is possible to argue that this system gave the artist a *more relevant* freedom than that to which he succeeded, and that it ensured the direct relation of art with at least some part of society, so that the sense of 'belonging' gave more than was taken away by the subsequent market obligation 'to please'. However this may be, the change was certainly felt, and the proclamation of autonomy seemed a necessary defence. Wordsworth wrote in the preface to the second edition of *Lyrical Ballads*:

> *Such faulty expressions, were I convinced they were faulty at present, and they must necessarily continue to be so, I would willingly take all reasonable pains to correct. But it is dangerous to make these alterations on the authority of a few individuals, or even of certain classes of men; for where the understanding of an author is not convinced, or his feelings altered, this cannot be done without great injury to himself; for his own feelings are his stay and support.*

In the conditions of the time, it is difficult to see what else could have been said. As Wordsworth wrote again:

> *Still more lamentable is his error who can believe that there is anything of divine infallibility in the clamour of that small though loud portion of the community, ever governed by factitious influence, which, under the name of the PUBLIC, passes itself upon the unthinking, for the PEOPLE. Towards the Public, the Writer hopes that he feels as much deference as it is entitled to; but to the People, philosophically characterized, and to the embodied spirit of their knowledge ... his devout respect, his reverence, is due.* (Essay Supplementary to the Preface, 1815)

This conception of the People is, of course, in terms of social theory, pure Burke. And the relation provides us with one more strand in the development of the idea of Culture. The artist could proclaim that 'his own feelings are his stay and support', but his confidence was greatly increased if he felt that his final appeal was to 'the embodied spirit . . . of the People', that is to say to an Idea, an Ideal Reader, a standard that might be set above the 'clamour' of his actual relations with society. 'The embodied spirit', in fact, was a very welcome alternative to the market. For the free play of genius found it increasingly difficult to consort with the free play of the market, although, ironically enough, very much the same forces had produced both. Adam Smith had written:

> *In opulent and commercial societies to think or to reason comes to be, like every other employment, a particular business, which is carried on by a few people, who furnish the public with all the thought and reason possessed by the vast multitudes that labour. (Quoted Klingender:* Art and the Industrial Revolution*)*

The artist, similarly, had become a specialist, in the general emphasis of the process of division of labour which the new industrial system required. His work, as Adam Smith had said of knowledge, was 'purchased, in the manner as shoes or stockings, from those whose business it is to make up and prepare for the market that particular species of goods'. This was not the intention, but it was the result. And so, as Sir Egerton Brydges commented in the 1820s:

> *It is a vile evil that literature is become so much of a trade all over Europe. Nothing has gone so far to nurture a corrupt taste, and to give the unintellectual power over the intellectual. Merit is now universally esteemed by the multitude of readers can attract . . . Will the uncultivated mind admire what delights the cultivated? (Quoted Q.D. Leavis,* Fiction and the Reading Public*)*

The *cultivated* and the *uncultivated*: there was the new issue. The artist might feel with Carlyle:

> *Never, till about a hundred years ago, was there seen any figure of a Great Soul living apart in that anomalous manner; endeavouring to speak forth the inspiration that was in him by Printed Books, and find place and subsistence by what the world would please to give him for doing that. Much had been sold and bought, and left to make its own bargain in the marketplace; but the inspired wisdom of a Heroic Soul never till then, in that naked manner. (*On Heroes, Hero-Worship and the Heroic in History*, p 383)*

This was the background of complaint, but the terms in which it was to be worked out were those used by Tom Moore to Wordsworth in 1834. He spoke of the 'lowering of standard that must necessarily arise from the extending of the circle of judges; from letting the mob in to vote, particularly at a period when the market is such an object to authors' (quoted Q.D. Leavis, *Fiction and the Reading Public*). He drew the distinction between 'the cultivated few' and 'the mob', and then in

1837 invented the significant new term for the latter, 'the masses'. From the difficulties of their own position, in fact, many artists were being driven towards the idea of Culture; and this had now to be defined in social terms, in terms of the relations between classes.

(iv) Culture and Classes

10. Coleridge, in defining Cultivation as the standard of health in society, defined also the idea of a minority to whom the business of Cultivation must be primarily assigned. This minority was the Clerisy, or national Church, which 'in its primary acceptation and original intention, comprehended the learned of all denominations; the sages and professors of . . . all the so-called liberal arts and sciences' (*On the Constitution of Church and State*, p 49). These were the third estate of the realm.

> *Now as in the first estate* (landowners) *the permanency of the nation was provided for; and in the second estate* (merchants and manufacturers) *its progressiveness and personal freedom; while in the king the cohesion by interdependence; and the unity of the country, were established; there remains for the third estate only that interest which is the ground, the necessary antecedent condition, of both the former.* (On the Constitution of Church and State, p 46)

The maintenance of the Clerisy, whose business was Cultivation, was to be assured by a specifically reserved portion of the national wealth, which Coleridge calls 'the Nationality'. This would be its Establishment, as a National Church; but the Church was not to be understood as merely the 'Church of Christ', for this would 'reduce the Church to a religion', and thence to a mere sect. Theology would give 'the circulating sap and life', but the object of the class was general cultivation.

This idea of a special cultivated and cultivating class was to be taken up, in a slightly different context, by Carlyle. Carlyle spoke of writers as 'the real working effective Church of a modern country', and urged the need for an organic Literary Class. He doubted the best arrangement of this, 'but if you ask, Which is the worst? I answer: This which we now have, that Chaos should sit umpire in it; this is the worst' (*On Heroes, Hero-Worship, and the Heroic in History*, p 394). It is not a question of 'money-furtherances', of securing to the artist a living:

> *The result to individual Men of Letters is not the momentous one; they are but individuals, an infinitesimal fraction of the great body; they can struggle on, and live or else die, as they have been wont. But it deeply concerns the whole society, whether it will set its* light *on high places, to walk thereby . . . . I call this anomaly of a disorganic Literary Class the heart of all other anomalies, at once product and parent.* (On Heroes, Hero-Worship, and the Heroic in History, p 396)

These ideas, of Coleridge and Carlyle, are deeply significant of the situation in the new society. It is, in the first place, very significant that even Coleridge did not see in any *existing* class the capacity for maintaining and extending culture. The landed classes might provide permanence, but they could not provide this. As for the new middle class, as Mr G.M. Young has written, 'The English *bourgeoisie* had never been isolated long enough to frame, except in the spheres of comfort and carnal morality, ideals and standards of its own' (*Portrait of an Age*, p 85). The demand, then, is for an endowed *élite*; and nothing could be more significant of the disintegration of traditional society. We were not yet to hear of an *intelligentsia*, which as a word did not appear in English till 1914, but the idea of 'an intellectual' had appeared in 1813, at about the same time as 'a genius' and 'artist' in the new sense. The word from the beginning had a derogatory tone, like the later 'high-brow', which was imported from the U.S.A. in the early years of our own country. The uneasiness is quite understandable, because it reflects the uneasiness of the rest of society at certain qualities being set aside as the prerogative of a distinct class; a class, moreover, for which, in spite of Coleridge, no clear *economic* basis could be perceived. In view of the subsequent importance of the idea of an *élite* in the general Idea of Culture, these circumstances of its immediate origin deserve pondering.

There is another way in which the idea of Culture is significant of changing relations between classes. At the time when Coleridge and Newman were writing, the industrial working class was beginning to be felt as an organized force. As a necessary consequence, the existence of this force was beginning to affect questions of education. It had, indeed, already offered a token in the flourishing Mechanics' Institutes. Reactions to this development were various. Macaulay, for example, argued that the 'ignorance' of 'the common people' was a danger to property, and that therefore their education was necessary. Carlyle, on the other hand, rejected any argument for education on grounds of mere expediency: 'as if . . . the first function [of] a government were not . . . to impart the gift of thinking'. The issue is very clearly put by F.D. Maurice, in his address to the Manchester, Ancoats and Salford Working Men's College in 1859:

Now while we were thinking about these things, and thinking earnestly about them, there came that awful year 1848, which I shall always look upon as one of the great epochs of history . . . I do say that when I think how it has affected the mind and the heart of the people of England; yes, of all classes of Englishmen . . . I hear one intelligent man and another confessing: 'Ten years ago we thought differently. But all of us have acquired, since that time, a new sense of our relation to the working-class . . . It did cause us to fear, I own; but it was not fear for our property and position; it was the fear that we were not discharging the responsibilities, greater than those which rank of property imposes, that our education laid upon us . . . We believed and felt that unless the classes in this country which had received any degree of knowledge more than their fellows were willing to share it with their fellows, to regard it as precious because it bound them to their fellows, England would fall first under an anarchy, and then under a despotism . . .

Maurice goes on to speak of the Mechanics' Institutes, evening classes, etc., through which education might be shared, and adds significantly:

> *. . . What we wanted, if possible, was to make our teaching a bond of intercourse with the men whom we taught. How that could be, we might never have found out. But the working men themselves had found it out. We heard in 1853 that the people of Sheffield had founded a People's College. The news seemed to us to mark a new era in education. We had belonged to colleges. They had not merely given us a certain amount of indoctrination in certain subjects; they had not merely prepared us for our particular professions; they had borne witness of a culture which is the highest of all culture . . . (Quoted in* Continuation Schools in England and Elsewhere; *Sadler, 1908, pp 38-9)*

The importance of this speech of Maurice's can hardly be over-stressed; for in it, after a very clear diagnosis of reactions to rising working-class power, he proposes, as an alternative to 'anarchy', not merely education, but Culture, which is something 'beyond subjects'. The preparation of the ground for Arnold hardly needs comment.

Maurice, of course, was speaking as a conscious ally of the new forces. But by many who were not allies, the type of education which the working-class was evolving for itself, in response to the pressures of an industrial society, was distrusted. It was distrusted because of its 'mechanical nature', because of its technological and vocational bias, and because of its appearance of miscellaneity in the absence of a guiding general idea. The great religious controversy over education, as a whole, is not only a matter of sectarian passions; it is also, and particularly in Coleridge and Newman, the response to the felt danger of the lack of 'a humane ideal' in the new education of the people. The idea of Culture was, among other things, the way in which this response was formulated and expressed. In a society characterized by rapidly changing class-relations, in which change could by no means be separated from violence, and complicated further by the expansion of new economic techniques and of ways of thinking which these techniques engendered, the idea of 'a spiritual centre', an agreed Culture towards which the processes of education and cultivation might be directed, was seen by minds of the character of Coleridge and Newman as vital. The Idea of Culture, with its elements of continuity and of the search for perfection, received the necessary stress.[2]

Notes

1. I have had to exclude here, for reasons of space, details of changes in the sense of art, artist, and genius; and of the development of artistic, artistical, aesthetics, aesthete, and the arts. It is difficult to appreciate fully the nature of the changes in attitude without this evidence from langauge, but the

tendency throughout is to distinction and dissociation of art and the artist; to generalization about hitherto separate arts; and the growth of the idea of art as a 'special kind of sensibility', rather than a skill. Art, in fact, becomes an absolute at about the same time and in much the same terms, as Culture; and in general the decisive period of change in the words is c. 1780–1880.

2. This article is a shortened version of the Introduction to a book of the same title, now in preparation. The book will deal with theories and ideas of culture that have been put forward in England since the Industrial Revolution. It is argued that in an industrial society the problem became essentially new, both in content and in expression; and the consequent revaluation of the relevant work of Arnold, Ruskin, Morris, Eliot, Read, the English Marxists, and some others, differs from the traditional estimate. The book will include also an estimate of the effect of the abstract idea of culture on the theory and practice of literary criticism, with particular reference to the issue of tradition, and to the various ways in which the 'standard of perfection' has been critically expressed or assumed.

The New Party Line?

From: *Essays in Criticism*, 7, I, 1957, pp 68–76

The Outsider, by Colin Wilson, Gollancz

We look, in each generation, not only for those works of original thought or imagination by which our immediate literary tradition will be formed, but also for works of an inferior kind which by their very lack of individual quality are in a sense characteristic: novels which consolidate an achieved territory or exploit a registered feeling; general works which represent the impact, on an ordinary articulate mind, of the medley of contemporary voices. Such works, when they appear, seem to many readers exceptionally important – a known way of seeing appears to be mapped, a familiar attitude appears to be well documented – but what, at this level, is an understandable valuation can become, very quickly, a familiar kind of nonsense. With literary journalism as it is, and with the application of techniques of commercial advertising and personal publicity to literature and publishing, certain books, which are capable of being immediately reduced to symptoms, can become, almost overnight, what passes for a literary or an intellectual movement. The celebrations are alike extensive and sustained, and which of us, sitting down somewhere alone, can feel with any confidence that his judgment, or his word, will matter a damn in such a storm? At times, even, there seems a kind of fixed alliance between sciolism and advertisement, and in the case of Mr Colin Wilson's *The Outsider*, for example, it is difficult to get at the text, and at thinking about the text, past Mr Philip Toynbee ('truly astounding'), Mr Cyril Connolly ('most remarkable'), Dame Edith Sitwell ('astonishing') and the usual addition sums in magenta on lemon. On the front jacket *The Outsider* is 'an inquiry into the nature of the sickness of mankind in the mid-twentieth century', and on the back jacket it is 'a blueprint' (really) 'of the malaise of the soul of mankind in the mid-twentieth century'. It is not clear whether Mr Wilson thought the book was either of these things; one hopes not, for of course it isn't. All the same, one has to reach the book through this kind of storm.

Actually *The Outsider* is a kind of scrapbook, or an anthology with a thesis. Mr Wilson has selected a point of view, which he calls that of the 'Outsider', and has written what is in effect a linking commentary on literary illustrations of it. The illustrations range from Blake to Camus and there are some biographical illustrations from George Fox to Nijinsky. Most of the examples are in fact from the nineteenth century, which makes the 'mid-twentieth century malaise' even more difficult to swallow. To his tasks of selection and commentary Mr Wilson has brought great enthusiasm, a certain expository clarity, and a seemingly genuine conviction. Moreover, the Outsider's 'fundamental attitude: non-acceptance of life, of human life by human beings in a human society' (p 18) is, in theory, quite widely held, so that both the examples and the commentary can be associated with a body of serious and important writing. Yet, if criticism now means anything, this is exactly the kind of book which might notably benefit from it; it is this process, as always, that the fixed alliance impedes.

The Outsider is *not* a critical work. Mr Wilson uses, in his examples, work as different as Wells's pamphlet *Mind at the End of its Tether* and Dostoievski's *Brothers Karamazov*, without seriously considering whether differences of intention and success modify (as they must do) the apparent thesis. Further, in his analyses of particular works, he is not free from the familiar error of detaching extracts from their dramatic context, or of failing to take this whole context into account: the dream at the end of *Crime and Punishment*, for example, might be thought a relevant comment on the idea of the outsider, but Mr Wilson does not mention it – he is busy with his continuous straight-line illustration. And, if it is not a critical work, it is hardly, in any serious sense, a philosophical work. Certainly it expounds an attitude, makes classifications within it, and recommends it. But the classifications are in fact vague, and the central attitude itself is, by the end of the book, rather miscellaneous. As for the recommendation, it is simple and largely unargued; there is a certain amount of bluff about the 'once-born bourgeois', the 'healthy-minded man', the 'do-gooder', and the 'average plumber or stockbroker', all likely apparently to undervalue the Outsider, but all, obviously, rather unpleasant things to be. There is also something called 'the Marxian attitude' (p 242) which it is doubtful if any Marxist would recognize. Such gestures lend an appearance of debate, but the Outsider, in Mr Wilson's image of him, never in fact encounters any arguments stronger than those of Aunt Sally, that notorious *femme moyenne sensuelle*. In an anthology, none of this would matter, but the book doesn't look like an anthology – it looks like thinking.

Taking it as a kind of anthology, however, one has still to observe certain important faults. The mistakes are sometimes misprints ('Varities of Religious Experience', p 260) ('Ecce Home', p 139); sometimes rather more than misprints ('Recherche de Temps Perdu', p 38) ('Professor F.O. Mathieson', p 110); sometimes quite serious, as in the belief that Blake wrote:

I wander through each dirty street
Near where the dirty Thames does flow
And on each human face I meet
Marks of weakness, marks of woe. (p 164)

But these are trivial errors beside such a howler as this:

> *The revolutions in thought, brought about by the Victorian sages, J.S. Mill, Huxley, Darwin, Emerson, Spencer, Carlyle, Ruskin, seemed to presage endless changes in human life, and man would go forward indefinitely on 'stepping-stones of his dead selves to higher things'. Before we condemn it for its shortsightedness, we survivors of two world wars and the atomic bomb, it is as well to remember that we are in the position of adults condemning children. The rationalism of the eighteenth and nineteenth centuries was not a sterile, boring state of mind; it was a period of intense and healthy optimism that didn't mind hard work and pedestrian logic . . . (p 47)*

Carlyle? Ruskin? I would guess that the procedure in Mr Wilson's mind at this point was (1) the Victorians believed in Progress; (2) some Victorian writers were Mill, Huxley, Darwin, Emerson, Spencer, Carlyle, Ruskin; (3) 'The revolutions in thought brought about by the Victorian sages, etc.', in a firm, adult hand. Otherwise, if Mr Wilson has ever read, say, Carlyle, what on earth are we to think of him as an expositor? He might at least, even now, be referred to *Sartor Resartus* (written 1831), where, in addition to some early illustrations of his theme, he would find, in Chapters VII and IX of Book II, the phrases 'The Everlasting No' and 'The Everlasting Yea', which, in their Nietzschean form, he takes over and uses freely.

I do not want to be intolerable to Mr Wilson, although, as the extract just quoted shows, he can at times be pretty cavalier, not only with his facts, but with his judgments of other men's work. It is more useful, however, to pass to the main thesis of *The Outsider*, and to discuss it. I have indicated that I find Mr Wilson's statement of the thesis something less than precise (the headings of the argument can be followed on pages 15, 18, 27, 82, 93, 105, 116, 143, 147, 161, 196–7, 202, 242, 243–4, 256, 261, 273, but whether from this skeleton or from the whole book the thesis is often vague and miscellaneous, being brought back to a seeming order by such phrases as 'the fundamental attitude', 'the only important distinction', 'the Outsider's chief desire', 'the Outsider's one need', 'the Outsider's problem', which are often, if you care to look them up, quite different things). Yet the mood, in spite of this, is clear enough. It is the mood of rejection of what is supposed to be the average version of reality, in favour of a truer and deeper vision, which sees not only chaos, but sometimes the possibility of recovering order. This mood, as commonly, amalgamates and confuses two different propositions: that some men see more than others, which I suppose is true; and those who see chaos, and who therefore cannot accept 'human life lived by human beings in a human society', are those who see more.

As a matter of fact, it is doubtful whether Mr Wilson adduces any literary work of importance which embodies this particular kind of rejection, even if it is supposed to be one of the Outsider's 'fundamental attitudes' among which the book, involuntarily, allows us to choose. Yet the gloss is easily associated with works of unquestionable power and intensity, which either include convincing perceptions of delusion, limited vision, unreality, and the 'world without values', or which, in certain rare cases, are almost wholly compounded of such perceptions. Such works are of an entirely different quality from those in which an evident personal inadequacy (often local and temporary) is projected as the inadequacy of all life, wherever lived. Mr Wilson's thesis suffers from the fact that he has made no such critical distinctions. He makes, however, a general progression of attitudes, from the simplest kind of inadequacy (what I would call the vagrant) through more radical kinds of rejection (what I would call the exile) to what is in effect a breaking of the Outsider's detachment – certain kinds of religious or quasi-religious acceptance. It seems to me very doubtful whether the retention of a simple term, the 'outsider', is adequate for the description of this immense range. One could say of Dostoievski and Blake, for example, who are both stressed in the later chapters of the book, that their 'fundamental attitude' is an acceptance of 'human life lived by human beings in a human society', not indeed in terms of the proffered ideologies, but in terms of an achieved compassion, relationship, and capacity for extending relationships – qualities which have little place in any psychology properly described as that of the outsider.

The experience of the outsider (the feeling of separation, isolation, and personal or social frustration) is, of course, not rare, as Mr Wilson claims, but common, and even, in certain situations, normal. The resulting detachment will often produce valuable perceptions of the general life that is being observed. But, on communication, these perceptions will, quite properly, have to undergo the scrutiny of other men (including such other men as psychiatrists and sociologists, in spite of Mr Wilson's fashionably arrogant dismissal of them). In practice, a great part of the more valuable descriptions of the outsider's situation, and of his ways of seeing, has come, on Mr Wilson's own evidence, from men who have ceased to be outsiders, in the simple sense; men who, in spite of everything, have accepted 'human life lived by human beings in a human society', leaving behind them records alike of the tension and the despair, and of the hard-won terms of acceptance. The phases of ratification and communication are, in terms of literature, virtually indispensable, and Mr Wilson's simple concept would need radical modification to be adequate to the diversity and complexity of such experience.

It is not, though, that he has not read about this diversity and complexity; in form, he acknowledges it, although it does not drive him back to review his initial formula. The reasons for this failure seem to me to lie in certain significant passages in which he discusses his own feelings, rather than the recorded literary work of others. He does not seem, moreover, to realize in any full sense that he is discussing his own feelings; he puts the points down as if they were self-evident general truths. This, of course, is the normal procedure of the simple Outsider. The passages I have in mind occur on pages 155, 196 and 232, and their general theme is the familiar modern construction of the 'masses'. Consider, for example, this:

Most men live from moment to moment, with no foresight or hindsight. Immediate physical needs occupy all their attention, just as with animals. The average man is distinguished from dogs and cats mainly

because he looks farther ahead: he is capable of worrying about his
physical needs of six months hence, ten years hence.

This familiar kind of point (the animal connection is interesting, and
typical; on page 196 there are ants and lice) is significant here because it
is put down with such casual certainty; it doesn't have to be argued about,
it is just known. But in fact what Mr Wilson thinks he knows about the
average man is evidence only of Mr Wilson; evidence in fact of the simple,
and as yet valueless, outsider.

Or take this, which is even more familiar:

These men travelling down to the City in the morning, reading their
newspapers or staring at advertisements above the opposite seats,
they have no doubt of who they are ... They have aims, these
men, some of them very distant aims: a new car in three years,
a house at Surbiton in five; but an aim is not an ideal. They are
not play-actors. They change their shirts every day, but never their
conception of themselves ... These men are in prison: that is the
Outsider's verdict. They are quite contented in prison – caged animals
who have never known freedom; but it is prison all the same. And
the Outsider? He is in prison too ... but he knows it ... And, of
course, the final revelation comes when you look at these City-men
on the train; for you realize that for them, the business of escaping is
complicated by the fact that they think they are the prison.

Well, of course, we have all read *East Coker*, and know what to think
about our fellow-passengers when we travel by tube. But it is still alarming
that this kind of stale cant should be offered, and accepted, as a serious
discussion of the condition of man. It is so general, though, this seeing of
men in block form, as 'masses', that it is easy to understand why Mr Wilson
thought he could write it down without argument. When we realize this,
we are in a position to add a comment on the general 'outsider' formula.

There are in fact no masses, whether of City-men or plumbers; there
are only ways of seeing people as masses. If this is not obvious in itself,
we must invite ourselves to remember that, to other people, we also are
masses; we also read, stare, have aims, and worry about physical needs.
If we know that we do more, we have to ask whether this will be evident
to the young man in the corner-seat, who may imagine himself to have
some final revelation when he looks at us. (If only we could tell him
that we, also, are looking at him!) A student once wrote an essay for
me, in which she described the drab, mindless masses, whom she had
seen with particular clarity while waiting for her husband at a station:
his train was late, and crowds of unknown people poured out at her,
but not the person she wanted. Unfortunately, she mentioned the station,
the day, and the time, and I had to admit that I had arrived on a train
during that period, and had poured out with the others, mindless and
drab. This sort of admission makes a difference, if you try it, to the
formula. One remembers, quickly, that modern industrial society offers

an unusually high number of opportunities for just this feeling: of physical contiguity to numbers of people whom we do not and cannot know, so that there is a sharp contrast between our own aware existence, and an apparently mindless, automatic, virtually animal, mass. This is a norm of the 'outsider' feeling, which contemporary ideology rationalizes with its formulae of 'masses' or 'the man in the street' (the man in a modern street is less of a man, less himself, there, than almost anywhere else). Multiple transmission, a concept very difficult to grasp, is similarly rationalized as mass communication. And it is not, of course, that the feelings and the difficulties are not real; what is important is that they can be recognized, and to some extent controlled, unless we have some other reason, personal or social, avowed or unavowed, for wishing to write off as insignificant the majority of our fellow beings.

There are in fact (to adapt a phrase from one of Mr Eliot's plays) perceptions of unreality and delusion that we can go on from, but some from which we must simply, and as soon as possible, return. The Outsider, unquestionably, is an aspect of contemporary man; but, while he can begin almost anywhere, he can end either as a Blake, or as a Hitler, or even as a Mr Podsnap, and it is the differences that are important.

Mr Wilson's book needs criticism because it may, with the aid of the Sunday thinkers, put into circulation yet another simplification of the facts of our common experience. The facility of his formulation reminds me, curiously, of the formulations of Christopher Caudwell (a more extensive thinker, but one very similar to him in intellectual method), and of other recent pseudo-Marxists. The image then was the Fighter, who alone saw reality, which was hidden from the deluded bourgeois, petit-bourgeois and recalcitrant intellectual. In much the same way, the image was made out of a closed system of abstractions, with supporting literary illustrations. The insights of a Marx or a Plekhanov, like the very different insights of a Blake or a Proust, are too important, in the common stock of experience, to be diluted or forced into a temporary cry. The detail and vitality of original work matches the difficulty and complexity of the life being interpreted, but the simplification has advantages in that it can be quickly taken up, and passed from mouth to mouth, as the thing to be. We may, I think, during the next few years, see this happening to the Outsider; there are already several such whom it is fashionable to be seen about with, and being an Outsider ('just feeling that way') may be one of the quickest ways to becoming an Insider and being supported by the fixed alliance. It will be a long way from doubt, despair and the struggle to communicate, just as the formula as we have it is a long way from significance and virtue. And this will not be wholly, or perhaps even mainly, Mr Colin Wilson's personal fault.

A Kind of Gresham's Law

From: *The Highway*, 49, February 1958, pp 107–10

Some of the most radical questions about our present society are questions about its culture. Yet, for a number of reasons, these are still largely open questions: we have a long way to go not only in practical enquiry but also in theory. This work can be done; some of it is already in progress. But the field is made difficult, not only by its actual problems, but also by the existence of certain formulas of interpretation, that never had much evidence behind them, but that are nevertheless, for other reasons, repeated and apparently relied on. I shall briefly examine one of these formulas, which I think is particularly misleading: what is known, in discussions of culture, as 'a kind of Gresham's law'.

Gresham's Law is a proposition in economics, and the name attached to it is that of Sir Thomas Gresham (1519?–79), a financier who founded the Royal Exchange. We can read with interest of his energetic and not always scrupulous transactions in the service of several English courts, but unfortunately he did not make his Law. We first hear of Gresham's Law, in fact, in 1858, in a book called *Elements of Political Economy*, by Henry Dunning MacLeod (1821–1902). The ascription to Gresham is a mistake by MacLeod: the proposition in question had been well understood long before Gresham, and had appeared in print in Oresme and Copernicus. The Law is, in its popular form, that bad money drives out good, but it will be convenient to take one or two more exact definitions:

(i) 'Where two media come into circulation at the same time, the more valuable will tend to disappear.'
(ii) 'The worst form of currency in circulation regulates the value of the whole currency, and drives all other forms of currency out of circulation.'

These, of course, do not say the same thing, but in the present context the difference is not relevant, since the application of the law to culture was in the most general terms. The application is an analogy: just as bad money drives out good, so bad culture drives out good. The terms of the definitions quoted will show how tempting the analogy was, especially as we use terms like 'currency' and 'circulation' quite ordinarily in relation to ideas.

The analogy was first made, so far as I know, by Sir Norman Angell, in the late 'twenties, in his book *The Press and the Organization of Society*.

He was concerned with the effect of bad newspapers, and drew attention to

> *'a psychological Gresham Law; just as in commerce, debased coin, if there be enough of it, must drive out the sterling, so in the contest of motives, action which corresponds to the most primitive feelings and impulses, to first thoughts and established prejudices, can be stimulated by the modern newspaper far more easily than that prompted by rationalized second thoughts'.*

This is confused, but from the general argument we know what is in question: the fear that irrational thinking, and opinions masquerading as facts, will, in their widespread dissemination by bad newspapers, make rational thought and informed judgment more difficult; may even indeed, if the dissemination is wide enough, make them practically disappear. This is a fear that had often expressed since the new journalism began in the 1850's.

But the analogy was not to rest there. The phrase, Gresham's Law, was taken up by F.R. Leavis and others, and has since been widely repeated as Leavis's influence has grown. I see it now quite often in newspapers, in magazines, and in reports of speeches. When it reached a speech in the House of Lords, it seemed that it had been finally taken into the establishment. In its repetition, its scope has been expanded. 'A kind of Gresham's Law' is now a very usual way of expressing disquiet at the amount of bad art, bad entertainment, bad writing, and bad argument in our culture, and of fearing that this flood will sweep away the kind of traditional culture that we value. The facts are serious enough, but it is a mark of our theoretical poverty that 'a kind of Gresham's Law' has been grasped so eagerly. In a field that is in fact chaotic, it sounds reassuringly scientific and authoritative.

Is There any Real Analogy?

We should look first, not at the analogy itself, but at the facts which it offers to interpret. There is, undoubtedly, a great deal of bad art in wide circulation. There are very bad newspapers, and these the most widely bought. The public level of thinking and writing is often, for a democracy, dangerously low. There is, further, a powerful body of opinion, affecting these matters, which can be best expressed by adapting Pope:

> *For ways of valuing let fools contest:*
> *Whate'er is best distributed is best.*

I will not, in questioning the analogy, join in any apologia for these facts.

Yet is there any evidence, we must now ask, that this bad culture is driving out, or tending to drive out, the good? We should need a very detailed enquiry to answer this question adequately, and this is where 'a kind of Gresham's Law' is in practice so dangerous, for it assumes an answer which is not based on evidence, but on an analogy from another field, and the assumption leads to very questionable social attitudes. My own view in these matters is that there has been an increase in the distribution of both good and bad cultural products, in a notably expanding culture, and that this increase, both of good and bad, may be expected to continue. More people than a hundred years ago now listen to bad music, read bad novels, see bad dramatic works, and look at bad visual art, because all of these things have become technically easier to distribute, and leisure to receive them has greatly increased. Yet, also, more people than a hundred years ago now listen to good music, read good novels, see good dramatic works, and look at good visual art. These facts can be easily checked by comparing attendances at concerts, galleries and theatres of all kinds, or the sizes of publishers' editions. I know of no case in which the audience for good work has declined, or indeed failed notably to increase. It is true also, of course, that the audiences for bad work have increased in a spectacular way, over the same period, and that many hopes, based on a simple formula of extending the good life, have been falsified, or not yet realized. This does not mean, however, that the experiment in universal literacy, or in making a popular culture, has failed. It is just this conclusion of failure, with the consequent adoption of other social allegiances, which is the really damaging product of 'a kind of Gresham's Law'.

I will take one example: from the Press, since it was there the analogy started. In 1851, when *The Times* was at the height of its virtual monopoly of the Press, it sold 40,000 copies in a population (England, Wales and Scotland) of some twenty millions: a ratio of 1 to 500. In 1870, when the monopoly had been broken, and not only a serious provincial daily press but also a cheap metropolitan press had been established, this ratio had improved to 1 to 390. Today, with a vast popular press, and other good newspapers as competitors, the ratio has further improved to about 1 to 165 (on the latest available figures). Not only has the mid-twentieth century *Times* more than seven times as many readers as that of the mid-nineteenth century, but, when the rise in population has been allowed for, the rise in circulation is about threefold. This hardly suggests any direct working of 'a kind of Gresham's Law'. Indeed, one may be tempted to what may be called the John Walter III Law (as expressed in *The Times* of 1847):

> *It is commonly said that cheap things do not interfere with the sale of good things, but that they rather diffuse a taste for the article, and in that way ultimately enlarge the class of consumers. We believe it to be so in our case.*

It has been so, with *The Times*, but we must add the next sentence:

They who start with a twopence halfpenny, or threepenny, or fourpenny journal, will soon not be satisfied with anything under a fivepenny journal.

With the ratio of the *Daily Mirror* or *Daily Express* at about 1 to 12, and still rising, we can hardly share the optimism of that 'soon'.

The fact is, surely, that we are faced with two versions of cultural change, the Utopian and the Apocalyptic, and that, on the evidence, we can accept neither. It was expected, by reformers, that cultural expansion would quite quickly produce the results *The Times* had predicted, and, when these hopes were disappointed, there was a relapse into the despair of 'a kind of Gresham's Law'. Yet the necessary theoretical revision is in fact something quite different. It would seem that in our kind of expanding culture we must expect increases in the rate of distribution of both good and bad work, and that, in the early stages of the expansion, the rate of the latter will be higher than that of the former. Historically, it still seems to me that we are in the early stages of this cultural expansion. In the case of the cheap press, for example, the penny *Daily Telegraph* was the first wave of expansion into new sections of the middle class (242,000 in 1875), and the halfpenny *Daily Mail* the next wave (400,000 in 1898, 1,000,000 in 1915, 1,845,000 in 1930). It is only with the figures from 1915 on that we find large-scale expansion into the working class, and this did not reach its peak until the 1939–45 war and the subsequent years. In the case of fiction, we are not yet beyond the stage reached in newspapers in 1900; in the theatre rather behind this, in music some way beyond. The cinema is in line with the Press, and television is rapidly becoming so.

It is understandable to be impatient with what is happening, especially since in a narrow sector there has been very rapid cultural mobility and advance, in direct relation to exceptional educational opportunities. But, through the impatience, we must keep our eyes on the whole process, and refuse to surrender to an apocalyptic formula. Of course the wide distribution of bad work is affecting the good, in particular in relation to rates of profit, as the necessary capital in an expanded culture rises, and the system of production and distribution is still largely capitalist in nature. We are faced with important social decisions, as the effects of the cultural expansion become clear. But nothing, finally, is to be gained by the Gresham analogy. Bad cultural products are not really like bad money: the complex of values to which they refer is inexpressible in a single standard. There is, in fact, no simple opposition of bad and good, but a great variety of levels, the majority of which are accepted as good at the cultural level at which they are received. All criticism now is social criticism, and it is vitally important which way criticism goes: either to the assertion of cultural class distinctions, or to the direction of an expanding common culture. The key critics are those who have experienced cultural mobility, in their own persons. It is easy, in the tension which mobility causes, to go wrong in either of two opposite ways: to adopt Gresham's Law, which leads to the rejection of a 'mass culture' and confuses the democratic allegiance; or to resign, in a latter-day Utopism, pretending that bad work is not so bad because it is enjoyed by good people. The necessary balance is difficult, but it is not impossible. Values are not a kind of gold standard, but living affirmations and conclusions. If we look at our culture as it is, we may come to understand, in affirmed detail, the process and problems of cultural expansion, and to find an adequate theory in our work to enrich the change.

Culture is Ordinary

From: N. McKenzie, ed., *Conviction*, McGibbon and Kee, 1958, pp 74–92

The bus-stop was outside the cathedral. I had been looking at the Mappa Mundi, with its rivers out of Paradise, and at the chained library, where a party of clergymen had got in easily, but where I had waited an hour and cajoled a verger before I even saw the chains. Now, across the street, a cinema advertised the *Six-Five Special* and a cartoon version of *Gulliver's Travels*. The bus arrived, with a driver and conductress deeply absorbed in each other. We went out of the city, over the old bridge, and on through the orchards and the green meadows and the fields red under the plough. Ahead were the Black Mountains, and we climbed among them, watching the steep fields end at the grey walls, beyond which the bracken and heather and whin had not yet been driven back. To the east, along the ridge, stood the line of grey Norman castles; to the west, the fortress wall of the mountains. Then, as we still climbed, the rock changed under us. Here, now, was limestone, and the line of the early iron workings along the scarp. The farming valleys, with their scattered white houses, fell away behind. Ahead of us were the narrower valleys: the steel rolling-mill, the gasworks, the grey terraces, the pitheads. The bus stopped, and the driver and conductress got out, still absorbed. They had done this journey so often, and seen all its stages. It is a journey, in fact, that in one form or another we have all made.

I was born and grew up halfway along that bus journey. Where I lived is still a farming valley, though the road through it is being widened and straightened, to carry the heavy lorries to the north. Not far away, my grandfather, and so back through the generations, worked as a farm labourer until he was turned out of his cottage and, in his fifties, became a roadman. His sons went at thirteen or fourteen on to the farms; his daughters into service. My father, his third son, left the farm at fifteen to be a boy porter on the railway, and later became a signalman, working in a box in this valley until he died. I went up the road to the village school, where a curtain divided the two classes – Second to eight or nine, First to fourteen. At eleven I went to the local grammar school, and later to Cambridge.

Culture is ordinary: that is where we must start. To grow up in that country was to see the shape of a culture, and its modes of change. I could stand on the mountains and look north to the farms and the cathedral, or south to the smoke and the flare of the blast furnace making a second sunset. To grow up in that family was to see the shaping of minds: the learning of new skills, the shifting of relationships, the emergence of different language and ideas. My grandfather, a big hard labourer, wept while he spoke, finely and excitedly, at the parish meeting, of being turned out of his cottage. My father, not long before he died, spoke quietly and happily of when he had started a trade union branch and a Labour Party group in the village, and, without bitterness, of the 'kept men' of the new politics. I speak a different idiom, but I think of these same things.

Culture is ordinary: that is the first fact. Every human society has its own shape, its purposes, its own meanings. Every human society expresses these, in institutions, and in arts and learning. The making of a society is the finding of common meanings and directions, and its growth is an active debate and amendment, under the pressures of experience, contact, and discovery, writing themselves into the land. The growing society is there, yet it is also made and remade in every individual mind. The making of a mind is, first, the slow learning of shapes, purposes, and meanings, so that work, observation and communication are possible. Then, second, but equal in importance, is the testing of these in experience, the making of new observations, comparisons, and meanings. A culture has two aspects: the known meanings and directions, which its members are trained to; the new observations and meanings, which are offered and tested. These are the ordinary processes of human societies and human minds, and we see through them the nature of a culture: that it is always both traditional and creative; that it is both the most ordinary common meanings and the finest individual meanings. We use the word culture in these two senses: to mean a whole way of life – the common meanings; to mean the arts and learning – the special processes of discovery and creative effort. Some writers reserve the word for one or other of these senses; I insist on both, and on the significance of their conjunction. the questions I ask about our culture are questions about our general and common purposes, yet also questions about deep personal meanings. Culture is ordinary, in every society and in every mind.

Now there are two senses of culture – two colours attached to it – that I know about but refuse to learn. The first I discovered at Cambridge, in a teashop. I was not, by the way, oppressed by Cambridge. I was not cast down by old buildings, for I had come from a country with twenty centuries of history written visibly into the earth: I liked walking through a Tutor court, but it did not make me feel raw. I was not amazed by the existence of a place of learning; I had always known the cathedral, and the bookcases I now sit to work at in Oxford are of the same design as those in the chained library. Nor was learning, in my family, some strange eccentricity; I was not, on a scholarship in Cambridge, a new kind of animal up a brand-new ladder. Learning was ordinary; we learned where we could. Always, from those scattered white houses, it had made sense to go out and become a scholar or a poet or a teacher. Yet few of us could be spared from the immediate work; a price had been set on this kind of learning, and it was more, much more, than we could individually pay. Now, when we could pay in common, it was a good, ordinary life.

I was not oppressed by the university, but the teashop, acting as if it were one of the older and more respectable departments, was a different matter. Here was culture, not in any sense I knew, but in a special sense: the outward and emphatically visible sign of a special kind of people, cultivated people. They were not, the great majority of them, particularly learned; they practised few arts; but they had it, and they showed you they had it. They are still there, I suppose, still showing it, though even they must be hearing the rude noises from outside, from a few scholars and writers they call – how comforting a label is! – angry young men. As a matter of fact there is no need to be rude. It is simply that if that is culture, we don't want it; we have seen other people living.

But of course it is not culture, and those of my colleagues who, hating the teashop, make culture, on its account, a dirty word, are mistaken. If the people in the teashop go on insisting that culture is their trivial differences of behaviour, their trivial variations of speech habit, we cannot stop them, but we can ignore them. They are not that important, to take culture from where it belongs.

Yet, probably also disliking the teashop, there were writers I read then, who went into the same category in my mind. When I now read a book such as Clive Bell's *Civilisation*, I experience not so much disagreement as stupor. What kind of life can it be, I wonder, to produce this extraordinary fussiness, this extraordinary decision to call certain things culture and then separate them, as with a park wall, from ordinary people and ordinary work? At home we met and made music, listened to it, recited and listened to poems, valued fine language. I have heard better music and better poems since; there is the world to draw on. But I know, from the most ordinary experience, that the interest is there, the capacity is there. Of course, farther along that bus journey, the old social organization in which these things had their place has been broken. People have been driven and concentrated into new kinds of work, new kinds of relationship; work, by the way, which built the park walls, and the houses inside them, and which is now at last bringing, to the unanimous disgust of the teashop, clean and decent and furnished living to the people themselves. Culture is ordinary: through every change let us hold fast to that.

The other sense, or colour, that I refuse to learn, is very different. Only two English words rhyme with culture, and these, as it happens, are sepulture and vulture. We don't yet call museums or galleries or even universities culture-sepultures, but I hear a lot, lately, about culture-vultures (man must rhyme), and I hear also, in the same North Atlantic argot, of do-gooders and highbrows and superior prigs. Now I don't like the teashop, but I don't like this drinking-hole either. I know there are people who are humourless about the arts and learning, and I know there is a difference between goodness and sanctimony. But the growing implications of this spreading argot – the true cant of a new kind of rogue – I reject absolutely. For, honestly, how can anyone use a word like 'do-gooder' with this new, offbeat complacency? How can anyone wither himself to a state where he must use these new flip words for any attachment to learning or the arts? It is plain that what may have started as a feeling about hypocrisy, or about pretentiousness (in itself a two-edged word), is becoming a guilt-ridden tic at the mention of any serious standards whatever. And the word 'culture' has been heavily compromised by this conditioning: Goering reached for his gun; many reach for their cheque-books; a growing number, now, reach for the latest bit of argot.

'Good' has been drained of much of its meaning, in these circles, by the exclusion of its ethical content and emphasis on a purely technical standard; to do a good job is better than to be a do-gooder. But do we need reminding that any crook can, in his own terms, do a good job? The smooth reassurance of technical efficiency is no substitute for the whole positive human reference. Yet men who once made this reference, men who were or wanted to be writers or scholars, are now, with every appearance of satisfaction, advertising men, publicity boys, names in the strip newspapers. These men were given skills, given attachments, which are now in the service of the most brazen money-grabbing exploitation of the inexperience of ordinary people. And it is these men – this new, dangerous class – who have invented and disseminated the argot, in an attempt to influence ordinary people – who because they do real work have real standards in the fields they know – against real standards in the fields these men knew and have abandoned. The old cheapjack is still there in the market, with the country boys' half-crowns on his reputed packets of gold rings or watches. He thinks of his victims as a slow, ignorant crowd, but they live, and farm, while he coughs behind his portable stall. The new cheapjack is in offices with contemporary *décor*, using scraps of linguistics, psychology and sociology to influence what he thinks of as the mass-mind. He too, however, will have to pick up and move on, and meanwhile we are not to be influenced by his argot; we can simply refuse to learn it. Culture is ordinary. An interest in learning or the arts is simple, pleasant and natural. A desire to know what is best, and to do what is good, is the whole positive nature of man. We are not to be scared from these things by noises.

There are many versions of what is wrong with our culture. So far I have tried only to clear away the detritus which makes it difficult for us to think seriously about it at all. When I got to Cambridge, I encountered two serious influences, which have left a very deep impression on my mind. The first was Marxism; the second the teaching of Leavis. Through all subsequent disagreement I retain my respect for both.

The Marxists said many things, but those that mattered were three. First, they said that a culture must be finally interpreted in relation to its underlying system of production. I have argued this theoretically elsewhere – it is a more difficult idea than it looks – but I still accept its emphasis. Everything I had seen, growing up in that border country, had led me towards such an emphasis: a culture is a whole way of life, and the arts are part of a social organization which economic change clearly radically affects. I did not have to be taught dissatisfaction with the existing economic system, but the subsequent questions about our culture were, in these terms, vague. It was said that it was a class-dominated culture, deliberately restricting a common human inheritance to a small class, while leaving the masses ignorant. The fact of restriction I accepted – it is still very obvious that only the *deserving* poor get much educational opportunity, and I was in no mood, as I walked about Cambridge, to feel glad that I had been thought deserving; I was no better and no worse than the people I came from. On the other hand, just because of this, I got angry at my friends' talk about the ignorant masses: one kind of Communist has always talked like this, and has got his answer, at Poznan and Budapest, as the imperialists, making the same assumption, were answered in India, in Indo-China, in Africa. There is an English bourgeois culture, with its powerful educational, literary and social institutions, in close contact with the actual centres of power. To say that most working people are excluded from these is self-evident, though the doors, under sustained pressure, are slowly opening. But to go on to say that working people are excluded from English culture is nonsense; they have their own growing institutions, and much of the strictly bourgeois culture they would in any case not want. A great part of the English way of life, and of its arts and learning, is not bourgeois in any discoverable sense. There are institutions, and common meanings, which are in no sense the sole product of the commercial middle class; and there are art and learning, a common English inheritance, produced by many kinds of men, including many who hated the very class and system which now take pride in consuming it. The bourgeoisie has given us much, including a narrow but real system of morality, that is at least better than its court predecessors. The leisure which the bourgeoisie attained has given us much of cultural value. But this is not to say that contemporary culture is bourgeois culture: a mistake that everyone, from Conservatives to Marxists, seems to make. There is a distinct working-class way of life, which I for one value – not only because I was bred in it, for I now, in certain respects, live differently. I think this way of life, with its emphases of neighbourhood, mutual obligation, and common betterment, as expressed in the great working-class political and industrial institutions, is in fact the best basis for any future English society. As for the arts and learning, they are in a real sense a national inheritance, which is, or should be, available to everyone. So when the Marxists say that we live in a dying culture, and that the masses are ignorant, I have to ask them, as I asked them then, where on earth they have lived. A dying culture, and ignorant masses, are not what I have known and see.

What I had got from the Marxists then, so far, was a relationship between culture and production, and the observation that education was restricted. The other things I rejected, as I rejected also their third point, that since culture and production are related, the advocacy of a different system of production is in some way a cultural directive, indicating not only a way of life but new arts and learning. I did some writing while I was, for eighteen months, a member of the Communist Party, and I found out in trivial ways what other writers, here and in Europe, have found out more gravely: the practical consequences of this kind of theoretical error. In this respect, I saw the future, and it didn't work. The Marxist interpretation of culture can never be accepted while it retains, as it need not retain, this directive element, this insistence that if you honestly want Socialism you must write, think, learn in certain prescribed ways. A culture is common meanings, the product of a whole people, and offered individual meanings, the product of a man's whole committed personal and social experience. It is stupid and arrogant to suppose that any of these meanings can in any way be prescribed; they are made by living, made and remade, in ways we cannot know in advance. To try to jump the future, to pretend that in some way you *are* the future, is strictly insane. Prediction is another matter, an offered meaning, but the only thing we can say about culture in an England that has socialized its means of production is that all the channels of expression and communication should be cleared and open, so that the whole actual life, that we cannot know in advance, that we can know only in part even while it is being lived, may be brought to consciousness and meaning.

Leavis has never liked Marxists, which is in one way a pity, for they know more than he does about modern English society, and about its immediate history. He, on the other hand, knows more than any Marxist I have met about the real relations between art and experience. We have all learned from him in this, and we have also learned his version of what is wrong with English culture. The diagnosis is radical, and is rapidly becoming orthodox. There was an old, mainly agricultural England, with a traditional culture of great value. This has been replaced by a modern, organized, industrial State, whose characteristic institutions deliberately cheapen our natural human responses, making art and literature into desperate survivors and witnesses, while a new mechanized vulgarity sweeps into the centres of power. The only defence is in education, which will at least keep certain things alive, and which will also, at least in a minority, develop ways of thinking and feeling which are competent to understand what is happening and to maintain the finest individual values. I need not add how widespread this diagnosis has become, though little enough acknowledgment is still made to Leavis himself. For my own part, I was deeply impressed by it; deeply enough for my ultimate rejection of it to be a personal crisis lasting several years.

For, obviously, it seemed to fit a good deal of my experience. It did not tell me that my father and grandfather were ignorant wage-slaves; it did not tell me that the smart, busy, commercial culture (which I had come to as a stranger, so much so that for years I had violent headaches whenever I passed through London and saw underground advertisements and evening newspapers) was the thing I had to catch up with. I even made a fool of myself, or was made to think so, when after a lecture in which the usual point was made that 'neighbour' now does not mean what it did to Shakespeare, I said – imagine! – that to me it did. (When my father was dying, this year, one man came in and dug his garden; another loaded and delivered a lorry of sleepers for firewood; another came and chopped the sleepers into blocks; another – I don't know who, it was never said – left a sack of potatoes at the back door; a woman came in and took away a basket of washing.) But even this was explicable: I came from a bit of the old society, but my future was Surbiton (it took me years to find Surbiton, and have a good look at it, but it's served a good many as a symbol – without having lived there I couldn't say whether rightly). So there I was, and it all seemed to fit.

Yet not all. Once I got away, and thought about it, it didn't really fit properly. For one thing I knew this: at home we were glad of the Industrial Revolution, and of its consequent social and political changes. True, we lived in a very beautiful farming valley, and the valleys beyond the limestone we could all see were ugly. But there was one gift that was overriding, one gift which at any price we would take, the gift of power that is everything to men who have worked with their hands. It was slow in coming to us, in all its effects, but steam power, the petrol engine, electricity, these and their host of products in commodities and services, we took as quickly as we could get them, and were glad. I have seen all these things being used, and I have seen the things they replaced. I will not listen with patience to any acid listing of them – you know the sneer you can get into plumbing, baby Austins, aspirin, contraceptives, canned food. But I say to these Pharisees: dirty water, an earth bucket, a four-mile walk each way to work, headaches, broken women, hunger and monotony of diet. The working people, in town and country alike, will not listen (and I support them) to any account of our society which supposes that these things are not progress: not just mechanical, external progress either, but a real service of life. Moreover, in the new conditions, there was more real freedom to dispose of our lives, more real personal grasp where it mattered, more real say. Any account of our culture which explicitly or implicitly denies the value of an industrial society is really irrelevant; not in a million years would you make us give up this power.

So then the social basis of the case was unacceptable, but could one, trying to be a writer, a scholar, a teacher, ignore the indictment of the new cultural vulgarity? For the plumbing and the tractors and the medicines could one ignore the strip newspapers, the multiplying cheapjacks, the raucous triviality? As a matter of priorities, yes, if necessary; but was the cheapening of response really a consequence of the cheapening of power? It looks like it, I know, but is this really as much as one can say? I believe the central problem of our society, in the coming half-century, is the use of our new resources to make a good common culture; the means to a good, abundant economy we already understand. I think the good common culture can be made, but before we can be serious about this, we must rid ourselves of a legacy from our most useful critics; a legacy of two false equations, one false analogy, and one false proposition.

The false proposition is easily disposed of. It is a fact that the new power brought ugliness: the coal brought dirt, the factory brought overcrowding, communications brought a mess of wires. But the proposition that ugliness is a price we pay, or refuse to pay, for economic power need no longer be true. New sources of power, new methods of production, improved systems of transport and communication can, quite practically, make England clean and pleasant again, and with much more power, not less. Any new ugliness is the product of stupidity, indifference, or simply inco-ordination; these things will be easier to deal with than when power was necessarily noisy, dirty, and disfiguring.

The false equations are more difficult. One is the equation between popular education and the new commercial culture: the latter proceeding inevitably from the former. Let the masses in, it is said, and this is what you inevitably get. Now the question is obviously difficult, but I can't accept this equation, for two reasons. The first is a matter of faith: I don't believe that the ordinary people in fact resemble the normal description of the masses, low and trivial in taste and habit. I put it another way: that there are in fact no masses, but only ways of seeing people as masses. With the coming of industrialism, much of the old social organization broke down and it became a matter of difficult personal experience that we were constantly seeing people we did not know, and it was tempting to mass them, as 'the others', in our minds. Again, people were physically massed, in the industrial towns, and a new class structure (the names of our social classes, and the word 'class' itself in this sense, date only from the Industrial Revolution) was practically imposed. The improvement in communications, in particular the development of new forms of multiple transmission of news and entertainment, created unbridgeable divisions between transmitter and audience, which again led to the audience being interpreted as an unknown mass. Masses became a new word for mob: the others, the unknown, the unwashed, the crowd beyond one. As a way of knowing other people, this formula is obviously ridiculous, but, in the new conditions, it seemed an effective formula – the only one possible. Certainly it was the formula that was used by those whose money gave them access to the new communication techniques; the lowness of taste and habit, which human beings assign very easily to other human beings, was assumed, as a bridge. The new culture was built on this formula, and if I reject the formula, if I insist that this lowness is not inherent in ordinary people, you can brush my insistence aside, but I shall go on holding to it. A different formula, I know from experience, gets a radically different response.

My second reason is historical: I deny, and can prove my denial, that popular education and commercial culture are cause and effect. I have shown elsewhere that the myth of 1870 – the Education Act which is said to have produced, as its children grew up, a new cheap and nasty press – is indeed myth. There was more than enough literacy, long before 1870, to support a cheap press, and in fact there were cheap and really bad newspapers selling in great quantities before the 1870 Act was heard of. The bad new commercial culture came out of the social chaos of industrialism, and out of the success, in this chaos, of the 'masses' formula, not out of popular education. Northcliffe did few worse things than start this myth, for while the connection between bad culture and the social chaos of industrialism is significant, the connection between it and popular education is vicious. The Northcliffe Revolution, by the way, was a radical change in the financial structure of the press, basing it on a new kind of revenue – the new mass advertising of the 1890's – rather than the making of a cheap popular press in which he had been widely and successfully preceded. But I tire of making these points. Everyone prefers to believe Northcliffe. Yet does nobody, even a Royal Commission, read the most ordinarily accessible newspaper history? When people do read the history, the false equation between popular education and commercial culture will disappear for ever. Popular education came out of the other camp, and has had quite opposite effects.

The second false equation is this: that the observable badness of so much widely distributed popular culture is a true guide to the state of mind and feeling, the essential quality of living of its consumers. Too many good men have said this for me to treat it lightly, but I still, on evidence, can't accept it. It is easy to assemble, from print and cinema and television, a terrifying and fantastic congress of cheap feelings and moronic arguments. It is easy to go on from this and assume this deeply degrading version of the actual lives of our contemporaries. Yet do we find this confirmed, when we meet people? This is where 'masses' comes in again, of course: the people *we* meet aren't vulgar, but God, think of Bootle and Surbiton and Aston! I haven't lived in any of these places; have you? But a few weeks ago I was in a house with a commercial traveller, a lorry-driver, a bricklayer, a shopgirl, a fitter, a signalman, a nylon operative, a domestic help (perhaps, dear, she is your very own treasure). I hate describing these people like this, for in fact they were my family and family friends. Now they read, they watch, this work we are talking about; some of them quite critically, others with a good deal of pleasure. Very well, I read different things, watch different entertainments, and I am quite sure why they are better. But could I sit down in that house and make this equation we are offered? Not, you understand, that shame was stopping me; I've learned, thank you, how to behave. But talking to my family, to my friends, talking, as we were, about our own lives, about people, about feelings, could I in fact find this lack of quality we are discussing? I'll be honest – I looked; my training has done that for me. I can only say that I found as much natural fineness of feeling, as much quick discrimination, as much clear grasp of ideas within the range of experience as I have found anywhere. I don't altogether understand this, though I am not really surprised. Clearly there is something in the psychology of print and image that none of us has yet quite grasped. For the equation looks sensible, yet when you test it, in experience – and there's nowhere else you can test it – it's wrong. I can understand the protection of critical and intelligent reading: my father, for instance, a satisfied reader of the *Daily Herald*, got simply from reading the company reports a clear idea, based on names, of the rapid development of combine and interlocking ownership in British industry, which I had had made easy for me in two or three academic essays; and he had gone on to set these facts against the opinions in a number of articles in the paper on industrial ownership. That I understand; that is simply intelligence, however partly trained. But there is still this other surprising fact: that people whose quality of personal living is high are apparently satisfied by a low quality of printed feeling and opinion. Many of them still live, it is true, in a surprisingly enclosed personal world, much more so than mine, and some of their personal observations are the finer for it. Perhaps this is enough to explain it, but in any case, I submit, we need a new equation, to fit the observable facts.

Now the false analogy, that we must also reject. This is known, in discussions of culture, as a 'kind of Gresham's Law'. Just as bad money will drive out good, so bad culture will drive out good, and this, it is said, has in fact been happening. If you can't see, straight away, the defect of the analogy, your answer, equally effective, will have to be historical. For in fact, of course, it has not been happening. There is more, much more bad culture about; it is easier, now, to distribute it, and there is more leisure to receive it. But test this in any field you like, and see if this has been accompanied by a shrinking consumption of things we can all agree to be good. The editions of good literature are very much larger than they were; the listeners to good music are much more numerous than they were; the number of people who look at good visual art is larger than it has ever been. If bad newspapers drive out good newspapers, by a kind of Gresham's Law, why is it that, allowing for the rise in population, *The Times* sells nearly three times as many copies as in the days of its virtual monopoly of the press in 1850? It is the law I am questioning, not the seriousness of the facts as a whole. Instead of a kind of Gresham's Law, keeping people awake at nights with the now orthodox putropian nightmare, let us put it another way, to fit the actual facts: we live in an expanding culture, and all the elements of this culture are themselves expanding. If we start from this, we can then ask real questions: about relative rates of expansion; about the social and economic problems raised by these; about the social and economic answers. I am working now on a book to follow my *Culture and Society*, trying to interpret, historically, and theoretically, the nature and conditions of an expanding culture of our kind. I could not have begun this work if I had not learned from the Marxists and from Leavis; I cannot complete it unless I radically amend some of the ideas which they and others have left us.

I give myself three wishes, one for each of the swans I have just been watching on the lake. I ask for things that are part of the ethos of our working-class movement. I ask that we may be strong and human enough to realize them. And I ask, naturally, in my own fields of interest.

I wish, first, that we should recognize that education is ordinary: that it is, before everything else, the process of giving to the ordinary members of society its full common meanings, and the skills that will enable these meanings, in the light of their personal and common experience. If we start from that, we can get rid of the remaining restrictions, and make the necessary changes. I do not mean only money restrictions, though these, of course, are ridiculous and must go. I mean also restrictions in the mind: the insistence, for example, that there is a hard maximum number – a fraction of the population as a whole – capable of really profiting by a university education, or a grammar school education, or by any full course of liberal studies. We are told that this is not a question of what we might personally prefer, but of the hard cold facts of human intelligence, as shown by biology and psychology. But let us be frank about this: are biology and psychology different in the USA and USSR (each committed to expansion, and not to any class rigidities), where much larger numbers, much larger fractions, pass through comparable stages of education? Or were the English merely behind the queue for intelligence? I believe, myself, that our educational system, with its golden fractions, is too like our social system – a top layer of leaders, a middle layer of supervisors, a large bottom layer of operatives – to be coincidence. I cannot accept that education is a training for jobs, or for making useful citizens (that is, fitting into this system). It is a society's confirmation of its common meanings and of the human skills for their amendment. Jobs follow from this confirmation: the purpose, and then the working skill. We are moving into an economy where we shall need many more highly trained specialists. For this precise reason, I ask for a common education that will give our society its cohesion, and prevent it disintegrating into a series of specialist departments, the nation become a firm.

But I do not mean only the reorganization of entry into particular kinds of education, though I welcome and watch the experiments in this. I mean the rethinking of content, which is even more important. I have the honour to work for an organization through which, quite practically, working men amended the English university curriculum. It is now as it was then: the defect is not what is in, but what is out. It will be a test of our cultural seriousness whether we can, in the coming generation, redesign our syllabuses to a point of full human relevance and control. I should like to see a group working on this, and offering its conclusions. For we need not fear change; oldness may or may not be relevant. I come from an old place; if a man tells me that his family came over with the Normans, I say 'Yes, how interesting; and are you liking it here?' Oldness is relative, and many 'immemorial' English traditions were invented, just like that, in the nineteenth century. What that vital century did for its own needs, we can do for ours; we can make, in our turn, a true twentieth-century syllabus. And by this I do not mean simply more technology; I mean a full liberal education for everyone in our society, and then full specialist training to earn our living in terms of what we want to make of our lives. Our specialisms will be finer if they have grown from a common culture, rather than being a distinction from it. And we must at all costs avoid the polarization of our culture, of which there are growing signs. High literacy is expanding, in direct relation to exceptional educational opportunities, and the gap between this and common literacy may widen, to the great damage of both, and with great consequent tension. We must emphasize, not the ladder but the common highway, for every man's ignorance diminishes me, and every man's skill is a common gain of breath.

My second wish is complementary; for more and more active public provision for the arts and for adult learning. We now spend £20,000,000 annually on all our libraries, museums, galleries, orchestras, on the Arts Council, and on all forms of adult education. At the same time we spend £365,000,000 annually on advertising. When these figures are reversed, we can claim some sense of proportion and value. And until they are reversed, let there be no sermons, from the Establishment, about materialism: this is their way of life, let them look at it. (But there is no shame in them: for years, with their own children away at school, they have lectured working-class mothers on the virtues of family life; this is a similar case.)

I ask for increased provision on three conditions. It is not to be a disguised way of keeping up consumption, but a thing done for its own sake. A Minister in the last Labour Government said that we didn't want any geniuses in the film industry; he wanted, presumably, just to keep the turnstiles clicking. The short answer to this is that we don't want any Wardour Street thinkers in the leadership of the Labour Party. We want leaders of a society, not repair-workers on this kind of cultural economy.

The second condition is that while we must obviously preserve and extend the great national institutions, we must do something to reverse the concentration of this part of our culture. We should welcome, encourage and foster the tendencies to regional re-creation that are showing themselves, for culture is ordinary, you should not have to go to London to find it.

The third condition is controversial. We should not seek to extend a ready-made culture to the benighted masses. We should accept, frankly, that if we extend our culture we shall change it; some that is offered will be rejected, other parts will be radically criticized. And this is as it should be, for our arts, now, are in no condition to go down to eternity unchallenged. There is much fine work; there is also shoddy work, and work based on values that will find no acceptance if they ever come out into the full light of England. To take our arts to new audiences is to be quite certain that in many respects those arts will be changed. I, for one, do not fear this. I would not expect the working people of England to support works which, after proper and patient preparation, they could not accept. The real growth will be slow and uneven, but the State provision, frankly, should be a growth in this direction, and not a means of diverting public money to the preservation of a fixed and finished partial culture. At the same time, if we understand cultural growth, we shall know that it is a continual offering for common acceptance; that we should not, therefore, try to determine in advance what should be offered, but clear the channels and let all the offerings be made, taking care to give the difficult full space, the original full time, so that it is a real growth, and not just a wider confirmation of old rules.

Now, of course, we shall hear the old cry that things shouldn't be supported at a loss. Once again, this is a nation, not a firm. Parliament itself runs at a loss, because we need it, and if it would be better at a greater loss, I and others would willingly pay. But why, says Sir George Mammon should *I* support a lot of doubtful artists? Why, says Mrs Mink, should I pay good money to educate, at my expense, a lot of irresponsible and ungrateful State scholars? The answer, dear sir, dear madam, is that you don't. On your own – learn your size – you could do practically nothing. We are talking about a method of common payment, for common services: we too shall be paying.

My third wish is in a related field: the field now dominated by the institutions of 'mass culture'. Often, it is the people at the head of these institutions who complain of running things at a loss. But the great popular newspapers, as newspapers, run at a loss. The independent television companies are planned to run at a loss. I don't mean temporary subsidies, but the whole basis of financing such institutions. The newspapers run at a heavy loss, which they make up with money from advertising – that is to say a particular use of part of the product of our common industry. To run at a loss, and then cover yourself with this kind of income, is of the essence of this kind of cultural institution, and this is entirely characteristic of our kind of capitalist society. The whole powerful array of mass cultural institutions has one keystone: money from advertising. Let them stop being complacent about other cultural institutions which run at a smaller loss, and meet it out of another part of the common product.

But what is it then that I wish? To pull out this keystone? No, not just like that. I point out merely that the organization of our present mass culture is so closely involved with the organization of capitalist society that the future of one cannot be considered except in terms of the future of the other. I think much of contemporary advertising is necessary only in terms of the kind of economy we now have: a stimulation of consumption in the direction of particular products and firms, often by irrelevant devices, rather than real advertising, which is an ordinary form of public notice. In a Socialist economy, which I and others want, the whole of this pseudo-advertising would be irrelevant. But then what? My wish is that we may solve the problems that would then arise, where necessary things like newspapers would be running at something like their real loss, without either pricing them out of ordinary means, or exposing them to the dangers of control and standardization (for we want a more free and more varied press, not one less so). It is going to be very difficult, but I do not believe we are so uninventive as to be left showing each other a pair of grim alternatives: either the continuance of this crazy peddling, in which news and opinion are inextricably involved with the shouts of the market, bringing in their train the new slavery and prostitution of the selling of personalities; or else a dull, monolithic, controlled system, in which news and opinion are in the gift of a ruling party. We should be thinking, now, about ways of paying for our common services which will guarantee proper freedom to those who actually provide the service, while protecting them and us against a domineering minority whether political or financial. I think there are ways, if we really believe in democracy.

But that is the final question: how many of us really believe in it? The capitalists don't; they are consolidating a power which can survive parliamentary changes. Many Labour planners don't: they interpret it as a society run by experts for an abstraction called the public interest. The people in the teashop don't; they are quite sure it is not going to be nice. And the others, the new dissenters? Nothing has done more to sour the democratic idea, among its natural supporters, and to drive them back into an angry self-exile, than the plain, overwhelming cultural issues: the apparent division of our culture into, on the one hand, a remote and self-gracious sophistication, on the other hand, a doped mass. So who then believes in democracy? The answer is really quite simple: the millions in England who still haven't got it, where they work and feel. There, as always, is the transforming energy, and the business of the Socialist intellectual is what it always was: to attack the clamps on that energy – in industrial relations, public administration, education, for a start; and to work in his own field on ways in which that energy, as released, can be concentrated and fertile. The technical means are difficult enough, but the biggest difficulty is in accepting, deep in our minds, the values on which they depend: that the ordinary people should govern; that culture and education are ordinary; that there are no masses to save, to capture, or to direct, but rather this crowded people in the course of an extraordinarily rapid and confusing expansion of their lives. A writer's job is with individual meanings, and with making these meanings common. I find these meanings in the expansion, there along the journey where the necessary changes are writing themselves into the land, and where the language changes but the voice is the same.

Our Debt to Dr. Leavis

From: *Critical Quarterly*, 1, III, 1959, pp 245–7

We must try to pay our debt to F.R. Leavis, whether or not he will acknowledge us as debtors. The influence of his writing and teaching seems to be growing year by year, even though the first generation of Scrutineers is being succeeded by a more varied or more motley generation, on whom he is a major influence, but who combine what they have learned from him with other elements that he would probably reject. He is not a politician, to count his influence by numbers; the questions he naturally asks are questions of quality, and he is quick to the point of touchiness in rejecting associations and derivations where these would involve him with work to which he cannot assent. In my own case, I have both learned from him and criticized him, and though I do not know whether he would want me to do so, I repeat what I have written over the past twelve years: that he is the most interesting critic of his generation, that his educational influence has been central to the best work of his period, and that his life's work is a major contribution to our culture.

I was never directly taught by him; indeed I have only twice heard him lecture and once talked with him. When I went to Cambridge, in 1939, my own college, Trinity, had nobody to supervise me in English, and so I was sent out, as a day-boy, to an establishment down the road, which could have been Downing but wasn't (I had then never even heard of Leavis). I can't say he was immediately drawn to my attention; in those years, at any rate, it didn't happen quite like that. But I bought *Scrutiny*, in a bookshop, and began reading his articles and books, as if he had been a teacher in Oxford or Toronto. I think it was the critical radicalism, even perhaps the aggressiveness of *Scrutiny* that made the first connection, and it is as well to say this because I am sure it has been so with countless others. I know now, in reasonable detail, the complicated story of Leavis's battle with the Cambridge establishment, to say nothing of his battle with Bloomsbury, and I agree that some of the early attacks on him were exceptionally offensive: particularly the indirect attack, in an official publication, using his wife's work as the immediate text. When this has been said, however, I see little point in the interpretation published by one or two of the minor Scrutineers: that here was an obviously fine man viciously and wantonly attacked. If ever a man came out fighting, Leavis did: this, to many of us, is one of his major virtues, because of the importance of the things he was fighting for. With others, he was working to make English grow to its place as a central subject in a contemporary humane education, with the emphasis on criticism and on cultural history rather than on academicism and the vagaries of 'taste'. He was as uncompromising as he was urgent, and as angry as he was determined. Reading him in my first years at Cambridge (I am more used to him now) was the succession of shocks which Q.D. Leavis has noted as characteristic of reading a good novel: 'a configuration of special instances which serve as a test for our mental habits and show us the necessity for revising them'. Leavis's idiosyncratic sentences would again and again jump from the page, with just that kind of challenge, and the aggressiveness, often the open rudeness, were at least elements of the process. This has had its unfortunate effects, for in lesser hands the manner has degenerated into simple nastiness, and into arrogance. Leavis, from the beginning, offered his own deeply felt values, his own illuminating readings; he was as far as a man could be from the formula of 'We, the Illustrious Dead'. The point is crucial, because the critic really is not Shakespeare or Marvell or George Eliot, and to knock down contemporary writers as if he were is both offensive and ridiculous. Unless in his own work the critic lives his values he has little claim on our attention, but, leaving certain Scrutineers aside, this is precisely what Leavis was doing. In all his writing, early and late, this deep engagement is the central quality. When he speaks of intelligence and sensibility, these are not counters, but alive in his own work. When he speaks of the vitality of great literature, you can feel, in this and that discussion, both his own sense of life and the depth at which the experience of the literature has been re-created in him. There is plenty of discipline in the ordinary run of academic criticism, and some eminent persons must wonder why Leavis, often making more mistakes than they do, nevertheless evokes in his readers a quite different response: the kind of excitement, the emotional engagement whether of conviction or dissent, which is characteristic of reading literature and not of reading textbooks. *New Bearings, Revaluation, The Great Tradition, The Common Pursuit, Education and The University, D.H. Lawrence, Novelist* are certainly required reading in any academic English course, but the fact is that they can be read in a quite different way, for though he writes about 'his subject', he is always essentially writing about his experience, and the result is more interesting, more relevant as literature, than all but a comparatively few of the imaginative writers of his period, with whom he could have been contrasted as 'merely a critic'. We can, that is to say, think of Leavis as we think of Arnold: as a man who communicates a whole experience, a distinctive way of thinking and feeling, to the life of his generation.

This is the measure of our debt, and it is better put in this way than in others that are more commonly suggested. The stress on his critical method I am now rather doubtful about, though when I went back to Cambridge after the war, and had close friends who were his students, this seemed the central point. Certainly he has written many good pieces of critical analysis, of 'the words on the page' kind, but especially in his later work, while not exactly breaking the rules as sometimes narrowly set down, he has ranged very freely. When he writes about Lawrence, he writes, through the work, about English life, setting his own responses beside

Lawrence's, and looking as closely at men and events as at the words. I see this as a broadening, not a lapse, from critical analysis as sometimes narrowly interpreted. In his writings about contemporary culture (which extend through his whole publishing period) there is the same breadth, with detailed analysis as only one line of approach, though of course a vital one (his extension to the analysis of newspapers and advertisements is a decisive educational contribution). I am far from agreeing with all his cultural conclusions, and I agree much less than I used to (I never altogether agreed) with some of his specifically literary judgments. But it seems now of secondary importance whether one agrees of disagrees with him, whether one has the 'right' judgments arrived at in the 'right' way. His work is there, in a central English tradition; the thing is to read it, not try to learn it. Many of us are directly indebted to him in respect of the interests he has emphasised, the insights he has communicated, the approaches he has opened. Over and above this, his outstanding integrity, in the course which he has set for himself, is a constant landmark, to which, even if set on different courses, we do well to refer. But finally, if we speak of debt, we have to speak in the only terms in which such debts can be paid: we cannot repay him, but we can try to serve the tradition of English writing and thinking to which he, with others, has given his whole energy.

Fiction and the Writing Public

Review of Richard Hoggart, *The Uses of Literacy*
From: *Essays in Criticism*, 7, iv, 1957, pp 422–8

Do your friends say 'You ought to write a novel' when you tell them an anecdote? . . . If so, post this form.

When Thomas Huxley first spoke of an educational ladder, he was not, I suppose, thinking directly about Jacob and the angels, but about democracy and the needs of an industrial society. But the moon has been shining for some years now, and the number of those who have gone up the ladder and down the wall has steadily increased. Not many, of course, have come out to play: the majority have done what Huxley expected of them; a few, like Richard Hoggart, have stood and looked around, preoccupied. The moon, after all, takes its light from elsewhere; the wall is still high, the ladder narrow; back there, where we came from, an extraordinary party seems to be in progress, and Hoggart stands listening to it, like a sober son watching his family get drunk. In a serious group, he is an unusually serious person. And what this group manages to get said, in its own accents, has a major directive importance. When others are giving up democracy, or defining culture as its antithesis, the strains in this group are crucial, for here, as in any future England, there must be loyalty to both. Hoggart is particularly admirable, because he sees the ladder as Jacob saw it, and neither as a convenience nor a technique.

The real importance of *The Uses of Literacy* is not that it is a comprehensive and intelligent account of contemporary commercial writing. As such, certainly, it is welcome: a natural successor and complement to, say, *Fiction and the Reading Public*. But Hoggart has attempted to go beyond this, to issues in which the methods of professional criticism (in which he is fully competent) do not serve. It is fair to say of Mrs Leavis's admirable book that the reading public is really only present in the title; the documents in the case are her real centre of attention. Hoggart, similarly, attends to the documents, but he also seeks to see the reading public as people, and to judge the documents with this reference. The result is not a better book than *Fiction and the Reading Public*, for the concentration on documents at least made questions of form and procedure more simple. But in extending the range of the discussion, Hoggart has encountered literary problems – which I do not think we can say he has solved – that are of exceptional contemporary interest.

106

The distinctive world of the writers of Richard Hoggart's generation and background is a complex of critical habit, recording ability, and imaginative impulse. This is, I think, the current mainstream of English writing, and one which is likely to broaden and deepen. The effect it is having on the forms of contemporary writing has not yet been assessed, although the symptoms have been noticed. A common reaction to many of the poems in *New Lines*, for example, is the complaint that the 'poetry' is muddled or inhibited by critical judgments, critical itches, theories of communication, observations on a culture. Certainly these elements are visible in some of the poems of Enright, Wain, Davie, Larkin and Holloway. Or again, in a novel like Amis's *That Uncertain Feeling*, there are times when the ordinary progress of the fiction is cut across by similar judgments, observations and itches, often in the significantly popular form of parody. Now in Hoggart's book, which is primarily a critical work, the analysis of documents is cut across by pieces which are very like this kind of fiction: sketches of 'allegorical figures' in the cultural situation; wry accounts of personal feeling; parodies and generalised comments, in a similar feeling-tone. What has been normally observed about this apparent confusion of forms takes a heavy pejorative emphasis. There was the same thing in Leavis, where the outbursts towards the end of *D.H Lawrence, Novelist* were quite widely thought to disfigure an otherwise sound critical work. In Orwell, again (from whom Hoggart, in terms of literary method, seems to have learned a great deal), there was a curious amalgam of personal observation and social generalisation, which offered itself as a whole but which was not, in its parts, uniformly valid or even uniformly assessible. It has in fact been easy for academics (the real literary historians, who treat literature as documents) to blame this group of mixed critics for getting distracted by life and politics and the British Council and other irrelevancies, which disturb the sweet clear line of an exposition. Similarly it has been easy for novelists and poets of an older minority to blame the new novelists and poets for having got mixed up with literature and education and cultural questions ('some of them, good God, actually have experiences *while reading*') which again disturb that sweet clear line. It is a curious situation, complicated by the undoubted fact that there are radical differences of skill and integrity among writers of this kind. Thus Leavis's outbursts, while sometimes private or matters of rote, are normally the pressure-points of the whole body of his work. It is for just this capacity to get angry about situations which it might be convenient to class as 'not my field' that we respect him. On the other hand, Orwell's similar capacity to get angry, on personal evidence, about whole institutions, is sometimes valuable, sometimes silly and even harmful. In the poems of *New Lines*, sometimes the pressure of this complex produces honesty or even intensity; at other times, silliness and pose. The novels in this category are critically simpler to assess: uniformly entertaining, uniformly inadequate in any permanent respect. But, when these distinctions have been made, it seems to me to remain true that the attempts to express and articulate this particular complex of interests and pressures are in fact the vital contemporary mainstream. The gaucheness and posing are not always failures of integrity; sometimes, at least, they are the by-products of the most honest attempts we have to communicate new feelings in a new situation.

The feelings and situations with which Hoggart is concerned are in fact relatively new in writing. The analysis of Sunday newspapers and crime stories and romances is of course familiar, but, when you have come yourself from their apparent public, when you recognise in yourself the ties that still bind, you cannot be satisfied with the older formula: enlightened minority, degraded mass. You know how bad most 'popular culture' is, but you know also that the irruption of the 'swinish multitude', which Burke had prophesied would trample down light and learning, is the coming to relative power and relative justice of your own people, whom you could not if you tried desert. My own estimate of this difficulty is that it is first in the field of ideas, the received formulas, that scrutiny is necessary and the approach to settlement possible. Hoggart, I think, has taken over too many of the formulas, in his concentration on a different kind of evidence. He writes at times in the terms of Matthew Arnold, though he is not Arnold nor was meant to be. He has picked up contemporary conservative ideas of the decay of politics in the working-class, for which I see no evidence at all: the ideas merely rationalise a common sentimentality – the old labour leaders were noble-hearted, less materialist, fine figures of men, but they are seen thus because their demands are over. (It is worth remembering that working-class materialism is, objectively, in our circumstances, a humane ideal.) He has acquiesced, further, in ideas of the working-class as a bloc. He says, for instance, that 'in working-class speech "I" sounds like ae (as in "apple")', though in fact there is no such thing as 'working-class speech': the only class speech in England is that of the upper and middle classes; the speech of working-class people is not socially but *regionally* varied. Finally, he has admitted (though with apologies and partial disclaimers) the extremely damaging and quite untrue identification of 'popular culture' (commercial newspapers, magazines, entertainments, etc.) with 'working-class culture'. In fact the main source of this 'popular culture' lies outside the working-class altogether, for it was instituted, financed and operated by the commercial *bourgeoisie*, and remains typically capitalist in its methods of production and distribution. That working-class people form perhaps a majority of the consumers of this material, along with considerable sections of other classes (all, perhaps, except the professional), does not, as a fact, justify this facile identification. In all of these matters, Hoggart's argument needs radical revision.

Yet Hoggart's approach, though involving a relative neglect of ideas, admits very valuable evidence which a concentration on ideas alone would neglect. The analytic parody of commercial writing, which most of us can now do, quickly becomes mechanical unless it is deeply correlated with personal and social observation of a feeling kind. The value of Hoggart's book is the quality of this observation, but here again we must make a distinction. There is social observation, which can properly be generalised, as for instance in Hoggart's chapters, 'There's no Place Like Home', 'Self-Respect', and 'Living and Letting Live'. Hoggart is much more reliable on all this than Orwell: he writes, not as a visitor, but as a native. But this is an observation of *mores*, which can properly be spoken of in class or group terms. The correlation between this and the newspapers and magazines is, as a result, exceptionally valuable: in particular Hoggart's note on the exploitation of 'neighbourliness'. Yet, beyond *mores*, there are further regions of social and personal fact – the world, shall we say, of the novelist, rather than of the sociologist. It is when he enters these regions that Hoggart tends to enter fiction. It is not that he becomes unreliable (though in one or two instances I think he does), but that he is now dealing with whole situations involving individuals rather than with the structures of such situations which are the *mores*. It is less easy to see this distinction because so much recent fiction, particularly the work of this general group, often offers a kind of personalised account of *mores* rather than a whole account of individuals within social situations. I will take some instances where I think Hoggart is thus mistaking his material.

The section on 'Mother' is satisfactory, and moving, in a way that the section on 'Father' is obviously not. The successful section is partly observation of *mores*, partly personal re-creation: the interaction of these produces something almost comparable with successful imaginative creation in its own right. The section on 'Father', on the other hand, is meagre and generalised, and the false personalisation – the usual position at the mirror – at once enters: the 'small . . . dark . . . whippet' of a man (the generalised caricature) becomes, in feeling, as a kind of meditation, Lucky Hoggart, trying on a cap and neckerchief. A more serious instance is the section 'Scholarship Boy', which I think has been very well received by some readers (and why not? it is much what they wanted to hear, and now an actual scholarship boy is saying it). Certainly we can generalise in some respects about scholarship boys as a group, but the portrait which Hoggart offers goes very far beyond these, and becomes, in the wrong way, personal (wrong, because offered as a general account). The problems of sexual delay, of the intellectual's isolation, of unease and the sense of exile, of the constrained smile at the corner of the mouth, of nostalgia, careerism, phantasy: these, certainly, are socially affected, but I cannot imagine where Hoggart has been if he has not noticed these things as characteristic of a group much wider than that which he offers to describe. They are familiar to us in fiction, from Gissing and Joyce to Huxley, Orwell, and Greene, and in life the spread is as wide. Moreover, while some of these matters can be socially characterised, others are clearly individual, in the full sense, and need a fully individualised substantiation to be read with much respect. At such moments in the book one feels Hoggart hesitating between fiction or autobiography on the one hand, and sociology on the other. The sociological method worked for matters apparently close to this, but once matters involving the myriad variations of individual response are in question, it breaks down. It is when this happens that one wishes Hoggart had written an autobiography or a novel: even if unsuccessful, it would have been an offering in relevant terms.

My argument returns to an earlier point: the confusion of forms which the new complex of feeling has affected. In *The Uses of Literacy* we find, first, the professional critic, who gets through his work with a really intelligent mastery; second, the social observer, who has a fine, quick descriptive talent which lends a background and depth to the critic's observations; then third, the man, the writer, seriously committed to the recall and analysis of direct experience, seriously concerned with personal as well as social relationships, and with their interaction; involved, finally, in imaginative creation, as he draws figures from the world he has experienced and attempts to set them in a theme. I am not blaming Hoggart for this variety, but since the condition is general, I am trying to insist on the distinctions we shall all have to make, if the voice of this generation is to come clear and true. We are suffering, obviously, from the decay and disrepute of the realistic novel, which for our purposes (since we are, and know ourselves to be, individuals *within* a society) ought clearly to be revived. Sound critical work can be done; sound social observation and analysis of ideas. Yet I do not see how, in the end, this particular world of fact and feeling can be adequately mediated, except in these more traditionally imaginative terms. Of course it cannot be George Eliot again, nor even Lawrence, though the roots are in both. But there, I think, is the direction, and there, under the fashionable lightness of parody and caricature, this solemn, earnest, heavy voice that one hears, at the crises, in Hoggart, is a voice to listen to and to welcome.

Working Class Attitudes

From: *New Left Review*, I, January, 1960, pp 26–30
Richard Hoggart and Raymond Williams

*Revised transcript of a recorded conversation between Richard Hoggart
and Raymond Williams, August Bank Holiday, 1959.*

R.W.: I'm glad that at last we've managed to meet. Since *The Uses of
Literacy* and *Culture and Society* came out, many people have assumed
that we knew each other well, though in fact I think it's been no more
than exchanging perhaps half a dozen letters in the last twelve years, none
of them, it seems, while the books were being written. Of course it's natural
that the two books should have been compared and connected, but such
relationships as there are have come out of the general situation, and not
from our knowing each other. Can we just clear up the dates of writing and
publication? *The Uses of Literacy* came out in the spring of 1957, *Culture
and Society* in September 1958. Actually I began *Culture and Society* (then
The Idea of Culture) in 1952, after an earlier try in 1950. I finished it in the
autumn of 1956. I was actually writing the Conclusion during the weeks
of Hungary and Suez. So, though we were often writing about the same
things, we hadn't each other's books to refer to.

R.H.: *The Uses of Literacy* was originally finished in the summer of 1955
– the delay in publishing was caused by clearing some passages which might
have been libellous. I had begun in 1952 too, by writing one chapter which
doesn't appear. I was thinking then of something quite simple in scope and
size – a series of critical essays on popular literature. Soon I began to feel
that I wanted to relate this material to the day-to-day experience of people.
After this, a strange thing happened . . . things I'd been writing since 1946
(bits of a novel and some unconnected descriptive pieces) began to fall into
place in the new book.

R.W.: It's interesting, the way the books were built. I can remember my
own first impulse, back at the end of the 'forties. I felt very isolated, except
for my family and my immediate work. The Labour Government had gone
deeply wrong, and the other tradition that mattered, the cultural criticism
of our kind of society, had moved, with Eliot, right away from anything I
could feel. It seemed to me I had to try to go back over the tradition, to look
at it again and get it into relation with my own experience, to see the way
the intellectual tradition stood in the pattern of my own growing-up. As I
saw the cultural tradition then, it was mainly Coleridge, Arnold, Leavis and

the Marxists, and the development, really, was a discovery of relationships inside the tradition, and also a discovery of other relationships: Cobbett and Morris, for example, who brought in parts of my experience that had been separate before. Getting the tradition right was getting myself right, and that meant changing both myself and the usual version of the tradition. I think this is one of the problems we're both conscious of: moving out of a working-class home into an academic curriculum, absorbing it first and then, later, trying to get the two experiences into relation.

R.H.: Yes; though I have a feeling that someone brought up among village working-people may be able to bridge this gap more easily than someone from the working-classes in a large industrial city. Or perhaps I'm ascribing to social differences what is really due to a difference in personality. At any rate I felt from your book that you were surer, sooner than I was, of your relationship to your working-class background. With me, I remember, it was a long and troublesome effort. It was difficult to escape a kind of patronage, even when one felt one was understanding the virtues of the working-class life one had been brought up in – one seemed to be insisting on these strengths in spite of all sorts of doubts in one's attitudes. One tried consciously, in the light of day, to make genuine connections, to see deeply and not just to feel sentimentally ... but it was a running argument.

R.W.: We both came from working-class families, but otherwise, really, from very different ways of life. I don't know, I'd like you to look at Pandy and I at Hunslet. I think the bridge is easier in Wales, in some ways. There's the respect for education among most ordinary people, and in the general life, as I knew it, less exclusion of certain kinds of art and intellectual interest: popular, certainly, and in many ways limited, but still serious, in the sense that these things were part of an ordinary life. I know this was so in my own home, though I suppose we never owned more than half-a-dozen books until we got our *Daily Herald* set of Dickens. And I know when I went out, there was no sense of going right against the grain. It was an unusual world I was entering, but still it was basically approved.

R.H.: I think working-class life may change when a town reaches more than a certain size. I talked about this once with Asa Briggs who comes from a smallish industrial township in the West Riding, a wool town. He is the same age and a scholarship boy; the family had a corner shop which, I believe, failed in the '30's. The points he made about working-class attitudes in his township seemed more applicable to your Welsh village than to my big city, Leeds.

His, and many like it, were very tight townships with their life based on wool or some ancillaries to wool. They had a sort of unity. Even physically, the most striking difference between the bosses' houses, the foremen's and the workers' was one of size – they all had a similar style, a common comeliness and dignity. The communities had a kind of organic quality, closer and more varied relations between the social groups than we had.

I've noticed too how many of the men have an air of great self-respect. The trade turned out experts – this man knew how to feel the differences between types of wool, this one to keep the machines going well and so on. You can see much the same air in a main-line express driver of the old type. He's got a craft and he is important. If you go into the pubs in the West Riding mill towns you're struck by how many of the men have this sort of air.

R.W.: Yes, and that's how I remember the men of my own village. They were important, and felt themselves important, because they lived there and knew each other. They'd call nobody 'Sir', in any ordinary circumstances, and I notice this difference, in Southern England at least, where so many people seem to take up a servant's attitude quite naturally: I still can't stand it when people call me 'Sir' on the bus – at least they do when I've got my suit on. But I remember the men at home – a whole attitude in a way of dress. Good clothes, usually, that you bought for life. The big heavy overcoat, good jacket, good breeches, leggings, then a cardigan, a waistcoat, a watchchain, and all of it open, as a rule, right down to the waist. Layers of it going in, and of course no collar. But standing up, quite open. They weren't, really, people with a sense of inferiority.

R.H.: Of course the class system there would be different.

R.W.: Yes, the best-off people were the larger farmers, and most of them tenants even when they could have afforded to buy. Of course the odd retired English Home and Colonial: bustling around, but not I think really affecting the life. A large village, about five hundred people, scattered over miles, and the middle-class settlers so very few; not like Sussex, where there's one behind every hedge, or a wall if they can afford it. The chapels set the standards, in almost everything, and that, really, was the ground of seriousness. You can't expect people who haven't had a long education themselves, and no access to a variety of books, to develop a high culture. But it's a question whether high culture is compatible with the ordinary values. What is the attitude, for example, to a child going on with his education, when it's discovered that he's 'bright'. Is this considered odd, or is it regarded as a gift?

R.H.: In Wales it is a gift I suppose?

R.W.: I've gone over this pretty carefully. With the girls, of course, it was different, though they'd go on to High School from the farms and the cottages, if they got scholarships; then some would drop out early, if they were wanted at home. But I can't think of any boys at the grammar school who dropped out like that. I can think of one case from the elementary school, a boy I thought bright, who came from a very poor family, right up on the mountain – three miles walk down from the mountain to school. He wasn't allowed to go in for the scholarship, he was needed – it mightn't even then have been anything but straight economic need. It's interesting, you see, that most of us didn't regard ourselves as poor. My father was getting two pounds, two pounds ten, a week, as a signalman, but we didn't think we were poor.

R.H.: You'd be all right for a pension too. I know we used to look up to railwaymen and policemen.

R.W.: Yes, my father was offered a job, in the late 'thirties, as a school attendance officer, but he didn't take it, because of the pension. But in any case we had no normal middle class, as a class, to compare with. To us the poor families were perhaps half-a-dozen in the whole village, with very bad cottages – I remember one with an earth floor; usually very large families, and the man was ill, or drank, and didn't get a regular job, just odd jobs and the harvest. So we weren't poor, most of us, in our own minds. But the other consciousness, that of being working-class, is more complicated. Basically, I think, it centred about the railway. There, as a new element, you had a group of men conscious of their identity in a different way. And in fact, at the two stations, you get the growth of political and trade-union attitudes of a quite mature urban kind.

R.H.: That's extraordinarily interesting. You think it only came in with the railway?

R.W.: Well, the self-government tradition in the chapels disposed many people to democratic feeling; feeling, really, rather than thinking. Someone like my father who grew up in a farm labourer's family, outside the tradition that brought conscious trade union attitudes, still got, I think, the feelings that matter. There was just enough local and practical democracy, but even more there was this sense that to be a man in this place was to be important; that this mattered more than any sort of grading on a social basis. Of course when he came back from the first war he was much more definite politically, and then on the railway it was the Labour Party, the union, the understanding of what a strike was, what it implied.

R.H.: The differences seem to me striking. Leeds in my day had just under half a million people. A great many of the working-people seemed to belong to families which had originally come in from the surrounding countryside between, I suppose, 1840 and 1880. Once there they began to live in new ways, segregated into districts. As we know, their districts grew up round the works, near canals, rivers, railway yards. The better-class districts were up the hill or on the right side of the wind. Generally one gets the impression, looking at this sort of city, that this physical separation illustrates less obvious separations between the various social groups. You don't have the sort of relations I called 'organic' when I mentioned the mill towns. What you have in a town like Leeds – or Sheffield or Manchester – is much more a sense of great blocks of people. Of course each block would be shot through with all sorts of distinctions and differences. Among working-people you had extended families, often overlapping; and particular neighbourhood loyalties; and you had distinctions between say the transport men, the heavy engineering men, those who laboured for the Corporation and so on and so on. The distinctions were very fine and very complicated. But still you could see first this large rough distinction – that industrially the area was a block, or a pool, of general labour for the city's industries – the human equivalent of the private reservoirs at the side of some of the big works. In our area there were a lot of men who hadn't served an apprenticeship, who weren't skilled workers – or not really skilled – but who could turn their hands to a number of jobs within related heavy industries. They felt two main kinds of connections, with their neighbourhood and with the industries they worked in; but the neighbourhood connections were stronger for most. They felt they belonged to a district more than to a trade – though not in the way country workers feel they belong to a village. We talked about 'our' kind of people in 'our' kind of area. You see this in the Institute's study of Bethnal Green too. Still – they were villages of a kind, and remarkably tiny villages. You knew exactly where your boundaries were.

R.W.: The most difficult bit of theory, that I think both of us have been trying to get at, is what relation there is between kinds of community, that we call working-class, and the high working-class tradition, leading to democracy, solidarity in the unions, socialism. As I saw it, this came from the place of work: in my village, the railway. I suppose this is always likely to be so. But is it the case that the high tradition is stronger where there are certain kinds of community: the mining villages, for example? To what extent can we establish a relation between given kinds of working-class community and what we call working-class consciousness in the sense of the Labour movement? There are discouraging signs, aren't there, in places where people have come together from all over, and live in very mixed and probably anxious communities? The men may be working-class at work, but not necessarily at home. The wives may not in their own minds be working-class at all.

R.H.: This I find complicated indeed. As I've said, the sort of group I grew up in was intensely local. You felt you belonged to Hunslet if you were in the middle of Leeds, outside the Town Hall; but when you were in Hunslet you only belonged to one-and-a-half streets. This was one sort of connection and a powerful general influence on attitudes. But it seemed to have very little political significance. Political solidarity came out of industrial situations. And in my experience those people who were politically active – and there were few of them – were regarded as slightly odd in the neighbourhoods. There was a terrific streak of small conservatism. This may have been fed by a desire for independence. There were many industries and they were continually swopping men. Some of the men liked to feel completely free to swop as and when they wished. My grandfather called himself a Conservative, I think; he also tended to show his independence at intervals by downing tools, telling off the foreman and going elsewhere.

Perhaps one important way in which political consciousness can grow strongly is where you have a large body of men who both feel locally that they are one and can also make wider – perhaps national – connections with others in the same job. The obvious instance is coal-mining, where you had a body of men who felt themselves solidly working-class, who had a lot of pride and dignity and self-consciousness, and who made strong connections with others right across the country.

R.W.: Yes, and of course new industries – the motor industry, for instance, may be producing different patterns again. I know I watch every strike for evidence on this question; whether the practice of solidarity is really weakening, or has been really learned. But then of course it isn't only at work that these class attitudes matter.

R.H.: Yes, some of the more striking instances of working-class political solidarity seem to have occurred not only in the larger and unmistakeably working-class industries but also to have gained from a sense of continuing local – using this now to mean quite a large area – traditions, loyalties, consciousness. A minority from these groups were able to work within these groups, making active connections between the local solidarity and political solidarity.

Today people are moving around more; many of the old areas are being split up; new industries and new forms of industry are recruiting people from all over, offering good wages and a much more fluid range of opportunities. What we want to know is what replaces the old channels by which political consciousness expressed itself – the local, the homogeneous, the solidly 'working-class' feeling, the minority. Or does much of the old feeling carry over?

R.W.: I think we can say that so far as trade union organisation in concerned, the increase in jobs of a new or more skilled kind isn't weakening the unions. Indeed some of the most active unions since the war, and most to the left politically, are the skilled workers. There, at any rate, the principles are being carried through. But that's only part of it. There's this whole question of a rising standard of living, and its effect on working-class social ideas. With more goods available, steadier employment, and so on, you can reasonably set your sights on a more fitted, a more furnished life. And of course the formula is: the working-class become middle-class, as they get their washing machines and things like that. I think myself that what the *Economist* calls 'deproletarianisation' is very complicated. If you test it by voting Labour, the facts are that through all the misery of the inter-war years, in a supposedly more 'proletarian' situation, the Labour vote was much less than now. In 1924 five-and-a-half million; 1929, eight-and-a-half million; 1931 six-and-a-half million; 1935 eight-and-half million, and now, since the war, twelve million in 1945, nearly fourteen million in 1951, back by 1955 towards twelve million again. Voting is only one kind of test, but it's interesting, as we've seen for ourselves, that there's no kind of automatic correspondence between being working-class, objectively, feeling working-class, and voting for a working-class party. Now what is meant, at the moment, by saying the working-class is becoming middle-class? Which kind of consciousness is pointed at? You could say, objectively, that in fact the middle-class has become working-class: that many more people who feel themselves middle-class are in fact selling their labour than in the nineteenth century, when, outside the professions, it meant having a bit of property, or working on your own, the small farmer or shopkeeper, or of course small businessman. And the middle-class, nowadays, take very readily to common schemes, in their use of the welfare state, for instance, as Abel-Smith showed in *Conviction*. Perhaps both 'working-class' and 'middle-class' need radical new definitions, to get into line with the facts of our society. Not that class feeling has gone, by any means, but it's in a different situation, when nearly everybody lives by selling his labour, yet in fact 'feeling' middle-class and 'feeling' working-class still goes on, buttressed by hundreds of differences in status and social respect. We could be a very much more unified community, if we mostly depend on our labour, and if we accept common provision for our social needs. All I'd say is that major principles, that matter for our future, have in fact come out of the high working-class tradition, supported by many aspects of ordinary working-class life. I mean the sense of community, of equality, of genuine mutual respect: the sense, too, of fairness, when the humanity of everyone in the society is taken as basic, and must not be outraged by any kind of exploitation.

R.H.: True. But today there are so many forces which foster other assumptions – such strong and persistent pressures towards making pretty well everybody accept a group of workable and convenient attitudes. This is not just a matter of advertising trying to make us all live the other-directed life rather than the communal life, or to keep up with the Jones's rather than being independent – it's part of the sheer pressure of any highly centralised society (and that itself is reinforced by the international situation).

Let's go back for a moment to the statement that the working-class has become middle-class, though I suspect it as much as you do. I think the main forces here are economic. Prosperity does seem likely to weaken that sense of solidarity which had its origins in a feeling of common need and could be reinforced by living together industrial district. Again, one has only to remember family and kinship. If you spend some time on a new housing estate you are aware of a kind of break, of new pressures and tensions – but also of new opportunities. A great deal has been cut away, and it's difficult to take the proper measure of the new prospects. How does one – how should one – live in a place like this, people seem to be asking unconsciously.

I'm not surprised that working-class people take hold of the new goods, washing machines, television and the rest (this is where the statement that they have become middle-class is a statement of a simple truth). This is in line with working-class tradition and isn't necessarily regrettable or reprehensible – what one does question is the type of persuasion which accompanies these sales, since its assumptions are shallower than many of those people already have.

A lot of the old attitudes remain, but what one wants to know is how quickly these new forces – steady prosperity, greater movement, wives going out to work – will change attitudes, especially among younger people. I've talked to a lot of working-class adolescents recently and been struck not only by the fact that they didn't see their industrial and political situation in the way their fathers did at their age (one expected that), but by the difficulty in getting any coherent picture of their situation out of them. Everything seemed open, and they seemed almost autonomous.

But by the time they've married and settled in with commitments a great many forces encourage the picture of a decent, amiable but rather selfish, workable society – the New Elizabethan Age. In this Mr Macmillan is one with Sir Robert Fraser, with many people in Personnel Management and a great many other elements . . . the Green Belt World of cosy suburban assumptions which is neither really communal, nor really individual.

R.W.: I agree, and this is why I think the cultural argument, that you and I have been trying to develop, is now so crucial. To understand this society, we have to look at its culture, even for political answers. We have to ask whether this pressure to 'unify' us isn't just a kind of low-level processing. They want to breed out difference, so that we become more predictable and more manageable consumers and citizens, united in fact around nothing very much, and the form of the unity conceals the basic inhumanities: in respect, in education, in work. The system is much less easy to identify, and it isn't only the old-style boss or group of bosses. Except when a scandal comes up, we hardly know who the controllers are. It's much more impersonal, yet it passes itself off as a natural order. It's built in so deep that you have to look for it in the whole culture, not just in politics or economics.

R.H.: Yes, they are the problems of prosperity. Though we hear this so much we can forget how many areas there are in which the situation isn't really much different from the 'thirties'. You can still find exploitation in England, especially in some of the hordes of small works – but they are outside the main new trend.

R.W.: Also unprotected people, the people not in the unions, the people not working, pensioners and so on.

R.H.: Yet when we've allowed for that, the new situation is seen best of all in the great Corporations. You can see there an increasing stratification – distinctions being made at each level from apprentices all the way up. I know one manager who says the most snobbish people in his works are the apprentices – selected from the foundry floor for extra training and given some privileges.

R.W.: The stratification at work is reproduced, physically, in new communities. You can see it at Margam. This really beautiful making of steel, and everything round it as ugly as hell. The main workers' estate is there in the mill's shadow, but the managers and executives drive away to live in 'unspoiled' places like Gower or Porthcawl.

R.H.: All this opens up a whole range of work for anyone interested in the relations between culture, work and society . . . all the way up to the way 'high art' is taken in and done for at the due level. They say automation will soon make it possible to produce variety – a predictable recurrent variety – within mass production. In much the same way you feel the new system allows for a few varieties of pseudo-non-conformists to be built into the pattern.

But to get to problems within industry. The same manager I mentioned before says he can get into touch with most of his staff – if they are at some point they can recognise on the ladder, with someone below them. But he says he feels lost with – can't get in touch with – the boys who haven't been selected. They've contracted out of the scheme and their lives go on elsewhere.

I'm constantly struck by the strength of our sense of class. We find it very hard to shake off – it's like pulling yourself up by our own bootstraps. So I wonder whether many of us are transferring it – the need for a sense of social class – to the new kinds of industrial or functional stratification . . . and so helping along that stratification. We don't need to feel it consciously, but simply to accept the notion of grade seeping all through society. We seem to have three-tiered minds: upper, middle and lower class; high, middle and lowbrow; Third, Home and Light. The new stratifications by function probably gain a lot of power from our traditional assumptions about class.

R.W.: Yes. One interesting thing is the way this kind of status thinking is remoulding the Conservative Party. A good deal of this new Conservatism is of course just a selling-line; the hard-core of preserving a class society is still there. But still one notices how many contemporary Conservative MPs would have seemed to a Conservative of say 1900, or even the 1930's, not their kind of men at all.

R.H.: And some of the Labour Party talk in this way too, with less justification or – luckily – conviction.

R.W.: The emphasis the Conservatives put is quite strong and attractive: that the competitive society is a good thing, that the acquisitive society is a good thing, that all the style of modern living is satisfying and a real aim in life. They seem to believe these things a lot more strongly than the Labour Party believes in anything. Labour seems the conservative party, in feeling, and it's bound to remain so unless it really analyses this society, not to come to terms with it, but to offer some deep and real alternative, of a new kind. I think it all centres on the nature of community, and when people say you and I are nostalgic, or whatever, I want to get this completely clear. We have learned about community, in our own ways, but we're not interested in the business of reproduction: it's the principle that's important. The fact is that communication is the basic problem of our society, even on narrow economic grounds, where failure to communicate, in any real sense, causes major waste of resources. But it's no answer to go about it as they're now doing: 'how can we put this which we want to say, or have done, in communicable forms that even the simplest person can take?' Like looking for a contraceptive that an illiterate can take by the mouth; and most mass-communication techniques, and personnel studies and so on, are just that. I believe that communication cannot be effective if it is thought of as simply transmission. It depends, if it is to be real – between people rather than just units in production or consumers on a market – depends on real community of experience, and the channels open, so that we are all involved. Not selling a line, but sharing real experience.

R.H.: Mass communications help to process people not just because they see them in large blocks but – because I think this is your point – they naturally tend to subordinate what is being said to the way of saying it . . . because they are so struck by the fact that millions can be reached if only one finds a way. The stress goes on presentation. I think of it as the replacement of virtue – the heart of what is being said, by virtuosity – the manner of saying it.

R.W.: Yes. And just to bring it back finally to ourselves. You're absolutely right about the system permitting, even needing, pseudo-non-conformists. In the last eighteen months or so I've felt a situation like they set up in their colonies, where they have members for native affairs, who are not going to influence decisions, but who are encouraged, even petted, to show their robes every so often. Being cast for this role of member for working-class culture is just as insulting and as useless as that. Obviously the available channels must be used, as well as trying to build new ones. It's easy to say I'm not available to be fingered, to see whether I'd suit the establishment. At the same time, there the system is, and we all live in it. I think we have both found – you've often said – how many people are trying to play it straight, trying to get it clear and the fact that the system excludes so much, in real human terms, means that the response against it, even if confused and partial, goes on inevitably being built. There, for us, is what matters, wherever we can find it. Yes, we reject the constitution that would place us and use us, but it's not any kind of simple gesture of revolt. It's a long effort to keep certain experiences, certain possibilities, alive. Not even as a minority, though clearly we have more time: this is our ordinary work. But because we know the human version we are offered is sterile, and that many people know this, and that to try to clarify it, try to act where we can, makes a life.

The Press and Popular Education

From: *The Highway*, April 1959, pp 183–8

In theory, the responsibilities of the press in popular education are easy to define. A democratic society assumes that its members are competent to understand and to judge the many and complex public issues about which decisions have to be taken. The nature of these issues is commonly such that there is an absolute dependence on reliable information about matters which are too distant or too general to be personally apprehended. With its advanced techniques for the collection of news, and with its ability to disseminate this news very rapidly over a wide area, the press is obviously a principal medium in this fundamental operation of a democracy. Broadcasting and television have achieved even more rapid, indeed virtually immediate, dissemination, but, in issues of any complexity, the durable printed word, which allows re-reading and exact consideration, retains its advantages. For news of a detailed kind, there is no substitute for the press.

Again, it is necessary that as an aid to the formation of individual opinion, a wide variety of opinions and arguments should be available, again in a reasonably durable form. For this function, the press in its widest sense, from daily newspapers to specialized periodicals, is clearly indispensable. It is no accident that throughout the history of the struggle for democracy, a free press has been at once a leading agent and a constant symbol of hope.

Even at the level of theory, however, certain major differences of interpretation of this function become apparent. As I have defined it, the function of the press is the provision of facts and representative arguments, as the raw material for decision by the individual citizen. It is clear, however, that something apparently resembling this, yet in fact very different, has often been both proposed and practised. The press can be regarded, not as providing the raw materials for judgment, but as providing a judgment in itself, a substitute for individual judgment, and the object of the press is then not to educate public opinion, but to mould it in certain directions which those who control the press believe to be desirable. This substitute function can be carried out at different levels of responsibility. It can be, in the best sense, paternal, seeking to mould opinion but providing a fair summary of the original facts, and a fair representation of alternative opinions. Or it can be, on the other hand, a medium of simple mass persuasion, in which the facts are predigested into a particular form, and certain classes of opinion are

121

either wholly omitted or seriously diluted and misrepresented. In the worst examples of the mass-persuasion newspaper, there are omissions and distortions of fact, as well as omissions and distortions of alternative opinion.

We can see, then, three major definitions of the actual function of the press, and only two of these can be represented as popular education. The press of mass persuasion is not in any sense educational, because any adequate definition of education must include not only the intention of fostering individual and independent judgment, but also the provision of the necessary materials for this. Where the press seeks simply to persuade, to mould and ultimately to control public opinion, it is not only not a part of education, but may even be its enemy. This is the case in the press of a totalitarian country, but the same essential process is visible also in a press mainly dominated by commercial considerations.

The two alternative definitions are those of a paternal press, and of a democratic press. These can both be plausibly described as educational in tendency, but at this point the radical question of the nature of popular education clearly emerges. If we see popular education as education of the majority by a minority – as the education of the people not by the people but by some smaller group, and not necessarily for the people but conceivably for the interests of that smaller group – then we see both the claims and the limitations of a paternal press. Such a press is very different from a truly democratic press, in which the overriding intention, at every point, is the provision of materials for individual judgment and decision, and in which it is fundamental that every citizen has access to the channels through which news and opinion are disseminated, so that he may, as he wishes, take his full share in the process by which his society educates itself.

A democratic press, in the sense described, hardly as yet exists in this country. Its models can be seen in certain small journals, ordinarily associated with some voluntary social or intellectual organization. Our conception of a press in a democracy has not, ordinarily, moved beyond the principle that opinion should be free; that there should be no censorship or control. This, while valuable, is really no more than a negative criterion. The positive principle, of a press that belongs to its readers, is still largely speculative. Yet, when we are considering the press in relation to education, this relative immaturity of the press is important. For, in education, and particularly in adult education, a more mature principle is already operative. Education is seen as a social institution, under democratic control, and teaching is a profession, with its own clear standards of qualification and conduct, in a way that journalism has as yet only occasionally reached. The distinction is vital because it is at this point that the difference between any theoretical statement of the press as an instrument of popular education, and the state of the press as it actually exists, becomes most apparent. We cannot expect the press to be a full part of popular education while its aims, as an institution, are still quite differently defined.

The Popular Press since Northcliffe

The problem can best be seen in the light of the great change brought about by Northcliffe, in the 1890s, which was the development, as the financial basis of a cheap newspaper, of a new kind of advertising – mass advertising. The whole basis of this new advertising had to be a very large circulation, and the newspaper which could attain this found itself in possession of a very large revenue which enabled it to become, technically, much more efficient. The newspapers which followed this course moved to very large national circulations, and those newspapers which did not make this change were either forced out of existence or left relatively very weak.

The educational importance of this change was radical. The primary intention of the press was now no longer the provision of news and opinion, but the achievement of a large circulation to attract the mass-advertising revenue. This tendency, so far from diminishing, has sharply increased in the subsequent half-century. The progression has been uniformly in the direction of lower standards of journalism and smaller proportions of serious news and opinion. The change is not due to the extension of literacy. There was substantial adult literacy in England before this process began. It is a question of the fundamental nature and intention of the press as an institution, and since the 1890s at least, this has not been educational, but commercial. We have not allowed our educational system to be governed by the pressures and methods of the market, but we have allowed our press to be so governed, to the point where many now see the press, not as an ally of formal education, but in certain respects as its enemy.

It is true of course that the popular press has sought to mould public opinion, and its apologists argue that this, after all, is what education, of any kind, seeks to do. But the crucial distinction is that, in education, not merely opinions, but the facts and skills necessary to arrive at an opinion for oneself, are at the centre of the process. The popular press has achieved a clever facsimile of this, but what it is really doing is making a selection of facts and opinions, and by the skilful use of powerful techniques – devices of emphasis in different kinds of type, devices of composing a page so that attention is very subtly directed in certain required ways, devices of illustration which exercise a very powerful visual appeal – seeking not to educate but to influence. The methods of the popular press in England are virtually indistinguishable from the methods of mass commercial advertising, which is also defended on the grounds that it is educating the public. But with the example of real education constantly available to us, we are not likely to mistake this facsimile for substance.

Popular Education versus Mass Persuasion

Popular education, in any worthwhile sense, begins from a conception of human beings which, while recognizing differences of intelligence, of speed in learning, and of the desire to learn which is clearly affected by differences of environment, nevertheless insists that no man can judge for another man, that every man has a right to the facts and skills on which real judgment is based, and that, in this sense, all education depends on the acknowledgment of an ultimate human equality. This has been the guiding ideal of our English adult education, and the right of students to control the processes through which they learn has, from the beginning, been central and fundamental. On every side, now, we see this ideal challenged, but its most formidable opponent is not the old paternalism, but the new mass persuasion. It seems to me deeply significant that, with increasing emphasis and certainty, the ordinary people should be openly described as 'masses'. This word, this formula of description, excludes by its very nature that conception of the worth and importance of individual human beings on which a real popular education can alone be based. It is true that we need constantly to learn new ways of teaching which are appropriate to very different kinds of intelligence and personality. We can acknowledge that, in certain respects, the mass persuaders have discovered techniques of exposition and presentation which are indeed generally useful. We certainly acknowledge that the new means of communication – the newspaper, the radio, the film, television – are wonderfully valuable in a society dedicated to democracy and to common improvement. But neither the new practical techniques, nor the means of dissemination, are a substitute for educational intention. They can be used to educate; they can be used to influence or control. The deepest social threat of our existing culture is the attempted replacement of the old ideal of popular education by the new conception of the organization of public relations with the 'masses'. Unless we are very clear about the values on which our own educational effort is based, we shall be powerless against this rising conception, which is already endowed with great material resources and with the approving sanction of all those who fear real democracy and who, alarmed by the development of popular power, seek only to tame and control it in directions favourable to themselves.

The Ideal of Responsibility in Education

Meanwhile, an older conception of responsibility stands as a possible alternative. The paternalist ideal of education shares with the practice of mass persuasion the conception of ordinary people as 'masses', but, guided not by desires of profit or power, but by its own firm conceptions of the good and the true, seeks to mould the majority towards these conceptions. Despite all pressures, certain institutions have held to this ideal. Our best newspapers, in England, have been of this kind and the BBC is explicitly committed to this ideal by its charter.

I do not want to criticize institutions of this kind, though in certain important respects I find their conception of responsibility – based perhaps on preserving traditional values against mass pressure – inadequate. I would draw attention only to certain important recent trends. Our best newspapers are based on a particular section of society, which in general comprises those who have had the longest period of education. It is not solely a question of intelligence, because the relation between intelligence and length of education is still not exact. As educational opportunities have widened, there has been a significant rise in the readership of the best of these newspapers, which a highly-educated class requires. This is most welcome, but we can no longer assume that the future holds a steady development of a range of newspapers, at different levels corresponding to differences of education and interest. For, alongside the rise in many of the best papers, there has been a startling contraction in the circulation of those middle papers which seek to be both responsible and popular. We have seen, in England in the 1950s, a kind of polarization, by which the best papers have gained slowly, the worst papers have gained rapidly, and the middle papers have substantially lost. It is not impossible that within a generation there will be in England only minority papers and mass papers, and, while the former may become stronger, meeting the needs of the more highly educated, it is clear that such a development would not only be irrelevant to popular education but would in this field mark its abandonment.

The situation is made graver by the severity of financial pressures, within existing methods of organization. The constant technical improvements continue to raise the amount of capital required to exploit them. In the related field of television, we have seen a startling example of the weakness of paternalism, in our kind of economy. The success of commercial television, indeed the very fact that it could be introduced in an England formerly governed, in this field, by firm paternalist ideals, show an all too probable pattern of our future. The huge revenue from advertising – £365,000,000 annually in all media – confers a power and an incentive which popular education, whether paternal or democratic, cannot hope to rival. Similar financial pressures on the press are becoming more severe. It seems absurd that a newspaper with more than a million buyers should be financially threatened. Yet the revenue from buyers is often less than half the total revenue: the rest comes from advertising, and the advertising money goes, relentlessly, to the organs of largest circulation. There is thus a constant pressure on all those who control and use these media, not to engage in the necessarily slow and careful process of popular education, but rather to seek the quick results, the easy influence, the continual simplifications and distractions of the alternative conception – the exploitation of human weakness and natural inexperience, for profit or power.

At such a time, it seems almost frivolous to recall the democratic ideal. The success of alternative conceptions is so marked that we can easily feel beaten before we start. Yet it is only in the democratic ideal, and in the serious and continuing example of real popular education, that we can find strength to keep alive an alternative future. The power of democracy is ultimately very great, and we need not fear the future if we are able, frankly and wholeheartedly, to identify ourselves with it. It is ironic that these great media of popular communication, which to the pioneers of democracy would have seemed a marvellous dream, should in our time be so deeply equivocal: at once the greatest opportunity ever given for real popular education and yet the source of deep and justified fears that this ideal will be abandoned in favour of new kinds of domination and control. Perhaps what we learn, finally, from our study of the contemporary mass media, of the press as of the other forms, is that a conception of education is inseparable from a conception of society, and that now these great powers have been loosed, we are launched too far for any kind of compromise. We can no longer afford either partial education or partial democracy. Neither has the strength to stand against these new powers. The only strengths that will be adequate are the strengths of full democracy, of a full and wholehearted popular education, which we are learning to conceive, and which we must, with urgency, go on to bring to life.

London Letter: The New British Left

From: *Partisan Review*, 27, 1960, pp 341–7

I wish I knew enough about Britain to be able to say with any confidence what is really happening here. The difficulty, as usual, is that too much is being said by too few people. The English literary world is supposed to have broken up since the war, but I know of at least some efficient if shallow channels, along which the best opinion of the time is supposed to flow, and I know one or two places where you can sit and watch it flowing. As I hardly ever do this, though, I can't be certain that I know what is supposed to be going on. I could, like somebody living outside Britain, get my sense of movement from print, but apart from the fact that this is always likely to be misleading – circulation still follows capital, and capital ownership in Britain is still certainly unrepresentative – I find that even the little I know about cultural groups here modifies the value of the evidence to such an extent that any plain reading is difficult. I get most of my evidence from discussions with audiences to whom I lecture, and from what can be generalized from the indisputable public facts.

I think the essential factor in any reading of contemporary British opinion is one of generation. If the average age of contributors were printed on newspapers and journals, it would clarify many things. It is important, for example, that the *Guardian* (which used to be the *Manchester Guardian*) seems now to be mainly run by youngish men, and I know when I read its book page I find it nearer, in tone and opinion, to people I actually meet than any other British paper. *The Spectator*, also, seems to belong to this generation. In other papers and magazines, few are untouched by the manner and opinions of the generation now under forty, but the mixture takes place in different ways, from modification to absorption. The *New Statesman* seems to fluctuate – still mainly the valuable organ of the older Left Establishment, but sometimes including the thinking and feeling of the younger Left, sometimes reviving, in spectacular ways, the features which drove this younger Left away from it. The *Observer* has a settled if filleted mixture of the most improbable page-fellows, but manages to look pretty young and radical (it certainly isn't the latter) beside the monumentally aged *Sunday Times*. In several of the best periodicals there is a characteristic contemporary tone, which ought to be relevant evidence, but that particular flavour, compounded of London and international contacts, seems oddly to have very little to do with Britain, at least the Britain I am interested in. I watch people I have known disappearing into that world, and there it is. I get an occasional message back that I am insular (it used to be 'provincial' but too many writers in demand now live in the provinces), and I interpret this as meaning that I route my international contacts other than through London, and also that I have as many friends in the Soviet Union as in the United States, which is not at all a civilised and cosmopolitan thing to do. But also I am frankly insular in the sense that I am primarily interested in British society and in what manages to get culturally expressed of *that*, and Port Talbot and Manchester and places like that seem to me more really productive of evidence.

Anyway, through these cross-currents, the difference between generations still emerges quite strongly, and everyone under forty believes the tide is flowing his way. But what way? In politics, for example, there are two important young groups: the Bow Group of Conservatives, who are interestingly liberal on colonial matters in ways that have little to do with solid Conservative opinion, and the New Left, which I think I belong to myself. It may be that British politics in fifteen or twenty years will consist of the conflict now existing between these two new approaches, but a lot can happen to start other directions. Broadly, the Bow Group seems to be the expression of a progressive pragmatism within the terms of the existing society: easier and more open about class, tired of the old Imperialism but rather liking the new, full of appetite for a fast-moving and affluent commercial society. To get any fair account of it you would have to ask one of its people; what I have seen and heard of it is pretty mixed, and there may be some organizing principle, other than that of decorous modernizing adjustment to small-power capitalism, that has escaped me. Meanwhile I could try to give some account of the New Left, from my own bias, and see what you make of it.

After long discussions, two independent journals – the *New Reasoner* and the *Universities and the Left Review* – joined forces recently to produce the *New Left Review*, which is to come out six times a year. Typographically it may not be very clear, but the emphasis is a review of the New Left not a new Left Review; reference back to the *Left Review* of the 1930's is not intended. The two original periodicals had very different beginnings. The *New Reasoner* succeeded the *Reasoner*, which began as an opposition journal inside the British Communist Party. Its editors originally were Edward Thompson and John Saville, from Halifax and Hull respectively. John Saville is an economic historian; Edward Thompson has written a long and excellent book on William Morris – a combination of history and literary criticism. Thompson and Saville came to defining Stalinism as a distortion of communism. The breaking point came with their support of the Hungarian Revolution, but it seems this was only the climax of a longer history of democratic opposition. Many British intellectuals came out of the Communist Party at about that time, and energies that had been locked up in the apparatus soon invigorated the traditional non-Communist Labour Left. At the same time, the non-Conformist Labour Left has long seemed uncomfortable resting-ground for intellectuals. Theoretically very weak, it made up in good-heartedness what it lacked in social theory, but was still subject to a jerky emotional opportunism, characteristically expressed by powerful leader-figures like Aneurin Bevan. Bevan's apparent desertion of the Left in 1958 on the issue of Britain's hydrogen bomb exposed this weakness and dependence dramatically. Meanwhile thinkers on the right of the Labour Party, especially C.A.R. Crosland, won easy if hollow victories, with the Labour Left theoretically impoverished.

The *New Reasoner* marked the reorganization of democratic socialist theory in Britain, and the wonder to me is that the people who wrote for it could have stayed in the Communist Party for so long. The question really was one of alternatives. If you were really interested in socialism, where could you work for it in Britain, with the official Labour Party steadily slipping away from it, and with the Labour Left in the condition described? Moreover, it must be said quite clearly that the long parade of ex-communist recanters was so truly miserable to watch, seemed so obviously not just a political change but a collapse of feeling and hope, that the incentive to stay attached was probably strengthened in many of the best men. I can only speak from the experience of several old personal friends, who hung on to their Communist cards through an increasingly bitter disillusion but hung on because, with the alternatives as they were, it seemed a test of plain human strength. I know no better people in postwar Britain than these, though I could not share their actual loyalties. If communists or ex-communists are suspect because they are not natural democrats, I can only say that I find men like Edward Thompson the real democratic fighters in a period in which the formal democratic assent was much too often a simple compromise with capitalism and the military alliances. The tension they have been through is, of course, still unresolved. The *New Reasoner*, for me, was still much too involved in arid fights with the Party Marxists, and occasional articles came through in which nothing at all seemed to have changed. But also there were signs of socialist *thinking* again, in the terms of actual contemporary British life, and that was the valuable strand.

The *Universities and Left Review* was always very different. It started from Oxford, after the Hungary-Suez crisis, and its editors were all new to politics. The eldest, Charles Taylor, a Canadian, was a fellow of All Souls and a philosopher. The others were recent graduates: Stuart Hall, from Jamaica, in English; Gabriel Pearson in English; Ralph Samuel in politics and economics. The magazine took some time to find an identity, but eventually became the channel of two distinct lines of work: economic description of contemporary British capitalism, *The Insiders* and Michael Barratt-Brown's *The Controllers*; and the cultural analysis – the bringing together of sociology and literary criticism. The former would have tied in easily to the best work of the *New Reasoner*; the latter was a bit more doubtful.

Three books appeared, in these formative stages, that had some effect. Richard Hoggart's *Uses of Literacy* and my own *Culture and Society* set off some of the cultural analysis in *Universities and Left Review*, but it is clear, looking back, that this would have come through anyway. The fact of cultural poverty is inescapable in contemporary Britain, and Hoggart had very thoroughly documented it. But not all of us were willing to describe this as 'mass culture': this is still our main point of difference from American radicals with whom otherwise we have much in common. Hoggart himself seemed uncertain about this, and it was easy to read his book as if the old working-class community feeling was the only alternative to the new classless 'mass culture'. I disagreed, and argued mainly that certain ways of thinking, including some radical thinking about 'the masses', were the sickness of a particular society, and that there was an alternative to these, not so much in the old working-class communities which were in any case breaking up, but in the democratic institutions which, however tarnished, still composed the British labour movement. This argument is not yet resolved, though Hoggart and I have learned from each other and we are now rather nearer a common position (one that had been assumed, quite wrongly, much earlier when Richard Hoggart and Raymond Williams got to be used like the name of a joint firm). The tying-in of this new strand with the other developments noted is also not complete, but some clarification came with the third book, *Conviction*, a series of essays from a rather different range of authors. Hoggart and I were put page by page with young Labour Party sociologists and economists (Peter Townsend, Peter Shore, Brian Abel-Smith), and on the whole it seemed like a group, though the contributors had never met as such, and in several cases had not met at all. Iris Murdoch's argument for a new effort and emphasis in socialist theory came close to this mood, and to some of the work in the two magazines. It began at last to look as if a new Left existed or was on the edge of forming.

The *New Left Review* was launched in December 1959, and its main job is to continue this search for new common ground, as well as continuing and extending the particular lines of work opened up. The encouraging thing is that it seems already to be something more than a magazine. The *Universities and Left Review* had already begun an extremely successful meeting-club, and also a coffee-house, *The Partisan*, in London. In recent months, New Left Clubs have been opening in many places all over Britain, and there are also many *New Left Review* readers' groups meeting regularly in different parts of the country – a form of organization that has not existed in Britain since the Left Book Club groups of the 1930's. Some breadth has also been added by three other developments: the Free Cinema movement (now disbanded as a group but spreading its influence as its directors establish themselves elsewhere); the encouraging revival of plays and novels about areas of ordinary British life which the cultural Establishment had neglected – the obvious names are Arnold Wesker, John Braine, Shelagh Delaney, but there are many others; and, above all, the Campaign for Nuclear Disarmament, which is in no way a creation of the New Left, but which, in the wonderfully successful marches from Aldermaston and in scores of crowded meetings, is bringing thousands of young people into politics, but politics of a new and independent kind which the traditional parties are hardly in touch with. It is all a glorious and lively muddle, changing in character continuously, full of serious differences within itself, but recognizable as a social mood absolutely different from that obtaining at the beginning of the 1950's. The main thing is that a good many people under thirty have bypassed or recovered from the real failure of nerve which deadened social and intellectual argument in Britain between 1945 and 1955. If the New Left does its job in the provision of the solid thinking which must succeed its lively evocation of a mood, the general effect could be considerable. A library of socialist books is now being started, which over five years could amount to a new statement of democratic socialist theory and policy in Britain. This could be of some international importance.

What are the relations between the New Left and the Labour Party? Distinctly odd, I think, though most New Left people work in the Labour Party, and some of its emphases have already passed into official Labour policy, particularly on the less minestrewn cultural sector. The fact is that most young socialists and radicals regard the Labour Party as a part of the Establishment they are against and will have to change. The conditions for healthy development seem to be: a new grasp of social and cultural poverty in an otherwise prosperous society; a renewal of belief in active participating democracy as the means of reform – neither the State board nor the compromise with powerful private monopolies, but the building of democratic institutions in industry, in the cultural apparatus, and in our heavily bureaucratic communities; an imaginative growth, finally, of a new attitude to international politics which will stop centering relations on military alliances and nuclear armaments. In the next five years, the official Labour Party could well be changed in precisely these ways; if so, it would itself be the New Left. If not, the Labour Party will almost certainly continue to decline. Reformed Conservatism, with the Bow Group as its pilot, will leave hardly any room for the moderate policy on which Labour lost three elections.

The difficult stage is now, when the New Left, pleased by its first successes, might easily sit back and become exactly like the Old Left which it sought to invigorate and clarify. The crucial test it still has to pass is that posed by the many communists who look on it all as little more than a game. Can you create contemporary and effective socialist theory, they ask, without in effect coming back to us? More important, can you do anything with it, even if you have created it, as a miscellaneous group or writers and young people? These are real questions, with no certain answers. Until the New Left makes sense to industrial workers (it is certainly trying to do this now), its potential is severely limited. But we think that all over the world two threads of development have snapped and are useless: Stalinism on the one hand (on issues of power and freedom), simple democratic evolution on the other (we get richer but not more free, and communicate more easily but often at the price of a culture so bad that it can destroy us). Facing our own problems, we find echoes not only from the United States, but from the Soviet Union and Poland. The gradual definition of new problems, the recovery of nerve to face radical change, seem carried to us by many winds.

Or so it seems to me from this crowded island we are trying both to discover and to change. If I am wrong, we shall all know about it, but the effort is pretty exhilarating.

Section 3:
Teaching and Learning

This section demonstrates clearly how important Raymond Williams considered his role as an educator of adults and how seriously he took his teaching. Produced between 1948 and 1953, the years when Williams was learning his trade, this writing constitutes 'a craftsman's notebook' in which problems of approach and method are debated and passed on to others for similar trial and readjustment. These pieces remain indispensable for understanding Williams's development as a literary critic/social critic.

Leavis had emphasised the importance of a university School of English and the teacher training colleges. Williams wanted to take the approach of Leavis and *Scrutiny* into adult education to provide working people with the tools to analyse literature, drama, film, radio, newspapers and advertising, and with the techniques to discriminate. So armed they might enrich their own lives, lift the deadening weight of the apparatus of manipulation and create a better society. The power of criticism must be taken by the people. Replenished with that the self-organisation embodied in the WEA could be extended to remaking a good and democratic popular culture. The techniques of criticism could become the tools for control. Cultural change required social and therefore political change.

The early extracts suggest how fervent, crusading and implacable was Williams's commitment to close reading in these years and how staunchly in this regard he still stood at Leavis's shoulder. 'Sorting that out', he was to remark later 'and eventually rejecting it, took the next ten years'.[1] Hoggart's **Some Notes on Aim and Method in University Tutorial Classes** and Williams's response, **A Note on Mr Hoggart's Appendices,** demonstrate Williams's insistence on the text, the responsive reading – for its own sake, not to illustrate problems, technique or general argument – and judgement. His position is outlined more fully in **Some Experiments in Literature Teaching**. The student and the text must be at the centre of the class. The tutor is a prompt and exemplar, not a commentator on either 'background' or the required response. Williams's pedagogy, which could bear further examination by educators, eschews the lecture. The student is central, the student must do the work. What is essential is 'progressive reading rather than progressive exercises in reading' if the response is to be living and authentic. The teacher cannot substitute for the student; a second-hand repackaged response is sterile. The text must come first and second – only then comes correlation to economy and society. The Cambridge tests – evaluate, compare, judge – are central. The reading of literature needs no justification – or obeisance to history or politics.

Compared with Hoggart and most other tutors this focus on the text was unusual, even obsessive. The extracts from **Reading and Criticism** (1950) which follow further demonstrate this commitment. The book is an assertive statement of allegiance to practical criticism. Intended as a case-book for adult educators it progresses from reading paired examples, George Eliot and Lawrence, to reading complete works. Williams believed you could not properly judge the part in isolation from the whole work to which it was essential. Conrad's *Heart of Darkness* is taken as a study in reading an entire work. With hindsight Williams lamented the split between the individual and the social this approach entailed. In retrospect he observed that **Reading and Criticism** 'shows the limits of that kind of critical analsyis – what it can and cannot do. For ironically Conrad's text poses quite crucial issues – about imperialism, for example – which concerned me greatly later on but which I did not discuss at all then, and which in a way could hardly be discussed within a procedure so completely focussed on use of language or thematic organisation'.[2]

His approach of the late forties and early fifties, 'get to the text . . . keep to the text', is boldly affirmed in **Literature in Relation to History**, reflections on an extremely high-powered conference Williams organised at Hertford College, Oxford in the summer of 1950. The list of participants highlights the resources that could be mobilised by adult educators in this period. Williams is critical of the defensiveness, timidity and lack of faith in their vocation of his fellow literature tutors. These comments also implicitly indict the limitations of many historians – despite the impressive galaxy of historical erudition assembled. Comparison between Williams's views and the humanism Edward Thompson brought to the writing of history is irresistible. Williams was the following year involved in jointly teaching a long course on 'Victorian Literature and Society'. Adult education, he continually asserts, was a field in which experiments could and, therefore, must be undertaken.[3]

The courses Williams taught under the rubric 'Culture and Environment' and 'Culture and Society' in the late 1940s were a major experiment. **Books for Teaching Culture and Environment** illustrates the hopes Williams held for critical analysis and the particular path his intellectual searching, strengthened by the publication in 1948 of Eliot's *Notes Towards a Definition of Culture*, was taking at this conjuncture. Much of the terrain he maps was not in fact new. At least some of it had been covered in adult education classes in the 1930s. The last section 'Culture and Civilisation' and his comments on Ruth Benedict's *Patterns of Culture*, however, show him heading into the hills from which he was to return with *Culture and Society*. But note, too, the numerous social critics addressed in that book who are absent from his bibliography at mid-century. Note also, despite the apparent continuing sway of Leavis, Williams's self-situation: he is in some ways, he feels, nearer to Marxism.

Williams's thinking certainly placed him in the optimistic stream of the tradition of cultural criticism. Unlike a pessimist such as Eliot he was working intensively in his teaching and organisation with a wide range of students for whom culture was ordinary but vital. It is interesting to

recall Eliot's own enthusiasm for the future when he himself had attended
extra-mural classes at the University of London three decades earlier.
Writing about his fellow students he exclaimed: 'These people are the
most hopeful sign in England to me.'⁴ This sentiment stimulated Williams's
work in these years and was to remain its bed-rock.

The Teaching of Public Expression is a succinct and robust statement
of Williams's attempt to unite practical criticism and adult education.
He wants to democratise the *Scrutiny* approach and take it beyond the
academy by handing out important weapons from the academic armoury
to be developed and used by workers in the way they wish, for *their*
ends. Williams's comments sum up the fundamental problem of adult
education. Is its purpose essentially to civilise and control in the interests
of a maintained *status quo*, inducting workers into high culture? Or is it
essentially to provide the conditions which will facilitate a free choice in
terms of social and economic organisation for workers and the making of
a new popular culture?

> *Does one impose on a social class that is growing in power the syllabus
> of an older culture; or does one seek means of releasing and enriching
> the life experience which the rising class brings with it? If the latter as
> I choose then the WEA has a lot of its thinking in front of it.*

'More than anything the films'⁵ . . . that was how Williams remembered his time at Cambridge. It was natural that he should extend his
concern for literary criticism to another nerve centre of popular culture.
Film as a Tutorial Subject provides a detailed case study of Williams's
philosophy, organisation and teaching technique. Finally the short pieces
from *The Tutor's Bulletin*, a forum for exchange between practising adult
educators, demonstrate a scrupulous attitude to polemic and, in 1953, his
continuing adherence to practical criticism, an adherence which was to fall
away by the mid-fifties.⁶ By that time Williams was critical of the isolation
of the text and the passivity in the face of it which this vigorous variant of
practical criticism imposed on the reader. This was reflected in a broader
approach to teaching which sought to integrate text and context.⁷

Notes and References

1. R. Williams 'My Cambridge' in R. Hayman, ed., *My Cambridge*, Robson
   Books, 1977, p 67.
2. R. Williams *Politics and Letters*, 1979, pp 237–8.
3. For Humphrey House see pp 21–2. C.J. Holloway 1920– was a Fellow
   of All Souls and later Professor of English Literature at Cambridge.
   J.B. Bamborough 1921– , a Fellow of Wadham College, later became
   Principal of Linacre College, Oxford. W.W. Robson 1923– was a Fellow
   of Lincoln College and later Professor of English Literature at Sussex and
   Edinburgh. Professor G.M. Young 1882–1959, a famous Victorian historian,
   was a Fellow of All Souls. Sir Isaiah Berlin 1909– was a Fellow of All Souls,
   later Chichele Professor of Social and Political Theory and a world-famous
   political philosopher. For Asa Briggs see p 30. Raymond Postgate 1896–1971
   was a Plebs Leaguer, a socialist, sometime communist, historian and pioneering

food critic. Sir Maurice Powicke 1879–1963 was retired Regius Professor of History at Oxford.
4. V. Eliot, ed., *The Letters of T.S. Eliot, Vol. 1, 1898–1922*, Faber and Faber, 1988, p 120.
5. R. Williams 'My Cambridge', p 60.
6. 'Text and Context' and Williams's letter are not listed in the indispensable and otherwise exhaustive bibliography in A. O'Connor, *Raymond Williams: Writing, culture, politics*, Blackwell, 1989.
7. See J. McIlroy, 'Border Country: Raymond Williams in adult education', pp 270–323, this volume.

Some Notes on Aim and Method in University Tutorial Classes

By Richard Hoggart
From: *Adult Education*, XX, 4, June 1948, pp 187–94

General Approach

It is a truism that we suffer today not so much from a lack of information as from an inability to handle all the information which is offered to us. That most of this information is presented in a purely sensational manner aggravates our condition: there is rarely any suggestion that responsible decisions or action should follow from the reader.

It should surely be no less a truism that in liberal adult classes the tutor's purpose is primarily to impart not matter but a method. If the tutorial class teacher does not insist on a strict discipline of study to this end he may see his students leave their last class talking about Proust or Palestine, but their talk will have no more significance than their workmate's gossip about football pools – and it will be touched with the snobbery of the partly informed.

It follows that for the adult tutor the problem of communication is of the first importance. Internal lecturers may, and one knows that in fact they sometimes do, fail to connect with more than two or three of their hearers. The external tutor, on the other hand, needs to think as much about *how* things shall be said as about *what* shall be said: he needs to pay much attention to questions of teaching technique. This is not to suggest that he attempts to explain the ineffable; there are places where words are no longer relevant, but most of us have still a lot to learn about communication in atmospheres less rarefied than those.

The Students

This section is inserted here because any notes on method will have little reality unless they take into account the special nature of our students.

Some time ago a speaker, pointing out that many of these students cannot read with critical intelligence, said that in our classes we should not concern ourselves solely with 'the cream' who can so read. I do not wish to comment on his specific point but mention the statement because it contains a common, and, I believe, regrettable assumption – namely, that those who come to us with sharp critical intelligence are 'the cream' of our students. For our kind of work that seems a very suspect hierarchy in which intelligence, or more accurately critical intelligence, ranks so high. The students I consider my best are respectively an elementary-school-trained boy in a steelworks office, an honours graduate in English with a research M.A., a forty-odd year old village-school-educated farmer's wife, and a sub-editor on a provincial paper who went to a minor public school. Their common quality (which they share with almost all the other students) is neither intelligence nor academic knowledge.

We are not out to create an intellectual elite, and must take care to avoid fostering a narrow snobbery of intellect and information. The best type of tutorial class student is one with a certain disposition of mind which may be found in the educated and the uneducated, in the intelligent and the not-so-intelligent. It is – for want of a better phrase – a potential of sensibility. By that last word I mean more than is normally implied by its use in discussions about literature or aesthetics; I mean a certain purity of intention, a sincerity which marks an undefiant kind of moral courage. How often one finds, as one begins to know a class, that in some way or another almost every student has the advantage in his approach to the work. If we so arrange our teaching that we always bat on our own wicket we may be able to maintain a guard that will deceive even ourselves. Once we move on to the students' ground we are humbled to note the places at which their sensibility, their depth, their wit, are more finely developed than ours.

With almost all, then, is to be found this 'potential of sensibility', sometimes informed by a fine intelligence, sometimes by an intuitive sense of fitness, sometimes by little more than energy and good intentions. It is this common possession of a questioning heart – questioning because of some want, some lack, some foretaste of joy, some reaching out after greater possessions of the spirit – which sends our students to the discomforts and ardours of the tutorial class. That is why it is true to say, as has been so often said, that in the end the basis of our work is spiritual. It is here that we come upon the relevance, both to the students and the tutor, of Carlyle's 'a loving heart is the beginning of all knowledge' and of Maritain's 'I must know where I am, and who I am, before knowing, and in order to know, what I should do'.[1]

It would not be appropriate to go on to the wider discussion of ends to which that last paragraph tempts. But its final sentence should at least preclude us, when we begin to discuss subject-method, from repeating with G.D.H. Cole: 'the rest – history, literature, the arts – should arise out of these basic studies, and should not be pursued independently of them, or

---

1 To a consideration of method Carlyle's other well-known dictum also applies: 'all that a university can do for us is still what the first school began doing – teach us to read.' Maritain, *Redeeming the Time* (Bles), quoted E.F.F. Hill in *Transformation Two* p 24.

apart from conceptions of current social purpose and meaning'.[2] Let us say no more now than that, though there are great differences in students, there is an important underlying unity, which brings them voluntarily to these classes, prepared to comply with their exacting demands.

Some Considerations on Method

Throughout this section I shall, since I am a literature tutor, draw most of my examples from the teaching of that subject. But the principles illustrated are, I hold, of general application.

Three preliminary demands must be made of all students. We have, firstly, to disappoint bitterly any desire for magisterial indoctrination. Their real education has begun when they realize that though the tutor may tell them the truth and nothing but the truth he is very unlikely to tell the whole truth; when they realize, too, that the further pursuit of that truth is as much their task as his. Secondly, our students must be persuaded to withhold judgment where their tools are inadequate: in literature this will mean that their first major effort will be to enter into the experience which is being communicated, to see exactly what the writer is getting at. Thirdly, students of any subject have to learn to read more slowly since nearly all, when they join a class, have only one reading-gear, that which allows them to eye-read by whole blocks of phrases. They have to learn to bring into play finer and finer sets of gears, to lose the habit of reading simply at top-gear, the eye skimming across the page, the brain operating at surface tension as lazily as a cyclist turning the pedals on a fine downward slope, letting a stroke register only occasionally, content if many of them are only rote movements. They must be brought to see that on the difficult bits top-gear lets you down, the wheels make no further impression; rider and reader give up.

For the tutor too there are, I think, at least three important rules of method. The first of them is contained in Bacon's, 'He that cannot contract the sight of his mind as well as disperse and dilate it, wanteth a great faculty.'[3] For we have, before any lecture, to work back from the place which we aim to reach, through our own half-forgotten assumptions and submerged foundation-knowledge, back to the point where this knowledge connects, by no matter how tenuous a thread so only it be a valid one, to the students' own experience. To call this preliminary process 'simplification' is to give a wrong impression; it is rather a working-back to a legitimate starting-point.

Perhaps it would be truer to say that one works back to a point just ahead of the student's existing awareness, and from there beckons to him.

---

2   G.D.H. Cole, *Plan for Living*, Essay No 1 in 'Plan for Britain', a collection of essays by the Fabian Society, 1943.

3   Bacon, *Advancement of Learning*, quoted I.A. Richards, *Interpretation in Teaching*, p 216.

Because the second stage is the journey itself, the mountain climb, the exploration of the chosen theme. Here again it would be wrong for the tutor to *lead* the students, in no matter how careful and friendly a fashion, to the top of the mountain; he has rather so to guide their progress that they are impelled always to stretch to the next point upwards (always the guide, never the cheer-leader, should be the motto). They may thus come to the end of each climb the richer not simply by the knowledge of its particular detail but by the grasping of the principles behind it; they will have been given notes towards a general method, not a set route for one more journey.

For the tutor this demands more than thinking back mechanically. It requires us to bear in mind that it was not the steady dressing of facts which quickened our own minds so much as the oblique comment, the seminal phrase, the clarifying correlation. The matter counts less than its presentation, the material less than the significance of its ordering. To change the metaphor, we have to try to find the points at which the curious mind will itself seize on the revealing correspondence and leap across the gap. We have, continually, to *connect*. It is easy, for instance, to say largely that our society is in danger of collapse, and that without the exercise of certain disciplines, the practice of the principles of democracy, etc., etc., etc ... in class we must reduce those abstractions (no doubt heavy with meaning for us) into understandable terms. We have to be continually staging the battle in a comprehensible form, so that our students may see its nature and the principles behind it. The moment for abstract statements, and that for their intellectual brother the generalization, come rarely and only after preparation (see Appendix A).

All this moving from the happy valley of the surface approach is very slow work. For the students it may seem that only a little ground has been covered, and that there are constant halts whilst detailed examinations are made of small areas. On the tutor the demands are heavy; the method requires not only the careful preparation of class lectures but the planning of discussion, the framing of pointers and leading-questions for each week's home reading, and the adjustment of each piece of written work so that it fits into the stage so far reached and does not require the student to tackle a job with inadequate equipment. In a more profound sense it is for the tutor the way of humility. With much patience and self-denial he has so to prepare the clues that the student can from them evolve the way up, and gaining assurance at each stage, by the effort of his faculties, not by external help, lever himself on to each successive ledge. This is a difficult process, especially for those of us who are strongly tempted to exhibit. It is flatteringly easy to see the students, faced with a problem which they cannot answer, a ledge hopelessly beyond their reach, look in hopeful ignorance for the tutor to produce the necessary ladder. Far more to the point is to give them a chance to reach that ledge by their own efforts, the self forgotten whilst working out the steps by which their judgment, given a fair chance, may grapple from problem to problem.

We must not so much indicate conclusions as frame questions (see Appendix B).

The Tutor

It seems likely that the conduct of the university tutorial class, if only because of the great demands it makes, will pass more and more into the hands of the staff-tutor. There will always be, one may suppose, a few part-time tutors who run extremely good tutorial classes, together with some young men who feel drawn to adult teaching and decide to try it out before they attempt to take up full-time work. One hopes that such arrangements will continue; among other things they will help to ensure that the conduct of tutorial classes does not become too formalized.

To run one such class well demands a large amount of preparation; to run four or five is in every sense a full-time job. The class session is then almost entirely taken up with the detailed running of the courses, so that there is little time even for reading. The external tutor, no less than the internal lecturer, needs time in summer for reading, writing, research and general recuperation. I include recuperation because the adult tutor's is a life with its own special strains, particularly the strain of isolation from professional colleagues and the weight of constant and peculiarly intimate relations with so many who are promising or lonely or unhappy or who need a leg on.

But surely the isolation has in the past been unnecessarily great. The newcomer to adult work looks in vain for a written tradition to which he can refer. There is a tradition, of course, but it is fragmentary, carried on in the main by the single excellent tutor who works on his own and compares his results with no one. There is, for instance, a curious lack of publications on the technique of the work. Almost all the books on adult education are written by administrators and deal with general ends. There are, as we all know, many such books, and it is useful for the tyro to read one of them for background. But of books which would allow us to compare methods, or of textbooks written with the special needs of the tutorial class in mind, or of books seriously getting down to the problem of popularization without vulgarization, we have almost none. I do not want to suggest a formalizing of method, but I do plead for a fertilizing discussion of technique by a group of people who are already kept unnaturally apart from one another.

Appendix A – 'On staging the battle in a comprehensible form'

In case my metaphor is not clear enough here is an account of a simple attempt on my part to follow this principle.

Among the first obstacles in literature classes are the students' attempts to cover a failure to use the tools of critical analysis by slipping in moral condemnation from unexpressed value-judgments; and, conversely, when value-judgments are in place, to shove them off as 'matters of taste'. The problem is to show the necessity for distinguishing between these, without adding further to the confusion by simply jingling abstractions. I can only indicate the stage which my attempts at a solution have so far reached – with help from several who have written on the matter, particularly Dr I.A. Richards. Since the problem is not peculiar to literature classes other adult tutors have no doubt gone further.

The students are asked to think of the work of an NSPCC inspector and are presented with four apparently similar statements on that work, viz:

(1) 'That man's work is intermittent' – i.e. cases for investigation occur at irregular intervals.
(2) 'That man's work is pleasant' – i.e. he spends much time travelling in the open, which the speaker enjoys.
(3) 'That man's work is obscure' – i.e. the complicated administrative process puzzles the speaker.
(4) 'That man's work is good/valuable' – i.e. he is succouring children, which the speaker believes to be morally good.

They are asked to distinguish between the sentences and are given some help to that end, e.g. certain questions which they might ask are suggested. Afterwards a detailed analysis of the nature of the four sentences is made and the dangers of shifts of meaning pointed out (especially between sentences two and four and three and four, since sentence four, as was suggested earlier, is often either used in a bastard fashion or reduced to 'a matter of taste'). Finally, the students are asked to notice how some of these four elements are interwoven in most of the statements which they make on their reading, and are invited to watch for the spurious statement which relies on a shift of meaning to hide a disinclination to use the proper tools.

Appendix B – 'On working back and the way of humility'

This awful example of the way in which some exercises were modified may illustrate my meaning.

Anxious to make early use of exercises in critical discrimination, I began by reading to the class contrasting passages, one from a good and one from a bad author. After inviting comments, I verbally debunked passage b., with no clear separation of technical from moral judgments, and with great enjoyment to myself. The class were left not with an increase of grasp but hurt because they were aware that something which they cherished had been mocked and derided without their understanding why.

Learning slowly, I began to look for exercises which did not easily lend themselves to shifts of judgment; I issued stencilled copies of the exercises to each student and allowed them a long time in which to read the passages; I stopped asking them to comment in class unless they felt sure of themselves – this to avoid embarrassment. Sometimes I gave the exercise as written work with at least a fortnight before they had to hand it in. At one point I found that all the answers seemed to me good. Impossible that they could all advance so quickly and uniformly – clearly, they were getting my measure and giving the answer which they knew I would like.

There have been some intervening changes but at present, and with new classes, I do this: issue contrasting passages in which the comparison involves not primarily the making of value-judgments but a distinguishing between content, aim, tone, manner and so on. To use an analogy from textiles: I no longer flash across their line of vision a piece of real silk and a dazzling imitation, and then proceed to show them how hopelessly they have been misled. I give them a piece of woollen and a piece of cotton fabric, and forbid them to make value-judgments until they are able to express the difference between them in terms of texture, weave, weight, feel, etc. If these exercises are done in class, plenty of time for reading them is given. If they are difficult they are read aloud, since so many new students are unable to give body to their eye-reading. Then each student writes down as honestly as he can what he sees in the passage. No one sees his findings so there is no tendency to try to satisfy the tutor. After this I make a careful oral analysis of the difference between the two passages as I see them. The strength of their convictions will decide whether, after this, any of the students wish to add to or dispute the analysis.

Again, there is much more to be done on this, and I am sure that other tutors have gone further. I reveal my own scars so as to draw evidence from those who are more expert.

A Note on Mr Hoggart's Appendices

From: *Adult Education*, XXI, 2, 1948, pp 96–8

Mr Hoggart's *Notes on Aim and Method in University Tutorial Classes*, which appeared in the June number of this Journal, seemed to me very perceptive. Where I have reservations I hesitate to urge them: first, because actual theoretical differences are difficult to argue on such limited ground – it is perhaps a criticism of Mr Hoggart's notes that their generality eased their acceptance and that at crucial points there was a sufficient lack of specificity to make one wonder rather than disagree; second, because I suspect that my reservations are largely questions of tone, a certain uneasiness about a method of argument of which the texture is largely that of the haphazard impact of metaphors. I thought, for example, that Matthew Arnold had finished *ineffable* for serious writing; *spiritual* I hear so often from politicians talking about food that I now turn away from the word. *Wickets, questioning hearts, gears and cyclists, mountains, ledgers, ladders, woollens* and so on: these as terms of educational discussion I do not understand.

But to ignore Mr Hoggart's article on these grounds would not, in fact, be wise. His appendices, to which I now wish to add a note, were most useful, and were a specific illustration of the value of his appeal for facilities for the exchange of detailed information on teaching methods.

Mr Hoggart's method of analysis of the nature of various statements, as explained in his Appendix A, seems to me to be admirable. I should like to know, however, how much time, in various types of class, he would devote to work of this local analytic nature. I have often attempted to solve the problem of demonstrating shifts of ground in condemnation or defence, since, as Mr Hoggart emphasizes, it is 'among the first obstacles' – I would say myself it is the major obstacle – to the intelligent study of literature. But I have not recently attempted to do it as an exercise in itself. It seemed to me that students realized the distinctions with more force when they were distinctions which arose out of a difference of opinion in the course of analysis of a particular poem or piece of prose. Perhaps this is a defect in my own training; and I know how possible it is to mistake one's own benefit and interest for one's students'. But it seemed to me that the problem was one which students were better able to handle when their interest in the thing about which the statements were being made had been engaged.

This point, of course, extends into a general problem. I used to think that one should collect a number of popular assumptions about literature (say, 'That the purpose of the novel is the revelation of character', 'That the persons of a drama should, to be acceptable, be true to life', 'That only modern poetry is difficult to understand'), and then arrange the reading of works selected to show how eccentric, or in most cases untenable, these assumptions are. I used later to think that one should list the stages of an approach to a theory of literary criticism, and then arrange the readings of works designed to demonstrate each stage. Perhaps both those methods are still right; they are methods, it will be seen, which are technically similar to Mr Hoggart's methods of distinction of the nature of statement. But I no longer very much believe in teaching *Criticism* to general classes of adults, nor do I think it wise to convey to them an emphasis – while they are studying literature – on an abstract discipline. I suppose that I still choose the actual works to be read in my literature courses on the same principle and framework as before. But I ignore the framework so far as explanation to the class is concerned. I do not say that we will read *Wuthering Heights* in order to find out if the characters in all good novels are lifelike; I try to let the point that they are not arise and become established when the response to the text has been made. I try, that is, to concentrate on the fully responsive reading of the particular work for its own sake, and not in order to point a stage in a general argument. There has been criticism of this, which usually comes back to the sense of guilt which most literature tutors have that theirs is not really a useful subject and that it must be made to resemble social history or philosophy or logic before it can fully accepted in adult education. I feel certain that Mr Hoggart will not need convincing that the discipline of reading – with no other end in view than that of adequate response to an important literary text – needs no reservations educationally.[1]

Mr Hoggart's remarks on the use of exercises for discrimination have the rare virtue – on this ground – of detail, and seem to me to be sound. The only point at which I would differ is contained in the phrase 'forbid them to make value-judgments until they are able to express the difference between them in terms of texture'. I do not want to be doctrinaire, but it would seem to me that this is impossible. One can separate analysis and evaluation only with a great effort. The three questions one might put to a class as a guide in the discussion of a passage: *What does it say?; how does it say it?; why is it saying it?*: these, too, involve a separation, a listing of elements which in fact are integrated and perhaps inextricable. Probably the way Mr Hoggart actually conducts such discussion would not be open to the criticism of abstraction or of suppression of value-judgments. But I think *forbid* in his context is much too strong. The mistakes which he lists, and which presumably led up to this forbidding, were, surely, failures of tone or sensibility such as one constantly discovers in one's teaching of

---

[1] For a fuller account I may now refer those interested to an article in the current *Rewley House Papers*.

literature and which, of course, one has to try to put right. But to diminish the function of primary value-judgment in analysis seems to me – to address Mr Hoggart in terms which he would seem to prefer – to throw the baby out with the bathwater.

There is a need, which perhaps he was trying in this way to meet, for analysis with elementary classes which does not involve value-judgments of the more complex and intricate kind. I would say myself that this need is better satisfied in what I call pre-literary analysis than in the actual study of literature. I mean that one can make all the necessary points with reference to a newspaper article, or an advertisement, or a paragraph from a book on economics or popular science. Value-judgments are, of course, immediately involved here also, but they may be handled in a simple way on such material with less harm than on a piece of literature. After some weeks of such work any normal class should be able to proceed to the study of quite complex pieces of literature, and the danger of an eviscerated response may, with time and effort, be minimized.

About actual procedure in what I prefer to call reading, rather than analysis, of the few short complete works, and the one or two longer complete works, which make up my course, I ought perhaps to give a more adequate account. But the trouble is, and I hope Mr Hoggart will agree, that there really is no procedure. Each particular work demands different kinds of specific response. Mr Hoggart's way of dealing with an extract, as described in the last sentences of his penultimate paragraph, seems to me to be right. But when one goes on – as I am sure one must quite quickly go on – to the reading of complete works I think one can perhaps do no better than say that one will settle down and read the thing. With novels or plays one will discern from this reading certain representative and crucial passages, which one will then analyse (approximately as with an extract) and go on to relate to the structure of the whole work which appears to emerge from one's equally close, but less articulated, reading. How all this settles down in practice varies with every class and every text.

Whether for his scars or his appendices, literature tutors ought to be grateful to Mr Hoggart.

Some Experiments in Literature Teaching

From: *Rewley House Papers*, II, X, 1948–9, pp 9–15

In the teaching of English Literature the last fifty years have produced fundamental controversies and a variety of experiments. Adult education travels light, with little that is settled in the way of institutions, with a variety of material shortages, and with a wide freedom to experiment. In the last fifty years the teaching of Literature to adults has accordingly been both battlefield and laboratory.

To summarize these long events, to place them in their context, or to attempt to restate the basis of Literature as an educational study, is not my intention here. I wish instead to offer comments on a variety of methods in Literature teaching which I have experienced in adult classes, and perhaps to suggest certain provisional conclusions. Because some of my experience would seem, by the sign of public discussion, to be representative, the account may have some general relevance.

It is necessary to begin from what one may call the sense of guilt of the Literature tutor. In adult education especially, among a variety of useful specialists, the Literature tutor is sometimes regarded, and as often regards himself, as a person for whom apology must be made. My own experiments in method were at least partly occasioned by this guilt, and it is necessary to allow for it in the subsequent examination.

As an undergraduate one has no common need to justify anything one may wish to do, and one reads literature for a degree without a backward look. It is only when one goes on to do the same thing and to be paid for it, and when one begins to be asked leading questions at conferences, that the retrospect begins. The first point is one's first course.

Literature, whether or not it has been adequately separated from linguistics, is normally taught as a branch of history. What is offered is a list of names, dates, and classifications (of authors, books, and styles instead of kings, treaties, and systems), and then summaries of certain of the major documents. This is orthodox in the adult class as elsewhere. So that a course will deal with a period of literature, dividing its material into from six to seventy-two equal parts, and proposing a lecture on each topic until the series is completed. For the tutor this is convenience itself, for he will be able to use, in some cases without amendment, the lecture-notes, examination answers, and essays which he made for his degree. There are certain technical difficulties sometimes; and in particular the extreme unlikelihood of the tutor's having been instructed in any literature written since 1900, and the unfortunately opposed desire of his average students to be introduced to precisely that literature. But with the aid of the usual introductions, and by private reading, this can be avoided. So that one's course will remain thoroughly sound, and be fully justified academically.

The first Literature course which I took myself was one of twenty-four meetings, and was on 'The Novel since 1800'. Now I began with certain doubts about the established methods of Literature teaching in the Universities. I knew, for instance, that in the English school of 'Practical Criticism Cambridge' I had done five-sixths of my year as required, and that it had not been necessary for me to read any English literature at all. I knew, moreover, that I had written examination answers about some authors whose works I had barely read, and had been not unhandsomely rewarded. I knew that I was not alone in this. And I was accordingly wary.

I restricted that first syllabus to twelve novels and novelists; gave a series of thoroughly sound (and only now and again second-hand) lectures on them; made sure that as many texts as possible were in the book-box; and quoted frequently from the actual novels. But I knew all along that it was no good. It is the discussion period, probably, which provides the first evidence against this method. Not that there will not always be discussion; much is certain to be said. And not that it will be anything but animated and pleasant. But what will it be *about?* Rarely, in my experience, about the literature in question. About the *actual* literature, that is. For how, in normal circumstances, could it be? How could even a minority of the students have read the actual works during the period of the course? I had thought I was playing safe in restricting myself to twelve novels and novelists. Yet the attentive reading of twelve novels during a six-month period (the copies having been readily obtained, which is an impossibly ideal circumstance) is, in my view, a task beyond the normal non-specialist adult. That two or three students in every class will be able to do the reading may reassure the tutor, and the discussion will proceed between him and them. The rest of the students, who will not have read the texts, will be doing little more than improving their occasional conversation. It is true that in some subjects the survey given to beginners is valuable; but this value is strictly limited in Literature. Inspiration of a familiar kind there may well be; but the event will normally be no more than one of those incidental distractions with which the margin of literature is closely filled.

So that one turned over *Felix Holt*, and remarked that it was sub-titled *Portrait of a Radical* – an interesting link with life there; Chartism! – and then it followed that the name of George Eliot was really Marian Evans, and that she had lived, unmarried, with George Henry Lewes, and was a leading member of that group of neo-Comtist thinkers of the 1850's; Herbert Spencer was one of her friends and had exempted her works alone from his ban on fiction in the London Library, and she translated Spinoza and Strauss, and made a hasty late marriage with a young Mr Cross, and declined in her later years from the fresh vigour of her rural reminiscences to the dryness of abstract speculation, and had been called a 'bleak wit', and might well, indeed, be due for a revival (after all there was Trollope, much inferior, but then the great classics cannot be reprinted in the paper shortage and how are we going to overcome that; a question of dollars? – no, book paper comes from North Africa) and wasn't she, George Eliot, didn't . .?; well here was a portrait one had brought along; yes, indeed, if one wished to be unkind, she *did* look rather like a horse.

One can, that is, provide the illusion of information about literature in a great variety of ways. Whenever there has been insufficient reading, discussion of literature degenerates to gossip. But I had thought to allow adequate time in restricting myself to twelve novels; even this programme had been too large. I wondered what happened in those courses of which I had been an external spectator, courses which proposed the examination, even the 'intensive examination', of eighteen, twenty-eight, even in one case fifty-three novels, in the same thirty-six or forty-eight hours. And the position was similar with plays and poetry. I had seen *As You Like It* the subject of one period, *Paradise Lost* of the next, *Songs of Innocence and Experience* of the next, and *Four Quartets* of the next. I had seen courses stretching from Cervantes to the Sitwells in twelve lessons, and lectures on W.B. Yeats (who wrote nine volumes of poetry) in one evening. I had even come to regard with comparative favour such an entry as this:

> LECTURE THREE: *James Joyce – Irishman, poet, dramatist, novelist, exile; the nature of his experiments; readings from* Dubliners, Portrait of the Artist, Ulysses, Finnegans Wake, *and* Pomes Penyeach. *To be followed by discussion.*

And I hid in my backmost drawer my own – less spectacularly notorious – entries.

What was certain was that most Literature courses attempted to cover too much ground; they proposed an examination of literature at the rate, and with the generalizations, of orthodox literary history. The accumulation of marginal facts concealed a very widespread inability to read the central matter. For as has happened wherever the test has been tried, persons who seemed able to talk interminably about poets as unacknowledged legislators or about the tradition of wit, were normally unable to read intelligently an unnamed piece of verse or prose that might be set before them. If the adult Literature class was not attempting to train this central and vital capacity, it seemed probable that it was wasting its time.

What seemed to be needed, for students with limited time for reading and without any or any recent close attention to a work of literature, was an actual *course in reading*. And here there was a body of work to which one could refer: the experiments of Richards, Leavis, and others at Cambridge and elsewhere. Adult classes, I found, worked well at a series of progressive exercises in reading. One had sheets of poems and prose extracts printed or duplicated, and discussed the extracts in class and set them as exercises for written work. After certain mistakes of tone by the tutor, it was seen that such exercises should not often be 'demonstrations', as I was once unwise enough to call them. The normal method came to be an almost complete passivity by the tutor, so that the group would venture confidently into extended comment. The tutor would say nothing of importance until the end, when he would summarize reactions, distinguish between what seemed to him false and valid *approaches*, set out differences in actual value-judgements, offer his own judgement, and bring back the group for further comment.

Certainly the results of such courses, and their whole tone, seemed much preferable to the survey of surveys. Yet could one stop at that? With undergraduates such exercises had been freshening tasks within a framework of orthodox study. Again, with one's limited time, would one be forced into what is ultimately a method of abstraction? I found that a course of exercises in reading could be imperceptibly turned into a course in the study of poetry, since poems were usually short enough to be handled directly within the period of a class. With prose, however, one was restricted, it seemed, to extracts; and the fact was that a number of important obstacles to good reading were never encountered because of this.

My first decision about the course of reading was that it ought to have an explicit critical programme. There were two clear alternatives: either one arranged a course in criticism, which would raise in turn those questions which occur in critical practice and theory, and so planned one's series of extracts that the desired problems would be raised in an orderly and manageable way; or, one listed a number of popular assumptions about literature ('that all good novels have lifelike characters'; 'that speech in a play ought to sound natural, as in life'; 'that poetry, except modern poetry, is clear at a first reading, and ought usually to rhyme and not to be obscure' and so on), and then devised a series of pieces by which these assumptions might be tested and so upheld or disproved.

The difference between these approaches was one of emphasis. I thought that the latter would be easier with adult classes, since the tutor had only to say 'Character' to elicit the usual assumptions; and then he could go on with the class fully engaged. In fact, I would say that the former approach seemed most welcome, since interest in critical theory seemed overwhelming. In either case the courses went on, and seemed both successful and sound.

Yet it was experience in the former alternative, in a course given shape by an explicit critical programme, which made me question this whole method. The interest in critical theory was, as I have said, overwhelming; and rather frightening. One came to be picking up a play to look for an objective correlative; or ticking off a poem at first reading into sense, meaning, and tone, with a double entry in ambiguity. One's approach, in other words, had gone abstract, dead. It was again the 'one of that group of neo-Comtist thinkers'. And this could not pass.

I decided eventually that one must drop, absolutely, so far as the class is concerned, any programme of this kind. One can write it out to go into the files, but it must be kept from the class. What the tutor has to do is to help his students to respond adequately to certain works of literature; that is his overriding purpose; distraction from it into a theoretical formulation is a denial of the particular qualities for which literature is valued and studied at all.

Then must one say: away with this modernism and with Leavis and all his works? Not at all. That is a usual subterfuge. One must rather plan a course in which one leads students through poems and paragraphs of prose, to longer poems and to short prose works such as short stories, and then to dramatic poems and to novels and perhaps to prose plays. Progressive reading, rather than progressive *exercises* in reading. Let the problems arise, as they must inevitably arise if they are real, from responses to, and difficulties with, actual texts. For the tutor, the same emphasis. To the class, a quite different one.

After experiments in different classes I found that the following time-factors were governing. In a normal two-hour class (whether composed of beginners or tutorial-class students seemed to make little difference) one could adequately read and examine: one or at most two short poems (sonnet-length); one short story (up to 5,000–6,000 words); one crucial chapter, or two or three crucial paragraphs, from a novel; one or two scenes from a play. So I offered a course based on these figures, and varying in content according to type of class and requests from students. I may give, for example, a course in some prose work, planned for twenty-four meetings:

A. *Paragraph from* The Dead*: Joyce.*
    Paragraph from Richard Feverel*: Meredith.*
    Paragraph from Body in the Library*: Christie.*
    Paragraph from Felix Holt*: Eliot.*

B. Mr Pim and the Holy Crumb *(short story): Powys.*
    Odour of Chrysanthemums *(short story): Lawrence.*
    The Lifted Veil *(short story): Eliot.*

C. Heart of Darkness*: Conrad.*
    Wuthering Heights*: Brontë.*
    Bleak House*: Dickens.*

There are certain comments to be made on this method, which is my most recent experiment and on which I am still collecting evidence. First, resistance from students. This is certainly considerable because most people like to see something much more impressive on a syllabus than this little list, which is really all one can put down. The demand for the immense or even the reasonable-looking survey is persistent, and one can only go on explaining why both are impossible. Then, once the course is begun, there are complaints about the pace. Usually I find that there is insufficient time; but as often as not this is demonstrated by complaints that there is *too much*. For the fact is that most students are quite unprepared for reading of this degree of attentiveness. They 'read through' a book as they have always done, and are left with time on their hands. Back, unless one is careful, come George Henry Lewes and the paper shortage. Of course, the training towards a capacity for close reading is one's purpose; the complaints, which usually diminish with the weeks, are a natural resistance to that exacting discipline.

Second, resistance from other quarters. In my own case, I have had ideal conditions, but I have been told that courses like this sometimes turn administrators in their graves, and throw the Ministry of Education into a conscientious flurry. On this I offer no comment.

Third, as to method. I begin with the short works, which can be read aloud, both paragraphs and stories. During these weeks (the first six or eight of the course) students are reading in their own time the longer works, of which one has fixed the order. In this way, given reasonable fortune, it is possible to begin the examination of a novel with all students having read it. Then one can examine and discuss crucial chapters, without too much abstraction.

In conclusion I had better anticipate the charge of narrowness. I have not commented on those many attempts to relate Literature to Life or Society which have occupied many tutors. I am convinced that correlation is necessary, and that adult education is a good place for it. But when it comes to correlation, let us have something to correlate. In relating literature to social history one ought to begin with the abstractions of the latter and fit the former by judicious quotation to them. (It seems to me that this is what most courses of the kind do.) One looks for the facts of the history, and also for the facts of the literature. But the disciplines differ; and the discipline of attention to fact in literature is the discipline of close reading. If it is wished to offer adult students any important correlation involving literature, a course of close reading is inescapably necessary. The extension from that ought then to be as wide as is reasonable. Nobody really knows how this ought to be done; it is an important field for experiment.

In a different interest, a course in reading may be applied to such institutions as newspapers, advertisements, popular fiction, pamphlets, etc., and its methods of analysis adapted to examine films, buildings, and broadcasting. This is one of the most directly useful forms of specifically social training which the literature tutor can offer; and experiments in it seem to have been successful.

And when there is immediately in mind neither correlation nor extension, and when Literature is again dismissed as the 'escapist' study, that sense of guilt of which I have spoken ought finally to be laid. Literature, as a coherent record of human experience, needs neither apology nor external justification. It is itself, and its study as such remains one of the permanently valuable disciplines of any education.

The Way We Read Now

From: Raymond Williams, *Reading and Criticism*, Frederick Muller, 1950, pp 9–18

It has been estimated that most people, in a country like Britain, read at least a million words a year. Yet rather less than half the adult population habitually read books. The bulk of our reading is contained in newspapers, magazines, advertisements, notices, circulars, and similar occasional material.

How many of us are what Aldous Huxley called 'reading addicts' is less easy to determine. Huxley wrote:

> We read, most of the time, ... because reading is one of our bad habits, because we suffer when we have time to spare and no printed matter with which to plug the void. Deprived of their newspapers or a novel, reading-addicts will fall back on cookery books, on the literature that is wrapped round bottles of patent medicine, on those instructions for keeping the contents crisp which are printed on the outside of boxes of breakfast cereals. On anything.[1]

It is at least likely that for a large and increasing number of people the supply of print has become as necessary as the supply of food or fuel. And the supply is met, the distribution is organised, in much the same way.

It would seem that only personal or limited evidence about the way we read this large amount of printed matter is available. But this is to ignore the most valuable evidence. If we want to discover the way the average reader reads we can do so by discovering how the average writer writes. In many ways, and for a variety of reasons, the serious writer is more detached from his readers in the present century than for many centuries before. But the bulk of our reading matter is not written by artists, but by journalists, copywriters, propagandists, and a class of writers whom we might describe as 'professional populars'. All these people are obliged, for their living, to write in a way in which the average reader is accustomed to read. The habits of mass writing are the habits of mass reading, and a study of such writing can provide valuable evidence of the way many of us read for considerable periods of our reading time.

---

[1] *Writers and Readers*, essay in *The Olive Tree* (1936).

We can start with a simple example of a successful contemporary advertisement. (We can know that it has been successful from the length of time it has continued to appear; advertisers do not keep a research organisation for nothing.) The advertisement is for a well-known brand of tea, which happens also to be a good tea. The product must not be confused with the words which advertise it, which are our sole interest here. The advertisement reads:

GOOD TEA HAS A CIRCLE OF LIGHT COLOUR AROUND
ITS EDGE.
LOOK FOR THE CIRCLE OF GOOD TASTE.

(A drawing then appears, of a cup of tea with the circle of light colour around its edge; and this is emphasised by a broad arrow.)

(BRAND) TEA.

The process of reading in this example would seem to be:

GOOD TEA.
CIRCLE OF LIGHT COLOUR AROUND ITS EDGE.
(*Visual confirmation*)
CIRCLE OF GOOD TASTE
SO AND SO'S TEA.

The points within which the statement moves are the initial GOOD TEA and the concluding SO AND SO'S TEA. That comprises the intention of the copywriter, and the impression of the reader. In the process of the statement appear one or two interesting assertions. Now we can assume, as argued above, that the advertisement has been successful, and that many people have been satisfied or convinced in reading it. But let us read it closely. What is the circle of light colour which is said to appear at the edge of good tea? With a little thought we realise that it is simply the reflection of the china cup in the dark liquid it contains. In any normal cup a reflection of light (circular as the cup is similar) will be cast on to *any* dark liquid. It will appear on good, bad or indifferent tea, on coffee, on beer, on dandelion wine, or on dirty water. Its appearance, then, is no indication of the value of the liquid as a drink. If it is an indication of value at all, it has reference to the quality of the china rather than to the contents of the cup. But this is not all. This circle of light is now equated with a circle of good taste. In one sense, this merely amplifies the original statement: good tea will, by definition, have a good taste. But *circle* and *good taste* have other associations. We talk of moving in the best *circles*; our capacity for discrimination in matters so various as art and personal behaviour is usually referred to as *good taste*. The tea, then, is not simply offered as something good to drink, but as a mark of social and individual distinction. And of course there has been no rational demonstration of either. The effect rests on nothing but trick statements and trick associations. And yet how often has it been read with a full realisation of this? If it had been so read, it would hardly have been profitable to pay for continued publication of it, and of hundreds of similar advertisements. Indeed, if the advertiser had had to reckon with a public which is accustomed to read with conscious attention, it would never have been written at all. But the trick is sufficient to delude readers who merely absorb impressions; it has enough slickness to invite only the amount of attention which it can stand.

It would seem highly probable that for many of us reading may be equated with the absorption of a series of general impressions, which are hardly ever related to any personal centre of intelligence, judgment, or value. Another piece of writing may be examined, this time from a newspaper:

STARTING ALL OVER AGAIN

Parliament reopens. It is a noteworthy landmark. For over a year the Socialists have ordered us around at will. Now they are about to start again.

What have they in store for the people this time? What will be controlled and who will be nationalised when the next opening of parliament comes along? These are questions to which it would be good to have the answers. Industry would feel less inhibited if it knew exactly what the Government intends to lay its clammy hands upon.

But, as in Matthew Arnold's sonnet to Shakespeare, 'We ask and ask: Thou smilest and art still.' While the Speech may cast some light on the darkness, the people may perhaps do a little guessing themselves about the sort of thing they can expect from Ministers during the coming months on their records to date.

Whatever else he does, they can count on that sugar-tongued Etonian, Mr Dalton, continuing soaking the rich. He does it, partly because he needs the money, partly to provoke his school-fellows, but mostly because he regards it as a sure way to win votes and applause. Raids on the rich, in fact, are to the Chancellor what jokes about mothers-in-law are to the uninspired comedian. Only whereas mothers-in-law go on for ever, quite soon there won't be any more rich.

Mr Shinwell will give us no more coal because he can't, and no more petrol because he won't. From Mr Strachey it would be logical to hope for more food, but on past form this seems unlikely. All he has given the country since he took office has been bread rationing and a mass of statistics.

The people of Britain are certain of only one thing. A further flood of legislation will add to the uncertainties of threatened but unimplemented, and perhaps unimplementable, nationalisation, and a rush of uncontrollable Orders in Council will further undermine the authority of Parliament.[2]

---

[2] *Evening Standard* leading article, November 12, 1946.

Now one's present concern is not the political aspect of this piece of writing. It is easy to disapprove of journalism if one disapproves its political trend, while approving, and hardly noticing, similar writing in one's own cause. In any case, one can hardly regard such writing as political argument at all. It is simply a *tour-de-force*, or an attempted *tour-de-force*, of the same nature as the tea advertisement.

First should be noticed such general points as the short sentences and the very brief paragraphs. The first paragraph is a perfect example of habitual journalistic practice in this respect. The tone (the author's apparent attitude to his reader) is indistinguishable from the tone of an advertisement or a poster. Perhaps the first point for detailed examination is the last sentence of the second paragraph. The words one needs to consider are *inhibited* and *clammy*. *Inhibited* has for the last twenty-five years been very widely used in popular writing[3], although few could perhaps define its meaning with any accuracy. It has become *cliché*. *Clammy* has not even this excuse. The figure of the Government laying its hands upon industry is an interesting assumption in itself; but description of these hands as *clammy* is quite insupportable. It is impossible to extract any relevant meaning from the adjective, and it is clearly used, not for conveying meaning, but for creating an impression: the impression, of course, is of something rather unpleasant, even rather disgusting. This is a conscious manipulation of irrationality.

The reference, in the next paragraph, to Arnold's poem, is a good example of the 'quotation-lifting' which is frequent in this kind of writing. It gives an air of knowledge and of culture, an impression of something 'old and true'. It is not necessary that the reader should know the poem or even the poet referred to. If, in fact, the reader had this knowledge, the effect of the quotation might be seriously diminished, since the next words are 'Out-topping knowledge', a quality which it hardly seems likely that the writer intended to attribute to the Socialist Government. *Cast some light on the darkness*, with its scriptural reminiscence, is, of course, a *cliché*, but serves the same purpose as the quotation. *The people may perhaps*: here is the characteristic assumption of the 'People', which serves always as the magniloquent disguise for the individual journalist; *may perhaps* introduces an impression of reticence and is intended to reassure the reader about the tone of the argument. But in fact this proceeds as before. The logic of the fourth paragraph is worth very detailed study; it is a perfect example of absolute inconsequence, sustained by the usual tricks of language: *sugar-tongued; soaking; partly . . . partly . . . but mostly; raids on the rich*. And so the piece proceeds to the final assertion. Once again the *people of Britain* are called in as an alibi, and then, with a variety of figurative language, an impression of Governmental violence is conveyed by the use of words like *flood, rush, threatened, uncontrollable* and *undermined*.

---

3   Cf. 'A look of intense relief mingled with awe passed over Florence's face. Her inhibitions left her. She gasped: 'Oh, *yes!*' ' (*Body in the Library*, A. Christie, p 134).

It is not with the unimportant writer of this piece that we need to be primarily concerned, but with the reader. For the example is typical of a large and important part of our total reading, and habits induced by writing of this kind are very likely to become permanent. The last thing which writing of this kind encourages is conscious and disciplined attention to the words which comprise the statement. Its staple is a series of associations and impressions, centred each on an emotive word or phrase, and linked by word-sequences whose familiar or 'impressive' (pompous) rhythms imply acquiescence. Automatic writing is subsidised by automatic reading. Neither has anything to do with literature or with language as a living means of communication.

It may be that automatic writing is found only in the most ephemeral productions: the daily paper, the poster, the advertisement. We may next examine a passage from a type of fiction which has achieved an astonishing popularity in this century:

> *Pendock did not even see her. He was taking the stairs three at a time, wrestling with the lock of the big front door, leaping the stairs and running out into the moonlit garden, sick with a horrible dread. Bunsen came across the lawn to meet him, white-faced with protruding eyes. 'This way, sir, down by the gate. My god, sir, it's dreadful; she's – her head . . .'*
>
> *She was lying in a ditch that ran by the side of the drive and down to the little stream; he could see her quite clearly in the moonlight, her legs at a dreadful angle, her arms bent under her, her head – her head had been hacked from her body and then clapped back again on to her neck; and on top of this dreadful, this bloodless lolling head was thrust, in all its absurdity, Fran's new hat. A mist like blood passed before his eyes; he closed them to shut out the horror of it, and falling at last on to his sagging knees, he started to crawl towards the horrible figure, going up close to it, flinging aside that frightful, that obscene gay hat; and pushing away the dark hair that hung, blood-clotted, across the face, he staggered to his feet and, at the side of the ditch, lay panting and vomiting till the world was still again.*
>
> *But it was not Francesca's lovely face that had leered out at him, dark and distorted, from the tangle of dripping hair; the body in the ditch, the severed head, the face beneath the brave little hat – they were Grace Morland's.*[4]

This is a very earnest piece of writing, dedicated to a publicly welcomed end. No opportunity for display is missed. Pendock does not simply discover the body; he *wrestles, leaps, crawls, falls to his sagging knees, flings, staggers, pants* and *vomits*. Pendock, moreover, *is sick with a horrible dread*; the eyes of his butler *protrude* (a usual gambit). The corpse itself goes to the limit. The legs (how?) are *at a dreadful angle*. The

---

[4] *Heads you Lose*, Christianna Brand.

head is *hacked* and *clapped*. It is *bloodless* and *lolling*, but the *dark hair* is *blood-clotted* and *dripping*. Even the *lovely* face might have *leered*. The hat, too, plays its part; it is alternatively *absurd, gay, brave*, and (a highly suggestive adjective) *obscene*. Although there is blood enough, one might think, over the corpse, Pendock's giddiness comes in a mist *like blood*. In addition to the words, devices of rhythm are used for similar effect. There is the very characteristic *she's – her head* . . ., where the dots have their necessary suggestive function. Later it is *her head – her head*. And in the organisation of the passage, it is noteworthy that the horror comes twice: in carefully described anticipation; and in the object itself.

Crudity of this order has its obvious, and disquieting, appeal. A large number of readers, clearly, find it satisfactory. It is worth observing that writing like this supplies the inescapable negative to the frequent rationalisation that crime stories are taken as 'an intellectual exercise', like crossword puzzles. If this were so, the subject of the mystery might be anything; yet in the vast majority of cases it is a corpse. Moreover, if the crime story were offered simply as a puzzle, the corpse need be no more than a counter, mentioned and taken for granted. In almost every story, however, the appearance of the corpse is described with loving care. It is either horrific, as here; or, if it was once relatively presentable, it is reserved (as in Mr Freeman Wills Crofts' *Inspector French and the Starvel Tragedy*) for an exhumation. There are many degrees of refinement. In Mrs Agatha Christie's *Body in the Library*, for example, the discovery of the corpse (which, unfortunately, I have been refused permission to quote) is accompanied by a series of ingenious associations. There is no blood on it, but we are told of the mascara on the *lashes*, and that the lips look like a *gash*. The fingernails are *a deep blood-red*. The sentences in which these descriptions occur, moreover, are packed with harsh consonants – sh, sc, ck, k – which have their own efficacy.

But perhaps crime books also are simply ephemeral (although one should remember the literary reputation of Miss Dorothy Sayers). In case this is true, we may next examine an extract from a book by a man whom it is probably accurate to describe as the most widely-known 'serious novelist' now writing in England:

A fat middle-aged woman, most unsuitably dressed and raddled, and an elderly painted buffoon, shouting and posturing, yelling in coarse accents their stale old jokes, busy vulgarising the sex instinct, performing without grace or wit. Gaping at the tiny stage, staring and nudging, guffawing and screaming, there are the thousands of workers of all ages, making what seem animal noises that yet no animal has ever made, and seeming all mindless eyes and ears, wide loud mouths and clapping hands. A strange and no doubt a deplorable scene.

Yet there was about it an air of release and innocent happiness; a kind of struggling goodness in it; a mysterious promise, not mentioned, not tried for, not even understood, but there somewhere all the time, of man's ultimate deliverance and freedom, a whisper of his homecoming among the stars. Nobody there was consciously aware of this, yet nearly everybody there, beneath the surface of the mind – that crackling surface where the jokes exploded, because of the absurdity of this life of ours – somewhere in the deep communal recesses, in the dark river of racial being, felt all this and was refreshed and restored by it.[5]

At first sight this might seem an impressive piece of writing; the ideas it handles are 'serious'. And yet a strain of falsity is everywhere apparent. The verbal terms of the initial description are in the reiterative hit-or-miss tone of the *gay, brave, absurd* of the crime piece. *Most unsuitably dressed and raddled* is misleading and strictly meaningless, but creates a quick impression. From then on the series is clear: *buffoon, yelling, coarse, stale, vulgarising, gaping, guffawing, animal, loud.* It is no use defending the crudity of the description as appropriate to the crudity of the thing described; that is simply a fallacy of the same order as that description of hysteria requires the writer to be hysterical. Here the writer's intention is simply to create a series of approximate impressions of vulgarity, on which the subsequent assertions of profundity can be superposed. The falsity of the second paragraph is particularly apparent. The initial rhythm – *Yet there was about it an air* – the deliberate structure of impressiveness, set the tone for the vague associations of the remaining sentences: *a kind of struggling goodness; a mysterious promise; ultimate deliverance; a whisper of his homecoming among the stars.* All through this vagueness run the assertive rhythms of pomp: *not mentioned, not tried for, not even understood.* From this it is only a step to *the deep communal recesses, the dark river of racial being.* It is writing which readers accustomed to the pompous style and mechanical rhythms of copywriter or journalist are instantly disposed to accept. That *crackling* surface?; where the jokes *exploded*? The absurdity of *this life of ours.* There is a difference in the literary reputations of the *Evening Standard* leader-writer, a writer of crime stories, and Mr J.B Priestley; but no difference in their methods which a reader deprived of the normal signals of prestige could discern.

Mr T.S. Eliot has written that 'every vital development of language is also a development of feeling'. The converse would seem to be also true. The crude or vague language, the pompous and mechanical rhythms, which we have discerned in these extracts, subsist – there is no other explanation – on crudity and imprecision of *feeling.* That vague or mechanical writing is profitable is amply proved by the economics of best-seller publishing. And such writing can only continue to be profitable where vague or mechanical habits of reading are widespread. It might be further argued that such inadequate reading proceeds from a deficiency in personal feeling. It can at least be said, with virtual certainty, that much of our reading has become dissociated from experience that is important to us in our directly personal living. In a society where reading is so universal and constant a habit, that is not a situation which we can afford to let pass unchallenged.

---

[5]   *Daylight on Saturday*, J.B. Priestley.

Critics and Criticism

From: Raymond Williams, *Reading and Criticism*,
Frederick Muller, 1950, pp 21–9

In a society in which art has seemed to move steadily away from the general
understanding the importance of the critic's function hardly needs stressing.
He is the mediator between the artist and the serious reading-public; his
criticism is the articulation of adequate response and trained evaluation.
But he is also likely to be increasingly concerned, the facts of mass reading
being what they are, with the growth of a serious reading public, with the
extension of literacy in its fullest sense. It is to critics and criticism, then,
that one should go for guidance if one accepts the evidence of mass reading
habits – habits which in greater or less degree will exist in oneself – and
wishes to improve one's reading.

But to say this is perhaps to say nothing. For: *who are the critics?;
which is the criticism? I have my favourites; you have yours. One man's
opinion is as good as another.*

Is this anarchy a fact? It is undeniable that critics are legion; criticism
has almost become the last-hope profession for the unplaceable son. There
are some signs that critics are on the way out and experts on the way in;
but that is merely a change of title. Certainly there is confusion enough
when both Mr Eliot and the film critic of the *News of the World* are to
be known by the same name. Yet such gulfs are readily distinguished. It is
with more delicate distinctions that one needs generally to be concerned;
and there the anarchy seems almost certain to begin.

So far as literature is in question, the general reader's acquaintance with
critics will often begin in the critical extracts which appear in publisher's
advertisements. It would of course be unfair to imply that all critics can
be adequately judged by sentences which certain publishers may have torn
from their contexts; but if one wants an idea of what criticism is not,
a review of such advertisements is worth brief attention. Looking at the
columns of a random issue of a weekly journal one reads:

> *insight and skill ... an intensity rare in fiction ... a cool and
> competent piece of work noticeable for its incisive style ... a disturbing
> book, because the author writes with a quick intensity, a closeness of
> contact ... a book that will commend itself to connoisseurs ... a
> new and remarkable talent ... a novel of extraordinary skill and
> power ... his work is always distinguished by a touch of the really
> creative imagination ... the passionate impetus of his writing ... This*

is his fifth novel; it is easily his best – a piece of literary work which is not only uncommon but also uncommonly good . . . a book that can only be described as sumptuous . . . this book is rich, and a proof of its richness is that it is difficult to say what it is about.

Lest I be accused of malice, I forbear from quoting the names which are attached to these snippets of opinion: they are sufficiently eminent for a mass attack on them to be reckoned as subversive. Yet of course the publishers may have distorted the actual reviews, choosing only those phrases which will sell the book. That publishers select favourable notices is understandable; the novel to which the third and fourth phrases refer has been described elsewhere as *trite, crude and dull,* which was also my own opinion of it. Since in the advertisement it is alternatively described as *close* and *cool,* variety would not seem to matter, but one understands the selection and omission. It is really surprising, however, that trite phrases like *new and remarkable talent* or *a novel of extraordinary skill and power* or *a disturbing book* should still commend themselves either to the reviewer or to the publisher or to the book-buyer. Words like *creative, genius, intensity, delicacy, passion* and so on have been widely misused, and in many contexts have lost any precise meaning. Reviewing is often a deadening business; but however excusable, the fact remains that a great part of it is no more than half-considered judgment, made on the basis of hasty reading, and expressed in terms of *cliché.* If one glances up from the advertisements in this very respectable journal to the actual reviewing columns one finds immediately: *it is an impressively disturbing book . . . a novel of extraordinary power and skill.* With a little attention, and particularly with attention to the actual works to which these fulsome phrases refer, one will come to assess the work of most reviewers as a minor antic, of no critical importance whatsoever. Yet to the general reader the work thus dismissed is 'criticism', and the persons dismissed 'critics'. Further, these writings and these persons commonly determine contemporary literary valuations. For almost a generation, the judgments and omissions of reviewers are likely to persist.

A few years ago a novel by Elias Canetti was translated into English under the title *Auto-da-Fe.* On considered judgment, I would put it among a small list – there are five or six names there – of great novels published in English since 1918. I am not able to demonstrate my judgment here; but the case is interesting as an example of what happens to an important piece of literature under the general treatment of reviewers. I read one review of it which, within its scale, offered a critical assessment. This review quoted an extract from the book and analysed its method. Having thus demonstrated what was 'new' and 'remarkable', it recommended the book to the reader. This seemed to me to be honest reviewing. But elsewhere one found the usual process. For example:

A mad, magnificent work which we are not able to endure, which perhaps we are right not to accept, but of which we dare not deny the genius or the justification.

What this sentence means I am at a loss to understand. If one *dares not deny* the *justification* of the work, it is curious that one is *not able to endure it* or *accept it*. The correlation of *mad* and *magnificent* is also not to be understood, except as alliterative rhapsody. The sentence, offered as a judgment, is no more than excited gossip. Then again:

> *If we believe it is the function of all art . . . 'to harmonise the sadness of the world'; then we may dare to say that* Auto-da-Fe *is, though a novel of terrible power, not a work of art.*

This seems and is more reasonable; it *dares* rather than *dares not*; but one must notice that it conceals an assumption which is highly questionable and not particularly relevant. In the imposition of concealed standards of judgment, reviewing perhaps does its greatest harm. It might be possible to distinguish between a novel of terrible power and a work of art, but it is a distinction that ought to be stated, not thrown off as an aside. A third extract is even more questionable:

> *It would be gravely irrelevant to judge* Auto-de-Fe *as a work of art, for any such intention is adjured in every line of it. The intensification of obsessions has nothing whatever in common with the process by which art intensifies real life. The purpose is denunciation, and it is most triumphantly and distressingly achieved.*

Here the first sentence, even granting reasonable exaggeration for rhetorical ends, is clearly nonsense. The novel is most certainly offered as a work of art. If it fails as such, this failure ought to be demonstrated. Instead, this writer offers a near-epigram which has more use as rhythm than sense, and concludes with a saving clause which again conceals a very large assumption about literature which ought not to be made if it cannot be demonstrated. These general pronouncements about the nature of art ought to be always suspect in such contexts. One feels that the reviewers, who are usually minor novelists, are often writing with an eye on their biographers rather than on the text.

And after these lordly shows, the usual dustcarts:

> Auto-da-Fe *is a disturbing masterpiece, a novel without precedent.*

> *Whatever its defects,* Auto-da-Fe *is the work of a remarkable talent.*

Now none of this can be seriously considered as criticism; yet the papers from which I have been quoting include *The New Statesman and Nation*, *The Spectator*, *The Listener*, *Time and Tide*, *Horizon*, *The Observer*, and *The Sunday Times*. These journals are generally considered to offer serious reviewing and to maintain high critical standards. On the evidence, which I think is in its necessarily small scale representative, one can discern neither. In most other papers a book like *Auto-da-Fe* is not reviewed at all.

Now the anarchy we are considering has often been noted. Virginia Woolf wrote in *The Common Reader*:

Reviewers we have but no critic; a million competent and incorruptible policemen but no judge.

In one sense this is true, but on the whole it is a misleading formulation. The question lies in the *competent* and *incorruptible*. Corruption in the ordinary sense is certainly rare, and it would need a long exposition of English literary politics to suggest any subtler forms of corruption. But the point is contained in the lines by Humbert Wolfe:

You cannot hope to bribe or twist
Thank God! the British journalist.
But seeing what the man will do
Unbribed, there's no occasion to.

The competence of a critic is a difficult issue. The universities give degrees in the study of literature, and one might assume, if experience both of the system and of the miscellaneity of its products had not been so mixed, that such graduates would be trained critics. But all critics are self-appointed, like all writers. It would be ridiculous to devise some scheme of professional qualification in the ordinary sense; literature covers too many human interests for that.

Criticism, however, is itself open to scrutiny. If it is possible to develop a first-hand judgment of literature it is also possible to do so in criticism. Reading capacity, that is to say, will ensure that one is able to discern at least the grosser irrelevancies and the more obvious falsities. The abstract question 'Is So-and-So a reliable critic?' is not likely to help. One can examine examples of his criticism, and judge them by one's standards.

But by now we have come full circle, and must ask ourselves once more: 'What are the standards?' This question could be treated theoretically, but a preoccupation with theories of literary judgment and value seems quite frequently to be of little relevance to the actual judgment of literature, however useful it may be to other branches of knowledge. Often, indeed, one has seen a theoretical interest of this kind distract attention from literature. I must not be understood as implying that all literary theory is distraction. It is my experience, however, that it is not in theory (of a kind) that the general reader is lacking, but rather in straightforward practical reading ability. I think that the negative functions of theoretical discussion – the dislodgment of literary mottoes – are the most important in this time and place.

One wishes to read adequately, and to set one's reading in order with relation to one's personal experience and to the experience of the culture to which one belongs. The basic standards one seeks are those traditional valuations which have been re-created in one's own direct experience. A scientific exposition of the basis of taste offers many difficulties, as does a similar exposition of intelligence or sensibility. Yet in a constantly recreated balance between traditional and personal experience one is recurrently aware of these forces as facts. All those general questions which arise when literature is relevantly discussed involve great and permanent difficulties.

Differences of viewpoint represent different attitudes to the human person and to society. Yet a large measure of agreement is frequently to be found across these general divisions. This is because it is possible to arrive at and state provisional conclusions about experience, and to assess new experience in their light. These processes will of course be subject to those standards of intellectual procedure which have traditional validity.

To the questions 'What are literary values?' and 'What are literary standards?' one can only reply 'they are literature itself'. By the application of intelligence and sensibility (in the function of which, although there is no orthodoxy, there is at least an effective traditional standard) one makes local valuations, and proceeds to form these into more general valuations which one is consistently concerned to refine. One seeks to describe one's experience of literature, and draws on the methods and terms of those who have in the past attempted similar descriptions. Where these terms and methods no longer seem adequate – for we must remember that literature is constantly being re-created and so, as an organism, changing – we must attempt to modify them in those directions which our experience indicates.

Mr George Orwell is too honest to be deceived by the processes of current literary politics, and so wrote recently:

> *I often have the feeling that at the best of times literary criticism is fraudulent, since in the absence of any accepted standards whatever – any external reference which can give meaning to the statement that such a book is* good *or* bad *– every literary judgment consists in trumping up a set of rules to justify an instinctive preference. One's real reaction to a book, when one has a reaction at all, is usually 'I like this book' or 'I don't like it', and what follows is rationalisation.*[1]

But a significant reference of literary value is not likely to be *external*. Standards are not rules which are brought from outside and imposed upon each work. They grow, rather, from a number of local observations and decisions; are formulated by the development of a literature. Such standards will, it is true, be inseparable from the values of the larger culture, which may well not be absolute. But because a judgment is not, in this extreme sense, absolute, it does not follow that it is without meaning. And the fact that judgment is difficult or unscientific is no excuse for calling the attempt at judgment *fraudulent*. Mr Orwell's *instinctive preference* seems to me a highly questionable quantity. *Instinctive* it will scarcely be. Mr Orwell's *instinctive preference* is, I am sure, quite different from the *instinctive preference* of a satisfied reader of Ethel M. Dell, because Mr Orwell, whatever modifications his experience may have forced on him, has inherited a system of value and judgment in literature which may not be easily formulable, but which is certainly not to be dismissed as *trumping up a set of rules*.

---

1 George Orwell: *Writers and Leviathan. Politics and Letters*, 1948.

D.H. Lawrence was as impatient of fraudulent criticism as Mr Orwell, but he did not dismiss the whole process as a rationalisation:

> *Literary criticism can be no more than a reasoned account of the feeling produced upon the critic by the book he is criticising.*
>
> *Criticism can never be a science: it is, in the first place, much too personal, and in the second it is concerned with values that science ignores. The touchstone is emotion, not reason. We judge a work of art by its effect on our sincere and vital emotion, and nothing else. All the critical twiddle-twaddle about style and form, all this pseudo-scientific classifying and analysing of books in an imitation-botanical fashion, is mere impertinence and mostly dull jargon.*
>
> *A critic must be able* to feel *the impact of a work of art in all its complexity and force. To do so, he must be a man of force and complexity himself, which few critics are. A man with a paltry impudent nature will never write anything but paltry, impudent criticism. And a man who is* emotionally *educated is rare as a phoenix . . . The more scholastically educated a man is generally, the more he is an emotional boor.*
>
> *More than this, even an artistically and emotionally educated man must be a man of good faith. He must have the courage to admit what he feels, as well as the flexibility to* know *what he feels . . . A critic must be emotionally alive in every fibre, intellectually capable and skilful in essential logic, and then morally very honest.*
>
> *Then it seems to me a good critic should give his reader a few standards to go by. He can change the standards for every new critical attempt, so long as he keeps good faith. But it is just as well to say: This and this is the standard we judge by.*[2]

There is much in this that it is not easy to accept outright, but there is a very welcome insistence on the essential nature of critical activity. For the establishment of standards is neither a casual nor a fraudulent process, but the attempt to define a *centre* to which one's experience has given meaning.

But what has this to do with the general reader, it will be asked. He is not required to become a critic, nor in most cases does he so desire. Here I return to a belief from which this book is written: that the activity of criticism is very largely the activity of good reading. The critic must usually define his response in writing and that requires other talents. But complete intellectual and emotional awareness, the 'flexibility to *know* what he feels', good faith: these are qualities that critic and reader need alike. If you are interested in literature, you can hardly fail to be interested in criticism. But it is necessary to draw a firm line, and to refuse to be diverted to those marginal activities of literary gossip which the inclusive name of criticism has too long dignified.

---

2   D.H. Lawrence: *Scrutinies*: 1928.

Criticism, we may note in conclusion, is essentially a social activity. It begins in individual response and judgment, needing the qualities of feeling, flexibility, and good faith which D.H. Lawrence has described. But its standards of value, if it is to acquire meaning, must be ultimately matters of agreement between many people: values which are instinct in the culture of a society. The doctrine of the self-sufficiency of personal taste is hostile to criticism for the same reason that the doctrine of individual self-sufficiency is hostile to society.

Literature in Relation to History: 1850–75

From: *Rewley House Papers*, III, I, 1949–50, pp 36–44

(i) Formal Report

A course for tutors on *Literature in Relation to History*, with special reference to the period 1850–75, was held at Hertford College, Oxford, between 1 and 8 July 1950. Thirty-one adult education tutors attended the course as students, fifteen of whom were members of the Oxford extra-mural staff. Nineteen of the tutor-students were primarily specialists in history; twelve in literature. The course was divided into six seminars, each concerned with a particular writer of the period, and conducted by the following tutors: Mr Humphrey House (Dickens and G.M. Hopkins); Dr C.J. Holloway (Ruskin); Mr J.B. Bamborough (Tennyson); Mr W.W. Robson (Matthew Arnold); Mr Raymond Williams, who was also Director of Studies (George Eliot). These seminars reported to two general discussions on the period as a whole. In addition to the seminar work, there were five lectures: Mr G.M. Young on 'Mid-Victorianism'; Mr Isaiah Berlin on 'Scientific and Philosophic Thought, 1850–75'; Mr Asa Briggs on 'Religion in England, 1850–75'; Mr Raymond Postgate on 'English Social and Political History, 1850–75'; and Sir F.M. Powicke on 'The Study and Writing of History, 1850–75'.

The ground covered in the course was very various, and there were many sharp differences of opinion. It is thus impossible to present a report of conclusions representing the views of the course as a whole. The seminar reports reached certain conclusions within themselves, but many of these were sharply challenged in the general discussion, and represent only local agreements. It was, in any case, not to be expected that anything in the nature of an encyclical on the period should issue from the course: the material was inevitably complex, and a large number of different value-judgments were involved. Nor was it the purpose of the course to produce an agreement of that nature. The course took its inception from the fact that, in classes, many history tutors were using literature as evidence and many literature tutors using history as background. It was felt that both practices were likely to have more validity if tutors in literature and in history came together in a common study of a specific period, each trying to understand the other's methods and disciplines. Moreover, many tutors were anxious to experiment in deliberately correlated courses in literature and history, in order to achieve the wider comprehension, unlimited by subject boundaries, which has been a traditional demand and objective in adult education. The experience of this specific course was intended as a control in such experiments, and as an exploration of possible methods.

It is probable that each tutor who attended the course would draw different conclusions in respect of these experiments. That again is natural, and is not to be regretted. We are teaching, after all, from certain specific and differing viewpoints; and we shall not achieve the wider comprehension of which we have spoken by any quick, rule-of-thumb uniformity. Nevertheless, the course achieved certain definite results: positive results, in its indication to many tutors of ways of correlation and of means of using secondary material, as well as in specific information and understanding of the period under discussion; negative results, in a demonstration of the inadequacy of certain kinds of 'correlation', and in an understanding of some of the dangers involved in appropriating material outside one's own specialism. These results justified the principle and practice of the course as a whole.

(ii) A Personal View

At this point, I wish to turn from generalized report to an explicitly personal evaluation of the course's work. I make no apology for the personal viewpoint, which should be sufficiently clear. It seems to me that there are certain things which need saying about the situation revealed by the course, and, when this is the case, it is not always right to miss an opportunity of saying them. I take my facts from my experience of the course itself, and from subsequent study of the written reports of seminars and of the general discussion periods.

I will begin from the report of the Dickens seminar, which summarized the following general conclusions: (i) that history is a corrective to literary study; (ii) that literature acts mainly as inspiration to the historian. (Perhaps I do not need to add that the Dickens seminar contained no literature tutors.) Now these conclusions, which seem to me to represent the opinion of the majority of the historians on the course, seem to me something very far less than adequate. I have searched the detailed report of the Dickens seminar with some interest in an attempt to discover how, for example, history may serve as 'a corrective to literary study'. I find, which no one disputes, that Dickens exaggerated many of his characters, that he was 'a cartoonist working within the truth'. I find also, and here again the facts are clear, that Dickens often constructed his situations for 'dramatic effect', and that he sometimes amalgamated situations of the twenties with sentiments of the forties. The facts are important, but in what sense are they 'a corrective to literary study'? They show that Dicken's method of characterization was not a photographically naturalistic one, but what literary study worthy of the name would conclude that it was? The fact is a corrective, not to literary study, but to general prejudice. It seems to me to be an important historical fact that a great many modern readers understand characterization in terms of a value based on 'lifelikeness'. I am not sure that I am wrong in detecting a residue of this kind of assumption in the present approach to Dickens. You do not need to correct the method of the literature by reference to an historical estimate of lifelikeness; the method is a perfectly familiar one, and is only inaccessible to persons with a naturalistic (and historically conditioned) prejudice. Again, the fact of Dickens's anachronisms is held to limit his value as a social historian. But he was not a social historian, he was a novelist; if he had been a social historian he would have written books of social history. The anachronisms are involved in a particular literary method, and an anxious correction of the method from a history book is a simple prejudice, supported by a similarly naturalistic assumption that 'the facts should be right'. What we have here, in fact, is not a corrective to literary study, but the need of a corrective to the non-literary study of literature.

This has always been my criticism of the approach of historians to literature. There is a frequent failure to approach a work of literature as itself, as a work subject to conditions of existence which only attention to the work as a whole will reveal. It is easy enough to see the distortion and fragmentation of literature in the work of a bad historian; he would, for example, be a bad historian who drew evidence of the radical movement in the 1830s from George Eliot's novel *Felix Holt*, without realizing that the movement is seen from the very particular (and historically distorting) viewpoint of George Eliot in the sixties. But a realization of this process does not dispose of *Felix Holt*; a perception of the fact merely informs us about a part of George Eliot's literary method. When we have accepted the literary method, as a result of attention to the text, we may then profitably ask if *the method* has any historical importance. Literary methods change; the preconceptions of readers change. It has always seemed to me that a study of these changes is more likely to be of use to the historian than a crude reduction of literature to the status of documents, with a subsequent careful comparison of the diet-table of a Dickens workhouse with the diet-tables on the records.

Perhaps I can best express the kind of attention which I have in mind if I say that all novels are historical novels, except historical novels. The explicit historical novel, whether it deals with a period long before the writer's birth, or with the society and manners and ideas of the writer's remembered childhood and adolescence, is not a novel expressing the history of the period chosen, but of that history seen through the consciousness of a particular and contemporary point in time. This also applies to plays; a good example is Ibsen's *Kongsemnerne (The Pretenders)*, in which the material of the action is taken from medieval Norwegian history, but is used to express a contemporary and personal theme. 'I cannot find that the Earl played any such prominent part in this business as Ibsen assigns to him', wrote William Archer, a thoroughly naturalistic critic. What Archer did not realize, and what some historians seem to me not to realize, is that the historical material was not used as historical fact (a kind of imaginatively forged document), but as a means of expression of a particular experience. The classical critical statement of this method is T.S. Eliot's:

The only way of expressing emotion in the form of art is by finding an 'objective correlative'; in other words, a set of objects, a situation, a chain of events which shall be the formula of that particular emotion; such that, when the external facts, which must terminate in sensory experience, are given, the emotion is immediately invoked.

It is in this way that many writers use historical material, and it is as irrelevant then to judge the material on grounds of historical accuracy as it would be to object, when a writer uses myth or legend for similar reasons, that the myth could not have happened. (*Nina: I am a seagull*; 'to me, physical impossibility'.)

All novels are historical novels, in the sense that the experience which they express and the literary methods of expression are events (even if only personal events) at a particular point in time. In this sense the explicit historical novel is also an event in history, and my earlier paradox breaks down. But the paradox may serve to emphasize the distinction I have been making. The historical novel may be based on accurate research, but the research is contemporary; elements of interpretation, or of exoticism, may enter, but they are of contemporary origin, the effect of the history on the personal consciousness, or of the personal consciousness on the history. The historical novel, like every other work of literature, is something made by a particular person at a particular point in time, and the making is part of human history. Perhaps the most convenient short statement of the matter is that all literature is history.

I have been criticizing the attitude of some historians to literature, but I find myself approaching the point at which I criticize their attitude to history. I was often amazed, in this course, at the scale of interest employed in the historical approach. 'This is where I get interested', said one historian in the George Eliot seminar, as the group considered in passing a letter by George Eliot in which she commented on the revolutions of 1848. He had no difficulty, no difficulty at all, in proving that George Eliot's remark would hardly pass muster in a contemporary Honours School of History. But is it as a commentator on international affairs that George Eliot is *historically* important? Is the limitation of judgement to be assigned to her alone? For my own part I know very little about history (I was brought up on Welsh history only, out of little books with the Welsh dragon sticking its tongue out on the cover, and learned all about the predatory and perfidious English in a manner which I am assured by my English historian friends was quite unsatisfactory). But I had thought that the study of dates and treaties and constitutions was now more widely recognized as only a part (if a valuable part) of the general study of human actions in time. I had assumed that historians would be naturally interested in an account of the nature and quality, at any given time, of specific, though unpolitical, human experience; or of the particular workings of social institutions; or of the effect of economic change upon differentiated individual persons, as well as upon a class. I had assumed this because it did not seem to me that the nature of the lives of the people I now know (the thirty people on the course, for example) could be adequately understood by a study of their personal incomes, their occupations, their expectations of life, and their opinions on the Atlantic Pact. The fact that experience, including social experience, had been shaped and assessed by the workings of an imaginative consciousness did not seem to me to make it any less important than experience which had passed through the statistical or generalizing process of the historical record. In certain cases, however, I was evidently wrong. There seemed to me to be a large element of original Bitzer (authentically ex-Gradgrind) in several historians' definitions of 'fact'. The survival was to me the most important piece of historical evidence which the course provided.

If there was a failure of human relevance in certain of the historical approaches, it seems to me, on reflection, to be due in no small part to the permission, by some of the literature tutors, of assumptions both about literature and about experience which were allowed to pass unchallenged. There is, for example, the very strange statement in the report of the Ruskin seminar that Ruskin was 'an intuitive rather than a logical thinker'. I had thought that since the work of, among others, the late Susan Stebbing, there was rather more care in the use of 'logical' as a definitive term. Its use here, with the obvious assumption that an intuitive thinker cannot be logical, seems to me to be very questionable. 'We talk as if thought was precise and emotion was vague. In reality there is precise emotion and there is vague emotion. To express precise emotion requires as great intellectual power as to express precise thought.' The whole distinction between thought and feeling, or between 'hard fact' and experience, seemed to me another simply historical phenomenon. It really seemed that one was learning more about the nineteenth century by observing certain twentieth-century approaches to it than from the period material itself. In reviewing the successive criticism of George Eliot's work, for example, one was constantly finding this crude distinction between 'thought' and 'feeling' being used to support the fashionable exaltation of her early novels at the expense of the later, and even being used in certain attempts to modify this fashion. But the distinction, when applied to the novels, seemed merely a prejudice. The discriminations one had to make in comparing, for example, *Janet's Repentance* and *Middlemarch* were not between 'feeling' and 'thought' but between vague emotion and precise emotion, as seen clearly in the relative quality of the language and in particular the imagery. Similarly, in comparing *Felix Holt* and *Daniel Deronda* with reference to their intellectual elements, the distinctions one had to make in each novel were between precise expression of 'the emotional equivalent of thought' and its imprecise expression.

The passing of inadequate distinctions was not the only limitation on the literary side. There was a very real failure to make clear the status of literature; the old sense of guilt of the literature tutor reappeared in an anxious attempt to conciliate the historians by an offering of hard facts, at whatever expense to the literature. I was very surprised to find (too late) that much of the literature was being read simply for possible historical references: a 'here-I-get-interested' attitude when a poem included a date. Now the correlation of literature with history had always seemed to me something rather different from this. One read the literature as literature; if not, it was better left alone. One tried to value it as literature, to determine its intrinsic importance. It did not matter, it seemed to me, if no convenient equations between the literature and the history became available during this process. But then one took the realized literature, and set it alongside the other products of the period: economic developments, political developments, social institutions, modes of thinking, intellectual conclusions, modes of personal behaviour. One then said: all these various facts were the product of a certain people living in certain conditions at a certain point in time; they were, however complex the whole which they form, nevertheless a whole. If one wishes to understand the whole, the parts must be accepted absolutely as themselves, and a new attempt made at understanding their relations. The poem which states in particular terms the fantasies of an adolescent is as much a part and a product of this whole as the novel which deals with the conditions of workers in an industrial town; and may indeed be just as valuable a clue to a general understanding. An incapacity for precise feeling may be just as important a fact to an understanding of a society as an incapacity for political stability. The 'change of heart' which Dickens may be said to have advocated as the basic social cure must be seen, not only in relation to the disappointments of Chartism, but also in an evaluation of its frequent personalization, in literary terms, as 'an innocent child' (cf., in particular, Sissy Jupe). What I am saying is that just as some of the historians seemed limited in their approach to an understanding by certain particular assumptions about 'fact', so were many of the literary approaches limited by an absence of literary criticism (an absence perhaps encouraged by a concentration on 'background' and on biography).

I must emphasize, having said so much, that this is what I have *learned from* the course; it needed so complete a demonstration to be able to assess one's ideas about method. I cannot hope that my arguments will be accepted, since the course made it quite obvious that the preconceptions I have been discussing are very strong. I would summarize my views on the future of such classes and courses in this way. Several history tutors who attended said that, while the subject interested them, they felt that they had already so much to do in teaching history in their classes that they could not find time to extend to literature. This seems to me a perfectly reasonable attitude, provided that one realizes that one is deliberately limiting one's field for the sake of emphasis. Other history tutors felt that they could find occasional uses for literature as illustration. On this I would only repeat what I have said before. From George Eliot, for example, one can find much illustration of social history: in her descriptions of country living in *Adam Bede* and *The Mill on the Floss*; of the country just before the coming of railways in *Felix Holt*; of provincial middle-class life in *Middlemarch*. She had a very keen generalizing eye for a social process, and great descriptive powers. But one must always enter the caveat: that there are frequent lapses and fusions of time; that the characters are part of a total reading of experience, and not simply social portraits; that as works of literature the novels have considerable complexity of theme, so that abstraction of a particular attitude often destroys the specific significance which the author has given it in its place in the total development. Again, one can abstract from George Eliot's works a kind of 'philosophy', which was valued in her own day and which is probably representative of a major tendency. But here again, the ideas are only part of a total organization: 'they can only be seen clearly in precipitate, but they are only valid in solution'. The particular temper of George Eliot's mind can only be realized by a full response to her work as a whole; the abstraction of 'leading ideas' can be very misleading.

So much for the incidental use of literature as illustration. There remains correlation in its full sense. Here one is concerned with society as a whole, including the social activity which is literature. One needs an insistence on disciplines of economic analysis, political analysis, social analysis, analysis of the religion and philosophy and science of the period, as satisfactory as one can achieve. One needs also, with reference to the literature, an attention to it as a thing in itself, as the only way of drawing from it full and adequate evidence, to be set alongside the evidence of other activities. I have tried to indicate something of what this kind of response involves. I should like, for emphasis, to indicate again one of its elements, which is the study of language. By this I do not mean linguistics, or linguistic history. Semantics, in so far as the study of semantics is definable, is rather nearer what I have in mind. But the particular method which is available is that of literary criticism and analysis. One is looking for changes in the use of language, what Mr House has called 'the idiom of the period': not changes in spelling or grammar or pronunciation, but rather the changes in language as a medium of expression, changes which reflect subtle and often unconscious changes of assumption and mental and emotional process. The change and continuity of a language, often seen most clearly in its use in literature, forms a record of vitally important changes and developments in human personality. It is as much the record of the history of a people as political institutions and religious and philosophical modes. Of all the evidence which literature can contribute to the study of human affairs, this evidence of language is perhaps the most important.

I do not suppose that the correlation of these various disciplines will be easy. To achieve adequacy in any one of them is sufficiently difficult. But there are some people, including some tutors who attended the course in question, who have perceived enough of the value of such an attempt to be willing to go on with the experiment. Adult education, with its considerable freedom for experiment, is in many ways a very suitable field. I think myself that the experiment will involve new thinking about the grouping of tutors, and about the arrangements for particular classes. No one proposes that the very suitable specialist work now being done should be limited because of the experiment. But there is willingness for such an attempt among some classes and among some tutors. It seems to me that the recent course advanced our readiness for such experiments more considerably than we have perhaps realized. The quarrels of specialists are sometimes negative, and even occasionally lead to bitterness. But the controversy over scope and methods is an essential part of the beginning of the process of correlation. I should not have been so deliberately controversial in this article (a deliberateness which does not at all cancel my very pleasant memories of the course) if I had not hoped, by attempting to restate the issues, to carry the experiment a further stage forward.

Books for Teaching 'Culture and Environment'

From: *The Use of English*, 1, 3, 1950, pp 134–40

Culture and Environment, the title of the book by F.R. Leavis and Denys Thompson, has become generally accepted as the title of a group of studies in which increasing interest is being taken. It is some way from being an ideal title, since each of the main terms has one or more general, and several specialized, meanings, and the intended force of their conjunction is likely to be missed by a majority of students. But it is the best title we have, and the studies to which it refers are in any case difficult to fit into existing categories. At the same time they are of fundamental importance, particularly to students and teachers of English.

The central activity of 'Culture and Environment' studies is, and must be, analysis. By analysis one means here the close reading of a literary text with a view to its fuller apprehension and to a detailed and demonstrated judgment. Literary criticism is the informing discipline of the studies as a whole, and it is criticism of the kind based upon analysis. Thereafter, education in 'Culture and Environment' involves an extension of this kind of analysis and judgment to a variety of cultural forms. First, there are those forms which, like literature, depend primarily upon words: newspapers, magazines and best-seller fiction, advertisements and propaganda. Second, there are those forms which, by reason of their influence, cannot be ignored, yet which do not depend upon the written word: broadcasting and the cinema; architecture and town planning. Extension to the first group is straightforward once the practice of literary analysis is understood; extension to the second group is not easy, although elements of analytic practice can in fact be carried over. In studies of the second group, critical experience from the visual arts can also be brought to bear, as in the first group it will be brought to bear on advertising.

The purpose of 'Culture and Environment' studies as a whole is the training of awareness and judgment in respect of these widely influential forms of expression: a training which is a necessary accompaniment to direct literary studies. Further, it commonly involves a judgment of the society in which these forms are characteristic, by means of an incursion into comparative sociology and social history.

I have made these definitions at the risk of repetition of what is already familiar, because it is clear that in writing about books for teaching 'Culture and Environment', as I have been asked to do, one is in fact

174

surveying an extremely large field and had better define where one can. Because of the fundamental nature of its educational concern the study touches a large number of other studies, all of which have their textbooks. In teaching the subject at all, however, one has, while respecting these specialisms, to refuse to be overawed by them. I will commit myself on the value of books in these various fields as I have found them in the experience of teaching adult members of university tutorial and W.E.A. classes. I would emphasize that in each case I am judging the books by their relevance to the main concerns represented by 'Culture and Environment'.

One begins any such study by examples of actual analysis. Here, for the teacher's reading, the standard books are F.R. Leavis's *Education and the University* (see particularly the chapter on Literary Studies) and the two books of I.A. Richards: *Principles of Literary Criticism* and *Practical Criticism*. For my own part I find the Richards books uneven. The attempt at a theory of value in the *Principles* seems to me both a distraction and badly done. In *Practical Criticism* there is, unfortunately, rather less analysis than documentation. But both books are stimulating and cannot be left unread. Leavis's book, in spite of what seems an unnecessary difficulty of expression, is excellent; and the chapter referred to is probably the best short explanation of literary analysis to be found.

It is important, in this kind of work, that teachers and students should provide the great majority of their casebook material. But, for literary analysis, books of examples are useful, having the advantage over anthologies that the names of authors will not appear to short-circuit judgment. Denys Thompson's *Reading and Discrimination* is very useful in this respect, although it tends to employ a kind of snap judgment which is somewhat inappropriate. E.G. Biaggini's *Progressive Exercises in Reading* has many useful passages, although those from popular novelists are a generation or two out of date. A book of my own, *Reading and Criticism* (to be published spring, 1950), has a fairly large appendix of examples for use in this way. The text of this book is a general introduction to critical reading on the basis of several pieces of analysis.

Reference to good examples of written criticism is a necessary guidance by the teacher. For literary criticism there are the essays by Empson and Leavis in *Determinations* (edited by F.R. Leavis); many of the reprinted pieces in *Towards Standards of Criticism* (edited by Leavis); L.C. Knights' *Explorations*; the essays in Parts III and V of T.S. Eliot's *Selected Essays*; the essay by Edwin Muir on Arnold Bennett in *Scrutinies*, I (edited by Edgell Rickword) – a book which still makes lively reading; and F.R. Leavis's sections on *The Portrait of a Lady* and *Hard Times* in *The Great Tradition* and on Shelley in *Revaluation*.

In conducting a study of 'Culture and Environment' with adult students I have always found it wise to begin with a reasonable amount of literary analysis. The alternative is to begin with analysis of newspapers and advertisements. There is not much to choose between these openings, but the teacher in any case must remember that in moving from one to the other he is taking a larger step than he may realize. Most analysis of newspapers and advertisements can be treated on a 'sense or nonsense' level

– the sort of thing which is done very well by Susan Stebbing in *Thinking to Some Purpose* and by R.H. Thouless in *Straight and Crooked Thinking*. Such work is important and excellent, but the distinctive feature of 'Culture and Environment' teaching is that in this matter it goes further than logical analysis and offers an analysis of quality – tone, method and effect – in pieces which cannot be faulted on the score of logic. It is relatively easy to take students to the 'sense and nonsense' level. The further range is more difficult, and can only be attained by a fairly concrete realization of certain values, which will be drawn in the main from literature (although, of course, not from literature alone).

It is this quality which makes Denys Thompson's *Between the Lines* and *Voice of Civilization* much the most useful books of their kind. *Culture and Environment* itself is still very useful, but I do not without reservation recommend the book as a whole, for reasons which I will discuss below.

Once analysis of newspapers is undertaken, one will have to some extent to deal with the Press on its own terms. The most useful general books seem to me to be Norman Angell's *The Press and the Organization of Society* and Jane Soames' *The English Press*. The P.E.P. *Report on the British Press* (1937) is still useful, although for many people it will appear superseded by the recent *Report of the Royal Commission on the Press*. The latter, however, would seem in many places to be no more than a document of attitudes which the teacher of 'Culture and Environment' will be concerned to combat. The results of the Commission's independent researches can be used separately from the Commission's conclusions on them; and subsequent comparison with the Commission's conclusions could be an interesting exercise. There are innumerable guides to the 'romance' of the Press, many by experienced journalists. *My Northcliffe Diary* is still an invaluable document. A book which might be expected to be capable, but which I find both disappointing and disquieting, is Kingsley Martin's *The Press the Public Wants*. Martin, like most journalists writing on the matter, is preoccupied with questions of organization, and evades the question of values in a way that makes his discussion seem irrelevant. It is important to direct the attention of students to the contemporary newspaper as an expression of certain typical responses to life; arguments about its ownership (or so it seems to me) can only profitably be discussed in that context.

On advertisements, there are, among reputable books: A.S.J. Baster, *Advertising Reconsidered*; F.W. Taylor, *The Economics of Advertising*; Stuart Chase, *Your Money's Worth*. *Prose of Persuasion* (by Thomas C. Steel) is a would-be serious anthology of advertisement writing which the teacher will find useful for analysis.

On popular fiction, of course, the standard work is Q.D. Leavis's *Fiction and the Reading Public*. The literary-sociological essays of George Orwell (reprinted in *Critical Essays*) are also useful. Also recommended is Unwin and Stevens' *Best-sellers – Are they Born or Made?*

For the analysis of propaganda, useful general books are: Norman Angell, *The Public Mind*; Lord Ponsonby, *Falsehood in Wartime*; Smith, Lasswell, Casey, *Propaganda, Communication, and Public Opinion*; Albig,

Public Opinion; and R.S. Lambert, *Propaganda*. There is, of course, no shortage at all of material for analysis.

Extension of 'Culture and Environment' studies to films and broadcasting is something the teacher must mainly tackle on his own. There is a certain amount of reasonable writing about films (Rotha's *The Film Till Now* (new edition), for example, or Winnington's *Drawn and Quartered*), but none of it can really be considered on a serious critical level. There are two quite recent books on the relations of films to society, M. Thorpe's *America at the Movies* and J.P. Mayer's *Sociology of Film*. The former is interesting, uncritical, partly relevant; the latter, although it contains an excellent body of documents of responses to films, is disappointing. It is badly organized and most indecisive. A general book, *Made for Millions* (edited by Laws), contains essays on films, radio, television, books, press and advertising. It is of very mixed quality and cannot be recommended. Among pamphlets, Marius Pope on *What's in the News,* Boris Ford on *The Reading Habit* and, to a limited degree, Frederick Laws on *Radio,* are useful contributions in the 'Current Affairs' series. The same cannot be said of C. McIver's pamphlet on *Advertising* in the same series.

It is inevitable, after a variety of particular studies in cultural forms, that a desire to undertake a fuller cultural analysis of our kind of society should arise. The orthodox general view, I suppose, is still that of Leavis and Thompson in *Culture and Environment*, a view largely derivative from the books of George Bourne (*Change in the Village, The Wheelwright's Shop* and *Memoirs of a Surrey Labourer*) and from the social criticism of D.H. Lawrence. Bourne's books are, of course, invaluable, and the relevant sections of Lawrence's *Letters* and of his *Phoenix* and *Fantasia of the Unconscious* must certainly be read. But this position, which is stated very well by F.R. Leavis in *Mass Civilization and Minority Culture*, is by no means the only one which can be taken up after studies such as those that have been outlined. When one reaches the position stated by G.H. Bantock in two articles in *Scrutiny* ('The Cultural Implications of Planning and Popularization', Spring 1947, and 'Some Cultural Implications of Freedom in Education', Spring 1948) one may well feel that though the elements are familiar and just, there is something very unsatisfactory about the view as a whole. I feel myself that the assertion of a 'minority' is by now largely irrelevant and, in certain social terms, idle and harmful. But it is not a question of suggesting alternatives. There is, potentially, a Marxist alternative, and one should, I suppose, read Caudwell's *Illusion and Reality* and *Studies in a Dying Culture*. As one who finds himself perhaps nearer to the Marxist than to the Leavis position, I would say, however, that Caudwell's books fall well below their reputation, and that they cannot really be taken seriously. Obviously I cannot fully argue these points here.

In any case, one ought to use books like those of J.L. and Barbara Hammond (*The Bleak Age* – which is excellent; *The Town Labourer* and *The Village Labourer*); and for the statement of settled and influential views, R.H. Tawney's *The Acquisitive Society* and Christopher Dawson's *Progress and Religion*. One can hardly avoid the work of Lewis Mumford, especially *The Culture of Cities*. There will be some who, like myself, find Mumford's tone embarrassing and his positives a little nebulous; there will be few, however, who will not find that his work brings much local insight. *Metropolitan Man* (Robert Sinclair) offers a broad analysis, but is hasty, unbalanced and frequently exhibitive. The two books by R.S. and H.M. Lynd (*Middletown* and *Middletown in Transition*) are essential and illuminating reading. Among recent articles, some which are relevant are 'The Letters of D.H. Lawrence' (Collins); 'The Politics of W.B. Yeats' and 'The Little World of J.M. Synge' (Freyer); 'Soviet Literary Controversy in Retrospect' (Williams); and the 'Critic and Leviathan' series – Winkler, Hill, Leavis, Elvin, Orwell – all in *Politics and Letters*, 1947–8. Matthew Arnold's *Essays in Criticism* and *Culture and Anarchy* are still important, and we may add to these T.S. Eliot's *Notes Towards a Definition of Culture*, which seems to me, although I disagree with sections of it, a far more definitive book than its title would suggest.

Finally, there is one book among many works of anthropology which seems to me so distinguished that it cannot wisely be omitted from an essential reading list in this field: Ruth Benedict's *Patterns of Culture*. Her book provides the method of comparative social evaluation which is necessary both to give the work of cultural analysis full scope and to keep it relevant.

Bibliography

GENERAL

Culture and Environment, by F.R. Leavis and D. Thompson. (*Chatto & Windus*, 1933): Education and the University, by F.R. Leavis. (*Chatto & Windus*, 1943): Principles of Literary Criticism, by I.A. Richards. (*Kegan Paul*, 1924): Practical Criticism, by I.A. Richards. (*Kegan Paul*, 1929).

READING AND ANALYSIS

Reading and Discrimination, by Denys Thompson. (*Chatto & Windus*, 1934): Progressive Exercises in Reading, by E.G. Biaggini. (*Hutchinson*, 1947): Reading and Criticism, by Raymond Williams. (*Frederick Muller*, 1950).

CRITICISM

Determinations (ed. Leavis). (*Chatto & Windus*, 1934): Towards Standards of Criticism (ed. Leavis). (*Wishart*, 1933): Explorations, by L.C. Knights. (*Chatto & Windus*, 1946): Selected Essays, by T.S. Eliot. (*Faber & Faber*, 1932): Scrutinies, I (ed. Edgell Rickword). (*Wishart*, 1931): The Great Tradition, by F.R. Leavis. (*Chatto & Windus*, 1949): Revaluation, by F.R. Leavis. (*Chatto & Windus*, 1936).

CLEAR THINKING

Thinking to Some Purpose, by Susan Stebbing. (*Penguin Books*, 1939): Straight and Crooked Thinking, by R.H. Thouless. (*English Universities Press*, 1936): The Comforts of Unreason, by Rupert Crawshay-Williams. (*Kegan Paul*, 1947).

THE PRESS

The Press and the Organization of Society, by Norman Angell. (*Minority Press*, 1933. Obtainable from Messrs. Heffers of Cambridge.): The English Press, by

Jane Soames. (*Lindsay Drummond*, 1936): Report of the British Press (1937). (*P.E.P.*): Report of the Royal Commission on the Press. (*H.M.S.O.* 1949): My Northcliffe Diary, by Tom Clarke. (*Gollancz*, 1931): Northcliffe, An Intimate Biography, by Hamilton Fyfe. (*Allen & Unwin*, 1930): The Press the Public Wants, by Kingsley Martin. (*Hogarth Press*, 1947): Between the Lines, by Denys Thompson. (*Frederick Muller*, 1939): The Reading Habit, by Boris Ford. (*Bureau of Current Affairs*, 1947): What's in the News? by Marius Pope. (*Bureau of Current Affairs*, 1949).

ADVERTISING
Advertising Reconsidered, by A.S.J. Baster. (*King*, 1935): The Economics of Advertising, by F.W. Taylor. (*Allen & Unwin*, 1934): Your Money's Worth, by Stuart Chase. (*Jonathan Cape*, 1928): Prose of Persuasion, by Thomas C. Steel. (*Grant Richards*, 1931): Voice of Civilization, by Denys Thompson. (*Frederick Muller*, 1943): The Anatomy of Advertising, by Colin McIver. (*Bureau of Current Affairs*, 1948).

POPULAR FICTION
Fiction and the Reading Public, by Q.D. Leavis. (*Chatto & Windus*, 1934): Critical Essays, by George Orwell. (*Secker & Warburg*, 1946): Best-Sellers – are they born or made? by Unwin and Stevens. (*Allen & Unwin*, 1939).

PROPAGANDA
The Public Mind, by Norman Angell. (*Noel Douglas*, 1926): Falsehood in Wartime, by Lord Ponsonby. (*Allen & Unwin*, 1930): Propaganda, Communication and Public Opinion, by B.L. Smith, Lasswell and Casey. (*Princetown University Press*. Obtainable from *Oxford University Press*, 1946): Public Opinion, by Albig. (*McGraw-Hill*, 1939): Propaganda, by R.S. Lambert. (*Nelson*, 1938).

FILM AND RADIO, ETC.
The Film Till Now (new edition), by Paul Rotha. (*Cape*, 1930. Revised edition to be published by *Vision Press*, 1949): Drawn and Quartered by Richard Winnington. (*Saturn Press*, 1948): America at the Movies, by M. Thorpe. (*Faber & Faber*, 1946): Sociology of Film, by J.P. Mayer. (*Faber & Faber*, 1946; *new edition* 1949): Made for Millions (ed. Laws). (*Contact Books*, 1947): Radio and the Public, by Frederick Laws. (*Bureau of Current Affairs*, 1947).

CULTURE AND CIVILIZATION
Change in the Village, by George Bourne. (*Duckworth*, 1920): The Wheelwright's Shop, by George Bourne. (*Cambridge University Press*, 1923): Memoirs of a Surrey Labourer, by George Bourne. (*Duckworth*, 1930): Letters of D.H. Lawrence. (*Heinemann*, 1932): Phoenix, by D.H. Lawrence. (*Heinemann*, 1936): Fantasia of the Unconscious, by D.H. Lawrence (*Heinemann*, 1923): Mass Civilization and Minority Culture, by F.R. Leavis. (*Minority Press*, 1931): Scrutiny: Spring 1947: 'The Cultural Implications of Planning and Popularization', by G.H. Bantock; Spring 1948: 'Some Cultural Implications of Freedom in Education', by G.H. Bantock. Illusion and Reality, by Christopher Caudwell. (*MacMillan*, 1937. *Reprinted by Lawrence & Wishart*, 1946): Studies in a Dying Culture, by Christopher Caudwell. (*John Lane*, 1938): The Bleak Age, by J.L. and Barbara Hammond. (*Longmans*, 1934. *Pelican Books*, 1948.): The Town Labourer, by J.L. and Barbara Hammond. (*Longmans*, 1917.): The Village Labourer, by J.L. and Barbara Hammond. (*Longmans*, 1911. *Reprinted by Guild Books*, 1948. 2 vols.): The Acquisitive Society, by R.H. Tawney.

(*Bell*, 1921.): Progress and Religion, by Christopher Dawson. (*Sheed & Ward*, 1929): The Culture of Cities, by Lewis Mumford. (*Secker & Warburg*, 1938.): Middletown, by R.S. and H.M. Lynd. (*Constable*, 1929.): Middletown in Transition, by R.S. and H.M. Lynd. (*Constable*, 1937.): Politics and Letters, 1947–48: Patterns of Culture, by Ruth Benedict. (*Routledge*, 1934.): Democracy in Industry, by Reavely and Winnington. (*Chatto & Windus*, 1947.): Essays in Criticism, by Matthew Arnold (1902). (*Reprinted by Macmillan*, 1938.): Culture and Anarchy, by Matthew Arnold (1869). (*Cambridge University Press*, 1948.): Notes Towards a Definition of Culture, by T.S. Eliot. (*Faber & Faber*, 1948).

The Teaching of Public Expression

From: *The Highway*, April 1952, pp 247–50

Public Expression is a term which, so far as I know, I invented. I was thinking about Public Speaking, and about the extent of its irrelevance to contemporary society. I wanted a term which would describe the modes of expression which we actually employ in the conduct of public affairs: speaking in branch meetings, committees, discussions, as well as in debates and public meetings; writing reports, memoranda, letters to newspapers, as well as articles and books. As a description Public Expression seemed accurate, and it was perhaps enough to stand a good chance of becoming familiar.

The WEA has a quite strong traditional objection to courses in Public Speaking; and on the whole I share the objection. As a voluntary exile from Wales I have probably reacted unusually strongly against rhetoric, but in general terms I think it is true that Public Speaking, in its understood sense of an address to a large meeting, is a dying craft. A training in voice production and elocution is occasionally useful, but to the training as a whole there are two objections: first, that it produces a mechanical voice style, in the manner of an average RADA actress (one makes the voice 'interesting' regardless of the interest of what one has to say); and, second, that while one might soon acquire a confident platform manner, there is on the whole a shortage of platforms. Meanwhile, for the less showy aspects of public communication one is not, under the old dispensation, trained at all.

It seemed to me that while these facts were quite widely recognized, the WEA was in danger of making a badly mechanical response to requests for training in public expression. When a group asks for a course of this kind, the agreed reply of a WEA District Secretary (I suspect he has a printed form for it) is that the group will be better equipped for public speaking when it has something to speak in public about, and that the proper prescription is a course in Politics/Economics/Philosophy/International Affairs. Now it is true that the mass meeting has declined in importance, and that as a result Public Speaking is hardly one of the humane studies. Can we say the same, though, of a training in speaking and writing which is specially directed to equipping members of working-class movements for the discharge of actual public responsibilities? It depends, I suppose, on your attitude to the working-class. It is theoretically fashionable, nowadays, to argue that the WEA must teach the worker Economics so that he will understand why he cannot have more wages; or Government (that passive phrase, '*How*

181

We Are Governed') to show him his place holding the ladder. I would not agree, and in this matter of public expression, I think workers often know quite well what they want to say or write, but find too frequently that they have not been equipped to express it. All this is a matter of fundamental choice, in which I as a tutor have taken my side. Does one impose on a social class that is growing in power the syllabus of an older culture; or does one seek means of releasing and enriching the life-experience which the rising class brings with it? If the latter, as I choose, then the WEA has a lot of its thinking in front of it; and part of this thinking, I submit, will be about education in public expression.

The tradition of tutorial classes, as I understand it, brings powerful support to this case. It is often said that the 'subject' of a tutorial class matters less than its fundamental procedure; that the class does not merely exist to supply information, but to develop individual powers of speaking, writing, thinking and study. I agree, and in all good tutorial classes I would expect to find a measure of the training which I am isolating as Public Expression. Why, then, am I isolating it? Because, first, in pioneer and short courses it is just this side of the work which is usually left out (for obvious reasons of time); and, second, even in tutorial classes, it is doubtful if one can provide the intensive development of faculties of expression which many active people will need. I am proposing courses in Public Expression which, first, will be of a pioneer or short-term nature, in WEA groups, in trade unions, and in Co-operative education; and, second, will be useful preparatory courses for a tutorial class in any subject.

I ought now to give an account of the syllabus I have in mind, and then of methods of teaching it. I set first a training in speaking and listening, which includes, on the one hand, the preparation and making of contributions to discussion and debate, of verbal reports, and of speeches; on the other hand, ways of following a verbal argument or exposition in any form. I set second a training in writing and reading: on the one hand, the preparation and execution of reports, letters to newspapers, articles, etc.; on the other hand, ways of testing and valuing a written argument or exposition, in newspapers, advertisements, pamphlets and books. In all these activities one is depending largely on an understanding of elementary logic of the kind which has often been taught in WEA classes as Clear Thinking. I include this training, and I add to it the essentially different kind of analysis which derives from literary criticism, and which is concerned with the valuing of tone, feeling, and sensibility. Then, as an extension of the range of the course, I include training in methods of study. Under this heading I include ways of approaching a new 'subject'; methods of access to information, and of testing its reliability; ways of using books and reports; methods of note taking; methods of organizing the knowledge that one has gained.

As to the way in which one will teach all this, I can only speak personally, although in fact there is a good deal of relevant WEA experience on which to draw. The training of speaking and listening is a matter of practical classwork, with arranged talks, discussions, verbal reports and so on. Writing is also done in class, starting with the simpler forms of notes for a short speech, log-book reports and short newspaper letters. Both for speaking and writing, a considerable amount of preparation procedure can be practically taught. I teach a standard procedure which can be summarized as:

(i) *Initial writing-down of points just as they come into the mind; and then numbering these points.*
(ii) *Looking through the list for leading ideas, allotting to each a letter, and then marking the numbered list with these letters.*
(iii) *On a new sheet of paper, setting out the lettered groups decided on; and arranging them in effective order, with the subsidiary points noted under each.*
(iv) *Making a check-list, on points for which one requires further information.*
(v) *Reconsidering the arrangement described in (iii) on the basis of the new information.*
(vi) *Allotting points to paragraphs, and then using these either as notes for speaking or as the framework for writing.*

There is nothing particularly original about this procedure; it is somewhat similar to that suggested by G.D.H. Cole in his recent *Hints on Reading and Writing* – although the later part, the second round, is perhaps new. But the exact procedure taught does not matter. I can only testify that my own students have found the adoption of *some* procedure both a novelty and a help.

Writing itself is a thing widely feared. I think one has to lay the bogy of Good English (cf. Yeats: 'the thing that gives words any literary quality is . . . the breath of men's mouths'). One has also to reassure students about grammar and spelling, reminding them that English is *their* language: no colonialism! At an early stage one can include exercises like the one I have based on the wage demands of the Mayfield and Ringmer labourers, quoted in the Hammonds' *Village Labourer*, Vol. II. Read these and rewrite them; then write a contemporary wages proposal. Or one can take union journals, and select passages for re-writing. As a counterweight, it is wise to include short exercises of description and report, based on personal and class experience. All correction of written work is, of course, done with individuals, not in class.

Underlying all this work is the training listed as Clear Thinking. One can use Thouless' *Straight and Crooked Thinking*, and then Stebbing's *Thinking to Some Purpose*. And then, because an argument can be formally impeccable but still bad, one includes as part of the training in reading and listening the making of simple value-judgments of the kind encountered in the early stages of literary criticism. For this I use my own *Reading and Criticism*, or Biaggini's *Exercises in Reading*. Part of this work is done formally; part as an element of the normal training.

Training in methods of study presents no great difficulties. Cole's suggestions are again useful, and I add to them my own suggestion of reading any important book backwards, an eccentric but often penetrating device. I suggest that in the class one selects a relevant 'subject' and textbook, and tackles them by way of example. It is also very important to provide information on sources other than books and periodicals, particularly for students who want to be able to negotiate current economic and political problems.

That then is an outline of my case and method. Courses based on it can range from three to twenty-four meetings, with appropriate selection of material. They are likely to be best when given a practical and *local* bias (a 'subject' which transformed a class in Hastings was the question of seasonal unemployment and light industries in Hastings itself; and questions like these lead naturally to further courses of a traditional kind). I can provide a more detailed account of method if it is required, but at the moment I am concerned merely to sponsor the idea. I should like to see it discussed by those concerned with trade union and Co-operative education, and also in the WEA.

Certain difficulties are obvious; among them the difficulty of finding tutors willing and able to do work of this kind. But the opportunities are also obvious, and I hope that they will not be missed.

Film as a Tutorial Subject

From: *Rewley House Papers*, III, II, Summer 1953, pp 27–37

'*Dear Editor: I have much pleasure in resigning my post as film critic, effective immediately. The fact is that 95% of all issued films are so bad that they cannot be written about at all; certainly not in any paper designed to be read while not at the same time chewing gum.*'

'*Well, have it your own way, but I've never heard such nonsense as a course in film appreciation. If this chap wants to study Betty Grable, let him do it where I do it from, the one-and-ninepennies, not expect to get subsidised out of public money*' (report of a meeting of an Education Committee).

'*The pictures? Well, it makes a change. I always go for a good rest myself.*'

The arts are still dangerous in education, as dangerous as real politics or as open psychology or as any valuing history. None of these things would ever have been allowed into any public education if it had not been possible, at the right moment, to pretend that each of them was something else. In adult education, the arts slipped inside, doing their best to look respectable, while the door was being opened for only one of their company, literature. Literature had been invited on the understanding that it was a 'bearer of ideas'. And certainly the ideas were there, and certainly literature had good references in society. Of course there was a certain amount of muttering, especially when literature was seen at last in its own right, and realized as an art. But by then it was too late to throw literature out; indeed the most urgent business of the orthodox was to discover and try to control the more open intruders, music, painting, architecture, theatre, film. That operation is now in progress, and it is certainly being conducted with skill and energy. But I think it is too late; too late to have anything more than nuisance value. Too many students have tried the study of the arts, and have found that it answers important needs. The dangerous quickening of experience which the arts represent may be atrophied, but it is never surrendered; any more than one surrenders the dangerous quickening of science and social understanding. Nor will those who have known this quickening be persuaded that there is any necessary opposition between the arts and the rest of adult and workers' education. The arts are among the emancipators, although at first their standards seem unfamiliar and their substance strange. What is important now, at a time when social studies are also of the first importance, is that honest effort should be made at reciprocal understanding.

The sentences which I placed at the head of this article are not a gage but a gift. The critic who wrote his tart resignation was almost right; his only immediate error is the percentage, which might be raised to 97 or even 98. The councillor, also, is more right than he deserves to be; a great deal of 'film appreciation' is little more than a rationalization of 'fan interest'. As for the lady who goes to the cinema for a rest, she is a representative figure, speaking for those millions who go there to get away from themselves and from others and from society. But then, if so much is admitted, how can film be claimed as a tutorial subject, or indeed as part of education at all? The answer is short, and, if occasion demands, sharp. In the first place, a high percentage of all art in the twentieth century is bad. That is why so much of the best contemporary criticism is necessarily destructive; the rubbish has to be cleared. The clearing process is important, as a practical testing-ground for values; and it is given point and worth by the discovery and affirmation of that small body of work which has permanent value. Of course it is true that this has nothing to do with 'appreciation'; it is criticism or nothing. Film appreciation, as it is commonly understood, is certainly not a tutorial subject; but then I would add that the mere appreciation of literature or of painting or of music is not tutorial work either. But the cinema has overtones; for reformers and conservatives alike it is conventional shorthand for depravity and cultural decay. Many fear that if education touches it, the taint will be indelible. It is a pretty fear; but if adult education cannot handle and assess an institution which weekly serves the leisure of twenty-five million British adults, and which deals well or badly, but at least with great emotive power, with the values of man and society, then adult education deserves to fade. The case for film as a tutorial subject is, first, that it provides opportunities for criticism, and that criticism is a major educational discipline; and, second, that the study of the cinema as an institution is an inevitable part of our sociology.

I will attempt to state more fully the case as it has reference to criticism. Fundamentally the case now being argued for film is the case for all the arts. Literature was welcomed in adult education, it seems to me, because of the fact that many of the greatest nineteenth-century writers were active critics of society; their writings had an obvious interest for those who demanded change. The only question was the level of seriousness; were not fiction and poetry self-defined as frivolity and escape? The question has continued to be put, for the Gradgrinds have accumulated (they could hardly do anything so frivolous as multiply); and had not the first sociologist, the great Spencer himself, banned all fiction from the new London Library as a waste of time (expecting only the works of his friend George Eliot)? But still, with the fierceness of Ruskin and of Morris against them, with Matthew Arnold quietly negotiating education in the name of culture, and with the strong tradition of self-educated working men still reading Bunyan and Shelley and Dickens, the accumulators were never sure enough of their ground. Literature stayed, and the best teaching of Ruskin and of Arnold developed into the practical criticism of our own generation.

The accumulators did not like it, but they could do no more than repeat the new word of abuse, 'aesthete', and this they could only sustain by reading Pater in quotation and by remaining firmly decontaminated from the actual experience of the arts. It came to be seen that the case for the arts in education was the case of criticism; that here, in the study of creative work, was a field of immediate training in the distinction of values; and that this was not some nugatory process of individual cultivation, but the process of decision *of a society* about the quality of its own living, in terms of the experience and embodiment of art.

Of course the appreciators muddled the issue. For them, art was a branch of deportment, and what mattered was that the uninstructed (the lesser breeds who read the penny papers) should learn under the guidance of experts the finer points of an art which must be accepted as absolute. In literature and in music and in painting there was indeed enough work of supreme value to make bardolatry at all levels seem satisfactory for a while, although the enervating process was always apparent. But the crisis came when attention had to be turned to contemporary work, for there no sifting of time, no classification of an Elton, served to provide the ready-made valuations on which the method depended. If contemporary art was to be dealt with at all, criticism was essential; and criticism was only possible if it rested on the whole tradition. And so, nowadays, it is widely enough recognized that a class in literature is a class in criticism; and it is agreed by anyone who has studied the practice that criticism is a discipline in the full educational sense.

I have said again my case for the tutorial class in literature because it is the necessary context for the present discussion of film. When in 1950 the Battle W.E.A. branch asked me to take a preparatory tutorial class in film, I tried to formulate the objections, my own and those of others. First, there was the objection that as material the film was not sufficiently important. Obviously there was something in this; there is perhaps no film which one can, without reservations, accept as an important work of art. But then important art is always rare; and there were, in the short history of the cinema, at least a dozen films which a critic could take seriously. There were many more, at least sixty, which had their own importance, and which provoked critical questions of some complexity. The importance, obviously, was not that of Dante or of Virgil or Shakespeare; nor even that of Bunyan or Shelley or Dickens. But let the comparison be restricted to the actual period of the film. Here again, the best work was clearly below the verse of Rilke or Valery or Yeats, and below the novels of Conrad or Thomas Mann or Lawrence. In twentieth-century drama, however, it was difficult to feel so certain. Was not the work of Pudovkin, Lang, Eisenstein, Dreyer, Clair, Pabst strictly comparable with that of Pirandello, Toller, O'Casey, Eliot, Fry, Anouilh? It seemed to me that it was, and indeed that if one had to maintain these artificial grades, *La Passion de Jeanne d'Arc* and *Mother* were more important, as works of art, than, say, *The Man of Property* and *The Good Companions* (which appeared in tutorial syllabuses), or even than *The Waves* and *The Power and the Glory* (which were taken without question). But it would misrepresent my position if it appeared that I was looking only for a small body of important work as a guarantee of respectability. Criticism is concerned with all work in a medium, and its importance as a discipline is not wholly determined by the importance of the material studied. There would be a case for a course of criticism in such bad films as *Brief Encounter, La Bête Humaine,* and *Panic in the Streets,* or in even worse films, like *Storm Warning, They Came to a City,* or *Quai des Orfèvres.* Nevertheless, although the process of criticism is valuable as such, it seemed to me that in film there was one difficult factor, the lack of a tradition. The serious film has been in existence for only thirty years or so; and within that short period there has been great technical change, so that one is faced at the start with two kinds of film, silent and sound, which are almost distinct forms. In these circumstances, it is necessary before undertaking general criticism to set up some provisional standards, on the basis of a few important works. Unfortunately, although much has been written about films, there is hardly anything that one can properly call criticism; and so any construction of standards is exposed to the dangers of isolation and eccentricity. From newspapers and trade reviews one does not expect criticism and the work of the best of these reviewers is distinguished only by the relative strength and attractiveness of the particular reviewer's personality, and hardly at all by any factors relevant to criticism. Again, there is a small body of serious appreciatory work – the writings of Rotha, Grierson, Lindgren, Manvell, &c.; and there is a fairly serious magazine, *Sight and Sound,* published by the Film Institute. But to one trained in literary criticism, this work, interesting and informed as it is, is likely to seem inadequate. It is usually technically expert (at least in the work of the actual film-makers), but this advantage is limited by a common failure to understand the place of technical analysis in a total judgement; so that what technical analysis there is comes usually as a separate kind of judgement – 'the film is interesting because of the emotional situation with which it deals; it is also, technically, very competent'. The worst result of this habit, in practice, is the passing of films which an integrated judgement would reject, but which in this artificial situation are praised for technical qualities which are somehow assumed to be in a separate category. After this fundamental error, it is not surprising that the normal staple of this criticism is summary of plot, charting of influence, discussion of character as if it were personality, and biographical study of directors and actors. To turn to this from the best contemporary literary criticism (the work of Eliot, Richards, Empson, Leavis, Knights, Murry, Levin) is to be reminded of the sharp cultural distinction between literature and film. What is more, it is a situation which cannot be remedied by mere allegiance to literature. It is fatal to attempt to carry over the substance of literary criticism into an art which is, in its essentials, very different. If we ever succeed in formulating adequate principles of film criticism, we can be sure that they will be different from the principles of literary criticism. The film may increasingly draw on words, and in this aspect we have the experience of good dramatic criticism on which to draw. But the best and most distinctive achievement of the film is essentially visual, and here (although some dramatic work will be relevant) a new critical method is clearly required. I believe, incidentally, that if film criticism is to develop in adult education, it will be wrong to regard it as an annexe to the work of literature tutors. We shall need specialists, and a literary training will not always be the best preparation. In any case, however, such tutors will need a certain maturity of general critical experience, and at least an awareness of traditional aesthetic problems and procedures; it is the lack of this experience and awareness which now vitiates most of the criticism associated with the Film Institute.

At the beginning of planning the Battle course, it seemed to me that the kind of critical discussion which it was necessary to promote (and which alone would justify film criticism as a tutorial subject) must be, first, integrated criticism, and, second, practical criticism; the two qualities, in fact, depended on each other. It seemed to me probable that one would encounter a difficulty of much the same kind as the familiar difficulty in literature classes; that is, a fairly general inability to read a particular work with adequate attentiveness and understanding. With a poem or novel one can always turn back the page, and a training in close reading is thereby possible. How would this be possible in film? There is no complete answer, but I decided to begin the course with a series of exercises designed to train attentive seeing and listening. I did not call them exercises; I called them filmshows, which was obviously more tactful. But the shows consisted of very short films and of short extracts; and the students were expected, in discussion and in writing, to describe accurately *the whole content* of each. Some of the short films were examples of the very early cinema (*The Well-Washed House, The Great Train Robbery, The Motorist*); but the historical interest, although real, was secondary. The valuable extracts prepared by the Film Institute (from *Caligari, Mother, Potemkin, Metropolis*) were used in the same way; there was a secondary interest in them as examples of early German and early Russian cinema, but their main function was the opportunity they provided for a manageable training in attentive and adequate response. The normal written work, in this part of the course, consisted of full and detailed description of a brief sequence, and it was very noticeable how quickly most students were able to improve their capacity for observing and recording a total rather than a selected content. I give in part one representative example:

> *I felt immediately interested when the extract began with the showing of the bowed figure. There was nothing in the background to distract the eye, therefore attention was completely on the central figure. The soles of her shoes were emphasised, and then came a dark circle opening out into light as if it were her mind's eye, and in this circle were shown men lifting the floor boards where the guns were hidden. Men then entered with the dead father: first we were shown the soles of his boots, and the legs of those carrying him, and the movements indicated the difficulty they were having in carrying him through the narrow door. Then again the soles were emphasised, and one saw the limp, dangling hand.*

This description of the opening of the extract from *Mother* is not quite full, but it is a considerable advance on normal observation and memory of a brief moment in a film. Of course it is not criticism, but to me it is the essential beginning of criticism; for what so often happens is that we abstract from what we have seen (often adding as well as omitting), and then base our comments on the abstraction, which by this time we have separated into content and technique, as well as into the usual categories of story, character, atmosphere, and all those things which the film is 'about'. Until students are able, fairly easily, to see what the film *is*, to see 'these images in this order', it is safe to say that the only critical method they will attain is the usual one of discursive comment.

This training continued for the first eight weeks of the course, and I found that students appreciated it once the end in view had been explained. It was necessary also, during this period, to provide a certain amount of information about film technique; but this was not in the manner of a series of 'peeps into the studios', but primarily given to provide a set of terms, so that 'these images' and 'this order' could be adequately realized and described. The next stage was the showing of complete films. I had laid down a normal timetable for the course which meant that films were seen at each alternate meeting, the intervening meetings being given over to discussion. On the evenings when films were shown there was a certain amount of preliminary discussion, but in fact the process of watching a film is exhausting and to some extent disintegrating from this point of view. The first real responses came in the written work, which was collected by the class secretary a few days after the class meeting, and posted on to me in time for examination and comment before the next meeting. At this meeting, I would begin a discussion of the film, based on the written work, and on my own reactions, and then pass the issue back to the class for the essential process of second thought and review. To begin with, each complete film that I showed was preceded, a fortnight earlier, by an extract from it. This allowed the process of attention to begin on a usefully small scale, and, when it was shown two of three times, provided a valuable introduction. I would not agree, myself, that it is best to begin with complete films, if only because in sheer profusion of detail they would be likely to overwhelm the student's capacity for critical attention and record. I can see that one might adopt, as an alternative procedure, the showing of the extract *after* seeing the complete film, and this might well work. But it would only work in the interests of critical discipline if there had been a considerable and thorough preparation of attention by the use of short films and other extracts.

When it came to stating and writing a criticism of a complete long film, most students drew valuably on their earlier training. Judgements were made, and made inevitably in terms of story, character, and technique; but at least these judgements were normally demonstrated by detailed analysis of the actual film rather than asserted by comment on the abstraction from it. And then, since one had actual material as a basis for discussion, it was possible to raise general critical questions: to examine assumptions about value; to inquire into the function of story and character and setting;

to discuss techniques. These meetings were, I think, valuable, because one cannot really understand such problems unless one has experience of detailed attention to the substance of a work of art; and certainly one cannot discuss them in any disciplined way unless one has common experience of a shared performance (whether reading or seeing or listening) as a basis. After a while, the class went on to a short series of complete films; having seen *Potemkin, Mother,* and *Metropolis* in extract and complete, we saw *La Passion de Jeanne d'Arc, The Italian Straw Hat, The Idea,* and *The Seashell and the Clergyman.* We also used two interesting composite films, *Drawings that Walk and Talk* (a history of drawn films which has material for a course in itself), and *Film and Reality* (a pleasant if rather perverse history of documentary and 'realist' films, which again gives scope for some genuine criticism). Towards the end of the course, the class agreed on three films which were being currently shown in local cinemas (*The Red Shoes, The Third Man, Panic in the Streets*), and students saw them, wrote about them, and discussed them in class in the same way as had been developed with the films actually shown in class time.

The class was a preparatory tutorial, and it would have been possible, I think, to go on to a tutorial in film alone. I advised against this, not because I doubted the value of the work, or because there was insufficient material, but because I preferred to gain more experience in the method before recommending a three-year class. In fact, the Battle group is going on to a tutorial in drama and film, which will include two sessions dealing mainly with plays, and one dealing mainly with films. Of course, the ultimate test of such work is the quality of criticism which the class reaches, and of this it is difficult, for practical reasons, to give evidence. I have a selection of written work which I will pass to anyone interested (the total volume of class written work exceeded 150 pieces); and for what it is worth, I have written a full analysis of Pudovkin's *Mother,* based on the critical method used in the class, and this will be published in the chapter on 'Film' in a book *Drama: Form and Performance,* which I am now planning.

The Battle course was in film criticism, but there is also the sociology of film, which I believe to be a valuable tutorial subject in itself. I think that a certain part of the training in criticism which I have described would be necessary even in the sociology course; the reasons for this are basically those set out in the discussion of the use of literature in other studies in my article 'Literature and History' in the last *Rewley House Papers.* The other material of the course would include, first, a discussion of the conditions of film-watching (an important subject, in which a good working basis is Mr Clifford Collins's formulation of physical and social factors – darkness; figures larger and louder than life; simultaneous appeal to eye and ear; the spectator's isolation within the audience; 'enclosure' and 'direct contact' in relation to the screen; shadows and 'finished' performances; all these conditions need investigation and assessment, and a class would be an excellent medium for trial, and for more complete and accurate description). Then, there would be the cinema as a social institution, for which some research material is already available; the economics of the film industry; and a study of the film as social expression, on the lines of Kracauer's *From Caligari to Hitler*, but carried out with a more rigorous idea of what is evidence. This last study has great potential value, and in the Soviet cinema of the twenties, the German of the same period, the French of the thirties, and the American since 1945, there are clear fields of work. I visualize studies of representative films alongside an analysis of social and political conditions; the correlation is not always obvious, but is always interesting. All approaches of this kind might be gathered together in a tutorial course on Film and the twentieth century.

Finally, as to administration, the Delegacy is affiliated to the British Film Institute, and can hire films at a preferential rate (roughly seven shillings for fifteen minutes). Books and records can also be borrowed from the Institute, which has a very valuable collection. The hiring charge makes film courses expensive, even where local authorities provide a projector free. This is an obstacle, but I think if the work shows itself to be valuable, it will be paid for. I should like, while I am on this point, to record my own gratitude to the Oxford Tutorial Classes Committee and its officers for their ready and practical help in the Battle experiment, especially since there were obvious and legitimate doubts about its value. I would say now that the experiment has succeeded, and that the work ought to be extended. The question of cost is hard; but I believe that we cannot afford to leave film to the councillor's one-and-ninepennies, or to resign like the tired critic. We cannot afford it, in terms of human cost, any more than we can afford to leave politics and economics to the newspapers, or literature to the Book Society, or science to the picture magazines.

Review of Drama from Ibsen to Eliot

by J.R. Williams
From: *The Tutors' Bulletin of Adult Education*, 91, June
1953, pp 18–20

One of the minor effects of Mr Raymond Williams's book is that it is a
stimulus to re-thinking on the problem of how to treat drama in our classes.
In the 'thirties some of us found it necessary to fight against the effects of
Terence Grayism, which bred the 'bad literature but good theatre' fallacy,
and at its worst produced such slogans as 'the script is the raw material
out of which the artist-producer creates the play'. The signs are that we
shall now have to wheel round and make a defence against extremism of
the opposite kind: the kind that says drama consists entirely of words.

From 'Reading and Criticism' we know what to expect from
Mr Williams, and this time he makes his position clearer by announcing
at the outset that his book is 'a working experiment in the application
of practical criticism methods to modern dramatic literature'. (Practical
criticism, he explains, began with Eliot, Richards, Leavis, Empson, and
Murry. He has forgotten Aristotle, Quintilian, Longinus, Dryden, Johnson,
Coleridge, Hazlitt, Arnold and a few others, but no matter.)

With this as the basis, we are not surprised to read, not merely that
'no separation of drama and literature is reasonable' (with which all but
mere theatre-addicts must agree) but more questionable statements such
as this:

> *'Literature, in its most general definition, is a means of communication*
> *of imaginative experience through certain written organisations of*
> *words. And drama, since it has existed in written plays, is clearly*
> *to be included under this general definition. A play, as a means of*
> *communication of imaginative experience, is as clearly the controlled*
> *product of an author – the control being exerted in the finalised*
> *organisation of words – as any other literary forms.'*

Up to a point, there is no legitimate quarrel with this conception.
The Bradleyite notion of 'character', for example, as something having
an existence independent of the verbal reality of the play, is scarcely to be
taken seriously nowadays. As Mr Williams says, 'character' and 'plot' are
abstractions from a whole – but he holds that the whole is a verbal one.
The trouble about this is not that . . . 'twere to consider too curiously, to

consider so', but that it is not to consider curiously enough. At this refined stage of analysis, 'words' themselves should be seen to be an abstraction – an abstraction from the author's total conception, which is a theatrical one, though it may contain (did contain in Elizabethan days) a preponderance of literary elements.

Mr Williams guards himself from an absolute denial of this ('performance is an essential condition of drama', he agrees) but he is unable really to accept it. For him the bounding line of a play is (or ought to be) a verbal one. To make the verbal element part of a larger conception is to deprive the author of 'control'. To this one can only say: 'too bad!' It is a deprivation from which Shakespeare was apparently content to suffer, for he had to rely on his actors not only to speak his verse according to a well-established tradition of declamation (so far the existence of 'control' must be conceded) but also to bring off, as parts of an expressive whole, dances, songs, shipwrecks, fencing-matches, battles, stranglings, tearings-out-of-eyes, grave-diggings and the like, over which pieces of business he (or at any rate his poetry) must have exercised very little 'control'. And how expressive – how artistically important – these non-verbal elements could be, is clear if one merely recollects the fencing-match in *Hamlet*, where the tension of the whole play – all the stress and struggle between the King and the Prince – gathers itself together in one superbly-conceived piece of mime, during the electrifying performance of which the poet is content merely to throw in such words as might have sufficed for a film-script (a very good film-script, that is).

Shakespeare is relevant here because, for most of us, Shakespeare is the norm. If Mr Williams were really consistent and bold, he would reject the Shakespearean method, as Yeats was not afraid to do when he found it unsuited to his own intense but narrow purposes. As it is, Shakespeare is the nigger in the woodpile who peeps out at every turn of the argument.

Take the question of 'naturalism', for instance. Mr Williams, though he admits, at one point, that naturalism is a convention like any other, nevertheless refers, elsewhere, to something called 'representation', as if assuming that some kind of literal reproduction of life is possible (Plato's mistake). The answer, of course, is that 'naturalism' represents a particular way of seeing life; and though you may like Clive Bell's definition, 'life as the green-grocer sees it', the important thing is that Shakespeare's vision (unlike that of Yeats) included the green-grocer's. Indeed if 'representation' be a sin, then Shakespeare was the most offending soul who ever lived. Similarly, though 'character' in a play is unquestionably part of its total pigmentation, and not something detachable and independent, it is of some importance that Shakespeare's colouring does appear to be related to that which the normal vision abstracts from life, and is not the expression of the emotions of an introvert (like Yeats) nor a means of release for a disordered personality (like Strindberg). Even Eliot, in his naive little essay on 'Poetry and Drama', holds that dramatic poetry must not lose 'that contact with the ordinary everyday world with which drama must come to terms.'

Mr Williams's book is, in fact, a fanatical plea for poetry in the theatre – poetry above everything and at the expense of everything. Everyone who fails to satisfy him in this respect goes down. Shaw, of course, is merely contemptible, Galsworthy apparently unmentionable, Chekov a suspicious character, Pirandello nothing but a camouflaged naturalist.

The laborious 'demonstrations' of the verbal inferiority of the rejected plays are mostly supererogatory. (Only Mr Williams's ear fails him when he says Shaw's nature-poetry in *Saint Joan* places him with the Georgians. It is pseudo-Synge.) Given the premises, most of this might have been taken for granted. But interesting questions still remain, as: whether art of any value can be made of meagre literary material cunningly placed amongst other material (what of the film, for instance?); whether, in Chekov, 'the poetry is in the action', as Schlegel said it was in comedy; whether comedy, which only occasionally 'lifts its voice' (and for which Mr Williams seems to have little taste) can achieve valuable effects other than practical ones. These are important questions for anyone who aspires to make a 'criticism of the naturalistic theatre', but for Mr Williams they do not appear to arise.

One of the oddest of the straws which show which way the wind of fanaticism blows is Mr Williams's objection to stage-directions in the published texts of modern plays. They belong to the technique of the novel rather than the drama, he says. True enough; but then the most chastely poetical drama becomes a novel when it is read (a Compton-Burnett novel, shall we say?). And no distinction is made between genuine stage-directions (to the actor, a legitimate guide; to the reader, an indication of what he would see when the play took on full life in the theatre) and pseudo-stage-directions such as Shaw often indulged in (which are parallel to the novelist's coming-before-the-invisible-curtain, and form no part of the real play). To Mr Williams, all stage-directions alike, it seems, are a mark of poetical impotence: an odd prejudice.

Most of us will find the book a fanatical overstatement of a by no means negligible case. The case is that literary standards are applicable in the theatre as much as anywhere else, in so far as theatrical art is verbal, and to this extent we must be as uncompromising as Mr Williams. But, since theatrical art is not entirely verbal, we shall, I think, in our exposition of theatrical art-forms, continue to hold it our duty to take cognizance of every element in them. Our range must obviously stop a long way short of pure mime, but 'impure' poetical dramatists like Shakespeare will continue to claim some of our attention.

Letters to the Editor: Drama from Ibsen to Eliot

From: *The Tutors' Bulletin of Adult Education*, 92, Autumn 1953, pp 29–30

Dear Sir,

At a point between his second and third descriptions of *Drama from Ibsen to Eliot* as fanatical, your reviewer (review-article writer, correspondent) finds what he calls –

> '*one of the oddest of the straws which show which way the wind (of fanaticism) blows*'.

This, he explains, is my 'objection to stage-directions in the published texts of modern plays'; and the fanaticism, apparently, lies in the fact that I make –

> '*no distinction ... between genuine stage-directions ... and pseudo-stage-directions such as Shaw often indulged in*'.

This is an odd straw indeed, for on page 158 of the book, I wrote, of a passage of Synge:– 'It is worth noting that the directions are real stage directions, and not pseudo-fictional comment;' and the same distinction is implicit on page 141 (your reviewer's point about Shaw) and on page 272. Since other reviewers have noted this distinction, and found it valuable, I cannot believe that my expression of it is wholly obscure. But (your reviewer continues):

> '*To Mr Williams, all stage directions alike, it seems are a mark of poetical impotence; an odd prejudice*'.

Odd is the word, but although the point is wholly relevant to the question of your reviewer's competence, I hesitate to ask for an apology. It is, I suppose, a writer's business to correct the more palpable and literal misrepresentations of his work; but with this kind of excited reviewer, an admission of an error of fact is, by common form nowadays, linked with an assertion (rather touching in the circumstances) that his 'main case still stands', or with the addition of a number of new, diverting opinions. Of that kind of bluster we have surely all had enough, while the essential critical discussion is better carried on in a more generally responsible atmosphere.

Yours sincerely,

Raymond Williams.

Mr J.R. Williams replies:–
I am content to leave it to your readers to judge whether it is reviewer or reviewed who is 'excited'. It is true I was lacking in alertness not to notice that Mr Raymond Williams had made (in a footnote) an admission that there can be such a thing as 'a real stage-direction' – an admission which (since it by implication recognizes the validity of the non-verbal elements in the drama) at once makes a puncture in his own case that good drama consists of words (dialogue). I do not find, however, that he gives this parenthetic admission any weight in his general argument, nor that he distinguishes *consistently* between genuine stage-directions and what he aptly calls 'pseudo-fictional comment'. His belief that he is making this distinction in the passages he cites from his book (pp 141 and 272, to which p 140 may be added) is itself an indication of his failure to see the need to distinguish between the legitimate and the illegitimate, not only as between author and author, but in the work of individual authors. He is discussing the crucial case of Shaw and, whilst rightly rejecting as irrelevant the pseudo-stage-directions, shows no sign of recognizing the genuine value of the passages which attempt to convey to the reader (if there must be readers) what will actually be seen in the theatre; but dismisses the entire method as 'eccentric': in short, matches Shaw's muddled practice and wilder theory with a muddled and bewildered analysis. This may look like poetic justice, but it is scarcely criticism.

And now sir, may I make two points of my own (one of which could be relied on to 'divert' Mr Raymond Williams) regarding my original article? Firstly, 'practical' in line 19 of page 20, should have read 'poetical'.

Secondly, you made two cuts in the article. If, as I understand, this was purely for reasons of space, could I ask you now to find room for one of the deleted passages, since it relates to a question which is of importance to anyone who is concerned to assess the value of the critical 'demonstrations' which are from time to time offered us in the name of 'Practical-Criticism'? My final paragraph ran as follows:–

Mr Williams is frankly of the nose-to-the-words-on-the-page school. Now in this book he writes of Norwegian, Swedish, Russian, German, Italian, and French dramas. A word of Russian or Italian here and there permits us to suppose that he reads them all in the original (and with an adequate sensitiveness to the subtleties of inflexion of each language). But the quotations (with the exception of those from Anouilh) are in English. For whom, then, is the book written, and in what sense are these judgments 'demonstrated' from texts? For a member of a school which attaches so much importance to its own feeling for verbal nuance to admit the validity of a single line of translation, is fatal. To make the copious use of it that Mr Raymond Williams makes, is to suggest that public hara-kiri *is part of the code of honour of this new order of* samurai.

Text and Context

From: *The Tutors' Bulletin of Adult Education*, 93/94,
December 1953 – March 1954, pp 19–22

It is probable that at any given time the slogans in common use in controversy confuse as much as they define. *Practical criticism* is a good example, its mode of operation closely resembling *the free world* or *drama is action*. The substance of the controversies in which each of these phrases is used tends to be hidden by the verbal organisation. Nobody supposes that drama is not action; the real controversy is about what kind of action. The political argument is about kinds of freedom, and kinds of law. The argument in criticism is not whether it should be *practical* – in its most obvious sense all criticism has to be – but about the kind of practice. It is ironical, looking back, to realise that I.A. Richards, who gave the phrase *practical criticism* currency, has hardly ever practised as a critic. The fact should give us pause as we sweat in our controversial deadlock.

Now to anyone who has written criticism – anyone, that is, who has tried to give relevant reasons for a judgment – the idea that there can be controversy about the position of the text will surely seem farcical. If the text is not central, one may be writing admirably about other things – oneself, the contemporary situation, the Industrial Revolution – but one will hardly be writing criticism of the work in question. Yet the real argument is not about this, but about what the slogan *the text is central* means. The physiological flourishes reveal this.

Keeping one's eye on the words on the page is light blue for the dark blue of *nose to the text*. Since nobody can read with his nose on a page, the users of the latter slogan feel they have made a point. What they mean, however – at least when they are serious – is that you cannot read any text unless and until you have also assembled its context. This is very reasonable, and I do not think those who practise, rather than argue, under the former slogan would deny it. The real argument, it comes to be seen, is the difficult one of the nature of context, and of its relation to the text.

The method by which I try to write criticism, and in which I try to train my students, recognises that criticism is a social procedure. An individual judgment is necessary, but one argues it in such a way that others, going over the same ground, may check in detail the way in which it was reached, and offer, again in detail, modification, amendment, or dissent. Since the text is the common ground, every judgment must be returnable to it in the short or the long run. This is, I think, the prerequisite for criticism as a liberal discipline. But it is also necessary to recognise that one is never, finally, *alone* with the text; nor is the text alone, but is always in relation with other texts and other facts. *Homo textualis*, indeed, is a fiction.

The difficulty, in practice, is both to recognise this, and yet maintain the essential discipline. It is, in fact, finding what other facts are relevant. There is always a tension between text and context, and we can, in writing or teaching, either draw from the tension, or succumb to it. In teaching, the problem is one requiring considerable tact. Does one *introduce* the text?; that is to say, put the context in before the text appears. Or does one first present the text, and then, from one's consciousness of its difficulties, or its margins, extend into context? In practice, I normally follow the latter method, because I think it makes it easier to ensure that the extension into context is relevant and useful. Ultimately, everything other than the text is context, but to practice under this principle would be absurd. The best way of selecting what parts of the context are useful in making judgment is, it seems to me, one's immediate awareness of what the text needs. As a matter of practical teaching, this method also seems to be useful; for I at least find it easier to learn something when I have realised, or have been shown, that I need to know it. Thus, if one is reading *Troilus and Criseyde*, it may be easier, and as an educational process more significant, if one goes to the mysteries of courtly love because one has been puzzled about the behaviour of Troilus; rather than feeling it necessary to prime oneself in courtly love before the poem can be read at all. I do not want to be dogmatic about this, but I think one is more easily aware of literature as an activity valuable in itself (not necessarily for itself) if, *when studying literature*, one goes to the context because the text sends one there. I have recently spent some months studying the construction of Greek theatres in the time of Sophokles, and have been taken in one direction to archaeological records, in another to the degrees of corruption among Alexandrine scholiasts and in another to the cults of Dionysus and their relation to the initiation ceremonies of Australian aborigines. I have found all this enjoyable, but I doubt if the journey would have been worth the carriage if I had not begun because I was interested in the text of the *Antigone*, and wanted to know in detail how it was performed. In teaching, one would hardly range so far, but I found, when teaching the play recently, that my students only wanted the context in so far as it made more clear, and more present, the text in which their interest had been engaged. In general, for students of literature, this will always tend to be so.

A class is single, and its emphasis must always be definite. I am always glad to see classes in, say, the history of the theatre, the psychology or social position of the artist, the anthropological origins of poetry, the social history of a period of literature, and so on. But my own classes are in the reading of particular works of literature, and my use of context is confined to problems that arise from that reading (whether to the students, or to me, or to others I know of, because any of us can fail to realise that there is a real problem of context in some apparently simple text).

Context includes society, belief, convention, conditions of publication or performance, biography: all will be approached, as and when one's own reading, or someone else's, has shown such an approach to be necessary, within reasonable limits of emphasis and time. Context also includes language, and here, except with contemporary or recent texts, there can hardly fail to be extension. One makes judgments about language (written or spoken) because it is the medium of the performance, and the result cannot be judged without real awareness of it. For works written in one's own language, in one's own time, one can make, in co-operation with others, reasonably definite points about the way in which the language is used, and these are important in the overall judgment. For works not in one's own language, or written in some period in which one was not alive, one is no longer, in this respect, one's own context; every text has to be supplemented by context in the formal sense. The context one can supply, by research, will, like context in any other field, be limited; and so will one's judgments be limited; but nevertheless, *the judgments are inevitably made*. Whether the text is Chaucer or Ibsen, the problems are the same, and all differences are merely of degree. One reads the text as well as one can, with the help of context in the specialised sense of language: that is to say, all one can assemble of the original language, of studies of it, of translations, commentaries, and paraphrase. Nobody who has done this, as in my work on the modern drama I was forced to do, is likely to underestimate its difficulties, or its essential limitations. But even in very difficult cases, it is possible, with care, to assemble sufficient context to make judgments possible and useful, although one never doubts that with further extension of the context the process of modification, amendment, or dissent – which is inherent in all criticism – will continue. The real difficulty comes in the communication of these judgments, and here, in foreign works, the difference becomes so wide as to be one of kind. The person one is addressing, whether he be student or general reader, cannot be assumed to know the original language. When I once quoted Anouilh in French, in a book (I did so because there was then no English translation, and to have made my own would have involved difficulties of copyright) I was at once accused of snobbery. When I recently read to a class a chorus of the *Antigone*, in Greek, two people left to catch an early bus. But is the alternative to deal with no foreign literature, and with no English earlier than, say, 1650? I think one has to recognise that there are degrees of recoverability in works outside one's own language and time. For my part, I am prepared to deal with foreign literature so long as I am satisfied that I am sufficiently aware of the context to make, and keep, the judgments relevant. In written criticism, if a translation has to be used for general communication, I take the original text, with a literal translation if I do not know the language well, and then read the available translations, in different languages wherever possible, comparing them with each other, and with either the original or the literal translation. Then, for exposition, the translation one has chosen becomes, for this immediate purpose, the text, with the most difficult of all cases of context. Every judgment from this text has to be checked with the context, and, where necessary, amended from it, by oneself or others. In teaching, one cannot always prepare so thoroughly but a degree of similar preparation (at least checking difficult translations) is usually necessary. Because this is only, essentially, a difficult instance of the perennial problem of text and context, I think in fact most people accept it as a reasonable procedure. The alternative is merely negative; and, further, one must not make a maximum of the kind of judgment one is restricted to when context is at its most difficult, and then attempt no other kind of judgment when the text more nearly stands alone.

To examine this whole problem fully is outside the scope of this note; but I wanted to say something about it, among colleagues, for reasons that I think will be understood.

Section 4:
Adult Education

Williams sometimes expressed impatience at the gap he saw between the work of adult education on the ground, the stimulus of growth in students, its real meaning, and the prolonged, sometimes sterile, sometimes acrimonious discussions about its organisation and finances. For him the politics of adult education too often bore little relationship to the doing of the work in the classroom. Nonetheless he accepted the necessity for such discussions – even if he disliked much of their ethos – as well as consideration of classroom practice. He privileged the latter and intervened in the former by means of his experience in the latter. His interest in the organisation of words and the difficulties he faced with his explorations of culture led him into historical semantics. This technique, which helped him produce *Culture and Society* and, many years later, *Keywords*, was developed with his students.[1] It was the means he used to analyse controversies about university adult education. This can be seen from the first three articles in this section.

In the immediate post-war years university extra-mural departments expanded, partially through providing more short courses. The possibilities of a consequent dilution of quality were already being questioned in the 1940s. In his book *The English Universities and Adult Education*, published in 1951, Sidney Raybould, Professor of Adult Education at the University of Leeds, developed a powerful and detailed critique of prevailing trends on the grounds that shorter could well mean worse. He questioned the trajectory of university adult education and urged universities to concentrate on three year tutorial courses. These provided the conditions for students to reach university level and allowed university standards of teaching to be applied. His position was debated at the 1951 WEA conference and provoked extensive controversy in the adult education journals.

Advocates of working-class education (amongst whom Raybould himself was numbered) as well as those who simply wished to increase enrolments, or could see no magic in courses of three years' duration, criticised this approach on a number of grounds. They were particularly worried that an insistence on length and an inflexible attitude to written work would drive away working-class students and that the conventional academic, subject-oriented approach needed adaptation if classes were to attract more trade unionists.[2]

The debates were extended, complex and convoluted. Williams's approach was characteristically low-key, indirect and thoughtful. His response was to go to the heart of the matter – for him the words. In **Figures and Shadows** he pursues the history of the educational ladder analogy which haunted his work in the 1950s and which is developed in *Culture and Society*. He relates the hierarchy and individualism evoked by the image to the context, 'reaching from the gutter' and the subsidiary analogy, 'winnowing out the chaff', to bring to the surface the social divisiveness contained in the success–failure signified by the word. Relationships between individuals are changed by education; between classes they are maintained. His sub-text is that a mechanical application of university standards would militate further against collectivism and solidarity in adult education.

Williams next addressed **Standards**, again approaching the issue through the shifting meanings of the word. His notes on its use as part of strategies of linguistic appropriation and imperialism, intended to disarm opponents, can be directly related to the debates in adult education: 'one gets the impression that one would be openly convicted of laxity or irresponsibility if one did not believe in *values* or in *standards* . . .' Yet the current uses of the word are imprecise and unanchored. The university itself is a contested concept. The onus, he urges, is on the proponents of 'university standards' to show what they mean by this invocation. Once again Williams's writing is useful both generally and specifically. **Standards** and the third piece on **Class and Classes** were both later developed as entries in *Keywords*.

Williams talks of 'a complicated kind of adult education politics', referring readers to Raybould's *Trends in English Adult Education* in his 1959 piece, **Going on Learning**. He accepts that the issues require discussion and action, 'but I wish more people discussed them in terms of the absolute necessity of an expanding culture'. Adult education can play a role in this; at the moment its politics are inadequate and insufficiently reflect its values and practice. He asserts the continuing relevance and underlying vigour of adult education. He is optimistic about its future, for its whole spirit, 'most admirably expressed by the WEA at its best, is of growth towards a genuinely common culture, an educated and participating democracy'. Embodied in a new generation on the left, renewed assertion of the democratic values of adult education would dispel the fog of prejudice and fatigue which threatened to arrest progress.

This is the mood of the valedictory **An Open Letter to WEA Tutors.** The message is straightforward: 'I may be leaving you in body – I am still with you in spirit, ready to help when called upon'. Adult education is a difficult, at times a depressing vocation: it is as necessary, relevant, urgent in 1961 as it was when the WEA was established in 1903. But in **The Common Good**, a talk given at the 1961 conference of the National Institute of Adult Education, Williams sounds a warning. Unless adult education can wrench itself from its present mental moorings, its self conception as special, almost superior, occupying a protected minority enclave, unless it can determine to broaden its appeal and its territory its purchase will be increasingly limited. It must become part of the mainstream of society by grasping the opportunities created by the communications revolution.[3]

The reviews grouped under the heading 'Reflections on Adult Education' find Williams taking stock. In **Sensible People** he finds himself risking 'the isolation of the heretic' by embracing the tradition of independent working-class education, a process no doubt deepened by his reading of Bill Craik's history of the Central Labour College, established in 1909 as an alternative for working people to Ruskin College and the Oxford University–WEA tradition. R.H. Tawney, 1880–1962, the subject of Williams's 1965 *Tribune* article, was a tutorial class pioneer and for many years President of the WEA. During Williams's tenure in adult education he continued his involvement as Vice-President of the Association. **Different Sides of the Wall** discloses Williams reflecting again on the nature of pedagogy and the relationship between his work in adult education and his teaching at Cambridge. The last short extract demonstrates his continuing enthusiasm for the Open University, of which he was an early and continuing advocate.

The final part of this section takes us to the end of the 1970s and Williams's interviews with *New Left Review*. The emphasis here differs from his analysis whilst working in adult education. He addresses the conflict which for many years divided adult education between, on the one side, the partnership between the universities and the WEA, and, on the other, the National Council of Labour Colleges, which believed in independent working-class education, refused state aid and condemned collaboration with the universities as purveyors of incorporation and bourgeois ideology.[4] The statement that the balance between these principles was still being fought out when Williams became an adult educator is correct. But, in retrospect, the advantages in terms of resources, expertise and respect which the universities possessed had already carried the field. Williams himself seemed to take little interest in the NCLC whilst he worked in adult education. Although a distinctive part of working-class life for three decades, it was in real difficulties by the 1950s and was taken over by the TUC in 1964. Despite the cogency of the comments on the limitations of university–WEA provision, the conditions for any healthy independent alternative have not existed since the 1940s.

Williams last reflections in **Adult Education and Social Change**,[5] written in the early eighties, reiterate many of the concerns expressed earlier. He repeats the need for adult education to rid itself of any missionary ethic, to rededicate itself to social change. It must, he argues, recharge its pedagogy. It must provide the tools for understanding not received understandings. The educational deficit, not only in the adult population but in higher education itself, remains, despite all the changes that have occurred since the 1940s. And if adult education is to contribute to social change then it will need to reorient itself and examine and seek to enrich popular culture and the quality of life in contemporary Britain.

Notes and References
1. See the discussion in the introduction to R. Williams, *Keywords*, Fontana, 1976. The help given by students is acknowledged on p 26.

Border Country

2. There was also some suspicion of Raybould, 1904– 1977, on the left because of the stance he had taken on 'objectivity' during the disputation between left and right in the Oxford Delegacy. See Roger Fieldhouse, *Adult Education and the Cold War: Liberal values under siege 1946–51*, Leeds Studies in Adult and Continuing Education, University of Leeds, 1985. Alan O'Connor, *Raymond Williams: Writing, culture, politics*, Blackwell, 1989, p 34, n 16, seems to consider the 'cold war' and 'standards' controversies as one. They were connected but distinct.

   Perhaps the best discussion of the 'standards' controversy is John Blyth, *English University Adult Education 1908–1958*, Manchester University Press, 1983, pp 249–64.

3. The reference to Dennis Potter relates to his book *The Glittering Coffin*, Gollancz, 1961.

4. For the background see, for example, A.J. Corfield, *Epoch in Workers' Education*, WEA, 1969; J.P.M. Millar, *The Labour College Movement*, NCLC Publishing Society, 1979; B. Simon, ed., *The Search for Enlightenment: Adult education and the working class in the twentieth century*, Lawrence and Wishart, 1990; 2nd edn NIACE, 1992.

5. This is the text of a lecture delivered on 17 September 1983 at a commemoration service for Tony McLean 1911–82; see pp 255–64.

Figures and Shadows

From: *The Highway*, February 1954, pp 169–72

I was listening recently to a broadcast report of the political conference in Bermuda: the announcer, in tones of classic authority, reported that Sir Winston Churchill had argued that there might be 'a New Look in the Kremlin', but that the American President had replied that 'the New Look might only be the Old Look with a stitch in it'. I was pondering this illuminating exchange, and wondering, heretically, if these dignified gentlemen in fact arrived in their aeroplanes, stood to attention for the military bands, inspected the tight-lipped guards of honour, and then went into a private room to say things like this to each other, when I recalled a remark of Mr Richard Crossman that one must always understand the proceedings of Cabinets and similarly august meetings in terms of one's own experience of the humblest committee meeting. If the broadcast report was at all accurate, one certainly had some relevant comparative experience. One has sat through discussions, in conference and committee, and read controversies in print, with the same awe and the same wonder. Awe brings the body to attention, but the mind may be elsewhere, in its own habits. We all have social responsibilities, main and marginal, and our functions correspond. Even a hermit has a social function, in that he may emerge from time to time and commit a stimulating indiscretion. Other trades, other habits, and I know myself, as I listen to controversies, I draw back quietly to my own trade, the use of words, and take notes. The result, in all kinds of controversy, may be useful; and since, as it happens, most of the controversies I hear are educational, the unity of theme soon allows one to try to organize the results. The first heading obviously must be Analogies, of the order of the President's stitch. One might compile, it seems to me, a sort of Natural History of Analogies, and have it printed, and then shuffle it among the papers at committee or conference. In education, my first three entries would be: the Ladder, Levels and Standards. Already, on these, I have done a certain amount of investigation. As an example of the kind of entry one might produce, I will set out my notes on Ladder; if they seem at all useful, Levels and Standards could follow, and of course beyond them the list could be greatly extended.

1. The Educational Ladder

The originator of this analogy appears to be T.H. Huxley (1825–95). In an address on *Technical Education*, delivered to the Working Men's Club and

207

Institute, December 1, 1877 (reprinted in *Science and Culture*, Macmillan, 1882, pp 65–85), he said:

> 'When I was a member of the London School Board, I said, in the course of a speech, that our business was to provide a ladder, reaching from the gutter to the university, along which every child in the three kingdoms should have the chance of climbing as far as he was fit to go. This phrase was so much bandied about at the time, that to say truth I am rather tired of it; but I know of no other which so fully expresses my belief, not only about education in general, but about technical education in particular.'

A few associated sentences make the use clearer:

> 'A small percentage of the population is born with that most excellent quality, a desire for excellence, or with special aptitudes of some sort or another; Mr Galton tells us that not more than one in four thousand may be expected to attain distinction, and not more than one in a million some share of that intensity of instinctive aptitude, that burning thirst for excellence, which is called genius. Now the most important object of all educational schemes is to catch these exceptional people, and turn them to account for the good of society. No man can say where they will crop up; like their opposites, the fools and knaves, they appear sometimes in the palace, and sometimes in the hovel .... Whatever (it) might cost, depend upon it the investment would be a good one. I weigh my words when I say that if the nation could purchase a potential Watt, or Davy, or Faraday, at the cost of a hundred thousand pounds down, he would be dirt cheap at the price. It is a mere commonplace and everyday piece of knowledge, that what these three men did has produced untold millions of wealth, in the narrowest economical sense of the word. Therefore, as the sum and crown of what is to be done for technical education, I look to the provision of a machinery for winnowing out the capacities and giving them scope.'

Comment

> (a) 'And Jacob went out from Beersheba and went toward Haran. And he dreamed, and behold a ladder set up on the earth, and the top of it reached to heaven: and behold the angels of God ascending and descending on it.' (Genesis *xxviii*, 10-12.)

The educational ladder is of the type derived from a figure in another context, rather than from a material process. Here it is the substitution that is interesting: *university* for *heaven*, and *geniuses* for *the angels of God* (who by the way both ascended and descended).

(b) The idea of educating persons of special ability could have been expressed, either in its own direct terms, or, if analogy were required, in terms of *taking them up a hill* (e.g. Donne's 'huge hill' of Truth. Huxley uses, later, 'a hand is held out to help him along any path'), or, if the implication of *higher* and *climbing* was not required, in terms of leading them into any special place. It is significant that *ladder* should have been chosen, and become popular, because the obvious fact about a ladder is that only one person can go up it at a time. *The educational ladder* is significant of a conception of education which is highly selective and, in effect, largely exclusive. Note the subsidiary analogy: 'machinery for winnowing out'. Grain is winnowed, and what is left is chaff, not other kinds of grain. The analogy enforces a conception of human beings in which differences of degree are made into differences of kind; and the use of *ladder* confirms the conception of a hierarchy. This is not only educational: 'every working lad can feel . . . that there is no barrier, except such as exists in the nature of things, between himself and whatever place in the social organization he is fitted to fill'. Society is similarly hierarchic, and one climbs (the shift in the analogy is unconscious) to the university and to a 'place in the social organization'. Thus, 'giving scope to the (intellectual) capacities' is made synonymous with 'promoting a career'. The idea of *purchasing* such a talent, and the justification in terms of profit ('untold millions'), is naturally associated with this.

(c) To use the analogy of *the educational ladder* is, it seems, to commit oneself to:

(i)   the idea of education as highly selective and largely exclusive: 'the most important object of all educational schemes is to catch these exceptional people';
(ii) the idea that intellectual distinction involves climbing, through the several stages of a hierarchic system, which is not only intellectual but also social;
(iii) the idea, at least in terms of Huxley's argument, that education is to be justified in cash terms, which in its turn will obviously influence selection of those who are to be given their chance to climb.

In the present educational system, a means of justifying our system of secondary education ('winnowing', and leaving the chaff); of justifying the argument that university adult education for working-class people is a false ideal ('if they had been any good, they would have been sent up the ladder'); of sustaining the belief (quite strong in some places) that adult education exists to pick out adult scholars for the universities; of justifying a general policy of restriction in education ('caution'), because everyone knows that if too many people try to go up a ladder it will break, or they will start fighting. In the social system, the tensions, as yet uncharted, of a man from a working-class home, who has climbed the ladder, and is asked to look back into the 'gutter'. Further, the apparently natural linking of intellectual distinction with economic advantage: 'if you cannot climb, it is absurd of you to expect to enjoy the view from the roof'. Finally, and perhaps most serious, if the idea of the ladder is always there, the effect on those who have not climbed: the encouragement of a feeling that they might, *as human beings*, have failed.

Counter-analogies and Embroidery

It was of course asked, eventually, if in addition to the narrow ladder outside, there was not also a lift, rather quicker and more commodious, for those already inside. Because a ladder must have something to lean against, whose is the house? Finally, when the figure was extended to the giving of economic opportunity: if a man is to go up the ladder (making money) who is to hold it while he climbs: 'the worker holds the ladder for the boss to climb'.

Huxley, we have seen, was tired of the phrase seventy-six years ago, but its use is still general. It expresses so well the assumptions about a necessarily unequal society, about education being something to which (like help in distress, with a means test) you have to prove your right, and about the human being as no more than an entry in a competitive system. There are many alternatives, but perhaps the most immediate is an explosive comment of Carlyle's: 'as if the first function of a government were not to impart the gift of thinking'. (In the full *Natural History*, refer now, immediately, to the entry under *Gift*. And remember of course that the compiler of these notes is a very partial person, who prefers certain ideas to others.)

Standards

From: *The Highway*, 46, December 1954, pp 43–6

Our modern word *standard* comes from two sources: first, from the Latin *extendere* = *stretch out*, which gave us our modern word *extension*, and which gave us, in the thirteenth century, *estaundart* and *standardus*; second, from *stand* = *to be erect*, which produced the noun *stander*, now commonly spelled *standard* (as in *standard lamp*) by confusion with the word from the other source. *Estaundart* and *standardus* meant flag, as still in *Royal Standard*. This is a physical description: the flag is *stretched out* from its pole. Usually, it was the *King's standard*; and in battles, where this was raised (the act of raising helped the confusion with *stander*) the place served as a centre of reference and command. From this, *standard* derived its sense of *a thing one refers back to; an authority; an agreed place to which one goes*. The term came to be widely used for weights and measures, like the *standard foot*; this kind of use began in the fifteenth century. At the same time, it was extended to other fields; *standard* came to mean 'an authoritative exemplar of correctness or perfection'. Thus we find, in the fifteenth century, mention of a *standard book*, in Alchemy.

The next main development came in the nineteenth century. In the 1850's, for reasons to be found in the changing relations of social classes, and in certain tendencies of an industrial society, we hear for the first time of *Standard English*: a particular use of the common language is designated as 'an authoritative exemplar of correctness'. Then, in the 1870's, comes the verb *standardize*, which is scientific in origin (standardizing the conditions of an experiment). The verb is then widely used in industry, of spare parts, screws, tools, etc. It expresses a particular idea of efficient production; but then, on the other hand, it acquires a derogatory implication: 'certain things can't be standardized' (people, feelings, ideas). Thus we can now talk of *standardizing* methods of teaching as a bad thing; but of maintaining *standards* in teaching as a good thing. At the same time, *standard* becomes a term for precise educational grading. In elementary education, from the 1870's, certain definite attainments in reading, writing and arithmetic are laid down, as *standards* (= *some definite degree of a quality*). The classes aiming at these standards are then called *Standards* Two to Six, in the schools. From this use, the idea of a *standard* is affected by the idea of a hierarchy; the *educational ladder* is contemporary with this new use, and one goes *up through the standards*. *Standards*, in this use, becomes like *grade, degree,* and *class*; the latter used socially and educationally as

211

a term of *grading*, and used also, more neutrally, as a term of *grouping*, with the question of grade tactfully or necessarily omitted.

At about this same time, or perhaps a little earlier, we get the new phrase *Standard of Life*; first used, it seems, in trade union activity, in relation to wages. By the 1890's this has become the *standard of living*, with which we are all politically and economically familiar.

This is the historical scheme of the word, but all the senses listed are active in contemporary English. When a word has more than one sense, it is normally defined by context: the ropes holds *fast*; the rope is *loose*; the woman is *fast*; the woman plays *fast and loose*. We are all quite at ease with this. And many writers, when they use *standard*, are careful to give it a precise meaning. In any activity, a standard can be agreed, and in some activities reference back to it is clear and useful. Where there can be precise measurement, of any kind, the term has no difficulties. But where such measurement is difficult, the figurative complexity of the word has its dangers, to the user.

A Noun With Three Tenses

One can briefly illustrate this with *standard of living*. It is probable that economists know what they mean by this phrase; but it is also used by quite common persons. One might say that *standard*, in this phrase, has the highly unorthodox property, for a noun, of possessing three tenses. There is *Standard Past*, in which we consult our authorities about the necessary minimum to maintain life. We look back at this *standard*, and we measure whether people are above or below it. I think *Standard of Life* was first used in this sense, in relation to the campaign for a minimum wage. In any case, it is *Standard Past*, as in all cases of weights and measures: the standard has been set, and we look back and consult it. Then, quite different, there is *Standard Present*. We investigate, and measure, actual aspects of living; we generalize from them, take a mode or an average, and are then in a position to talk of the existing *standard of living*. This is *Standard Present*; we do not refer back to any determined standard; we measure things as they are. Finally, there is *Standard Future*. The others come from *standard* as an agreed measure, or as a definite degree of a quality; this one comes from *standard* as a flag – we bear our standards before us; we aim, through a movement, to attain certain standards; we set up an ideal. We are fighting, in fact, for a *proper standard of living*: either the old measures, or the existing degrees, are inadequate, and we will scrap them and make new; or, there is something to aim at, to follow. All these uses, of course, are quite proper, but there are times when a discussion goes wrong because a speaker shifts unconsciously from one to the other. And, in *standard of living*, the use has not been made any easier by the extension from the reference to material standards to a reference to other standards: *standard of living* is now often used to describe the whole life of a society, in the sense of 'the quality of living' (*living* as opposed to *maintaining life*). We need, at least, to be clear which use we intend. Nor is the matter to be settled by reference to a dictionary, as so many people are in the habit of thinking. Of *standard of living*, the definition in the OED (the standard of all standard dictionaries) is: 'the view prevailing in a community or class with regard to the minimum of material comfort with which it is reasonable to be content' (i.e., Standard Past). Yet Standard Present is perhaps the most commonly used, and Standard Past perhaps the least.

Standards is sometimes an ordinary plural; that is, a number of agreed measures or definite degrees. But *standards* is also what I call a Nineteenth Century Plural. By this I mean a plural that is not really a number of separate, single things, but that operates, essentially, as a thing in itself. Another example is *Values*; for while *value* is a very useful word, to indicate a measure of worth, *values* (usually with a capital letter) is not always a number of such measures, but sometimes a quality, often an abstraction, which is commonly used without further definition. A *concern for values* is a very common phrase; but it is not common to find it used with any precise reference to actual measures of worth. *Values*, rather, operates as a blanket word, always with the sense of approval, but often without any clear indication of what is being approved. *Standards*, commonly, is in the same case. One gets the impression that one would be openly convicted of laxity or irresponsibility if one did not believe in *values* or in *standards*; but it is something quite different from believing in modes, averages, pounds shillings and pence, or the metric system. Cardinal Newman could use *standards* with some precision, because of his whole philosophical position:

> 'There is an ideal perfection in ... *various subject-matters, towards which individual instances are seen to rise, and which are the standards for all instances whatever.*'

If one can believe this, the use of *standards* or *values* has a clear meaning. Otherwise, however, the words are like *Culture* (also a nineteenth-century abstraction), which you either have or have not; if you ask what it is, that is a pretty clear indication that you have not got it. It is a nice procedure, throughout, but it is a great mistake to be awed by it. *Standards* is used again and again, in public discussions, as a bullying word; and, when it is so used, our reaction should follow the traditional recommendation for treating bullies. We will find, in many cases, that a speaker, when challenged, can show us what he means by *standards*; show us, rather than tell us, for the concrete is where standards are lived and agreed. In other cases, we shall do right to disregard him; as we are right when we doze at conferences when a speaker begins a complicated exercise in Nineteenth Century Plurals. Nor shall we be satisfied, immediately, if some adjective is added: *Western values; University standards*. Western society is a fact, although complex, and containing disagreements; universities are facts, although again complex and containing variations and controversies. We shall need to be sure what actual selection the adjective embodies, in each particular case; and also to know whether *Standards* (in the senses defined above) is *Past* (an agreed measure), *Present* (a taken mode or average) or

Future (an ideal). By the time we have got this far, it is probable that we will be discussing actual issues, which as a rule (though not always) is the object of the exercise.

The *process* of valuation, and the *process* of agreeing standards, are indeed to be cherished. We live as we choose, and we form relationships, and associations, by agreeing (often tacitly) our choices. The discussion of standards can promote control, and consciousness; but this very discussion can be hindered by failure to understand the complex operation of the word that we take as our title.

Class and Classes

From: *The Highway*, 47, January 1956, pp 84–6

The English word *class* is derived from the Latin *classis*, which meant, literally, a *calling-together*, or a *summoning of the multitude*. According to tradition, it was Servius Tullius (?578–534 BC), the sixth Roman king, who, for military purposes, divided the Roman people into five *classes*, according to property owned. With 100,000 *asses* a man in the first class; with 12,000 in the fifth. *Homo quintae classis* – *a fifth-class man* – came to be used later as a general phrase rather like our *tenth-rate* or *rag-tag-and-bobtail*. *Classis* came to be used of any division, and was often specifically applied to a naval fleet.

The first appearance of the word *class* in English was in fact in the sense of a *fleet*, but there is only one instance of this. The word became generally familiar in relation to Roman history, and is glossed in this sense, by Blount, in 1656. But, other than in this special reference to Rome, it was not the sense of *class* as a social division or grouping which first established itself in English. It was, rather, another sense which still survives: *class* as a group in education, which is fully established by the seventeenth century. Thus Wood, in 1691, writes of going 'through the usual classes of Logick and Philosophy' at Oxford; and at Harvard, in 1684, a teacher is assigned to 'ye class of ye Sophimores'. In 1741 we hear of 'boys of the upper classes', but this refers to their place in school, and not to their social position.

It is, indeed, as late as 1772 that we hear, for the first time, of *class* in the social sense, and then it is in a title which now has a familiar ring: 'Observations on the Causes of the Dissoluteness which reigns among the lower classes of the people'. Before this time, when writers looked down (at dissoluteness or its like) other phrases had to be used. From the fourteenth century there had been the *comen*, or *commun*, or *commune*, and later the *commons*, the *common herd*, and the *vulgar*. These terms were not necessarily contemptuous (apart from *herd*), but indicated the *common people* (itself first used as a phrase early in the eighteenth century) as distinct from those of rank or dignity. Contemptuous uses, however, were soon frequent. *Order*, which from 1300 had been 'a rank of the community', attached itself in the eighteenth century to *low*, which had been similarly used to *commun* and *vulgar*. In 1712 Steele wrote in the *Spectator* of a 'place of no small Renown for the Gallantry of the lower Order of Britons, namely, the Bear Garden'; and Fielding, in 1749, in *Tom Jones*, wrote of 'the controversies that arise among the lower orders of the English Gentry, at Horse-races, Cock matches, and other public places'.

These are the first uses of *lower orders* that have been traced, but the phrase joined with *lower classes* to pass into its long nineteenth-century summer. There was also, again in Fielding, the *lowest degree*.

From the end of the eighteenth century, the modern structure of *class*, as a word indicating social division, began to be built up. Burke, in *Thoughts on French Affairs* (1791), writes of the 'higher classes' (the first use of this kind I have traced). *Upper classes* followed in 1826. *Lower orders*, it seems, is still at this time making its way. Burke uses it, without comment, but in 1796 we find a 'skittle-ground filled with people of the lower order (according to fashionable denomination)'. In 1822, Cobbett writes: 'I will make your Aristocratic insolence bend before the superior mind of the "Lower Orders"; but in the same year the phrase is used quite naturally, in a sermon establishing a Savings Bank at Bury: 'the young women among the lower orders'. Meanwhile (in the earliest uses so far traced) Robert Owen has written of the *working classes*: 'the poor and working classes of Great Britain and Ireland have been found to exceed 12 millions of persons' (1813); and 'Two memorials on behalf of the Working Classes' (1816). And as early as 1795 we have *middle class* (Thomas Gisborne: *Enquiry into the Duties of Men in the Higher Rank and Middle Classes of Society in Great Britain*). In 1830, the Birmingham Political Union declares 'that the rights and interests of the middle and lower classes of the people are not efficiently represented in the Commons House of Parliament'. In 1831, in a speech, Brougham declares: 'By the people ... I mean the middle classes, the wealth and intelligence of the country, the glory of the British name'.

The terms became established, but their definition continued. Borrow, in *The Bible in Spain* (1843) writes: 'Several of these were of the middle class, shopkeepers and professional men'. Cockburn, in 1844, comments on what are 'termed *the* working-classes, as if the only workers were those who wrought with their hands'. In 1890 (*Act 53 and 54 Vict.*) we learn that 'the provision of section eleven of the Housing of the Working Classes Act, 1885 ... shall have effect as if the expression 'working classes' included all classes of persons who earn their livelihood by wages or salaries'. The attendant controversy about who was a *worker* or *workman* had been proceeding for some time.

Class, in the nineteenth century, became a focal word, often of strong feeling. There is not only Mr Gladstone, in 1886, writing that 'on these and many other great issues the classes have fought uniformly on the wrong side, and have uniformly been beaten'. This use (the contrast of *the classes* and *the masses*) was always a rather special one: the *classes* pure, neither *middle* nor *lower* nor *working*. More general, to indicate the word's focusing power, is the development of a number of derived words. Emerson, in 1856, wrote of *bitter class-legislation*. *The Times*, in 1861, commented:

> 'The word class, *when employed as an adjective, is too often intended to convey some reproach. We speak of 'class prejudices' and 'class legislation', and inveigh against the selfishness of class-interests.'*

Class-consciousness does not seem to have appeared earlier than a translation of Marx's *Capital*, in 1887. *Class-conscious* followed it, in the early years of our own century; but *class-conflict* and *class-war* do not seem to have been used until after the 1914–1918 war. But the descriptive *working-classes* had already, in mid-Victorian England, become the more self-conscious *working-class*. In 1869, we hear already of *working-class leaders*. Then, about the turn of the century, the old *upper, middle-* and *lower-* (or *working-*) class terms receive further definitions. In 1891 we hear of *the great body of the upper middle classes*, and in our own century *lower-middle class* takes the field.

Meanwhile, *class* in its earliest, educational sense had continued undisturbed. The refinements of *upper-middle* and *lower-middle*, in social terms, may well have been affected by similar niceties of grading within the schools: *Upper* and *Lower Fourth*, etc. (We do not yet have a social class called *Remove*, but it is an idea.) The school and university *classes* had also produced *classic* and *classical* – the *classic languages, Classical civilization*: i.e., the languages and civilization studied *in class*. This implication of value (things good enough to be studied at school or university) had produced *classic* and *classical* in their now wider senses of things of established value or outstanding merit. With the extension of education, *class* had also been used in the Methodist societies. Wesley, in 1742, wrote that

'the whole society should be divided into little companies or classes – about 12 in each class.'

In 1791, we learn that this has happened:

'Each society is divided into companies of ten or fifteen, called classes: each of which regularly meets the leader once a week.'

The minutes of the Wesleyan Conference of 1885 confirm that 'the quarterly visitation of the Classes is our most important official work'.

When, later, in adult education, we hear of a *tutorial class*, we can probably see the term affected by this Methodist use, although of course *class* was also familiar in the schools and colleges. And probably, somewhere, in the whole educational system, there has been a class on the classification of class; it has often been observed that class is a particular English preoccupation, and the history of the word may offer some evidence for testing this, and, more widely, for the general historian.

Going On Learning

From: *The New Statesman*, 30 May 1959

Old images never die; they have to be publicly broken. In the case of adult education, this is a matter of some urgency. Touch one button and you get a maddening engaged signal: 'Apathy.' Touch another and you get a high-pitched buzzing: 'Yes, when I was a tutor, in 1916, it was a fine movement, but nowadays, with all these Lucky Jims about ... Welfare State ... council houses ... materialism.' Touch a third, some little lion perhaps: 'Yes, of course, Mechanics' Institutes ... night school ... meat teas ... a wet Thursday in Swindon.' Touch a fourth, for a really smooth operator: 'Quite, adult education was necessary, as a remedial expedient. Naturally, now that we have full educational opportunity, it is withering away.'

Will the facts help? I hope so. But the psychological damage that has been done to adult education, not only by its natural enemies, but by its supposed friends, has a wider interest, showing regular patterns of distortion of what is happening in our culture and society. If I say what I can show to be true – that adult education since the war has expanded rapidly and vigorously, that it is now exceptionally fertile in experiment, that demand for it increases in direct relation to better basic education – the reaction to these facts, in any particular mind, will show the patterns and images of this culture clearly enough. What happens after that is that mind's own affair.

Three points stand out, to be discussed in detail: the nature of the expansion; the new problems in workers' education; the relation between adult education and such media as television and broadcasting.

The expansion is considerable, but because of the way it has happened it is difficult to compare it directly with pre-war. The Workers' Educational Association has had an increase in students, since 1939, of about 33 per cent. But its relations, with different universities, have radically changed in the same period. In some parts of the country, the traditional pattern of joint university and WEA provision, with the tutorial class at its centre, is still the rule. In other parts, it has been virtually abandoned. In Britain as a whole, the number of tutorial class students is about the same as pre-war. But in the Oxford extra-mural areas, for example, there is a threefold increase in tutorial work, and this is still steadily developing. Where it is still applied, the traditional pattern is vigorous and relevant.

There need be no conflict between this traditional activity and the new kinds of university extra-mural work which represent another part of the

218

expansion. There has been a rapid development of a new kind of extension work, partly in relation to specialised groups, partly in lectures and classes for a substantially new audience. This work shows very clearly that there is a large demand for adult education from the already better-educated. In London, for example, recent extension figures show 11 per cent of students as having been to university, and 62 per cent to Grammar Schools. This is extremely encouraging in one respect, for it shows that the longer the learning process has been encouraged in an individual, the more likely he is to continue to want to learn. Looking to the future this is the permanent case for adult education: that the man who thinks his education is complete at 15, at 18, or at 21, is not educated, and that there are now many less uneducated people about. It works in different ways: from the professional worker who wants to keep up with new research, or wants contact with related disciplines, to the man who knows how many questions – in politics, philosophy, religion, literature – come alive in new ways in adult experience, and that the universities, which among other things exist to keep this interaction going, can meet him on them, within the context of his ordinary living.

The extension audience is largely of a new kind, and represents a vital expansion. At the same time there has been another kind of expansion, in the work of the local authorities. Here again, there is a marked variation in different parts of the country. But, in different ways, with new short-term residential colleges, with adult education and community centres, with the expansion of the evening institutes, and with the provision of lecturers to thousands of voluntary groups, the local authorities are doing excellent work; again, with a largely new public. To this must be added the developing schemes of certain voluntary organisations themselves: notably the Women's Institutes and Townswomen's Guilds.

The growth is leading, naturally, to tensions between old and new organisations, to difficult readjustments, and to a complicated kind of adult education politics. (For an introduction to these see *Trends in English Adult Education*, ed. S.G. Raybould, Heinemann.) The issues are real, but I wish more people discussed them in terms of the absolute necessity of an expanding culture, which must obviously operate at very different levels and in very different ways. A large part of what passes for adult education theory is an extraordinary combination of sectarianism, special pleading, mythmaking and mortmain. In practice, fortunately, the difficult and continuous negotiation of the necessarily complicated working relations has been surprisingly successful.

Workers' education is a key issue. This has always been difficult, with the competing claims of Socialist education (by the spirited National Council of Labour Colleges) and university education through the WEA. It begins to look as if this long division may be ending: if it does, the gains will be great. Much of the post-war expansion of adult education has been in the expanding middle class, yet the WEA's present students include some 39 per cent who are workers in the sense that the TUC understands workers (from labourers and shop assistants to post office workers and draughtsmen). Another 11 per cent are teachers, and 35 per cent are housewives, of similar background to the majority of the men. This seems about right, but a decline in manual worker students is concealed within it. A great deal is being done to meet this situation, through the trade unions. I am sure this approach is right, for the working class, in spite of the Welfare State, is still socially alienated, to a marked (degree) by comparison with other groups. The social participation of the working class is still primarily through its own collective organisations. This is a fact of our culture more fundamental than television and/or council-houses.

Education through the unions is now an exciting growing point. Some unions, with the Transport and General Workers in the lead, have their own excellent schemes. Day-release courses, particularly with miners, are very successful, and are expanding. WEA pilot-schemes in South Wales and on Tyneside, are attracting young workers, especially through linked weekend courses. For many people, perhaps especially manual workers, this short-term residential work fits much better into post-war life than the evening class, and moreover it has certain educational advantages. In all this new work, teaching problems are difficult, but in the last ten years there has been something of a breakthrough, with courses related to specific industries (at Oxford we have a research programme to get these facts alone), teaching related to specific democratic activities (meetings, negotiations), and training in public expression – writing, speaking, skills of study – at a point where the unions' practical needs and a central process of humane education interlock. Given reasonable resources, this new workers' education, through unions, will develop in a radically important way.

There is no necessary opposition between (education) through the small group and the use of such new media as broadcasting and television. We all live at different levels of community, and a healthy culture needs a corresponding scale and variety of institutions. Broadcasting has helped adult education, both directly and indirectly. Television, at worst, has not harmed it. In the (US), television programmes of adult education, (directed) by universities, are successful; and, with the coming of a third channel, we should consider the same possibility here. Yet we do not necessarily want a television Third Programme. I was alarmed to read that the transfer of educational broadcasting to Network Three has reduced its audience to less than a tenth of its previous size. This is the result, surely, of a distorted kind of thinking, quite natural to a class society, which not only assumes divisions between people but then, by arbitrary separation, enforces them. A more useful way of thinking about the third channel is in terms of institutions other than the ordinary 'independent' congeries of newspaper, publicity and commercial interests. Other groupings might be considered, on a regional basis, from such institutions as universities, theatres, orchestras, county societies, the great voluntary organisations, local authorities, and the minority national cultural organisations. If the Labour Party is serious about a common culture (and it had better be: it is its one growing point) a proposal of this kind will get the most detailed and serious consideration.

Adult education, in its formal sense, will continue to serve its growing minority. But its whole spirit, most admirably expressed by the WEA at its best, is of growth towards a genuinely common culture, and educated and participating democracy. The images of prejudice and fatigue are now being powerfully challenged, by a new generation on the left. In certain things that are now happening, on absurdly limited resources compared with the powerful resources of a capitalism living on acquisition and display, we see a practical and desirable shape of our future. The miners come to Oxford to study the coal industry, and to join in an equal discussion with its leading officials, but they also join in, excitedly, on discussions of language and social class, or contemporary literature and politics. Nuclear physicists from Harwell ask for and attend tutorial classes in literature and philosophy (this is the educated response to specialism, and in it lies much of the case for future adult education). Packed audiences at Glyndebourne listen to resident producers and university lecturers discussing one of the seasons's operas. Sociologists, film-makers, archaeologists, local historians, astronomers and biologists find ordinary people eager to study and practise their skills. A neurologist, a philosopher and a writer meet to discuss with 50 members of the general public the bearing of their disciplines on the idea of a creative mind. And the most sustained and professional discussion of contemporary literature takes place, up and down the country, in adult classes of ordinary readers, to whom many of the writers come and discuss their work. These things, and many like them, are happening now, in 'Britain the unknown country'. It is in the growing pressure of their exciting reality that the old images will be broken.

An Open Letter to WEA Tutors

Published by the WEA, 1961

Dear Colleague

For the last fifteen years I have been working as a full-time tutor in adult education. I must have taught more than a thousand adult students, and I think I have taken every kind of class, from tutorials to short terminals, and helped in every kind of residential course, from summer to weekend schools. It has been a good job, but always, as for most tutors, it has been more than a job. At the risk of repeating what many tutors already know, I want to pass on a few reflections on the kind of job it is and the kind of life it is. This is the best way I know of telling other people about the W.E.A.

Almost all my students came to me through the W.E.A. I went to the District Secretary in Cambridge, when I returned there after the war, and he found me a class in a village in the Fens, mainly of farm workers. The same summer I went to the General Secretary of the W.E.A. in London, and asked him for similar work in the South West, where I was then planning to move. He put me in touch with the District Secretary down there, and some classes were arranged. Soon afterwards, however, I got a job with the Oxford Tutorial Committee, and went to meet another District Secretary, in the South East. Once again the classes were arranged. In fact, wherever you are in Britain, this organisation exists, and tutors can get in touch with it. But nobody, as I soon learned, should take it for granted. In the South East, I joined the W.E.A. District Committee, elected from the many branches in the area. I soon realized the problems of keeping this kind of voluntary organisation going: money problems, inevitably; problems of purpose, as the W.E.A. insisted on keeping its own standards of good work however many difficulties then arose; problems of spirit, as the struggling new branch, or the old branch in temporary decline, cast doubts on the viability of the whole enterprise but gradually gained strength from the experience and determination of the others they met. Any tutor who thinks the W.E.A. exists, ready-made, just to provide him with students, will soon learn differently. The branch at Portslade, the branch at Battle, the branch at Hastings, the student-group at Seaford: it sounds very formal on paper, but sometimes these are lively organisations with many people taking part, and sometimes just the odd individual, hanging on with a scratch committee, trying to keep the work going. And the difference isn't an act of God or an act of sociology; it has everything to do with the quality of people and the quality of their vision. I remember now, with deep respect, the very many people I met who gave their time to this work, who went beyond their job to encourage and strengthen it, and who are the W.E.A. Any tutor who gets in touch with them will be getting in touch with one of the best and deepest traditions in Britain: that of voluntary, independent, serious work. If he is a real W.E.A. tutor – a term we use among ourselves to cover many kinds of people but all with certain qualities of recognition and concern – he will be glad and proud to work with them.

There isn't any rule about how to do it; there never is, in any movement of actual and varying people. I have seen tutors build or save a branch, by giving enough of their students this sense of common purpose. Many tutors work with their local branches and districts, as members of committees or helping to organise special functions. But sometimes I have seen a tutor almost kill a branch, by regarding it as his private recruiting organisation, and by trying to do too much in the wrong way. If you go in as a tutor you must go in as an equal, trying to share in activity and to spread activity, in a common effort.

But why should tutors do anything like this at all? First, I think, because the W.E.A. represents a vital tradition which we are always in danger of losing and which we can never afford to lose. The organisation of social justice, and the institutions of democracy are worth working for, in the society as a whole. But haven't many of us realised, in the years since the war, that you can have some of these things, or approximations to them, and still not the spirit which is their real life? I've often defined my own social purpose as the creation of an educated and participating democracy. The W.E.A. taught me much, in defining these terms. It has always stood for the principle that ordinary people should be highly educated, as an end justifying itself and not simply as a means to power. Equally it has always stood for the principle that society is a method of common and general participation, and it exemplifies this in its own work. It does not see the good things in society as benefits to be handed down by an elite, or as bargaining counters to win the favours of an electorate. In the end, it has insisted, they will only be good things if people have made them for themselves.

This is worth repeating, in the 1960s, when many people will tell you that the W.E.A.'s historic mission is over. With the coming of better opportunities in the schools, the exceptional mind in the poor family is spotted young, and is given a real chance. Yes, but this was never at the heart of the W.E.A.'s purpose. Of course the exceptional minds must get their chance, but what about everyone else? Are they simply to be treated as rejects? The W.E.A. stands for purposes which some people, including some reformers, cannot even begin to understand. It stands for an educated democracy, not for a newly mobile and more varied elite. Its historic mission is as urgent and central today as it was in the 1900s, because its basic challenge stands out much more clearly, and is no longer propped up by simple missionary feelings, that the fortunate should help the unfortunate, or by simple class feelings, that the odd pearl should be picked out of the swineheap. The W.E.A. has never looked at the world in this way, and because it doesn't it is more up-to-date, more genuinely in touch with real needs, than the people who want to persuade us that its fundamental aspirations are simply old stuff. They are joined by the cynics who find it damnably easy to point out how little, comparatively, has been achieved; what a tough fight the W.E.A. is still having. It is quite true: we are fighting for our lives. But *for our lives*: that is the whole point. And it isn't what some abstraction called the W.E.A. now does. It is what we do, as tutors, students and friends.

There is another main reason why tutors should join and work with the W.E.A. This is a matter of the health of their own academic subject. There are some important examples here. There was the profound stimulus, to all the social studies, from the contact of men like Tawney and Cole with the realities of working-class life and history, through the W.E.A. There has been, more recently, the profound stimulus to literary and cultural studies, by the fact of contact between tutors trained in academic disciplines, affected sometimes by fashions, and students who live in less specialised cultural worlds and who force the tutors to follow the questions of value right through. This is the reality behind the claim that, in the W.E.A., tutors and students meet as equals. Of course the tutor knows his own discipline better, and wants to help the students to learn it, but he may not know how his discipline looks to people outside it; may not know the gaps between academic thinking and actual experience among many people; he may not know when, in the pressure of experience, a new discipline has to be created. Working with the W.E.A. is not just a matter of committees, important as they are. It is also a matter of constant experiment in teaching, and the W.E.A. is one of the very few institutions in which this is possible, because of its freedom from external requirements. Just because there can be no reward but increased understanding, the challenge to new and imaginative teaching is constant. This may be a new method in an experienced class, or the profoundly important work with new kinds of students, who have never before made much contact with formal education. In recent years I have discussed D.H. Lawrence with working miners; discussed methods of argument with building workers; discussed newspapers with young trade unionists; discussed television with apprentices in training. To me these have been formative experiences, and I have learned as much as I have taught. A whole world of work is waiting, of many kinds, for all who are ready to try it. The next few years may see a transformation in trade union education, which is of vital social importance. The development of work with women's organisations and young workers is also extremely promising. All this, of course, in addition to the familiar work in tutorial classes and residential courses, where experiment in teaching is often just as important. But none of us can sit back and wait for this to happen. It will only happen as widely as it needs to if we all get in and work.

I have mentioned various kinds of satisfaction and stimulus. I need hardly add that there are regular disappointments, and that the going is often very hard indeed. At the first tutorial class I ever took there were three people present, and one of these had only come to see the thing properly started. We had to join that class with one in a neighbouring village. And then there are the rows in branches, the jealousies, the intrigues, that you can chew over in all their bitterness during the long winter journeys. No good is done by concealing any of this, or the constant national rows about the best way to organise adult education, the sense of continual crisis. It's enough to put anybody off, until you get back a sense of proportion and remember the deep needs, the real pressures, behind it all. You must make up your own mind about this as about all the other things, but I can say, for myself, that if I had these last fifteen years back, to use as I liked, I would want to do the same work again, with my friends, students and colleagues in the W.E.A.: only trying to do it better, by understanding it better. Meanwhile if you think I can help at all, with any question or problem, do write to me, or come and see me. I can always be found care of the W.E.A.

Yours Sincerely
Raymond Williams

The Common Good

From: *Adult Education*, XXXIV, 4, November 1961,
pp 192–9

Sunday morning, about church time, and a man speaking to the converted: this combination of circumstances seems irresistibly to suggest a text. I begin at the eighth line of the second paragraph of the Agreed Memorandum of Remarks by the Minister of Education.

> '*He could not see why adult education should need a lot more public money for its development. Given that it was a good product, people had sufficient free money to buy it if there was adequate salesmanship for it . . . If one asked people what they thought about adult education, they were likely to describe it as dreary, and that was because it was not effectively advertised.*'

Now the words of the heathen are so easily refuted, within the temple, that they are hardly even heard. It is very easy, in a sense too easy, to meet dogma with dogma. We are suffering in adult education, as in education generally, from the fact that people working in it have a profound belief that their special interest is the common interest: but when they have to justify this belief outside the temple, then, because they are so shy of theory, they often find themselves in difficulty. The English have a great suspicion of theory, and a great love for the concrete and the practical. Yet the truest thing about our addiction to the concrete is that for a long time now we have been stuck in it. We are so involved in what we think self-evident propositions, leading to a clear course of action, that when we have to justify ourselves, in a very complex and changing society, and one with such deep divisions of belief and principles as now in Britain, then we can easily get lost.

I want to describe three strands of thinking about education, which have shaped our system, and which are still active. Until these are brought out into the open and compared, we shall not get practical agreement on what we are doing and must do.

First, there is the line of what I would call the Old Humanist, who believe that education is, above all, the repository of certain values, the true golden thread in the life of man. Education is an ideal process which should resist as far as possible the pushing claims of the world. What it has to do, at any time, is far more important than meeting temporary

226

practical needs, because its content, methods and relationships maintain an incalculably valuable tradition. This is often held to be most evident in subjects of the least practical importance.

The Old Humanists have been very powerful in English education, as indeed in most educational systems, and they are always people to listen to with respect. They have, however, done a vast amount of damage, because of the nature of the group by whom they were opposed. I would call this second group the Industrial Trainers. They are much more numerous and now seem to be in sole command of the field, at certain points where critical decisions about resources are made. These are the people who believe that the purpose of education is to fit people to earn their living – a view more commonly held, of course, in an industrial society than in a traditional, more stable, rural society. The battle in nineteenth century education was fought mainly between these two groups. The Old Humanists insisted that the push towards reform and extension of education was a denial of its essential values and would cheapen it: the Industrial Trainers said that it was quite impossible, in a changing country, to preserve a curriculum which, however appropriate it may have been to former periods, would not meet the hard demands of an expanding and competitive economy. All through the nineteenth century the Industrial Trainers won debate after debate, apparently very easily, because at each point they could say that there were simply not enough educated people to run the economy and the society. This is still true. There is a shortage of educated people in every part of our society, and the most persuasive argument for the extension of education has still to be put in terms not of values but of competitive economies: what Russia is doing, what America is doing. The nations are thought of as large firms, which have to put their training systems in order and arrange that the right number of people with the right number of skills are trained in the right quantities.

We had, in the end, of course, to effect a marriage, if only a shot-gun marriage, between the Old Humanists and the Industrial Trainers. Our modern educational system is the result. Our curriculum, so difficult to justify on rational principles, can be justified at once as the historical deposit of those two groups. On the one hand, its justification is its practicality; on the other hand, it is an ideal process which essentially does not have to justify itself.

I do not think that adult education can draw much sustenance from the arguments of either of these groups, and this has been one of its difficulties. The typical Old Humanist is very much afraid that if the values of education are extended too far, they will in the end be diluted and destroyed. Mr Eliot and others have argued that education is a process of great importance to a minority in the society, but that any attempt to extend it to a majority is destructive of the process itself. It is true that many an Old Humanist will admit that there must be people scattered around, here and there, who have the right kind of minority qualifications, and the provision ought to be made so that these people are not cut off from their natural life. But he will also argue that once the ordinary educational system is put right, these odd people will be picked up any way, and get their education at school and university; adult education is then not really necessary.

The Industrial Trainer, on the other hand, is equally not likely to believe in adult education as we ordinarily use the term in this country. He says that the main purpose of training and education is to fit people for the skills of work. A good workman must, of course, acquire certain character traits – responsibility and self discipline, for instance, as well as minor virtues like punctuality – but on the whole these things are best done young. Adult education might be found some specific technical job to do, or problems might arise in the work process which a little adult education would help to smooth out, but one could not expect, from an Industrial Trainer, adult education getting any kind of priority.

If, indeed, there were only these two groups, there would not be an adult education movement. But there is, fortunately, a third – active in the nineteenth century, mixed up in odd ways, fighting often on different sides, making allies of each of these two groups as opportunity offered – a group whom I would call the Public Educators. They say, with Carlyle, that it is the first duty of government to see that the people can think. This, from the beginning, is a radically different emphasis. It does not see education primarily as training for the existing tasks of the society, nor as an ideal process of values which must be kept to a comparatively small minority. Instead it sees the process of society as itself a process of education. But these phrases are so commonly used that they no longer mean very much. In any case, we say, it is only too evident that most people do not *want* to be trained to think. For there are people even in the adult education movement who take some pride in their minority position. In my years as a tutor, I have been shocked to find the odd student, and tutor, who by virtue of coming to class once a week thinks he is not as other men. The whole tradition of Public Education has at times been allowed to run underground, while we hold to one of those other definitions. Thus the most common argument against adult education at the moment, that it is no longer relevant to the common good, resolves itself into the thinking of either an Old Humanist or an Industrial Trainer. Adult Education is not particularly relevant to expanding productivity, nor to increasing the efficiency of the society in direct terms. It is not particularly relevant to the ideal process of the Old Humanists. It is wholly relevant to Public Education – but what *is* this? And then follows this other argument: adult education was relevant in a time of great social injustice when people were economically deprived, but it is not relevant now because there is no social injustice, and people are not economically deprived. Even good people have been caught by this argument. Of course, in Britain, the mere fact that adult education has been going for fifty years will ensure it another fifty, but none of us can be very happy with that sort of assessment of our chances.

To re-state the principle of adult education involves, I think, remaking an analysis of society. The Public Education tradition is, in one way, accepted. People say that this is a democracy. The decisions of society are, theoretically at least, in the hands of everyone. This is also a society in which there are very large and highly developed communication systems, so that decisions are not merely formal: the affairs of the country and of the world are regularly presented to the people. Again, quite outside the sphere of political and economic decision, it is becoming increasingly evident that the quality of art and the quality of thought in this country are going to be dependent on the quality of majority taste. It has been apparent for some time that we would reach this critical point. The tastes and preferences of the majority of our people are going to determine not only the directions of our society (a fact which those with that lordly disinterest in politics comparatively easy to cultivate in England might accept without a qualm), but are also going to determine quality in art and quality in thought.

The battle for quality in art and for quality in thought has now to take place on a majority stage or not at all. The idea that minority enclaves can be preserved within the society without grave damage to the minorities themselves is already a matter of history only. The whole issue of quality has moved into the field of majority decision, whether we like it or not. Our plays, our films, our television service, our newspapers, our government, our public life – the quality of all these is dependent on the active, or quite as often passive, preferences of the majority. In this situation, public education is not less, but surely much more, urgent.

The difficulty is to put this case in a way that is in touch with contemporary reality. Even the Public Educators themselves have often spoken with two voices. One of these, which I do not like, says that the majority of the population are depraved. This is one of those perennial springs of education, moral rescue. In the eighteenth and nineteenth centuries it was easy to get up funds for education by pointing to the depravity of the working classes – then it was drink, now it is television.

I admire temperance workers when they are working for temperance, but not when they are engaged in this essentially odd operation of saving the people. The crucial thing about English society today is that for the first time in history the working people are in a position where they can afford not to be saved. This is a profoundly important and encouraging fact, and the kind of thinking which has come from missionary work, while it has often been valuable in its way, is now utterly irrelevant and is one of the continual blocks between educators and their public. In the old days people could talk sincerely about the missionary, going out from this city of Oxford to those dark places beyond. It's a good image, but I cannot help thinking of one of our best young men – Mr Dennis Potter – who came here as an undergraduate and after three years of Oxford said it was one of the darkest places he had ever seen. I do not agree with him, but it is a sign of the times that he could say so, that he did not come from the Forest of Dean to Oxford as from darkness into light – and a good many people are finding the same optic registration.

All this means, quite simply, that if adult education bases itself on any one of three common principles, it is finished. If it bases itself on an Old Humanist principle, it is finished because it is denying its own premise. If you say that education is essentially the business of a very small minority, the rest of the society will turn round and say 'Good luck to you, we can forget about *you*'. Meanwhile, if adult education bases itself on the arguments of an Industrial Trainer, then, quite frankly, better ways will be found of doing it. If you want to increase skills you do not run WEA classes and evening institute classes and literary institute classes and so on – you get down to some training at the bench. And if adult education bases itself, finally, on the missionary principle, it is finished, even though at first it may appear to get an encouraging amount of support for what sounds a good cause. For between you and the people with whom you should be speaking is fixed something inherently destructive, so that you will never be able to speak to people as an equal again. The time has passed in British society when you could get away with speaking to people other than as equals, although there is still tolerance of inequality and all sorts of apparent deferences are made. The deep undercurrent of contemporary British life is the thing which is called apathy, but which I think is something different from that. It is a pretty massive scepticism with certain persistent if often unspoken questions: who are these people? What are they after? Why do they put it like that? What do they want? It is easy to deplore scepticism, which indeed in its present form is very dangerous, but you must also ask what people are being sceptical about. What they are being sceptical about is a process of being spoken to in ways which no self-respecting man could accept, unless he had to.

The problem is a problem of communication, and if we understand this properly it gives us so much promise for the future that we may come to look back on the last sixty years of adult education as only its prehistory. This field has to be very carefully explored, because we are offered an alternative – modern means of communication – which seems to make adult education in its old forms outdated. This is the most difficult one of all to think through. In the first place, we must get rid of the extreme hostility which has been too common in education towards the general communication services. In the classroom we are often very deferent about the past. We make nice remarks about the Essays of Elia, in an essentially genteel way, but when it gets to television, or the newspapers, or the advertisements, you wouldn't know us for the same men! How fierce we can be, how uncompromising, what vigorous radicals we all are! Although the relevant teaching, if you come to think of it, would be the relation between the Essays of Elia and the modern television personality – the methods involved are very similar. We have almost assumed it as our birth-right, because we are in education, to claim that the rest of this stuff is inferior. As Richard Hoggart has said: 'One has to try to keep open all lines which may allow for good development as well as to oppose those which are likely to lead to a dead smartness. At present most people with literary interests keep open less effectively than they oppose'. And who can honestly say that this is not true? On the other hand, say that, say television is one of the lines, and there are people who will sit back with relief and pat their pocket – the pocket is the operative word – and say, 'Ah, you're not going to criticise modern communications, you realise they have this vitally important part to play'. Yes indeed, on the right terms.

Let us look at the situation quite frankly. The development of the press, of broadcasting, of television, was the great hope of democracy. Without communication on that scale we could not build an active democracy, even as far as we have already taken it. This was the great hope – and yet now we tolerate with a quite fantastic apathy a situation in which all the large circulation magazines of the country are owned by one man; in which four out of every five copies sold of our daily newspapers are controlled by two men; in which, in almost every field, that sort of control is operative. And then, immediately we say a word about this, it's either 'Oh, you're an old fashioned person who doesn't believe in modern communications' or (and this is a beauty) 'You're threatening the liberty of the press'. Any discussion of the press in terms which suggests that it is not the best of all possible worlds is a threat to the freedom of the press. But the freedom of the press, in the only important sense of the term, no longer exists, except in minority forms. There is only one comment to make on this, the comment of Burke: 'You are terrifying yourself with apparitions while your house is the haunt of robbers. Wise men will apply their remedies to vices, and not to their names'. The vice is, quite simply, that we have a communication system wholly inadequate to democratic life, and I think that, so far from this being a temporary situation or a temporary crisis, all development over the last sixty years shows that it is a process with very deep economic roots, and a process which, so far from being finished, is still accelerating.

Adult education, in this situation, has to think hard. There is no easy way out. There is no way out along the path of saying 'Well of course, there will be these vulgar things like the mass press and the ITV and so on, but adult education will keep its own corner sweet'. In the reality of modern communication, there is no future in keeping corners sweet – we have to clean the house. Yet once we start thinking about this, we are up against blocks of a very severe kind. We have to redefine communication and education in terms of a society rather different from that we have been accustomed to thinking about, yet a society which should not be strange to educators – a society in which it is assumed that society itself is an educative process, that society is a method of association and co-operation in which the processes we separate out as politics, as economics, as communication, as education, are directly related to the reality of living together, and in which control over the process is in the hands of the people who use them. The relevance to adult education, I think, is this: if we conceive ourselves as a minority movement, on whatever principle, we are losing the biggest opportunity we ever had. This does not mean that some sudden change of mind could convert adult education into a majority movement. Growth is not of that kind. Growth is a slow business; it is necessarily long in time; it is work for at least one generation to expand even reasonably. But I want to feel sure that we are looking in the right directions and that we include in the purposes of adult education not only the maintenance of the kind of classes we have been doing, but the making of much more direct links with the new communication services. Some of the most hopeful signs in the last few years have been the chances that these links open up in television and in broadcasting. Eventually adult education will have to think in terms of the whole field of communications, including the press, as something it must judge by its own standards.

Simply, my case is this: I do not think that a movement which only makes sense in terms of majority education can have any future except in the direction of majority values and a deep concern with the values of the whole society. We cannot go on overlooking the fact that alongside our kind of service, alongside the education service as a whole, is a communications service very mixed in quality, very questionable in control, which is going to play a decisive part in moulding the quality of our general life, and not merely the life of the masses. I have hammered at the word masses over the last few years to the point of tedium, because it, too, is one of the ghosts that haunts us: the idea that if somehow we can keep the few people right, then the masses who are only interested in rather bad, rather silly things, can be left to their own devices – as Orwell left them in 1984. There were the 90 per cent of proles, outside the walls, but they never interfered. The one thing wrong with this analysis was the assumption that they would not interfere. It is becoming clear that, not necessarily by positive action but by the whole sum of our actions and failures to act, we the majority are going to settle the quality of this society; if this is so, adult education can be concerned with no less.

The Roots of Education

Review of Brian Simon, *Studies in the History of Education 1780–1870*
From: *The Guardian*, 14 April 1960

Teaching is one thing, and education quite another. Yet it is far from clear which is the more important. Teachers often complain of interference in their work, not only by educational theorists but also by politicians. It is easy to sympathise with the feeling (teachers are not the only individual craftsmen carrying a heavy apparatus on their backs), yet most schools were the creation of politicians, most subjects were the creation of theorists, and our current arguments about organisation and curriculum are all, finally, arguments about the structure and values of British society. We should all be much clearer about our immediate problems if an adequate social history of British education had in fact been written.

A new book by Mr Brian Simon, *Studies in the History of Education 1780-1870* (Lawrence and Wishart, 37s 6d), is an interesting indication of the kind of work that remains to be done. The period chosen covers a radical reorganisation of all parts of our educational system, in terms of a new industrial economy, a new social class structure, and new forms of democratic government. The technical history of education in these years has often been written, but only one previous book, A.E. Dobbs's *Education and Social Movements 1700-1850* (published in 1919 and unreasonably neglected), has brought to bear on the problems of curriculum and organisation an adequate sense of the movement, complexity, and conflict of the society which was shaping them. Anyone familiar with the technical histories will find few new facts, but will certainly find serious patterns of analysis and interpretation which bring many of the facts to new life.

Mr Simon's first chapter discusses the major educational contribution of the religious dissenters, running back to the English Revolution. *New Trends in Education in the Eighteenth Century* by N. Hans, is perhaps a better account of this movement, but Mr Simon's contribution is a convincing analysis of why this tradition only partly succeeded, to our great subsequent loss. The second and third chapters cover the new radicalism of the first half of the nineteenth century, both in educational theory and in the provision of institutions for the middle class and the urban workers. The analysis here is incomplete; Bentham and Mill were mean and narrow compared with Milton and Priestley, and the decline needs further exploration.

In his fourth and fifth chapters Mr Simon usefully covers quite familiar ground, in an account of independent working-class educational movements, from the Corresponding societies through Owen to the Chartists. This is a vivid period, well described. In his two final chapters, Mr Simon describes the major national reorganisation of all educational institutions between 1850 and 1870. The new structure of graded secondary schools, designed to serve and provide different social classes, is of crucial importance here, and Mr Simon's account, though drawing on familiar facts from the Clarendon and Taunton Commissions, is excellent in its detail and clarity. It is very much to be hoped that Mr Simon will continue the history from this point, since the line from these reports to our current secondary patterns needs to be traced and clarified until everyone concerned with educational decisions is aware of it.

Meanwhile, I hope this book will be widely read. It is the work of a frank and intelligent partisan, both in politics and in education, but it is also scholarly, full of interesting detail, very well illustrated, and clear and easy to read.

Sensible People

Review of J.F.C. Harrison, *Learning and Living, 1790–1960*
From: *The New Statesman*, 5 January 1962

Two generations of historians have worked on the political and economic institutions of the British working class. A great deal remains to be done, but a reasonable basis has been laid. On the cultural history of the same people, almost everything remains to be done. Many scattered contributions have been made, but there is still no history of this long and distinctive tradition in our literature, still no history of the independent working-class press, and still no history of working-class education. Until this work has been done, it is doubtful if we can fully understand even the political and economic history.

Professor Harrison describes his book as 'a study in the history of the English adult education movement'. He disclaims any intention of writing a full-scale history, and argues, quite reasonably, that the material is not yet available, in anything like adequate detail. His own approach is much narrower than his title suggests, but it is a very sensible approach. He takes all his material from one area, Yorkshire, and seeks to relate the development of adult education in the county to its changing social history.

In the main, and within the limits set, the book is successful. The thread of a familiar social history runs through the book, but the continuity of local investigation gives it an interesting sense of the particular. The links between adult education and actual social conditions, and between its pioneers and the very varied political movements and purposes which it was thought it would serve, are admirably illustrated. One early chapter on 'the Middle Class Image' is an original contribution to social history in its own right. It is not that the idea is new: we have realised for more than a century that a great deal of activity, apparently on behalf of working people, was really an attempt, as Shaw approvingly put it, 'to abolish them and replace them by sensible people' – the image of sensible people being taken, then as now, from current middle-class life. Professor Harrison shows the vitality of this attempt in early Victorian England: a vitality which it has never had since, for what I think is the obvious reason that the middle class, in that period, was itself engaged in a major constructive and creative effort, was itself still forming culturally and not the fixed pattern it later became.

It is interesting to follow this theme down to the emergence of the WEA, which, second only to the Labour Party, has been the battleground of fundamentally conflicting traditions. The strike at Ruskin in 1909 illuminates the whole issue, and ought still to be pondered. I have made up my own mind, recently, that the strikers, who refused to be made into 'sensible people', were right. All the resources and main tendencies of the society were, however, on the other side, and I can feel, in committing myself on this, the isolation of the heretic. Now, though, that the WEA is being cast off by its temporary friends, the whole issue seems to have re-opened, and perhaps its only future lies in a recovery of the independent yet powerful working-class tradition.

Professor Harrison continues his detailed and lively account to the present day. It was only in his last chapter that I lost interest. If it is true that newspaper reports of events within one's personal knowledge nearly always turn out to be inaccurate, I wonder if this is also true of contemporary history in which one has taken some part. The inaccuracy, if it is there, is not in matters of fact, but in the equally relevant questions of estimating consciousness and personality. Though it was done from the inside, Professor Harrison's account of the contemporary situation seems to me external and stilted. To be a lively historian and to have a really living awareness of the present may often, I suppose, involve separate qualities. Anyway, on the present, Professor Harrison has got all the names but very little of the life, whereas the life of the earlier chapters of his book – the long Yorkshire tradition of adult learning – is real and welcome.

Workers' College

Review of William W. Craik, *The Central Labour College*
From: *The Guardian*, 1 January 1965

At a time when we are again actively discussing the future of adult and workers' education, Mr Craik's book is especially welcome. It is the first detailed account of the early crisis at Ruskin College, Oxford, and of the work of the Labour College movement which followed the famous students' strike and breakaway in 1909. As a chapter of social history, it is essential reading for anyone interested in education and the Labour movement, and it is well told and illustrated. As a contribution to the current argument about the organisation of workers' education, which though given little publicity is of fundamental importance, Mr Craik's book is inevitably controversial and is much more than a voice from the past. The relation between the methods and content of traditional education, and between both and our continuing social conflicts, is still too little explored. This vigorous justification of a prolonged campaign and a tenacious principle needs to be read by many outside the particular field of adult education. Mr Craik was a railwayman who won a union scholarship to Ruskin in 1907, was prominent in the 1909 strike, and eventually became Principal of the Central Labour College. His book is a valuable record of a life, a generation, and a movement.

Voices of Socialism: R.H. Tawney

From: *Tribune*, 1 January 1965

Socialism, in Britain, is a unique combination of different traditions. The importance of Tawney is that he represents, in its purest form, the transition from Liberal to Socialist values. The historical importance of this transition hardly needs emphasis, but it is still, in fundamental matters, very imperfectly understood.

> *The problem now confronting us . . . is moral, and political, even more than economic. It is a question, not only of the failure of the existing order, but of its standards of success. It is not merely to restore the conditions of material prosperity, urgent though such a restoration is. It is to work out a new social synthesis which may do justice both to the values of the Liberal era and to equally important aspects of life, to which that era, for all its virtues, was too often blind. It is to provide more compelling motives for the sustained cooperative effort which, under modern conditions of mass organisation, civilisation demands, by relating it to common purposes of a kind to appeal, not only to the interests but to the conscience and reason, of all men of good will.*

This is Tawney's explicit acknowledgement of his kind of Socialism: as a development of Liberal values and an appeal to the 'conscience and reason, of all men of good will.' His greatest influence, it is now clear, was on those many men who, born into the hitherto politically responsible classes of British society, were disturbed by the scale of twentieth century poverty and inequality. In calling for an ethical renewal, as the necessary basis for the institution of Socialism, Tawney relied, consciously and unconsciously, on the inherited strength of the Liberal conscience.

He was deeply affected, in this reliance, both by his Christian habit of mind and by his experience in the war of 1914–18. Liberalism must get rid of its dogmas – in particular its 'acceptance of absolute rights to property and to economic freedom as the unquestioned centre of social organisation.' These dogmas, in practice, limited the freedom of too many other men, and prevented the achievement of any national sense of unity and purpose. Only the creation of new public institutions – public ownership in industry, public initiative in education and the social services – could extend and realise the traditional Liberal values. But 'institutions rest on psychological foundations' so that the new effort must be at once a practical shaping of these institutions and an ethical campaign to alter the national psychology.

The character of this effort, which represents all Tawney's major work, is now very familiar. It is a tribute to his influence that it is now the ordinary language of Labour in government. Instead of emphasising the reality of class interests, and the consequent struggle of classes as in the Marxist tradition, Tawney, and those who learned from him, argued that

> *social institutions . . . should be planned, as far as is possible, to emphasise and strengthen, not the class differences which divide, but the common humanity which unites . . .*

The nature of this appeal, as we have learned under successive Labour Governments, needs very careful analysis.

A call to unity in the service of absolute human values is indeed, at root, the permanent basis of Socialism. But everything depends on the way these values are related to actual experience. The ease with which Conservatives call for just such an apparent unity should make us all pause. It is clear that we have values, as men, which are more important than any class or sectional interests, but the whole question, in politics, is the actual operation of these values, in real circumstances.

No deeper and more moving moral appeal than that of Tawney has been made in this century, but it has been very easy to take the phrases and forget the substance. We have all heard the phrases of an appeal to set the common interest above a sectional interest being used, for example, against a strike in which real human interests are being defended in the only immediately available way. At such times, it is understandable if we react against this whole approach to Socialism, and return to the harder and more immediately valid language of conflict and interest.

Everything depends, in fact, on what we are being asked to unite for. It is a misuse of Tawney to take the language of ethical community and apply it to any particular definition of the common interest which happens to be current. If someone says that the common interest is membership of a nuclear alliance, or a productivity effort or incomes policy within the existing economic system, the only relevant response is to look at what is actually proposed, to see whether it is demonstrably a common moral interest. The language of morals, that is to say, cannot be used until the moral substance has been agreed. The strength of Tawney was his continual direction of interest towards this moral substance. His weakness, as of any ethical thinker, is that he can be used for purposes which actually negate his effort, behind a screen of praise of the very height of his argument and the nobility of his style. As he said of Ruskin:

> *Though later generations have sometimes acted upon his stray hints, which he let fall in following his main argument, they have not*

submitted to that argument itself, because it has seemed too hard for them.

What was that argument, in Tawney's own case? First, and essentially, this:

> *As long as men are men, a poor society cannot be too poor to find a right order of life, nor a rich society too rich to have need to seek it.*

The ethical and practical consequences of this basic position is, of course, that it is always false to argue that a society 'cannot afford' a particular measure of social justice. To say that we shall have social justice when we can afford it – in practice that admittedly necessary measures of reform must wait on and go step by step with our economic recovery – is, in Tawney's terms, not really to believe in social justice at all. To regard equality as dependent on the state of the economy is, Tawney argued, to put the economy first and human beings second.

> *When the press clamours that the one thing needed to make this island an Arcadia is productivity, and more productivity, that is industrialism. It is the confusion of means with ends.*

It is interesting to remember that that was written 43 years ago. Its point is not an airy indifference to the material facts of life. Simply, the argument is that the achievement of a 'right order of life' is the first and inescapable objective, and that to postpone it in the interests of production is to beg the whole question of 'common interest'. As he went on to argue . . .

> *So to those who clamour, as many now do, 'Produce! Produce!', one simple question may be addressed: 'Produce what?' Food, clothing, house-room, art, knowledge? By all means! But if the nation is scantily furnished with these things had it not better stop producing a good many others which fill shop windows in Regent Street? . . . What can be more childish than to urge the necessity that productive power should be increased, if part of the productive power which exists already be misapplied?*

This is the point at which the moral argument becomes intensely practical. To say that we haven't the resources for this or that (very desirable) enterprise, is to invite, in Tawney's terms, the simple reply: then why have we the resources to produce this or that which we now have and propose to continue? The actual distribution of human energy and resources composes, in fact, a moral system. Any existing economic system is an expression of real preferences. The attention of the moralist, and of anyone who offers to use moral language in politics, must be turned to these actual preferences, and not to an arbitrary argument in terms of total production, which obscures the real choices we are making or underwriting.

In *The Acquisitive Society* (1921) Tawney wrote the classic statement of this approach to politics, and it is remarkable how much of it can be applied, almost word for word, to the arguments now taking place within the Labour movement. It is small comfort to hear Tawney revered as a great teacher, and to see his actual teaching almost wholly ignored.

The case is similar on his other major point: the argument for equality. He took great pains to distinguish the old Liberal argument for 'equality of opportunity' from the new Socialist argument for 'equality of practice'. The former is merely a condition for beginning a race: the inequalities at the end of the race are taken for granted. But the moral case for equality, Tawney argued, lay in the proposition that

> *while [men] differ profoundly as individuals in capacity and character, they are equally entitled as human beings to consideration and respect.*

This consideration and respect must be shown, not merely at the start of a race, but at every point in life, and to be real it must be far more than a patronising kind of acknowledgement. The reforms Tawney proposed, in making a democratic educational system, and in creating democratic control in industry, are still radical. His challenge to a Labour Government to introduce democratic procedures into industry, using the nationalised industries as the obvious starting-point, still waits to be taken up. Here, as everywhere, the test must not be, in the first instance, efficiency, but right relations between men. For in the end, Tawney argued, even efficiency, the achievement of a genuine national effort, depends on those equal relations between men which create a real as opposed to a spurious national interest.

To re-read Tawney, in *The Acquisitive Society*, in *Equality*, in the collection of essays called *The Radical Tradition*, or in his major historical work, *Religion and the Rise of Capitalism*, is, then, to return to a great teacher, whose arguments, because of their moral basis, are still alive and relevant. But it is also to return to a major landmark in that still unfinished process, in Britain, of the transition from Liberalism to Socialism. His appeal to reason and conscience, beyond mere interest, has the ambiguity of this transition as a whole: not only, though most obviously, when it is simply misused; but also, more fundamentally, in its reliance on values as the creators of institutions, as opposed to seeing institutions as the creators of values.

No man could have gone further with the Liberal kind of moral analysis, and with its consequent appeal to action. But perhaps the transition to Socialism is only complete when morality is seen as a social process rather than as a set of individual values. We can at least be certain that Tawney lived and expressed his own position with unusual dedication and intelligence.

Different Sides of the Wall

From: *The Guardian*, 26 September 1968

I was standing with a miner, a man of my own age, in the university museum at Oxford. The others had gone on ahead, past the bones of the dinosaur, the neat glass cases of rocks. 'I can't explain to anybody what my work is,' he said suddenly. We had started that week talking about novels of working-class life, in a summer-school literature group. The trip to the museum was one of the regular afternoon excursions. Most adult tutors know how, with working-class students, it isn't a question of just teaching the formal hours. Until some other relationship has been made, no teaching begins. Yet I still wasn't sure what he meant. Was it a way of questioning the authenticity of the novels? We'd been discussing, that morning, why life in a working-class home is so often described, the work itself hardly ever. So I tried to bring what he said back to that. He went on looking past me.

'I can't,' he said at last, with emphasis. 'Not them. Me.'

'You mean you've tried describing it?'

'Yes, talking.'

'And not got it through?'

'No.'

The museum was very quiet. He was watching me carefully.

'All right, try it.' I said.

He smiled, without sympathy, and then told me quite quickly. He was a roadmaker, underground. He had to follow and build the road to the face.

'Yes,' I said, 'I get the general picture.'

'Do you?', he said, with an aggressive edge.

'I think so, yes.'

'All right. Draw it.'

He took out a pencil and paper and handed them to me.

'I don't draw very well,' I began to explain.

'Try it.' he said.

I made a rough sketch, and he watched me closely. It wasn't too bad, for he looked relieved, though he took the paper back and made a quick alteration of line. We waited some moments, and then went on to join the others. Some crucial point had been passed, and the rest of the week went better. Yet I still go over and over this episode, as I try now to think, in very different circumstances, about the crisis in education, about communication, and about the relations between education and democracy.

Shared Decisions

The first modern demand for what is now called student power came in adult education, for good historical reasons. It is an illuminating history, that long struggle by working men to get an education that answered their needs. Obviously they needed to be taught; they depended on men who through opportunity and training knew the things they wanted to know. At the same time, generation after generation, they insisted on sharing in the essential decisions: about what was to be studied, and how. Repeatedly, they set up their own institutions, and in this kind of self-organising there was always a close relation between education and democracy: not simply the internal conditions, deciding what was to be done, but the external conditions, the relation between learning and what it was for, what the social process was for. The corresponding societies, the Hampden clubs, the secular Sunday schools, the cooperative circles, the mechanics' institutes, the Workers' Educational Association, the labour colleges: we can learn more, now, from these, about the crisis in education, than from the more formal established institutions. For there was always a tension, of a most complicated kind. Some people always wanted to control them (it was often easy, through finance) so that what was taught was what the authorities decided.

But there was also authority of another kind: that which any teacher can feel, when a need for understanding is presented to him; that to get to D one must go through A, B, and C; that, from his experience, the best way of learning is in this way and this – that, which you ask about, can only come later. But isn't it possible, the student replies, not always politely, that you're simply prejudiced; that you're not interested in D; that the world has changed since you learned your order of things; that anyway, if it hasn't it looks different from where you are and where I am? At certain points of breakdown students have gone away on their own, distrusting established education and established teachers. 'Do you suffer from too much class consciousness?' the cover of *Plebs* asked ironically, at the time of a scheme for trade union scholarships at Oxford; 'try a term or two in the home of lost causes.'

I have been closely reminded of this history in the last year, in the new phase of the student movement and the free university. And there is some advantage in being able to see the problem from different sides of the wall. I had 15 years as an adult tutor; I am now in my eighth year as a university teacher. In adult education the class meets, before the session, and decides the syllabus with its tutor. This was sometimes a formality; sometimes a combination of skilful persuasion and briefing; but often enough a genuine participation in the definition of educational ends and means. When I came back to Cambridge, as a lecturer, I found something of the same atmosphere; optional papers, and the need for selection within papers, made a comparable process necessary. Again, I used to say as an adult tutor, that I was in the only kind of education where students voted with their feet; if the class wasn't right, they didn't come. I had forgotten the Cambridge lecture system, in which attendance is optional and where, in English for example, only half the students ever attend at all. This seems to me increasingly a negative freedom: the right to stay away (in fact often ignorantly or fashionably exercised) is no real substitute for cooperative decision. Teachers know too well the real errors, the glaring gaps, that follow from negative freedom. If some of them retreat into cynicism about students, which is now very widespread, they do not perhaps always realise that they too are victims of an inadequate system.

Reform and Discipline

I have tried in my own teaching – lectures, classes and supervisions – to use methods I learned in adult education. But the difficulty of which everyone is aware is the examination system, which exerts its own, often separate disciplines. To have been free of that in adult education, was of course an advantage, and it is not only because I hate examining (quite apart from not knowing what beta-plus-query-plus means) that I believe its radical reform is necessary. Yet it can only be changed, responsibly, if teaching is also changed, and these changes would demand more effort, more continuous and cooperative discipline, than the present system. Students have above all to convince their teachers that they are ready for this. It is the problem of all social change: that a system produces kinds of human being who then seem to illustrate the justification of the system. Breaking through to a different world involves not just the rejection of authority but the taking of authority, with all its consequent demands on oneself.

This new authority can come only from the difficult, prolonged, and of course untidy process of cooperative decision. As a teacher, in adult education or at the university, I have often believed that I know what needs to be done, to understand a particular issue, and that this can involve unwelcome postponements, or tough and even boring preparatory work. But I have never known this refused, by a group, when it is fully explained. The challenge that the work can be done without it is after all, easily met by detailed argument; or, if this is not so, if a proposed scheme can not be sustained, any teacher ought to know he must change.

The real difficulty comes when this process is short-cut by external administrative decision, as happened all too often in the bureaucratic structure of much modern adult education, and as happens all the time in universities, even where, as in Cambridge, the structure of the faculty is partly democratic (often, by that very fact, involving delays which can outlast any particular student generation). The toughest issue is not the complication of internal control, which with goodwill, patience, and of course a necessary militancy of demand, can be got right. It is the very complicated question of social demand, and hence social control, of a public educational system. There have been some ugly attempts recently to exert repressive controls; and in any case the sophisticated financial management, by which control is really exerted in Britain, is now very dangerous to the universities as it was constantly dangerous in the more exposed and poorer conditions of adult education.

Public Rows Needed

I agree, in principle, that a society has a right to make demands on its education system. I would like to see more public rows on this, not less, for I know I have to answer to, among others, that miner, on whose backs an expensive system, directly benefiting now only a minority, must be seen to rest. It is in its way of meeting this issue that the most hopeful part of the student revolt can be seen. What students are often blamed for, inside the universities, is, to quote the caricature, 'asking us to meet them about the syllabus and then, instead, demonstrating about Vietnam.' The indefinite and unargued extension from the syllabus to Vietnam is of course irrational. But, in this real movement, the right questions seem to me to get asked: not only the local questions about research contracts with outside bodies, or about the giving of money for this, the refusal of money for that. But also, more generally, about who is speaking in the name of society: what real public decision is involved in the giving or withholding of public money; what version of society is implied in what are called educational requirements and standards. I think the student movement has been right to identify the present educational and administrative structure with the values of the bourgeois society which, in the nineteenth century, created it: the rigid selection and distribution of specialised minority roles, as against the idea of public education, in which the whole society is seen as a learning process, and in which, consequently, access is open, not only for all people but for all their questions, across the arbitrary divisions of quotas and subjects. This is what adult education embodied, as a demand, at once educational and social; in fact political; and there is good evidence to show that, in its genuine form, this extending education makes higher rather than lower demands, not only in intellectual quality (which a specialism can protect but not extend) but also, and crucially, in human recognition and response.

This is what I think I learned, from my years in adult education, and that now helps me to see the true character of the university crisis. This is why I argue, in fact, not for student power but for democracy. What teachers have learned is also relevant, and will have to be part of any real reform; much can be lost in the sillier rhetoric of generations, and the teacher who pretends he is not a teacher (of course also with much to learn) is a pathetic and irrelevant figure. But if there is discontent among students, there is also discontent among teachers, since we are all victims of the same system, and even those who play along with it usually have, in private, few illusions about what is really happening.

In these uneasy months, I remember the history of men without rights and without property demanding the means to understand and alter their world; of the complicated interaction between their own self-organising institutions and not only those who could control or buy them but also those who knew, from direct experience, how hard, disturbing, and endlessly flexible any real learning is. How many useless supposed shortcuts there are in systems and in negations of systems. What I had to face with that miner in the university museum was the challenge to act as a man beyond a system of teaching, and yet to meet as we were, without either formality or pretence. It is what Tawney faced, in his adult classes in economics, on experience the discipline didn't yet include. Or, again, a generation of adult tutors, in the years since the war, on the real relations between culture and society, between democracy and education. The issues that at last, through a new generation, have reached the universities and that are going, not without difficulty, to change them.

Open Teaching

From: *The Listener*, 6 May 1971, pp 594–5

Any Sunday morning, at the press of a button, we can drop in on some of the Open University's lectures. It will be interesting to know, eventually, how many people do this, over and above the registered students. One of the important effects of having this work on television is that some aspects of the real work of universities are available for direct public observation. Nobody could say that universities haven't been in the visual news in recent years, but I often wonder what image has been built between the poles of student demonstrations and quiz shows like *University Challenge*. At least here, in the lectures, we are getting some of the preponderant routines.

It must be said at once that the television lectures are only a part of the teaching. There are also the radio programmes, the finely produced printed material – in course units and background books – and beyond these the whole system of assigned written work, study centres, tutors and counsellors and residential schools. As a combined exercise in educational communication it is genuinely experimental, and we shan't know its results for some years, until more than one generation of students have gone through.

What is being shown now are the Foundation Courses, in Social Sciences, Mathematics, Science and Arts. A good deal of work at something like this level is already transmitted on television in other ways. Interestingly, though, this other work is mainly science and arts. In economics and mathematics very little professional work ever penetrates beyond the education programmes. And yet it is not, for example, that economics is not endlessly discussed. On *The Money Programme*, on *Panorama* and *24 Hours* and *This Week*, on the Budget Specials, there is what often seems a perpetual economic conversation. But the number of professional economists who take part in it is very small. Political and financial journalists, and a few rather regular politicians, industrialists and trade-union leaders, go through discussions which, whatever else they might be, are never educational, in any sense. Difficult and controversial concepts are tossed along those studio tables in what has to be seen in the end as a sort of national game. Like much of the press, *The Money Programme*, for example, has included more and more share-tipping and company gossip, in a quite open way. I've calculated that in proportion we would need six or seven hours a week on the more popular form of gambling with pools coupons, though it's fair to say that the racing spots, on sports programmes, keep the expected ideological proportion between the sights of horses running and the calculation of chances and starting prices.

Such considerations are crucial in reviewing one obvious problem, which affects the relation between television education and general informative programmes. Ideology, in the form of known kinds of communicator and audience, gets into the general programmes quite frankly. But this is sometimes rationalised as not wanting too many bloody dons. It is a fact, for example, that a different kind of economic discussion, in the general programmes, could be quite easily arranged, if economists rather than journalists were more regularly invited. But think of watching it, people say around the studios and the offices. I do, and I also think of the party gossip we now get as a matter of course; some of the most boring television ever made or conceivable.

What ought to be happening, on the Open University courses, is something more serious, more sustained, more open. In general science and arts programmes we do usually get people with more real things to say – more authoritative people, if you like – than in the general political and economic discussions. But, in the hazards of programming, the subjects are often random, or a single subject is dealt with in one big programme, where genuine understanding might require a different method: more orderly, more progressive, more sustained.

This, then, is one of the ironies of some of the Foundation Courses. Offering an introduction to a very wide field, they can result, as last week, in John Dankworth on the instruments of the orchestra followed by an analysis of Bernini's *Ecstasy of Saint Teresa*. The Science and Mathematics programmes, as I understand them, are teaching basic units, concepts and procedures. So, it might be said, are the Arts and Social Science courses, but at what seems to me a rather different level. There is a problem of deep theoretical penetration from which alone any really founding introduction could follow, and it is a fact about our culture that some of this has been achieved in mathematics and the physio-chemical and perhaps biological sciences, while it has not been achieved in social sciences and the arts. So it has to be said that some of the Arts programmes, and in a different way several of the Social Science programmes, have been useful in particular ways but also in quite enclosed ways: that there is nowhere to go from them, towards the discipline as a whole. But then it must be added that the Open University is no different, in this respect, from other British universities. The whole problem in arts and social science faculties in recent years – and it has underlain a great deal of what has been stupidly received as Student Unrest – is precisely this question of relevance.

I watch the Mathematics and Science programmes as a layman. I am often baffled by details but I do get a sense of where the exposition is going. Last week I tried to follow a problem in the geometry of surfaces: introduced, by way of good will, with a film of an oil survey and then moving, by way of some instrument readings, to what were to me some truly formidable equations. Only duty kept me watching, but then the teaching began: a series of visual demonstrations of problems of minima and maxima, becoming more complicated but with a warning that it was involving simplification; and I then found to my surprise that at some different level of the mind a new way of seeing certain physical relations was beginning to form. I am sure I would have needed to follow it up, with exercises, but the working models and mobile diagrams seemed a clear advantage of television teaching.

Similarly in the Science programme on cells, where I already knew rather more. The detailed unpacking of a model cell, with very flexible visual interpretations of its structure, was clearer than anything I had previously seen or read. And the second part of the programme, showing procedures for getting actual material for analysis, took this beyond spectator science and at least some way towards the idea of an active discipline.

In some elementary economics, of the M=PQ/V variety, there was also a good use of diagrams, but as so often in that field there was an element of abstraction of a quite different order from that of, say, the surface geometry. The Social Science course in general has been very orthodox, and another way of saying that (in any university) is bad. Some terms – there was an early example in a demonstration, actually a misunderstanding, of 'cognitive dissonance' – have been presented more as instruction towards a phraseology than as analysis towards an understanding.

In the Arts course, John Dankworth's theme composed to demonstrate the various instruments was more interesting and clearer than several similar programmes I had previously watched. There were good earlier programmes on, for example, the use of primary historical materials, and on some of the elements and conventions of visual composition and recognition. An early programme on the Yorubas, offering to make a point about culture and cultures, was less successful, and like other things in this course, was not seriously followed up, at least at this stage.

As I've already said, the difference about these courses is that everybody can drop in on them. I think we are all in debt to these teachers, who are working right in the open. The use of television for real education has barely begun, and most of the signs are that it will be a real expansion of our resources, not just as a transmission system but in actual modes of understanding.

Adult Education

From: Raymond Williams, *Politics and Letters – Interviews with New Left Review*, New Left Books, 1979, pp 78–83

What was your immediate working environment in the WEA?
When I got my job in the Extra-Mural Delegacy at Oxford, which controlled a scattered region extending from Staffordshire in the North to Sussex in the South, I was appointed to East Sussex, and went to live in Seaford. The social character of my classes was extremely mixed. At one level there was the class that I ran in Hastings, essentially with the local Trades Council, which was called Public Expression and simply involved specific training in public writing and public speaking. There seemed little point in teaching the writing of essays; I taught the writing of reports, minutes, memoranda, and committee speaking and oral reports – skills relevant to their work. At the other extreme you would get a class of commuter housewives at Haywards Heath who wanted to read some literature. Perfectly serious in their interest, but an entirely different social composition. Then I had a fair number in which there was a mixture of the two elements, including of course the substantial number of wage earners one discovers, who at the third or fourth meeting produce their novel or autobiography, short stories or poems – an enormous amount of unknown writing of this sort goes on. It was a mixture I could live with.

How do you judge in retrospect the whole nature of adult education, as you experienced it in practice over a decade?
I remember G.D.H. Cole, who was a university representative, saying at the meetings of the Delegacy: 'I am damned well not interested in adult education, I am interested in workers' education.' That was the conflict. He was a minority voice and he lost. Of course, some would say the battle had been fought and lost long before this. I don't think so myself, but I can see the way of writing the history which would make it out to be so. The adult education movement split before the First World War, with the famous Ruskin strike, between a consciously socialist-affiliated workers' education which eventually produced the National Council of Labour Colleges, and the Workers' Educational Association which attached itself to the universities, and tried – I think with more success than the NCLC said was possible – to develop a working-class education which would draw on the university claim of exploring all positions rather than teaching from an affiliated position. Today, when I read of the Ruskin strike and the foundation of *Plebs*,

I think that the opponents of this WEA conception were right. They said: 'Do you suffer from class-consciousness? Come to Oxford and be cured.' They sensed that the universities could eventually incorporate the movement and that what would be taught in the name of academic standards and better learning would not be a socialist education. On the other hand there is no doubt that specifically class-affiliated education does in certain important respects run the risk of becoming subservient to particular party lines in particular periods, and genuinely losing some of its educational characteristics. The NCLC in certain areas was a more important working-class movement. In South Wales it produced far more educated militants than the WEA ever did. The WEA on the other hand tried to represent the notion of a distant affiliation to a class which yet had to be mediated by a kind of education that made no presumptions – in Tawney's phrase you follow the argument where it leads. The balance between those two principles was still being fought out in the adult education movement in the forties, when I joined it. There is no question which eventually won and the reason was in the end a very crude one. The universities could financially sustain their version of adult education and were unwilling to sustain the alternative definition. But this does not mean, as some histories suggest, that it all ended in 1911; that the WEA was always a mere liberal or reformist diversion. For every time a class came up with working-class membership, and there were still many such, what they wanted was the original WEA form of education; although they did not want – and I think they were right – dogmatic instruction, being taken through any *Short Course*; they wanted an open orientation. I think we were affected by that. So the experience of the WEA was always very ambivalent for me.

Presumably the WEA differed from area to area. What was the character of the Oxford Delegacy?
There was an important radicalizing presence in North Staffordshire, a strongly working-class area. Together with Kent it made possible a miners' summer school. In Oxford itself, Thomas Hodgkin ran the department, with a very strong and principled conception of how to develop a popular working-class education. He believed that essentially the people to do it were committed socialists. He fought hard to say that tutors had the right, when it was relevant, to declare their position in the class, but to ensure within the open structure of the class that this position was always totally challengeable, naturally subject to opposition and discussion. That approach was attacked very bitterly, of course. The whole Delegacy was seen as a Communist cell. There was a violent assault on its whole organisation and on Hodgkin in particular. Moreover, quite soon tutors were going out to West Africa and the Sudan – Hodgkin was an Africanist – practising this sort of education. So the Delegacy was perceived not simply as an internal conspiracy but as subversive externally. There was an extreme crisis within the institution during the late forties and early fifties. It was a sharp local form of the Cold War.

How did the conflict develop? What was your own role in it?
Well, of course I agreed that it would have been wholly wrong in classes not
to declare your own position; and equally that you made no assumption at
the beginning of the class that you shared anything else than an interest
in the subject. You can see very easily the dangers one way, of teaching
declining into a propaganda exercise. But in fact increasingly through
the fifties the dangers were the opposite. For like all the other welfare
services, the WEA started to become heavily used by the middle classes
as a form of leisure and education. There was nothing wrong in this,
except that in socially mixed communities they induced a quite different
cultural atmosphere from that of the working-class student. You had to
positively encourage specific working people's classes, organized round
trade unions and so on. This was done. But all the time there was constant
pressure from the university: you must improve academic standards, you
must get written work, there must be no crossing of subject boundaries.
As an adult tutor one lived on a very long lead. Living 100–150 miles
away from Oxford, you had a hell of a lot of practical autonomy. Still,
my syllabuses were constantly criticized on these grounds: of course a class
in English literature, but what is this other – including the first class in
which I started discussing the themes of *Culture and Society*? What sort
of class is this? The main spokesman for university standards was S.G.
Raybould, who wrote various books on the subject. The effect was to
tend to eliminate people without secondary education, since they found
difficulty in producing that sort of written work. We tutors had to certify
that such work was being produced in order to satisfy the conditions of
the class to be approved and funded by the university and the Ministry.
We replied, of course, that we were trying to create new standards of a
different kind of work. The controversies, if anybody wants to look them
up, are all there in the Adult Education *Highway* of the period – to which
I contributed.

Over the years there in the end occurred a pretty successful conversion
of the WEA into something that could be indifferently called Further
Education: any other emphasis was deflected, except in certain specialized
areas of trade union education. That only became totally clear to me when
I moved to Oxford in 1960 as what was called a resident tutor, which was a
kind of senior post. Immediately a plan was unfolded – it was quite explicit
– to create a residential college in Wellington Square, whose focus would
be on refresher courses for young graduates who had gone into industrial
management, and so on. This was suddenly no longer the mixed situation
I had lived in for fourteen years. When they moved to institutionalize these
dreadful refresher courses for managers, then of course adult education
ceased to have enough meaning. It was at that point that I knew that I
wanted to move on. Though it happened quite unexpectedly. I got a letter
saying I had been appointed a Lecturer in Cambridge, though I hadn't
applied for it. But I was ready to go.

*There is one question raised by your account that relates the WEA to
Politics and Letters. You've said that you took the position within the*

WEA, that as a teacher you would state your own views as a socialist but not impose these or assume that they were shared by your students. You would not, however, affect an unreal neutrality or suppression of your convictions. But in a way that is precisely what you did not do in Politics and Letters. *It would have been quite possible for you to declare that this was a socialist journal, but on the other hand that it would publish any strong or valid objections from other points of view. You did not do so. What was the balance of considerations which led you to that presumably very central and conscious choice in '46–7, which you later changed in the WEA?*

I would be happier if I could say that it was conscious in *Politics and Letters*. I am not sure that it was not the unconscious process of the emerging terms of the collaboration between left politics and 'Leavisite' criticism. I think that the bad influence of the *Scrutiny* connection on us was to accredit the whole idea of the disinterested intelligence. You can see the way in which one could move from this free-floating concept of disinterested intelligence to the very much more defensible position of an essentially open style of intellectual work which nevertheless includes the non-dominative declaration of one's own position. It was the blurring of those two concepts that was responsible for the particular weakness of the journal. It took me a long time to sort them out – to see that the disinterested intelligence is a fantasy which is different from the much more viable and correct position which sounds so much like it. Or can sound like it. But I don't want to confuse my own later choices with the actual developments of adult education. The WEA had certain positives as against any closed internal propagandizing education. Yet in the end you cannot be financed and academically controlled by those kinds of universities, and carry out a programme of education of the working class. The WEA itself had the same ambiguity as the programme of *Politics and Letters*. There is no denying that.

Can we ask a more practical question about your actual working routines? Presumably during those years you must have read and written during the day and taught mainly in the evenings. Did you find that more advantageous for a writer than the typical teaching situation which would involve contact hours during the day and trying to read and write in the evening?

I don't know. All I can say is that it is the only regime I have ever been able to operate. If I had to do other work in the morning at all regularly I would probably start drying up. Adult education was actually physically a very wearing job; I felt that particularly later. The travelling in the evening, particularly in post-war conditions, on late buses and trains was very tiring. But it did mean that every morning I could write and every afternoon I could read, before leaving most evenings to teach. From '48, when I pulled back from most collaborative work, this was a routine of extraordinary regularity. It was also a process of self-education: it was only from '48 that I got any extensive knowledge of English literature. The selective three year course at Cambridge, particularly the way in which I had done it, had not given me that. I remember I used to put 50 or 75 per cent new literature into my teaching every year so that I eventually knew I had gone through enough. These special conditions of work were very advantageous to me. But they meant that when I came back to Cambridge I adopted the very same routine and I still do – I could not now work in any other way.

Adult Education and Social Change

From: *Adult Education and Social Change: Lectures and Reminiscences in Honour of Tony McLean*, WEA Southern District, 1983, pp 9–24

There are two ways, perhaps, in which we can interpret the matter of the relation between Adult Education and social change. One, the evident and obvious one, is that Adult Education was instituted, developed and altered by social change in the sense of movements of the larger society. The other, less obvious but I think quite inner to its history, is that Adult Education offered to be, and at times was, part of the process of social change itself. It is much easier to talk about the history in terms of the first, in which Adult Education is the bottle with the message in it, bobbing on the tides and waves of history. It has its good phases and its bad phases and so on. But I think that kind of history and that kind of interpretation of its relation to social change, although inevitable and full of evidence, diminishes it. For, though in very different ways and leading into controversies which are not yet over, the central ambition of this process which was eventually called Adult Education was to be part of the process of social change itself. At many times, and especially by those who had become eminent in one of its previous phases, this ambition was denied or played down. Nevertheless I think the true dignity of its history is not to be found in what it was influenced by, although of course being so often marginal, precarious and under-funded, it was continually influenced in this or that direction – momentarily encouraged, often thwarted. Its dignity is in the more general sense that it kept this ambition to be something other than the consequence of change and to become part of its process.

Now, this distinction matters very much, in talking about a colleague like Tony McLean and about the generation to which he belonged; not that his was the first generation in which this intention was active. I think however that his was the first generation in which it became extremely controversial. There was a real complication of that ambition to be part of the process of social change at a time when the society also happened to be changing very rapidly, with changing and dividing affiliation. In respect for so good a historian I then take both those senses of history: history as the general record in which many voices, but only a few of them very loud, are active and influential; and that other sense in which the opportunity to intervene in history, with whatever puny resources, finds, as in Tony's case, a willingness to put oneself on the line but also to see what learning itself can contribute to an active process of social change rather than simply being its reflection. That I think, as I knew him, was Tony's sense of the matter. Since he was so good a historian, he had an exceptional sense of its complexity in the period he was working through.

One of my best remembered conversations with him was on one of our innumerable train trips to Oxford, when I said – and I was always more cynical in these respects than he – 'In the winter we teach English and History and Art and Ideas. In the summer we do Adult Education'. The distinction – which still seems to me a valid one – is that there is all the difference in the world between the set of teaching and learning practices which we tried to carry out, often in what seemed very marginal and precarious ways, and the body of formal doctrine of an institutional and ideological kind which was called Adult Education, which was waiting for us when we got off at Oxford Station and went into meetings and conferences and discussed large matters of that kind. It isn't that one couldn't acquire a knack at it, but there was something about that contact which underlined the fact that we lived most of the winter as independent intellectuals, taking our classes, and in the summer we were something quite different. There was that place, older than the rocks among which it was sitting, and full of ideas and prejudices which were even older than that. The arrival of these strange, outlying characters – who had been teaching some sort of classes somewhere out in the country – was bound to be mutually disturbing. The social problem was not so difficult; the ancient universities were such socially insecure places in spite of appearances that it was not a serious problem. It was primarily an intellectual problem. For what always seemed to me the case was that ninety percent of these definitions and propositions about Adult Education and its importance were produced only because an essentially normal activity was being challenged or questioned by somebody. Yet there really was extraordinarily little reason to have to justify it at any point. It justified itself. Still when you got to that level you had to spin out of your mind the most extraordinary propositions, assent to the calculations of this or that institution, find reasons of some official sounding kind for resisting yet one more exercise in cost cutting. So I made the distinction between the work, the real practice, and what was generalised as Adult Education and had this whole apparatus attached to it. That is why I said 'we do one thing in the winter, we do another thing in the summer'. But Tony, who was always more generous than I, said 'No, of course it is necessary. We have to discuss the general problems and put them right'.

But discuss them, how? Because this was just the point. I remember a key meeting of the Oxford Delegacy at which G.D.H. Cole, very much a surviving voice of an older tradition, said 'I don't give a damn about Adult Education, I am only interested in Workers' Education'. That was one of the interpretations of Adult Education as being part of the process of change which was at just that time colliding with the need which Cole, to be fair, did not see, for a kind of Adult Education which was wider than that of Workers' Education in the strict sense. But it was colliding also with a newly anxious respectability in which it was Adult Education that was expected to assimilate to the changed manners of the University rather than in any sense the other way round. What was at stake was the whole history of the educational challenges that Adult Education had made to those institutions which, in a way, because they do their own jobs so well, are always in danger of acquiring a very restricted and privileged and stagnant view of the world. The tension had to be worked through, the challenge had to be made, between equals. Whereas always in practice there were those unnoticed superiorities which do not belong to matters of the mind but to control of resources and committees and so on. The superiority always seemed to be coming from this other end and one of its results was that the very notion that an Adult Educator was contributing to the process of social change became suspect. This was so especially in that period of the forties and fifties when almost everybody put their intellectual resources well under cover. For it was a politically dangerous time.

Every such notion was controversial, and besides it was not made any easier to resolve by the fact that there were some crude versions of that active role around. There were indeed crude versions which would have converted this educational practice into ideological training and propaganda. But we can never be satisfied with that kind or argument between two false positions. The true position was, always essentially was, that the impulse to Adult Education was not only a matter of remedying deficit, making up for inadequate educational resources in the wider society, nor only a case of meeting new needs of the society, though those things contributed. The deepest impulse was the desire to make learning part of the process of social change itself. That was what was important about it. How to do it was always in question and always being changed, but if one forgets that underlying intention then it becomes just one of many other institutions with an essentially different kind of history.

It is true that the conscious organisation of a more literate and scientific culture in the nineteenth century was bound to throw up new kinds of institutions and eventually something that could be consciously called Adult Education. But I often recall a remark of Cobbett, at a very early stage, when people were collecting money for one of the early Mechanics' Institutes and he sent along £5.00, which is quite a substantial subscription if you translate the currency from the early nineteenth century. However, he added, 'I gave my £5.00 as a mark of my regard for and my attachment to the *working classes of the community* and also as a mark of my approbation of anything which seemed to assert that these classes were equal, in point of intellect, to those who had the insolence to call them the *Lower Orders*. But, I was not without my fears that this institution may be turned to purposes, *extremely injurious to the mechanics themselves*. I cannot but know what sort of people are likely to get amongst them . . . Mechanics, I most heartily wish you well but I also most heartily wish you not to be *humbugged*, which you most certainly will be if you suffer anybody but REAL MECHANICS to have anything to do in managing the concern. You will *mean well*; but, many a cunning scoundrel will get *place* or *pension* as the *price* of you'.

Now Cobbett on Education is no kind of automatic authority. He was a great adult educator in his own practice, a remarkably self-educated man continually engaged in the real business of adult education before it was officially named. But at the same time he was deeply suspicious of the process in ways that anticipate many of the later arguments, because he was never prepared to say that education was an unambiguous good. He didn't have that kind of intellectual swoon before the very notion of a leavening of cultivation. Always it was the true content of education and the relations which as a process it was itself instituting which seemed to him to draw the line between whether it enabled people to understand and have better control over their lives or whether it was part of what he called more generally and abusively and often loosely 'the comforting system'. This was to be echoed in that slogan of the Plebs' League, a hundred years after Cobbett: 'Do you suffer from too much class consciousness? Come to Oxford and be cured'.

I often think of Cobbett's phrase 'I cannot but know what sort of people are likely to get amongst them'. It is part of the real history of adult education that some very remarkable people have got amongst the mechanics and their successors and have contributed enormously to a better understanding of the world and an ability to act in it. It is also true that some of the people Cobbett foresaw got there too, and got there because they could see the sort of process it was going to be. The necessary entry of a new kind of organised learning for adults in an increasingly literate and scientific culture didn't stay at the early institutional phase. What interests me most is the very mixed case – I have thought about it a good deal in trying to understand my own practice and that of others – in the next phase, which really inaugurates the history of what we now directly call Adult Education, particularly as it began to relate to the Universities. It was obvious that there had to be some relation to the Universities. In that second phase, particularly in the hey-day of the Extension Movement in the last third of the nineteenth century, there was a very curious thing which I think helps one to understand that crucial difference in British culture between two ideas which sound so like each other that we often confuse them: on the one hand *social conscience*, and on the other *social consciousness*.

There is no doubt that a very large part of the Extension Movement was the product of a certain kind of social conscience, and this is in a limited way to be respected. People saw not only hard-working men living in poor and deprived material conditions but hard-working men of considerable intelligence and interest in learning deprived of the least opportunity in any sustained way to fulfill that kind of resource. If what followed from that included a missionary sense, the sense of going out to remedy a deficit, it has still to be respected but certainly not submitted to. For it sent out many good people who tried to humanise their own learning and to bring it into real relations with this hard-pressed environment. But also necessarily, and it is true of the majority in that phase (I would not like to estimate how long that kind of confidence persisted) they believed that they were taking *understanding* to people. Not taking the tools of understanding; not taking the results of certain organised learning; not putting these into a process which would then be an interaction with what was often very solid experience in areas in which the learned were in fact ignorant; but rather a taking of learning itself, humanity itself. It is surprising how often in the writings of that period people whose individual lives we can respect, talk about 'humanizing' or 'refining' people, of course mostly poor people. But the fact is that the real situation was never of that kind.

Everyone notices, in an unequal education system, the facts of deficit; notices the people who could do with more or better, more sustained education and who are in that sense deprived. But what few notice, because to have the opportunity to observe both sides of this divide is not common, is that in a society in which learning is unequal certain distinctive kinds of ignorance accumulate in the very heartland of learning. This heartland defines itself; it defines what learning is; it deems what is a subject and what is not. It knows what is evidence and what is not. We find Cobbett, if I may quote him again, thinking just about this in relation to history. The Histories of England, he says, 'are very little better than romances. Their contents are generally confined to narrations relating to battles, negotiations, intrigues, contests between rival sovereignties, rival nobles and to the character of kings, queens, mistresses, bishops, ministers and the like'. He was talking, he tells us, to a very clever young man who had read the history of England by many different authors and 'I gave the conversation a turn that drew from him, unperceived by himself, that he did not know how tithes, parishes, poor rates, church rates and the abolition of trial by jury in hundreds of cases came to be in England'. 'It is not stuff like this' Cobbett argued, 'but we want to know what was the state of the people, what were a labourer's wages; what were the prices of the food, and how the labourers were dressed?'

Now, again I don't quote Cobbett as an authority but the point he made was made again and was instanced without being made in hundreds of subsequent cases. For although the manifest relationship was that taking learning to a class seen as in deficit, or to certain stranded exceptional individuals as it was often interpreted, it was rarely noticed that the real deficit was on both sides of the account. For there was a positive deficiency in the centres of learning themselves. There were areas of the life of their own people about which they were profoundly ignorant. When adult education was seen only as the process of humanizing and refining, when people who went out in that missionary spirit hit (as they sometimes did, although they often got a lot of submissive respect, but as they sometimes did) the hard talk of men who did ask (and it wasn't a utilitarian question although it often tended to be reduced to it) 'Where does this learning tie in with my life?', then the notion of refining and humanizing could become anti-educational.

There was the anti-educational notion that you should soften the terms of the discussion; the anti-educational notion that you should exclude controversial current material. There was also the support of certain subjects, in that period and since, precisely because they moved people away from those areas which would put the status and nature of official learning in question.

Yet if you look at the next period from the turn of the century, there is not only that bust-up between the Plebs' League and the WEA, in which the Plebs' League saw the WEA, as at one time they called them, 'Lackeys standing in front of the university trying to divert the workers into this kind of university consciousness'. There is also what the WEA did, through its best tutors, to meet that centrality of response without, at least without intending, the responses of refinement or of humanizing a rather raw population. For that is not where real social change lies. As it came through with harder, better organised people, it has been true of the best Adult Education in this century that the idea of learning itself has been changed, and this has been one of the processes by which learning has contributed to social change rather than simply reflecting it.

The case of Tawney is now classical because Tawney had the intellectual honesty to admit that as already a major professional historian there were areas of the history of his people about which he knew little. It happened later, I believe, in economics. It certainly happened after the war in a period in which Tony and I were colleagues, when – if I may tell you this as a story – when I moved into internal University Teaching, when at about the same time Richard Hoggart did the same, we started teaching in ways that had been absolutely familiar in Extra-Mural and WEA classes, relating history to art and literature, including contemporary culture, and suddenly so strange was this to the Universities that they said 'My God, here is a new subject called Cultural Studies'. Tony McLean was one of the best of those who had been teaching Cultural Studies for years before the announcement of the birth of this new subject. But we are beginning, I am afraid, to see encyclopedia articles dating the birth of Cultural Studies from this or that book in the late fifties. Don't believe a word of it. That shift of perspective about the teaching of arts and literature and their relation to history and to contemporary society began in Adult Education, it didn't happen anywhere else. It was when it was taken across by people with that experience to the Universities that it was suddenly recognised as a subject. It is in these and other similar ways that the contribution of the process itself to social change itself, and specifically to learning, has happened.

Now it is very important to say this when we come to the post-war period in which the notion of deficit was dropped. It was said that since there was now universal education, since there was now every opportunity of access for what was still in that twinkling way called 'a bright child' to go wherever he wished, then there was a diminishing or vanishing deficit. The cannibals thus appeared to be dying out and there was therefore less demand for missionaries. The rough, naturally intelligent but unlettered were becoming a very small number, and the ones who were still like that didn't want to know anyway. Therefore – as if indeed that had been its only premise – adult education had reached its natural limit. It was the kind of thing that could be safely dropped and mythologised. Mythologised it was but also there were really very serious attempts to drop it, and still are.

This brings us to a real complexity, the relation between willingness and ability to learn and the forms of learning that are at any time presented. What is usually offered, in the crude state of official educational thinking, is the proposition that there is something called academic education and there is even something called the academic mind and, God help us, the academic child. Thus academic institutions exist for these potential academic persons and academic children, and those who are not academic persons or academic children will be very much happier not to be bothered. Under this wonderful alibi word 'academic' the problems about education which Adult Education and others raised can be simply evaded. For life is not like that, of course. It is not some simple process of offering and reception. There are always some blocks on learning. One of them is the relevance of the learning that happens to be available to what *you* want to learn. These complications eat so deeply into all educational systems that only somebody up to no good ever draws the stupid conclusion that you have reached the limit of the educable.

Actually the last time we had any records on this was in that otherwise unregretted period of National Service, when they gave recruits intelligence test; not that we should put any great faith in them but they indicate something. It is very interesting that then, in the late fifties, in National Service recruits' intelligence tests, half of those who were put by the tests in the highest intelligence categories had had no more than a minimum education. Yet this was in a period when if the institutional alternatives which were talked about as having ended this deficit had really done so, at least a good number of them would have been picked up. This is one kind of objective support for my own very strong belief that it is not just a matter of available intelligence and available learning interest, but that there is still an extraordinary lottery in the interlock between those and the kind of learning that is at any time available and the time of life at which it comes up. This is a point that adult educationalists have of course often made. It defeats the crude, ideological attempt to write the last chapter of adult education because all the bright boys and girls have gone through the system and up the ladder. Or rather it should defeat it, but in practice the crude ideology can be one of those self-fulfilling prophecies, as you put less resources into education, or as people subtly change their own attitudes to it and then you get less significant response and that seems to confirm the initial assumption.

Such changes are very different from the movements of large, objective forces such as the nature of work and the rise of modern communications systems and all those other things which have quite evidently changed the nature of education in any case. All of us must adjust to those, but this is very different from adjusting to the anti-educational ideologies. Indeed I sometimes feel when I look at the actual cannibals who are now powerful in the world of ideas and educational provision, that we could do with a few missionaries again, simply carrying social conscience towards deficit. But then if we accept their kind of analysis of the history, we shall be quite unprepared to analyse the very critical and complex situation that anything now offering to call itself Adult Education finds itself in.

It is very interesting in spite of the persistent echoes of that symbolic dispute between the Plebs' League and the WEA, and later the WEA and the Labour Colleges, about the feel, the tone, the content of education, and about who should control it, that although the WEA was the better funded organisation and had the key assistance of the universities and of official recognition, nevertheless people entered it, especially in the nineteen-thirties, with a strong sense of Adult Education as contributing to social change. These were people, and in my experience they were almost all good people, who went into Adult Education because they wanted to change the society in some specific ways. They were driven not by social conscience, in the old sense. It wasn't the missionary position of feeling sorry for the unfortunate. Instead they were interested in the process of building a social consciousness of an adequate kind, as they saw it, to meet new crises, the crises that were then defined as war and unemployment and Fascism but that in any case were seen as the crises of modern capitalist society. It was almost invariably seen like that, but they went into Adult Education, not to propagandise – they could have done that more easily in other institutions – but with that necessary consciousness as a kind of priority. The resulting complications – the emotional, intellectual and social complications of that generation, which entered with that kind of intention – have still, I think to be fully analysed. Because quite apart from the simplest things one can say about it – that it didn't turn out like that, that it became politically very difficult, and so on – the whole problem was that people arriving with a message, their kind of message in the bottle, had to learn, if they were to enter in any sustained way the experience of Adult Education, that even people who agreed that the point of Adult Education was the building of an adequate social consciousness didn't, in that sense, want messages. I mean they didn't want the conclusions of arguments: they wanted to reach their own conclusions.

But also in a rather later period, in the generation precisely of the adult work of Tony McLean, the whole problem was not whether the message would be accepted or rejected or modified but – and I don't mean this satirically – what the message should be. I mean that the very broadening of the material and of the subjects of Adult Education which occurred in that generation, was, we can say in retrospect, a kind of thinking arising from the complications of practice. It was a question not what the message should be so much as what would be the kind of evidence, what sources would you look for?

I would instance, for example, the shift that has happened in thinking about symbolic values, as in thinking about Art and Literature. Something of this kind had always been done in this work but usually as reflecting what happened elsewhere in the society. The new thinking was about just these practices, in any period, as part of the way in which a general social consciousness is formed, the way in which it actually gets embodied, not from other sources but from some general source in social life and yet they are still unmistakable as themselves and can only be addressed as themselves. The shift to that, as in much of Tony's later teaching, is part of the complication. There was a time as an adult tutor when you felt a second class citizen if you were not teaching Economics or Politics, because that had been the first interpretation of what the business of creating social consciousness was. I know in my own case, and I remember asking

Tony's advice, the first four Tutorial Classes I had were all in International Relations and in some curious way in the next year they had all become classes in Literature. The process by which this happened has never been satisfactorily explained. Yet I didn't get what might be called approval about this. And after all you can still see the case. Suppose you say now, 'What do we most need to be conscious about, since we are starting a class this winter?' You might easily ask if there is anything worth discussing this winter but the problems of nuclear disarmament and the problems of the British and world economy – I am not running any of those issues down – I am just saying the old assumption was that there and there only, and in those ways, was consciousness formed. And this was the curious change that happened in this post-war period, of which some of the political results are now taking some of the people who never noticed this shift by surprise. If I can again give one example, when I was teaching classes and writing about newspapers and advertising in the fifties one of my political friends said 'Well, I suppose it's amusing enough but what does it have to do with politics?' But if you look back from the eighties, having seen what newspapers have to do with politics, you can recall the really virgin innocence of people who thought themselves hard, mature, political analysts.

For the process of real social consciousness is always complex, and learning and getting through to the centres of consciousness of one's own time is always a matter of *contemporary* analysis. This will certainly renew many received things but it will also draw on kinds of evidence, kinds of influence, kinds of change which had previously been excluded. Yet the other pressure on us – I remember talking to Tony about this in the case of the History of Art – was to feel that this was the nice, good stuff, as against the chaotic and dismal muddle of Politics and Economics; that this was the beautiful material, these were the real achievements of humanity. But to be able to see in the shift of a style of painting or in the shift of a method in architecture or in a shift in a major literary form, that social relationships and people themselves are changing, and that people's symbolic values have a crucial effect on the ways in which they interpret all their other values and their other relationships and therefore contribute necessary evidence to it, this was the kind of change that eventually occurred. The simple version, that you went into Adult Education to build social consciousness, changed, not in its ideals but in its methods. Of course there were then also all the other changes: the supposed ending of the deficit; the development of an educational bureaucracy; the pressure, backed by funding, to train people for roles and jobs as preferable to the general education of human beings and citizens. Through all this there was also the pressure to make adult education respectable, in such limited terms. The old humanists were pushed away; the industrial trainers arrived; but still, under difficult conditions, the new humanists – the true public educators – survived.

Now it is in that respect, that the life's work of Tony McLean is still exemplary because he never in any crude sense thought that the contribution to social change was delivering people some kind of boiled-down pap which would indicate some already decided course of action to them. The building of social consciousness was of real consciousness, of real understanding of the world. And it extended beyond the simpler areas that were externally defined as Political and Economic. It is in lives like his and in work like that, that real Adult Education justifies itself. It is reduced if it is seen as merely the second-order consequence and reflection of social change. At its best it has truly contributed to change itself, and continues to contribute in a social order which has more need of it, being less conscious of its real situation than I think has ever been the case. For this is a social order which really does not know in what crucial respects it is ignorant, in what crucial respects it is incompletely conscious and therefore in what crucial respects this collaborative process of Adult Education is still central.

Section 5:
Retrospect and Prospect

In this section we look first at the past, at the context in which Raymond Williams worked in the years after the war. John McIlroy's 'Border Country: Raymond Williams in Adult Education' was written as a celebration in the immediate aftermath of Raymond Williams's death and first published in *Studies in the Education of Adults*, 22,2 and 23,1. Williams's intellectual history was complex. His early experience on the borders of Wales and England in a very specific kind of working-class community was crucial, and preoccupied him to the end of his days. The Cambridge of 1939–41, the years of war, the rediscovery of an active socialist community in the early New Left, the Marxist renaissance of the sixties were all important to his life and thought. But so too was his experience as an educator of adults. It provided space and stimulus at a crucial time, strengthening and purifying the radical populism of his early politics and encouraging breadth, intensity, active disregard for academic frontiers in his thinking and writing. The purpose of McIlroy's essay is the rehabilitation of this experience in assessing Raymond Williams. McIlroy examines the relationship between Williams's writing and teaching, his approach to pedagogy and the conditions in which his mature intellectual formation developed and the first landmarks in his life's work were produced. This provides an essential location for the texts in the previous sections of the book.

If the Williams of 1961 was already established as a coming force in social thinking, his untimely death at the age of 66 deprived us of a pre-eminent, popular intellectual. Already in 1979, it was estimated that his books had sold some 750,000 copies in UK editions alone. *Culture and Society* and *Communications* had each sold more than 150,000 copies. The reach of his oeuvre was complemented by its breadth. By the eighties, Williams was recognised as literary critic, cultural theorist, political analyst, social thinker, novelist and dramatist. In recognition of this *Politics and Letters*, published in 1979, was hailed by *The Guardian* as 'a new kind of book . . . a remarkable human achievement'.[1]

The road from 1961 to 1988 was long and crowded, and the Raymond Williams who faced the low, dishonest eighties was in important ways a different thinker from the proponent of *The Long Revolution* who had left the Oxford Delegacy for Jesus College, Cambridge 20 years before. Key to the changes was renewed engagement with Marxism. On the brink of the exciting, optimistic sixties Williams believed the success of Keynesianism and the post-1945 Welfare compromise guaranteed a strong measure of economic stability and working-class quiescence, rendering conventional

Marxist political analysis questionable. Economic problems, it seemed then, had largely been laid to rest. What remained were the problems of prosperity. Williams's scrutiny of the native tradition of Marxist criticism – Rex Warner, Alick West, Christopher Caudwell – in *Culture and Society* registered strong dissatisfaction. In his view the argument – last rehearsed in the controversy over Caudwell he had followed in the Communist Party's *Modern Quarterly* – was no further on than it had been in 1945. It still seemed to resolve itself into an irresolvable and unhelpful either/or choice between mechanical materialism or romanticism. Either the arts were passively determined by the mode of production or they forged consciousness which determined reality.[2]

Williams therefore continued to attend to the quality of life within capitalism, cultural renewal, gradual reform rather than economic transformation and revolutionary change. He saw as central an extension of democracy and participation, increased control by workers and citizens over decision-making in industry, the media and education. The quality of communication and learning could only be deepened by a reorganisation of industrial organisation, the work process itself, the burgeoning communications industry and the expanding education system.

The publication of new work in the early seventies, such as 'Base and superstructure in Marxist cultural theory', marked an important change.[3] After a period of activity in the Labour Party in the early 1960s Williams became disillusioned, resigning his membership in 1966. He was active in Cambridge Left Forum, The Vietnam Solidarity Campaign and the Mayday Manifesto working group, an activism reflected in such articles of the period as 'Why I am marching . . .' and 'Why do I demonstrate?'. Intellectually he was influenced by writings of Lukacs and Brecht first published in English in 1962 and 1964 and then by the work of Gramsci, Goldmann and Althusser. Capitalism was once more demonstrating economic and social instability and he was closely related to, if ultimately independent of, the renewal of Marxist culture in and around *New Left Review*.

It was now possible for Williams to return to and attempt to penetrate the apparent cul-de-sac he had retreated from in *Culture and Society*, to find a way through. In the Marxist metaphor where base determines superstructure and culture stands in thrall to economy, he revalued 'determination', moving away from the suggestion of a direct, imperative interaction between production and culture towards the idea of an ultimate circumspection and the exertion of pressure on culture by the forces of production. He reworked 'superstructure' in the direction of *relation to* rather than *reflection of* the organisation of the means of production. He reviewed the economic base not as the almost external inhuman organisation of production but as social and economic relationships created through conscious human endeavour, always in a state of development.[4]

This return to an open, humanist Marxism where culture was relatively autonomous and where 'no dominant culture in reality exhausts human practice, human energy, human intention' was in its turn transformed in *Marxism and Literature*, published in 1977. Here Williams defined himself as a 'cultural materialist'. The distinction between base and superstructure, he now seems to suggest, is inherently false and evasive. Culture and politics too are established by a process of direct material production. The concept of literature and the practice of criticism are rejected.

None of this – accompanied as it was by a more radical political stance – is without problems. Nor did it go without criticism. Raymond Williams remained an original and unconventional swimmer in the contradictory currents of Marxism; creative because undogmatic, always, first and foremost, a confident intellectual spokesperson for the Raymond Williams tendency. It took him, however, a fair distance from Oxford and *The Long Revolution*, where we left him in 1961. Yet, as we have seen, he never lost contact with adult education. It was often in his thoughts, and his continuing fertile criss-crossing of established disciplinary boundaries and denial of artificial academic compartments bear the enduring mark of the freedom he had enjoyed in his early years as a teacher. At a meeting of the Socialist Society in the early eighties he found time to discuss problems in trade union education, demonstrating a clear understanding of the issues and a sure feel for what was at stake. Shortly before his death he had promised the WEA an article for its journal suggesting future strategies for progress as it moved within sight of its centenary. And in his major work of the eighties he powerfully reasserted the optimistic humanist socialism which had endured through all the changes over four decades.

Towards 2000 recognised the crisis of the labour movement and hopes of socialist advance in the face of new confrontationist capitalist strategies. Yet Williams remains convinced that a new society is both essential and possible. Essential, because his look into the future discloses as the alternative a new epoch of wars and exploitation. Possible, because of humanity's enduring potential to create real, vital community – and here once more he asserts the validity of his early experience of working-class solidarity created in the border country and in the Welsh valleys under the most adverse conditions. The past is again used to affirm hope in the future.

This too was the theme of the imaginative work which fittingly took up Williams's last years. *Loyalties*, (1986) a journey from the thirties to the eighties, dwells, sometimes bitterly, on solidarity and betrayal, on how struggle cannibalises humanity, on the processes of false allegiance and self interest by which left intellectuals have remained foreign to and have thus far failed the working class. But the novel touches also on the resilience of embattled community and the necessity and inevitability, today, tomorrow, of continuing struggle against a system which continues to deny humanity. *Loyalties*, an underestimated novel, demonstrated the tenacity of Williams's socialism, his continuing allegiance to the people he came from and his faith in their ability to ultimately change our society. In the same year he spoke out impatiently against intellectuals on the left who were theorising 'new times' and a retreat from class; those who had:

produced that block diagnosis of Thatcherism which taught despair and political disarmament in a social situation which was always more diverse, more volatile and more temporary ... Is there never to be an end to petit-bourgeois theorists making long-term adjustments to short-term situations?[5]

Until his death Williams was working on his massive novel *People of the Black Mountains*, which he left incomplete, although the first two parts – *The Beginning* and *The Eggs of the Eagle* – have been published posthumously.

In a book about the past it is important to conclude by looking at what is to come. In a book dedicated to the work of Raymond Williams we do this through his eyes. Sallie Westwood's 'Excavating the future: towards 2000' urges the continuing importance of the voice of Raymond Williams in debating the challenges of the nineties. This final essay critically addresses Williams's last important work of social analysis, a book in which he returned to his work of the fifties to consider and develop enduring concerns. Westwood endorses Williams's emphasis on the need for a new kind of socialist movement. Anchored in a new definition of the general interest, it will have to unite the new social movements based on feminism, anti-racism and ecology with the institutions of organised labour. In relating to the processes by which a new politics will be forged in the way Williams prefigures, she argues, lies the best hope for a renewal of social change and the creation of a radical adult education.

Notes and References

1. These figures are given in R. Williams, *Politics and Letters*, New Left Books, 1979, p 7. *Keywords*, two years after first publication, had already sold 50,000 copies.
2. R. Williams, *Culture and Society*, Chatto and Windus, 1958, pp 258–75.
3. R. Williams, 'Base and superstructure in Marxist cultural theory', *New Left Review*, 82, 1973, pp 3–16.
4. See, for example, R. Williams, *Politics and Letters*, pp 324–58.
5. R. Williams, 'The uses of cultural theory', *New Left Review*, 158, 1986, pp 19–31.

Border Country: Raymond Williams in adult education

John McIlroy

Raymond Williams spent the first fifteen years of his professional life as a teacher in the education of adults. Those years, fundamental to his intellectual formation, saw the publication of his path breaking books *Culture and Society* (1958) and *The Long Revolution* (1961) as well as a substantial body of literary criticism and his first novel *Border Country* (1960). It is a commonplace that borders – between working-class community and the life of the intellect, country and city, England and Wales – permeate and structure Williams's life and production, and critics have noted, if only in passing, that the years of his professional youth, lived on 'the periphery of the academic establishment', in the borderland between England's oldest university and the wider community were 'crucial for the development of his work'.[1] Williams himself reflected, 'I first started to look at the idea of culture in an adult education class'.[2] On several occasions he remarked on the extent to which his understanding of what was really happening under the surface in post-war Britain was based upon discussion with his students.[3] In introducing his published material he regularly paid tribute to the degree to which it was 'based on methods and materials I had been using in adult education classes'.[4]

As Williams took his passage from border country into the heart of Cambridge academic life, his work continued to be impregnated by his experience of adult education. This was fundamental, as in his continuing emphasis on the need for a common culture, and in his continuing conception of the operation of the Workers' Educational Association (WEA) at its best as a model for the learning society, the educating participating democracy of the future; and it was sometimes incidental, as in the vivid painful picture Williams gives us, in *Second Generation* (1964), of the shop steward, Harold Owen, poring over his NCLC correspondence course, or the wry sketching of the antecedents of Mark Evans, the MP in *The Volunteers* (1978) who was a Labour College organiser before, somewhat incongruously, becoming Deputy Director of the Extra-Mural Department in the University of Wales at Brecon!

As late as the mid 1970s Williams in his best-selling *Keywords* (1976) reworked ideas and approaches first developed as appendices to *Culture and Society* and initially published in adult education journals as contributions to debates in that field in the 1950s.[5] In his later career

269

he continued to ponder the linkages within his adult education work and wider. He told a meeting in 1983:

> *We are beginning, I am afraid, to see encyclopaedia articles dating the birth of cultural studies from this or that book in the late fifties. Don't believe a word of it. That shift of perspective about the teaching of arts and literature and their relation to history and to contemporary society began in adult education, it didn't happen anywhere else.*[6]

Reflecting in his retirement on adult education, then and now, he reasserted its continuing relevance in the world of Margaret Thatcher, enterprise culture, mass unemployment, inner city riots and the Falklands War:

> *At its best it has truly contributed to change itself and continues to contribute in a social order which has more need of it, being less conscious of its real situation than, I think, has ever been the case. For this is a social order which really does not know in what crucial respects it is ignorant, in what crucial respects it is incompletely conscious and, therefore, in what crucial respects this collaborative process of adult education is still central.*[7]

For Williams in his last years it was still that important. Against this background it seems to me that the small mountain of tributes and longer appreciations which followed the death in 1988 of a man described as 'the most authoritative, consistent and original socialist thinker in the English speaking world'[8] and 'the most important thinker on society and culture in Britain',[9] paid little, certainly inadequate, attention to Williams's life as an adult educator and particularly to the context in which he worked. Mary Joannou[10] and Derek Tatton[11] provided us with very useful but brief notes. Alan O'Connor in his longer, stimulating survey of Williams's life and work addresses this period, but, at three pages, his is still a brief and at times uncertain sketch.[12] Williams's interviews with *New Left Review*, conducted in 1977–78, remain a fascinating and invaluable source of information. However the treatment of this part of Williams's life is, once again, lacking in detail. And it is sometimes coloured by the interviewer's preconceptions and what, at times, verges on a project of appropriation, designed to assimilate Williams to a particular school of Marxism, absorbing the early Williams into the different thinker of the 1970s.[13]

Williams's years in adult education, the man and his work, will eventually be the subject of definitive, original treatment, integrated in a longer biography. That is not the purpose of this paper. My objective is rather to systematise and develop some of the existing material on this period to provide a more complete, but still very much an interim picture, of Williams's work between 1946 and 1961. In particular, I shall seek to examine Williams's work as an educator in its context and relate it to his broader preoccupations. I hope this will be useful, not only to those involved in continuing education but also to those who approach Williams from other starting points. What characterised Raymond Williams was the wholeness of his thinking and writing whether on literature, politics or society. Some understanding of his largely hidden activities in these years is important to any assessment of his thought and his heritage.

Adult Education

In recent years I have discussed D.H. Lawrence with working miners; discussed methods of argument with building workers; discussed newspapers with young trade unionists; discussed television with apprentices . . . To me these have been formative experiences and I have learnt as much as I have taught (Raymond Williams).

Working towards the completion of his degree in 1946, Williams's original intention appears to have been to leave Cambridge to live in the South West where he would work on his novel *Brynllwyd*, the first version of *Border Country*, and write short stories and a film script. He intended to collaborate in producing a journal with his Cambridge friends Clifford Collins and Wolf Mankowitz, supporting himself and his family by teaching classes for the WEA. Williams's first involvement with adult education was while still a student. In 1945–46 he approached Frank Jacques, the WEA District Secretary in Cambridge, and was given a class in the Fen District, probably teaching 'The Novel since 1800'. His initial experience was salutary: only three students presented themselves and the class had to be combined with another in a nearby village.[14] The impending birth of his second child motivated Williams to seek more secure employment. In the summer of 1946 he was interviewed and appointed as a Staff Tutor by the Oxford University Tutorial Classes Committee 'to work in close association with the WEA', teaching literature to adult classes.[15]

The Oxford delegacy and the WEA

In consequence of its pioneering role in university adult education, Oxford had covered much of England and in 1946 it still served Kent, Lincoln, North Staffordshire and Sussex – as well as its present heartland of Berkshire, Buckinghamshire and Oxford. Williams was appointed to work in East Sussex and went to live in Seaford. The organisational arrangements in which Williams operated were complex and confusing to the outsider. The University Tutorial Classes Committee organised long classes in collaboration with the WEA. Meeting twice a year with the University Extension Lectures Committee, which directly organised shorter provision, it constituted the University Delegacy for Extra-Mural Studies. Historically, the full-time secretary of the Delegacy was joint honorary secretary with the general Secretary of the WEA of the Tutorial Classes Committee. This committee also appointed a full-time organising secretary. Williams's job involved organising classes through the branches of the WEA and teaching them. He reported to the Tutorial Classes Committee and also worked with the Joint Committee for Adult Education in East Sussex, which consisted of representatives of the university, the WEA and local education authorities.[16]

The ideology of the adult education Williams entered was powerfully social democratic. Set within a framework of optimistic belief in the ability of education to stimulate controlled and gradual social reform, its initial objective was to provide the working class with a rigorous liberal education, centred on the social sciences. The courses Williams was to teach comprised three-year tutorial classes conducted in the evening for two terms, one-year preparatory classes intended to funnel students into the longer rigorous tutorial classes, and a variety of shorter one-term and one-session classes. There were also weekend and summer schools. At the heart of the liberal approach was the conception of dialogue between tutor and students, trained intellect and experience.

The ethos surrounding the 1908 Oxford Report which had launched this work remained, in the immediate post-war period, a powerful one, reinforced by the election of the first majority Labour Government. Cole and Tawney were still actively involved, and many of those Williams was to work with, such as Frank Pickstock, had themselves come through the great days of the tutorial class. In the 1940s the chair of the Oxford Delegacy was first A.D. Lindsay, Master of Balliol, a veteran of Oxford adult education and chair of Williams's appointment committee, then Lucy Sutherland, Principal of Lady Margaret Hall. Among the delegates were such as G.D.H. Cole, while Thomas Hodgkin, Secretary of the Delegacy from 1945–52 and a Communist Party member from 1938–49, was influential. However, an alternative pole was constituted by Ernest Green, the WEA General Secretary, who stood firmly on the right wing of the Labour Party.[17]

After 1951 Hodgkin was succeeded by Frank Jessup, although much of the day-to-day administration was in the hands of Frank Pickstock, who became Organising Secretary of the Tutorial Classes Committee (TCC) in succession to Williams's friend, the historian of adult education H.P. Smith. The approach became more conventional and, while Pickstock was intensely interested in working-class education, he conceived of it in a far less radical fashion than Hodgkin. In the latter part of Williams's Oxford career the emphasis switched from the TCC to the Delegacy itself, as links with the WEA diminished: the Delegacy became more initiatory in joint ventures and provided more classes directly. The TCC was eventually abolished and the Delegacy, which in the years 1945–61 enjoyed a good deal of autonomy from the university, was faced with greater scrutiny. By the late 1960s it was felt that the Delegacy had 'become isolated from university life'[18] and in the early 1970s it became the Department of External Studies.

In his formative years in adult education Williams was an admirer of Hodgkin who possessed a passionate belief in the expansion of an adult education more organically rooted in the institutions of working-class life.[19] He had in Williams's view 'a very strong and principled conception of how to develop a popular working class education. He believed that essentially the people to do it were committed socialists'.[20] Others in Oxford at the time mention the affinity between Hodgkin and Williams and recall Hodgkin's 'energy and ambition for the development of mass popular education. I think Hodgkin saw Williams as having the qualities to do this in the field of literature . . . He spoke highly of his work.'[21]

Williams supported Hodgkin's approach and bracketed his attraction to adult education work with that of others who entered the field at this time.

> *This was the social and cultural form in which they saw the possibility of reuniting what had been in their personal histories disrupting: the value of higher education and the persistent educational deprivation of the majority of their own originary or affiliated class.*[22]

In intellectual terms he wanted to combine the cultural radicalism of Leavis and his own 'intoxication' with practical criticism with the development of a socialist cultural position; he saw adult education as an ideal forum for this. Williams wanted very much to work in adult education because of class loyalty and identification; because of a desire as an intellectual to make a new bonding with the class that had produced him; because of the specific form his passage from the working class had taken, which focused his attention on culture; and, because the four years of army life had provided a pause for pondering his origins and his passage from them. For Williams:

> *What other people in different situations might experience more directly as economic or political inequality was naturally experienced, from my own route, as primarily, an inequality of culture: an inequality which was also in an obvious sense an uncommunity.*[23]

Williams's elation at his appointment at Oxford still, if now tempered by experience, rings down the years:

> *When I heard of the possibility at Oxford, adult teaching of Literature for the Workers' Education Association and Thomas Hodgkin, a communist, was Secretary of the University Committee who interviewed me, it seemed unbelievably lucky as a job. It was not to turn out so but it seemed absolutely right. A lot of my subsequent work came out of that particular choice of jobs.*[24]

Adult education 1945–61

It was not to turn out so for a variety of reasons. The heady ferment, 'the sky's the limit' atmosphere, of adult education in the 1940s produced by the wartime radicalisation and influx of committed socialists[25] was real; but it was limited and temporary. Even in the 1940s there were those who wanted expansion to be aimed not only at the working class but also to meet the needs of the professions and of management. They argued for a greater distance from the WEA and that the universities 'could not regard their services as available exclusively to any one organisation or section of the community'.[26] Throughout the 1950s the university–WEA partnership catered more and more for leisure provision for the middle classes and vocational provision for industrial and welfare state functionaries. These trends were underpinned by the new affluence, consumerism, privatisation, depoliticisation and instrumentalism of the working class.[27]

In 1939 almost 30% of students attending WEA classes were manual workers and a quarter of these were attending the longer tutorial classes. By the time *Culture and Society* was published only 15% of manual workers were attending WEA courses and less than a fifth of these were in the longer more rigorous courses.[28] Without conceding to vulgar conceptions of class these figures underline the increasing absence of workers from mainstream adult education classes. As early as the mid 1950s it was possible to argue that 'university extra-mural work is developing into a public service provided for the benefit not of the educationally underprivileged but increasingly for those who have received the advantage of a full time education'.[29] And, as adult education became more professional and catered for the already educated, so pressures intensified to ensure that it became more assimilated to what happened inside the university.

Williams remarked, looking back on this period:

> the WEA started to become heavily used by the middle classes as a form of leisure and education. There was nothing wrong with this, except that in socially mixed communities they induced a quite different cultural atmosphere from that of the working-class student. You had to positively encourage specific working people's classes organised around trade unions and so on. This was done. But all the time there was constant pressure from the university: you must improve academic standards, you must get written work ... The effect was to tend to eliminate people without secondary education.[30]

These tendencies did not go uncontested. Williams himself fought them. There was a series of debates in the adult education world through the 1940s and 1950s on the issues of conformity in teaching, university standards and the absence of working-class students.[31] There was still room to do good work and good work was done. A number of experiments in working-class education most significantly centred around the development of day-release courses for workers and special provision for trade unionists was pioneered in Oxford by Arthur Marsh and Frank Pickstock.[32]

Space remained for radicals and for committed work – partly because of the overall expansion that took place. The number of staff tutors employed by the universities, for example, increased from seventy in 1939 to 207 in 1953.[33] The grant from the Ministry of Education increased from £240,000 in the year after Williams's appointment to £680,000 in the year of his resignation.[34] The number of courses increased from 1,584 in 1946 to twice that figure in 1961.[35] Oxford's full-time staff in this period fluctuated between twenty-seven and thirty-one, and its courses increased from 157 to 1946 to 269 in 1961, although in comparison with other universities it successfully maintained the longer three-year classes.[36]

Williams's career also witnessed a formalisation and improvement in the role of staff tutor. In 1946 tutors did not enjoy the same tenure, facilities, or opportunities for promotion as internal lecturers. But by 1961 assimilation was advanced, although it was only in 1960 that Williams secured a form of promotion. This reflected and reinforced the marginality of university adult education. Critics felt that this work 'is not of university quality'.[37] It was noted that 'extra-mural tutors, many of whom necessarily work at places remote from the university have little effective contact with their internal colleagues and are not in fact regarded as of equivalent status'.[38] At Oxford, Frank Jessup recalled staff tutors in the post-war period as being connected with the university but not of it, 'irregulars skirmishing on the periphery'.[39] There was still, by 1961, 'scepticism as to whether the work that is done is or can be of a quality justifying university sponsorship'.[40] Tutors often 'schizophrenically straddled two worlds'.[41] They had come some way during Williams's career but they still inhabited border country.

A golden age

The view that 'Williams' books from *Reading and Criticism* to *Communications* belong to a vibrant adult education movement'[42] or the belief that Williams's 'direct audience was in principle working class, taught by committed socialists who saw their educational practice in that light'[43] thus requires modification and respecification. A survey of tutors conducted in the year Williams left Oxford showed a majority to be 'moderate socialists' with all shades of labour movement opinion represented.[44] Throughout Williams's career the majority of adult education tutors was far removed from the positions of the editorial board of the *New Left Review* of the 1970s and, as we shall see, many were actively anti-Marxist. If we understand 'vibrant movement' as carrying some suggestion of magnitude we have to register the fact that there were only 1,359 enrolments for the Oxford tutorial classes in 1948 and 1,453 in 1949.[45] In the latter year there were only eighty-four classes in total (fourteen in literature) and even with expansion there were, in 1958, only 115 classes of which thirty-three were in literature.[46] Within the WEA, activism was declining not increasing and, as for social composition, in 1947–48 22% of the Oxford adult students were manual workers and ten years later 18%.[47]

Williams's audience, therefore, was not in principle working class – at least not in the way the term was perceived in adult education in these years. His programme had a mix of students and so did individual classes. But he most often encountered working-class groups in special short classes and sessions outside the mainstream tutorial class structure. Whilst Williams involved himself in the new trade union courses, most of his teaching consisted of evening tutorial work in which working-class students were a declining minority. Such classes in areas such as Bexhill, Brighton and Cuckfield attracted large numbers of largely middle-class women students: in 1948–49, in one class fourteen out of fifteen were women; in another sixteen out of twenty; in another twelve out of nineteen; and in another ten out of nineteen.[48] These were often on the model of, as Williams put it, 'a class of commuter housewives at Haywards Heath who wanted to read some literature'.[49] By 1958 27% of Oxford's adult students were categorised as housewives[50] and the flavour of some of the courses in the post-war period was well expressed by a WEA activist: 'I've never dared tell the ladies what WEA stands for, you know, or they'd never come. They think it stands for women ... Last year we were doing Russia and one lady reported us for Communism.'[51] As early as 1948 one tutor felt 'the WEA has become a very respectable, very middle class organisation'.[52] The view that Williams worked in the context of the WEA as an education movement that 'brought the masses into politics and led them into discussing momentous issues'[53] is an exaggerated and romantic one.

The limits of adult education and its radicals in this period can be seen from the attitude taken to the women who made up more than 50% of adult education's students in these years. The April 1952 issue of *The Tutors Bulletin of Adult Education*, for example, published a column which addressed itself to the problem of the middle-class housewives dominating classes in literature and drama.

> *The point is important for three reasons. First, it was not for* them *that the WEA was started; secondly, too many women make a bad class, lacking in bite and 'comeback', lacking, in a word, in guts. Thirdly, one gets the impression that the WEA tends to get only the women men don't want, the inference being that they are there not because they are impelled by a drive for education but because they hope for husbands or have nothing better to do.*[54]

Even though it was published in the journal of the tutors' trade union, the Association of Tutors in Adult Education, the piece drew no response from male tutors. The only critic was a woman who trenchantly replied 'What kind of snobbery is it that thinks a woman who is working ten hours a day in a house (middle class though it be) needs an educational life less than a man who is working rather shorter hours in a factory or mine?'[55]

If, in an era when literature tutors in adult education could casually remark 'Shakespeare is the nigger in the woodpile'[56] and the universities and WEA ran courses on 'How To Be a Good Housewife', Williams was no feminist, he showed no such prejudices in teaching classes of women.[57] He was prepared to live with what he termed 'this mixed situation'. When he felt that matters had moved decisively, that there was 'no longer the mixed situation that I had lived with for fourteen years',[58] that courses for graduates and managers and for those with a leisure consumption perspective were now dominant, he was ready to leave.[59]

A *dangerous time*

The general tendencies which moulded adult education in the 1946–61 period and which led to some disillusion on Williams's part were given specific weight and form in the Oxford Delegacy by the onset of the cold war and problems which began to develop in consequence soon after Williams arrived there. It has been estimated that by 1947 nine out of thirty full-time tutors as well as Hodgkin were Communist Party members or fellow travellers.[60] Concern was aroused in the government, the WEA and amongst right wing Labour tutors, particularly because of the activities of the left within the trade union work, in the developing work in West Africa[61] and also because the Communists were successfully recruiting existing tutors.[62] The ensuing faction fight from 1948 led to the non-renewal of the contracts of several left wing tutors, caused difficulties for several more, and influenced the resignation of Hodgkin.

It has recently been asserted that:

> the Delegacy's most gifted academic figure Raymond Williams be-
> longed to a notable band recruited by Thomas Hodgkin who justifiably
> complained that it was the victim of an early British McCarthyism . . .
> Michael Carritt and Williams were at the centre of this purge.[63]

There appears to be no evidence to suggest the centrality of Williams to these events. Having joined the Party in 1939, on going up to Cambridge, he had dropped out in 1941. While he later stated that in formal terms his political position throughout the war remained very close to the Communist Party he failed to rejoin. There seemed to be, underlying his actions, a sense that his too speedy entry into a Marxism which failed to answer his intellectual and emotional concerns meant he had to start over again.[64] He noted the similarity of the Communist Party's policies in 1945–47 to those of Labour, which provided little stimulus to membership, but also his 'contempt' for what he saw as the Party's 'manipulation and centralism'.[65] Though he has been relatively reticent about his experience of the war it appears to have exercised a profound effect on his character. 'I became much more qualifying and anxious and careful, always stressing complexities and difficulties . . . the absolute reverse of what I was in 1940'.[66] Between 1945–47 Williams had other personal and political preoccupations. He did not see the Party as an adequate vehicle for the popular cultural mobilisation of the Labour movement he wished to achieve in the immediate post-war years.

Instead his main attention in 1947 and 1948 was devoted to the two short-lived journals, *The Critic* and *Politics and Letters*, which he edited with his Cambridge friends, Collins and Mankowitz, who were also involved in adult education. He saw these journals, together with his teaching, as the main contribution that he could make to the development of a new form of cultural politics in tandem with Labour's hoped-for development in a socialist direction. The journals, intended to fuse left politics and Leavisite criticism, were quarterly and faced commercial difficulties. There were also differences amongst the editors. *The Critic* foundered after two issues and *Politics and Letters* after four issues. *The Critic* was intended to carry serious textual criticism, *Politics and Letters* to relate the issues to questions of political policy and realisation. The journals aimed at replenishing and developing existing channels of education and culture and were directed specifically at the new generation of socialist tutors coming into adult education and their students.[67]

Politics and Letters attracted distinguished contributors, such as Orwell, Leavis and Christopher Hill – as well as adult educators such as Cole, Henry Collins and Lionel Elvin. There were debates over cultural policy in the Soviet Union and the Leavisite 'loss of organic community'. Williams wrote a short piece 'The state and popular culture' prefiguring later work. He challenged Labour policy and urged the financing of organisations such as the WEA. Democracy, he argued, did not demand a cultural levelling down but discriminating aid to allow workers to develop their own concerns in education, the theatre, films and the press. Socialist advance required the extension of socialist values.[68] *Politics and Letters* attracted some attention in adult education and wider but the project was not successful.[69]

Williams felt the failure deeply. The additional inability to get finance for a film whose script he had worked on for Paul Rotha and the path of the 'objectively quite reactionary government'[70] produced 'a personal crisis'.[71] Williams experienced the years 1945–51 as years of defeat. On his own account:

> For a period I was in such a state of fatigue and withdrawal that I stopped reading papers or listening to the news. At that point apart from going on with the actual adult education teaching I felt I could only write myself out of this in a non-collaborative way. I pulled back to do my own work. For the next ten years I wrote in nearly complete isolation.[72]

The recollection of those such as John Vickers who were at the centre of the Oxford 'troubles' was that Williams played no part in them.[73] Neither was he involved in the Communist Party Adult Education Group which attracted a periphery of non-members in the late 1940s and early 1950s.[74] The fact that he was teaching literature would have provided insulation and, although there was some fallout in Sussex, the main battleground was in North Staffordshire.[75] After the removal of Vickers and Campbell and the departure of other left wing tutors the conflict abated. New limits had been drawn and a minority of Marxists would be tolerated so long as they did not come to exercise more than a minority influence. The episode had an enduring influence on Oxford adult education. One of Williams's colleagues in the South-East recalls that for some time after 'the tutors as a body were riven with antagonism'[76] and another feels that 'the witch-hunting of that period continued through until probably about Suez, though with decreasing force'.[77]

What already struck his colleagues about Williams in the late 1940s was his 'independence'.[78] Whilst he spoke at the time about leaving the Communist Party 'he always, however, made it plain that he retained his earlier political convictions. He was deeply influenced by his memories of his father's uncompromising trade union socialism'.[79] Williams himself emphasised the point that even in these conflicts he was again in border country:

> *What other people said was: 'you are a Communist, not a member of the Party, but still a Communist'. I did not know what to reply. Neither no nor yes was the right answer. They would even say 'With Party members we know where we are, but you are worse, a maverick'. During the disputes of those years that was how people cast me.*[80]

Williams was seen as an 'independent left', distinct not only in political but in social terms from the organised left in adult education. 'Perhaps his background separated him from the (largely) public school educated left wing tutors in the Oxford Delegacy at that time'.[81] There were political connections but cultural barriers and, conversely, Williams's roots in Welsh working-class community meant he sometimes felt at home with those on the right, such as Frank Pickstock who, like Williams's father, had been a railwayman and a participant in the General Strike.[82] In the land in between he was sometimes seen as a mediator between the warring factions, possessing the respect of the opponents of the left, such as Pickstock, who succeeded H.P. Smith as Secretary of the TCC. The recollected view from that side was 'I have to be quite categorical that Raymond gave no encouragement to divisive feelings and at no time supported the view that the WEA or the adult education movement at large should further a left wing ideology, Marxist or otherwise'.[83]

In 1976 Williams vividly recalled this period, emphasising the centrality of culture and experience to politics, his sense of marginality and his constant thinking, doubting, questioning independence:

> *I remember an extraordinary experience during the Cold War when the institution I worked in was almost evenly divided between Communist Party members . . . and Labour Party members. For internal reasons it became very bitter and there was both intrigue and witch-hunting. It was a curious phenomenon that at the worst moments I was the only person to whom both sides spoke: the Communists because I shared their intellectual perspectives and most of their political positions; the non-Communists – but there's the rub – because I, like most of them, was from a working class family and had the same tastes in food and drink and enjoyment, whereas most of the Communists (Marxists) were public school boys to whom much of our incidental behaviour was vulgar. I joined neither camp but I remember the experience.*[84]

Williams was aware of continuing, more subtle, pressures constraining adult education, pressures which he resisted such as:

the anti-educational notion that you should soften the terms of the discussion; the anti-educational notion that you should exclude controversial current material. There was also the support of certain subjects, in that period and since, precisely because they moved people away from these areas which would put the status and nature of official learning in question.[85]

It was against this that he had to struggle as an educator in the 1940s and 50s for, as he recollected at the commemoration for his colleague of those years Tony McLean, who had been in the Communist Party:

the very notion that an Adult Educator was contributing to the process of social change became suspect. This was so especially in that period of the forties and fifties when almost everybody put their intellectual resources well under cover. For it was a politically dangerous time.[86]

The Conditions of Intellectual Production

We begin to think where we live (Raymond Williams).

The staff tutor

In the late 1940s there were eleven Oxford staff tutors working in the Kent and Sussex area. There were four economists; three historians; one philosopher; one political theorist; one specialist in international affairs; and Williams as literature tutor. However, the rigid dichotomies of the internal academy were slacker here. Tutors were expected to possess, to one degree or another, an initial breadth, a general interest in the social sciences and in working-class education. Flexibility and an ability to follow changes in demand were expected. In 1946–47, faced with an inherited situation, Williams was teaching four courses in international relations, with such titles as 'Problems of peacemaking'. His colleague Tony McLean moved from social and political studies to teaching classes on the renaissance and art history. Economists Arthur Marsh and Fred Bayliss moved from tutorial classes into the new trade union education.[87] Williams seems to have fitted in well and his closest friends amongst his colleagues were McLean, a Communist Party member until he left in 1949, and Jack Woolford, a historian. He also worked well with Eric Bellchambers, the WEA District Secretary in the South-East, who had studied literature at Oxford.[88]

Those paid to judge him saw him as a competent and conscientious tutor, naturally adept as a teacher. During these years Williams appeared to fellow tutors as a man who knew where he was going and what he wanted to do and who was 'wholly committed to adult education'.[89] Some remember his warmth and increasing authority. Others found Williams 'distant', 'a loner' or 'highly companionable but with a built-in reserve – you only got so far'. He is sometimes, it must be said, remembered as arrogant, intolerant, 'a Cambridge intellectual' wrapped up in his work.[90] A fellow literature specialist felt that 'Early in his career he set a shield of reserve around himself so that he could save and pour his energies into the large scale scholarship of his writing'.[91] Williams's originality, strong character and developing reputation also incited behind his back references to 'prima donnas'.[92] But there seems to be unanimity among his former colleagues that his prolific scholarly output was not purchased at a cost to the quality of his teaching or the number of classes.

This period indeed saw a significant growth in the literature programme of the Oxford Delegacy. By 1950 it was noted that its growth 'represented probably the most striking advance in the whole of the Oxford province'.[93] On Williams's arrival literature was seventh in the league table of Oxford's most popular subjects. By 1949 it was topping the list, having overtaken such subjects as international relations, economics, modern history, economic and social history, psychology; it maintained a leading position throughout the next decade, dropping from the top spot only in 1955.[94] By that date the Oxford annual reports were noting 'The quality of the classes in Literature is something that is now taken for granted'.[95] Williams's teaching, therefore, kept him very busy and he was also willing to supplement his class teaching with additional individual tutorials.[96]

But here was no retiring, self-absorbed intellectual or absent-minded academic, but a man of great practical powers. He was a gifted organiser, did all that was asked of him in terms of administration of courses and membership of committees and 'worked closely and enthusiastically with and for the WEA'.[97] In an age when 'administrativitis' was beginning to creep into adult education, 'He was the scourge of administrators. He believed they were parasites quite unnecessary because any competent tutor could do all the necessary administration with a typist and a telephone – and he practised it'.[98]

Some saw Williams in the internal adult education world of the 1950s as 'an intensely political animal in a more general sense ... he found it intriguing to be a political go between'.[99] He was 'the natural chairman of the staff tutors' meeting reconciling differences of opinion with superlative lucidity and grace'.[100] Williams saw himself as 'retired from immediate politics'.[101] But if for much of his career in adult education Williams was inactive in a wider political sense, he brought his energies to bear in a trade union capacity as Tutor's Representative, a post he assumed in 1950–51. Here 'in the defence of colleagues under attack ... he was unmatched and unmatcheable. Underneath the always courteous and quiet-spoken advocate there was a ruthlessly logical and matchlessly briefed "prisoners friend"'.[102] In his role in the Tutors' Association 'the hereditary trade unionist'[103] in him came out and he demonstrated in disputes with the TCC and Frank Pickstock, over appointments and the grievances of part-time as well as staff tutors, an ability to bring to bear scheming and even the odd plot. Other tutors recall his vigour in:

representing the claims of colleagues upon their employers with a force of personality seemingly irresistible. In status and salaries everyone drew benefit at a time when these matters tended to be unfavourably separated into intramural and extramural categories.[104]

Even those who did not share Williams's concerns observe: 'He was very active indeed and a model of what a tutor at that time was expected to be'.[105] And despite conflicts: 'He and Frank Pickstock got on quite well as one politician to another and because Raymond was a good administrator in his own right and able to work the system pretty well.'[106]

The context

It has been recently remarked that in studying Williams 'it will not do to forget the material conditions of his work in adult education and the university'[107] and in this context the system had pluses and minuses. For example, during this period, Williams's intense concentration on difficult creative writing as well as organising and teaching placed a strain on him, particularly as he had a growing family and 'the pressure of an extreme shortage of money'.[108] On the other hand, he was spared having, '. . . to mark people and grade them, summing them up through the relaxed conversational teaching as possible firsts, poor seconds, straight thirds . . . None of this could be good for a man however necessary it might be'.[109]

Teaching adults from a wide variety of occupations and backgrounds, students who could bring accumulated insights and practical experience to bear on the study of literature and society, was invaluable. It has often been noted that what were, in many ways, the seminal works of the 1950s and 60s, Hoggart's *The Uses of Literacy*, Thompson's *The Making of the English Working Class* and Williams's *Culture and Society* and *The Long Revolution* were all produced by tutors in adult education. Thompson, for example, in the introduction to his classic, states, 'I have also learned a great deal from members of my tutorial classes with whom I have discussed many of the themes treated here'.[110] Williams himself noted in this period,

> the profound stimulus to literary and cultural studies by the fact of contact between tutors trained in academic disciplines, affected sometimes by fashions and students who live in less specialised cultural worlds and who force the tutors to follow the questions of value right through.[111]

The format of mutual exchange and the nature of the students provided advantages not possible in a life of lecturing the largely middle-class eighteen-to-twenty-one year olds of the 1940s and 50s for 'the object of such teaching was not only to present certain facts and methods of study but also to start a process of independent thinking and common discussion'.[112]

But the point should not be exaggerated, particularly as adult education developed through the 1950s. The changing kaleidoscope of students –

Williams's colleague Douglas Hewitt found himself teaching, in 1959, youth club leaders, US graduates, engineering apprentices, Swedish teachers of English and nuclear physicists as well as his mainstream adult classes – and the sometimes short and slight contact with groups could open the tutor to the dangers of superficiality.[113] There could be real problems facing students who had left school at fourteen or earlier. Application to written work, or the lack of it, could make life difficult for the tutor. Sometimes classes could collapse into the incoherence described so hilariously, but painfully, by Malcolm Bradbury in his short story *The Adult Education Class*.[114] In some cases there was pressure on the tutors to entertain rather than to educate. Williams reported on one course he taught constant requests to the tutor to talk or read himself 'as this is more interesting'.[115]

The tutor who argued that in 1946 there was probably 'not more than a half-a-dozen good literature classes in the country'[116] was exaggerating, but there were real problems that tutors like Williams had to grapple with. A good example was the requirement in the Ministry of Education's adult education regulations for tutors to certify that written work was being produced. As Williams noted, this created difficulties. The students often did not have time to do it or found it difficult. In consequence, some literature tutors argued that the requirement should be removed, as it became a barrier to attracting and retaining students and to the educational response of those who did attend.[117] Others – including students themselves – responded that it was essential. Sometimes they were not aware of what they thought, or how they felt, until they put pen to paper.[118] The position was uneven. At one extreme J.L. Carr's novel *A Summer Day* was written in a WEA class in the 1950s. At the other the requirement was honoured in the breach: '"You really ought to do written work", he used to say peevishly, "The District Office expects it". And I remember the class secretary used to hand in something most evenings.'[119] Through Williams's career written work overall declined but its pursuit in a situation where there were no sanctions and, often, no expectations on the part of the students, remained a nagging problem for the tutor.

On himself, Williams imposed a strict work regime. He adopted the system of insulating himself even from telephone calls until 1 pm while he was writing, and leaving as much of each afternoon as he could free for reading and class preparation.[120] During the October–Spring period Williams would be out teaching three or four evenings each week. This involved considerable preparation and, in the context of the transport conditions of the period and the area Williams had to cover, it was inevitably wearying. A survey published in 1958 noted 'The physical strain of too much evening work and long journeys often in remote areas in winter conditions cannot easily be over-estimated'[121] and it was cited as a barrier to sustained research work. A distinctive aspect of Williams's work was its geographical isolation from the university and from other colleagues. The itinerant tutor, travelling with bookbox around the small villages and towns of Sussex, could muster his efforts to use the time for thinking and reading – or fritter it away. Similarly, during the daytime, when formally free, the tutor needed a modicum of self-discipline to focus energies on his work. Some did not and the folklore of adult education is rich in tales of those who went feral. But for the independent spirit with the capacity for self-knowledge, strong motivation and a strategic approach to time management, the advantages in terms of personal freedom were immense.

Another danger was the burden of administrative and organising work which could fall on tutors. In 1952 Richard Hoggart, then Williams's counterpart at Hull, saw this as a potential problem. He asked:

> ... *by using good scholars on so much incidental activity do we not put a strain on them which will eventually either spoil their interest in adult teaching and send them out of the field, or make them much less effective as scholars and, therefore, as teachers? Few men can combine for long the hectic and immediate life of the organiser with that of a specialist in a subject and its teaching. In the event of friction do not the scholarship and teaching suffer because the telephone cannot go unanswered, or urgent letters unwritten, or a visit to a local office be left unpaid?*[122]

Against this, staff tutors in this period finished most of their teaching at Easter – although there was summer school work and organising for the following academic year. However, for many the breadth of concerns and the limited compatibility of teaching, organisation, administration and writing restrained a sustained approach to in-depth research. In my own personal experience over some years Frank Pickstock was aware of these problems and acutely conscious of the need for Oxford's Extra-Mural Department to provide high quality teaching and research. He urged tutors to make time for thinking and writing. Nonetheless, it was largely left, in the end, to the individual and Williams was only able to keep these problems at bay, to the extent of producing major work, through meticulous planning, strong determination and a natural flair for organisation. They meant that the published output of some adult education tutors in their own disciplines was minimal.

Another consequence of the marginality of the adult educator in the 1950s which applied increasingly to Williams was noted in 1951:

> *Heads of internal departments were often uninterested in the fields of research which seemed important to Extra-Mural tutors. The latter were influenced by their experience as tutors of adults and by the interests and experience of their students and this often seemed irrelevant to the lines along which the research of an internal department developed. The adult tutor, therefore, often had to play a 'lone hand' ...*[123]

Nonetheless, the contradictions could work for the adult educator if he or she was willing to develop some of the insights which flowed from the collision of codified knowledge with the experience and concerns of the student. All tutors, to some degree, had to pioneer, because, as Douglas Hewitt pointed out, 'much of what is taught in a university Faculty of English will obviously be irrelevant to my students'[124] or, as Williams put it,

> *the tutor may not know how his discipline looks to people outside; may not know the gaps between academic thinking and actual experience among many people, he may not know when, in the pressure of experience, a new discipline has to be created.*[125]

There were limits, but Williams felt that with the need to teach formal syllabuses to examinations he would not have had the same opportunity he possessed in this period to develop the work that became *Culture and Society* and *The Long Revolution*. In the introduction to *Communications*, published just after he went to Cambridge, he commented:

> *University teaching is extraordinarily stimulating but it is remarkable how much it excludes: both in the simple sense of the syllabus where this kind of work is only just beginning in England to enter the university field; and in the more complex sense of the cultural atmosphere of a university, in which there are strong pressures to confine oneself to the traditional interests and habits of minority education so that issues and institutions affecting the majority tend to fade.*[126]

But how far did one see oneself as a pioneer and how far a priest of a particular discipline? And if one was a successful pioneer when might one want, and be able, to go further, which often meant 'internal'? As subject-specialists, tutors, all too often, did have to play 'a lone hand' in adult education; over time the pressure of this could take its toll. Moreover, the official pronouncements of the Universities Council for Adult Education and the annual reports of individual departments emphasise, time and time again, the need for more resources. This acted as a constraint and irritant for many tutors. If university adult education was under-resourced it was also, as we have seen, under-esteemed. It had, on the other hand, its sense of mission. Its tutors had a sense of social commitment and movement. But as mission and movement declined, as adult education became more routine and institutionalised, then, as a career developed, the disadvantages might, in the audit of the successful pioneering intellectual, come to outweigh the advantages. And it was the internal university that controlled resources, esteem and the credentialling of quality and which, even in terms of pioneering, might well be perceived as the next field to conquer.

The 'lone hand' was in relation to one's discipline and its development. In relation to the teaching of adults and its organisation there was in the 1940s and 50s intensive and voluminous collective debate, informal and published, covering a wide range of problems which by comparison made internal university teaching appear unconscious and sterile. Like other tutors, but unlike most internal lecturers, Williams 'talked and argued endlessly about the content of curricula, about teaching method and teaching attitude'[127] and read and contributed articles on teaching method and problems to *Adult Education, The Highway* and *The Tutors Bulletin for Adult Education.*

The one novel I have been able to discover published in this period whose protagonist is an adult education tutor, Olaf Stapledon's *A Man Divided* (1950), is aptly entitled. For Williams the geographical isolation and the lonely intensity of the work during the twenty-four weeks of autumn and winter contrasted with the summer round of schools and conferences in Oxford to erect another boundary: 'In the winter we teach English and History and Art and Ideas. In the summer we do Adult Education.'[128] Williams often felt that 'Adult Education was waiting for us when we got off at Oxford Station – we lived most of the winter as independent intellectuals taking our classes and in the summer we were something quite different'.[129]

Williams mourned, in terms of subject discipline, 'the relative lack of intellectual exchange'.[130] This related not only to the absence in adult education of the largish group of subject specialists that characterised the internal university department, but to the way in which the concerns of adult educators burst the bounds of particular disciplines as internally defined. The advantage lay in 'the wide freedom to experiment'.[131] In his early days as a tutor Williams thought of his literature classes as 'a battlefield and a laboratory'.[132] But as he developed his concerns beyond conventional literature teaching he recorded 'I have been told that courses like this sometimes turn administrators in their graves and throw the Ministry of Education into a conscientious flurry'.[133] University adult education formally encouraged the breaking of boundaries and an inter-disciplinary approach, yet Williams felt 'my syllabuses were constantly criticised on these grounds: of course, a class in English Literature but what is this other – including the first class in which I started discussing the themes of *Culture and Society*? What sort of class is this?'[134]

Williams's problems with 'the authorities' on this issue are confirmed by former colleagues. Where others submitted an orthodox syllabus but taught as they saw fit in the classroom 'Raymond made it clear in his syllabuses what he was going to do in the classroom and these were sometimes returned to him unapproved'.[135]

The irony of the problems Williams faced in trying to go beyond literature was that in the 1940s 'among a variety of useful specialists the Literature tutor is sometimes regarded, and as often regards himself, as a person for whom an apology must be made. My own experiments in method were at least partly occasioned by this guilt'.[136] With the strong emphases on the working class and social studies, although this was to change, 'you felt a second class citizen if you were not teaching Economics or Politics'.[137] Once again Williams was the man in the middle caught in the crossfire. There was an opportunity to experiment but there were limits, as some in adult education became imbued 'with a newly anxious respectability in which it was Adult Education that was expected to assimilate to the changed manner of the university rather than in any sense the other way round'.[138]

Despite this, Williams was determined to live through the contradictions of his position to challenge the terms and definitions of university orthodoxy.

In the Classroom

In the university I have always thought him a writer and an intellectual before a teacher (Stephen Heath).

A revolution in method

As he began his first classes Williams encountered difficulties with the way literature was taught in adult education. It seemed to him that, all too often, tutors and students approached literature as a branch of history or sociology. Particularly popular – even the orthodoxy – was the survey style course in which the tutor lectured about a particular writer or period, with the emphasis often on the social and historical background or biography, rather than appreciation of the texts – these often seemed incidental to the real purpose of the class. Although the lecture was followed by discussion, the distinctive purpose seemed to be to provide students with information about writers and periods, rather than to develop the students' experience of literature. Williams's favourite example of this genre culled from a syllabus went:

> Lecture Three: *James Joyce –*
> *Irishman, poet, dramatist, novelist, exile; the nature of his experiments; readings from* Dubliners, Portrait of the Artist, Ulysses, Finnegans Wake *and* Pomes Penyeach.
> *To be followed by discussion.*[139]

Courses of twelve evenings stretched from Cervantes to the Sitwells and, in one case, a course lasting thirty-six hours covered fifty-three novels. This approach was partly the product of tutors' convenience in regurgitating their own degree work, thus skewing much of the curriculum away from modern literature, and partly the result of student demand for a 'Teach Yourself All About' approach and the emphasis in the WEA tradition on the social, historical and economic background. Williams's own course, 'The Novel since 1800', sought, as he afterwards observed to his own surprise, to cover 140 years in twenty-four meetings. With some inkling of the problems he restricted the syllabus of this course to twelve novels. He then gave a series of, in his own estimation, worthy if second-hand lectures, having made the books available in advance and directed himself to the texts, 'But I knew all along that it was no good.'[140]

The ensuing, often animated, discussions were often not addressed to the literature because only a handful of students had actually read the novels. They were, therefore, dominated by Williams and two or three students, with the rest, in his opinion, 'doing little more than improving their occasional conversation'.[141] On occasion, the passivity that tutor-centred methods induced could be even more crippling. Richard Hoggart describes one of his classes from the same period: having given a lecture which subsequently formed a chapter of his book on Auden, his announcement of 'Discussion' was greeted with a prolonged silence. One of the students eventually explained that he had left them with nothing to get hold of, nothing to discuss, 'I had talked over their heads'.[142] The abundance of such courses illuminated the limitations in practice of the dialectical, dialogue approach to adult education.

Williams therefore turned away from this vicarious approach to literature towards attempting to construct a course in *reading* based upon the practical criticism approach developed by Richards, Leavis and Thompson at Cambridge. Instead of, by proxy, giving students information *about* literature this was intended to directly engage the students' response to a poem or novel, develop their powers of understanding and discrimination in what they heard and what they read and, thus, intensify their critical awareness. In the canon of Leavis, enhanced critical awareness made for control over life, richer social participation and an improved and more vigorous popular culture: 'The reading of literature is the best means of improving one's capacity for living.'[143] Williams therefore followed the Cambridge approach by supplementing set texts with duplicated poems and prose extracts which were discussed in class and used as the basis for written work. The tutor became far more passive and the class more active and student-centred, with the tutor summarising, distinguishing between what he thought to be valid and invalid approaches and offering his own judgments before handing back to the group.

Williams then sought to give the course an explicit critical programme so that the exercises raised, in turn, questions which occur in critical practice and theory. Experience led him to question this method as it seemed to become an exercise in closed technique which, far from quickening student response, degenerated into an abstract and arid labelling: 'One came to be picking up a play to look for an objective correlative; or ticking off a poem at first reading into sense, meaning and tone with a double entry in ambiguity.'[144] Williams, therefore, sought to move away from what he saw as the distraction and cul-de-sac of theoretical formulation and to put at the heart of the course the need to help students respond adequately to the work. He did this by planning courses which led students through poems and paragraphs of prose to longer poems and short stories and then to novels and prose plays, 'progressive reading rather than progressive exercises in reading'.[145]

Williams encountered resistance from students as well as administrators in developing this approach which swivelled the class from transmission to self-direction and participation, from lecture to seminar. Yet his new approach, typified in a course where the class analysed in detail *Heart of Darkness*, *Troilus and Cressida*, *Four Quartets* and individual poems, appeared to achieve better results: 'The work of the class has been generally successful and the policy of restricting the scope of the syllabus to the revealed general rate of reading would seem to have been justified.'[146]

Williams appears to have somewhat exaggerated the dominance of the survey approach in the 1940s. Leavis and Thompson had aimed their training in critical awareness at the grammar schools but hoped that: 'Those interested in adult education too, may recognise here something that will help to solve some of their most difficult problems. Indeed one of the incitements to writing this book was the experience of work under the WEA.'[147] There had been discussion of the Cambridge approach in adult education in the late 1930s and early 1940s and it had been used by Tecwyn Lloyd in North Wales.[148] Moreover other tutors, such as Richard Hoggart and Cecil Scrimgeour, were developing a similar method simultaneous with Williams. In the Oxford Delegacy itself, progress was swift: by 1948, seven out of the fourteen literature courses were concerned with close scrutiny of a small number of texts.[149]

It has been argued that:

> *The influence of practical criticism becomes clearly discernible during the late 1930s and by the time the war years had passed, with the influx of young teachers employed to meet the growing demand for literature classes, the 'liberating' force of the new theory . . . had well and truly made its mark.*[150]

Williams's emphasis in these years was on the value and autonomy of literature. Reacting against the idea that the study of literature was a 'soft option', a deviation from the true and hard social curriculum of adult education, to be liquidated into sociology, Williams asserted, in terms which were pure Leavisite, that 'Literature as a coherent record of human experience needs neither apology nor external justification. It is itself and its study as such remains one of the permanently valuable disciplines of any education'.[151]

Culture and environment

Williams nonetheless wanted to develop the literature programme outwards and to utilise the tools of practical criticism to analyse and criticise contemporary popular culture. This emphasis flowed from literary criticism and was stated strongly, as early as 1946, by Williams's collaborator Collins with whom he initially planned to write what became *Reading and Criticism*. Collins argued that minds whose cultural experience was based on nothing more complex than the commercial cinema could not be expected to immediately accommodate Forster or Lawrence – unless their work was destructively simplified. Courses should train students initially in criticism and understanding of commercial culture using films, advertisement, newspapers and popular novels. They should also examine the media and the organisation of commercial culture, later moving through popular classics such as *Gulliver* or *Wuthering Heights*, to more difficult major works.[152]

To this emphasis on the critical analysis of the content and organisation of popular culture, Collins and Williams wished to add an excavation of the historical development and meaning of the idea of culture. They projected an examination of the tradition in which thinkers had sought through literary criticism to judge the way of life of their society, hoping to, 'where possible reinterpret this tradition which the word "culture" describes in terms of the experience of our own generation'.[153] Reinterpretation was driven by concern that those who had written about culture in this way had essentially, or ultimately, defended the status quo and the need to interrogate this conservatism. It was to be left to Williams to complete this project and he quickly set to work in his teaching.

The first course in which he sought to develop these concerns in some systematic way – actually entitled, after Leavis, 'Culture and Environment' – was one of twelve meetings held in Maresfield in the academic year 1946–47. The syllabus stated: 'The study of culture and environment is one of applied sociology but the method of application is cultural, based on literary analysis.' The topics covered included 'The Cultural Tradition'; 'The Modern Press'; 'Fiction as a Business'; 'Advertisements'; 'Commercial Cinema and Theatre'; and 'An Inorganic Society'. Williams offered courses in a similar mould in 1947–48 which covered 'The Functions of Education'; 'Word Functions'; 'Advertisements'; 'Cinema'; and 'The Problem of a Community'. In July 1948, at the Balliol Summer School, Williams lectured on 'The Politics of Popular Culture' and also taught courses on 'Culture and Environment' at Bexhill and Eastbourne. For Williams's first course entitled 'Culture and Society' we have to wait only until 1948–49, and he mounted other short courses under this rubric as part of the WEA South-Eastern District Schools at Broadstairs.[154]

These courses prefigured the concerns in Williams's later books. Many of the chapters in *The Long Revolution* 'were topics I had taught or was going to teach in adult classes – the reading public, the social history of writers, the press and dramatic forms'.[155] The writers Williams discussed under the rubric 'The Cultural Tradition' were Eliot, Leavis, Clive Bell and Matthew Arnold – only some of those examined in *Culture and Society*. In 1947 Williams had not fully uncovered the chain of thought about culture stretching back to the Industrial Revolution. His energies no doubt focused by the classes, between 1949 and 1951 he read back on a lot of the writers he eventually studied in *Culture and Society*. Even in the essay preliminary to the book – which he began in 1950 and which was published in 1953 – he states he was still working through this tradition of social thinking stimulated by experience of the arts.[156]

There was, thus, a clear dialectic between Williams's thinking, teaching, writing. But the courses themselves do not seem to have taken off on any significant scale nor to have constituted a major component of Williams's teaching. By 1959 it was recorded that:

> *Courses on 'Culture and Environment' deriving from Leavis' literary and sociological examination of the cultural scene which began to appear about 1946 have not yet been really fruitful at the tutorial*

level, though one knows that in residential work and on shorter courses they have done, and continue to serve, an important function, as preliminary work for students going onto other subjects. It may well be that there are possibilities here, as there are also issues. At the moment one must record that these courses beginning in 1946 have only produced ten tutorial classes to date.[157]

The development of this area was important, but on a scale less than many seem to assume. The statement hints at official lack of enthusiasm and the courses do not appear to have generated the popular support which might have overcome such reservations. Neither does Williams, in this period, appear to have attempted to stimulate formal debate on some of these issues within the adult education world.

This was attempted energetically by Edward Thompson who in 1949 deplored the lack of any genuine people's culture. On the one hand, there was a sterile pessimistic and backward-looking minority culture, on the other, a commercial market drugging the masses. He contrasted this with the activism and participation in the arts of workers in Bulgaria and Yugoslavia, with workers cheering and applauding street productions of Shakespeare. Organisations such as the WEA should see their purpose as, not simply personal development, but the encouragement of popular participation for cultural enrichment. 'The WEA', Thompson asserted, 'has a vital part to play in the establishment of a popular culture in Britain'.[158]

Just as the aspiration in courses in trade unionism, or the social sciences, was that the class should stimulate the student to industrial, political or social involvement, so students in classes on music or literature should be expected to join a dramatic or musical society or serve on a library committee. There should, indeed, be an active practical section at the end of each class. This would help to halt the march of commercial forces which were degrading standards. Courses should deal critically with the role of the new means of 'mass suggestion' and the WEA itself should act more as a pressure group for greater public expenditure on the arts, for subsidy to produce art more organic to the concerns of the working class and for greater popular involvement in the development and regulation of state cultural bodies – as well as involving local literary and dramatic groups in WEA classes. He noted the potential conflict between imposing culture from above, rather than stimulating its 'emergence' from below. Perhaps, he concluded, we needed a new society but progress could not wait on the millennium.[159]

Thompson thus reflected many of Williams's concerns, then and later. The mixture of Leavisite and Communist Party ideas was not fully realised and the perennial problems which engaged Williams as to whether progress involved an extension of existing high culture to the working class, or the development of a new distinctive working-class culture – and, if so, how the latter was to be developed – remained unresolved. But these short essays are of interest in demonstrating that other adult educators were thinking about these issues contemporary with Williams. And perhaps also, in showing the first link between two important mutually reinforcing influences on the social thinking of two decades later. However, despite a tradition of debate in the journal in which Thompson published this work and discussion within the WEA and the Tutors Association, his articles drew no formal response.

Practical criticism

Williams's major effort in these years, 1948 and 1949, was going into his work on literary criticism and drama while he also continued to work on his novel. His book, *Reading and Criticism*, was published in 1950 in The Thinkers Library, a series published by Mueller, aimed at adult education students and tutors.[160] The book was clearly based on the approach he had adopted in classes since 1946 and again emphasises the link between his teaching and writing. It was intended to disseminate that approach. Practical criticism was still gaining ground in adult education and Williams noted the similarity between his work and that of Richard Hoggart at Hull. But there was still a tendency to feel that literature 'must be *made to resemble* social history, or philosophy, or logic, before it can be fully accepted in adult education'.[161] And even among those who had moved from this, a tendency to try to teach critical principles rather than concentrate on 'the fully responsive reading of the particular work for its own sake and not in order to point a stage in a general argument'.[162]

The book consolidated and developed Williams's approach of the 1940s, discussing and comparing passages from Eliot and Lawrence to make the point that such isolated analysis was ultimately disruptive of the author's totality by a consideration of Conrad's *Heart of Darkness*. Its approach fell four-square within the Leavis canon and acknowledged its debt to Leavis – and to Denys Thompson who read the manuscript – in its introduction. It was generally favourably received in adult education as a sober, well-judged introduction[163] which presented 'a clear and convincing case for practical criticism in the extra-mural class',[164] although one tutor found its language too difficult. He preferred an existing book which tutors used, Biaggini's *The Reading and Writing of English*, as 'more sensitive to the students needs and free from the jargon of analysis'.[165] It was felt, however, that Williams's book would be a useful text, as 'one can still find in the adult movement surprising reluctance to approach literature through the critical reading of texts'.[166] But there were reservations as to the degree to which Williams wished to 'stay with the words'. It was felt that this was hardly possible without theoretical discussion and that there was a danger of remaining within the limits of the work and making no extension to life. Social context was important so as not to give the work 'an almost absolute, and certainly artificial, self sufficiency'.[167] And responses from students who claimed too rigid an approach interfered with the enjoyment of the work were also noted.

The publication of Williams's *Drama From Ibsen to Eliot*, in 1952, stimulated a renewal of these arguments. Continuing studies which Williams began at Cambridge, the book was a powerful plea for criticism of drama as literary criticism, 'a working experiment in the application of practical criticism methods to modern dramatic literature'.[168] Again a debt to Eliot, Richards, Leavis and Empson was acknowledged and contextualisation opposed: 'The biography can readily be used to gloss but not to explain or judge the literature.'[169] The message was essentially, 'Get to the text and never mind anything else'.[170] In cultural terms Williams's project remained Leavisite – the extension of minority culture through the development of 'certain qualities of living, certain capacities for experience ... drama at the present time if it is to be serious in the full traditional sense, is inevitably minority drama'.[171]

Adult educators had little quarrel with this framework but were critical of 'the words on the page, and no more' approach and Williams might be seen to fall within the category of 'extremist advocates of practical criticism'[172] by those who felt that history and biography could facilitate and deepen the personal response. In his teaching, as in his writing of this period, Williams placed a strong emphasis, perhaps too strong an emphasis, on immediate personal experience. In his classes on 'Modern English and European Drama', for example, which covered Ibsen, Strindberg, Chekhov (and ironically in view of the title) Synge and Yeats, he concentrated on the close textual analysis of a small number of plays. Few, if any, critical works were recommended to the students, presumably for fear that they would come between the student and the text and constrain the reader's response. The relationship, in any adult education which aspires to democracy, activity and individual growth, between immediate experience and wider discursive and conceptual knowledge is always a difficult one. But much is inaccessible to immediate experience and some adult educators felt that Williams was pushing the 'text itself' approach too far. The problem was compounded when dealing with drama which was not simply literature: plays, for many, were only fully realised when performed and the art and technique of performance were important as well as the words on the page in eliciting the full response.

Thus J. R. Williams, a literature tutor in the London Extra-Mural Department, critically reviewed the book as, 'a fanatical plea for poetry in the theatre, poetry above everything and at the expense of everything'. It was 'a fanatical overstatement of a by no means negligible case'.[173] Williams replied with a brief retort to 'correct the more palpable and literal misrepresentation' of his work[174] and then, later, at greater length in a judged and non-polemical restatement of his position.

The text, he argued, was central. It was *there*. The questions of what the context was and, if established, how it related to the text were real and difficult ones. If one could assemble the context should it appear, as in the practice of some tutors, prior to the text? He insisted not. People found it easier to study something when they understood the need for knowledge. His acknowledgment of the context appears cautious and limited. For him it would:

be approached as and when one's own reading or someone else, has shown such an approach to be necessary, with reasonable limits of emphasis and time. Context also includes language and, here, except with contemporary or recent texts there can hardly fail to be extension.[175]

He rejected the wider claim of the contextualists:

I am always glad to see classes in, say, the history of the theatre, the psychology or social position of the artist, the anthropological origins of poetry, the social history of a period of literature and so on. But my own classes are in the reading of particular works of literature and my use of context is confined to problems that arise from the reading.[176]

This position, that context must grow organically out of the text and that explicit exploration of context should be, at least to some extent, a separate matter, was seen in action at an inter-disciplinary conference of literature tutors and historians which Williams organised at the Oxford Delegacy in the summer of 1950. Williams expressed concern that some of his colleagues were selling literature short by their tendency to de-centre literary criticism in favour of background and biography. Literature was literature – not history or social science and it was, for example, the height of irrelevance to 'correct' Eliot or Dickens on grounds of historical exactitude. Williams enjoined the literature tutors to read the literature as literature – or leave it alone. True inter-disciplinary work meant working through the literature. Only then should the realised literature be set alongside the social institutions, economic structures and modes of thinking. Together they formed a cultural whole but, 'If one wishes to understand the whole, the parts must be accepted absolutely as themselves and a new attempt made at understanding their relationships'.[177] The emphasis on the autonomy of literature, the failure to grant any final determination to economics, the refusal of structure and determination, the hesitancy in suggesting any mode of integration showed the distance Williams had travelled from his youthful Marxism of 1939–41 and the distance he had to travel to the later Williams of *Marxism and Literature*.

Williams's position could be expected to arouse criticism, particularly at a time when tutors were experimenting with a variety of methods which emphasised the centrality of drama in performance, such as the creation of drama groups, visits to the theatre and, later, the study of television plays.[178] In this context, the emphasis on the words could be perceived as passive and restrictive. This is not to say that Williams was not interested in crossing frontiers. In the 1950–51 session, for example, he collaborated with an historian on a course 'Literature and Society in Victorian England', described as 'an interesting experiment although it was impossible to do more than make a few beginnings'.[179] However, it seems that the two strands were kept separate and attempts at synthesis were limited.

One of the criticisms later made of *Culture and Society* and *The Long Revolution* was that it was not possible to understand the total historical process and experience of capitalism simply by looking at literary texts, that by failing to examine the politics of the thinkers he examined in the context of wider social developments, Williams's interpretation suffered.

Moreover, while it was essential to replace the text at the centre of adult education classes, an understanding of the conditions of its production could explain the text more fully; too firm an emphasis on immediate experience, on allowing nothing to come between the collision of text and student could, similarly, place limits on a full explanation. It is clear that once practical criticism conquered the field and began to approach the status of a new orthodoxy in adult education, its proponents began to differ in emphasis and practical application. While much unified the literature tutors, Williams's insistence on the autonomy of the text seems to have constituted a minority position within the school of practical criticism.

Film

Williams's enthusiasm for film seems to have flowered at Cambridge where he sometimes saw two or three films a day and he tried to develop this in his work as a tutor.[180] Film had attracted attention as an area for adult education development immediately after the war,[181] although classes in film appreciation had been pioneered by Roger Manvell, at what was to become the Leicester Extra-Mural Department, long before that. The British Film Institute attempted to encourage adult education classes, and Manvell emphasised the potential: 'The production of a great film is socially more important than the production of a great novel because incalculably more of the community will share it.'[182]

Williams organised two short schools on film criticism in the academic year 1947–48. He organised and taught a twenty-four week preparatory tutorial class for the WEA branch at Battle in 1950. He began the class with a series of exercises, designed to train the students in seeing and listening, based on short films and extracts with the students expected to describe the content of each. The core of the course consisted of the showing of complete films: *Potemkin; Metropolis; Mother; The Italian Straw Hat; Jeanne d'Arc; The Idea.* Towards the end the students saw three films at local cinemas – *The Red Shoes, The Third Man* and *Panic in the Streets.*

The films occupied every second week, the class posting written work to Williams in the interim. Williams felt that the class had been successful, 'it was possible to raise general critical questions: to examine assumptions about value; to inquire into the function of story and character and setting; to discuss techniques . . .'.[183] He felt that it would be possible to mount further courses such as this in film criticism and others on the sociology of the film. Despite this optimism and the publication of Williams's book with Michael Orrom, *Preface to Film* (1954), little progress was made in this direction then or since and the course reports at Oxford disclose few incursions into this fascinating field.[184]

Public expression

Williams was involved in developing classes in 'Public Expression' early in his career. These courses were not new (indeed courses with this title had been taught by the Delegacy at least since 1919–20)[185] but the content and approach adopted by Williams was novel. Most of the earlier courses were essentially courses in public speaking and courses for new tutors in pedagogic techniques.[186]

As one contemporary noted, 'Raymond fell into the dilemma which is not uncommon with literature tutors who favour working-class education. This was, quite simply, that he was unable to get shop floor workers into his tutorial classes and he would very much like to have done so'.[187] If it was increasingly difficult to attract working-class students to the mainstream of provision, there was a demand from labour movement activists for courses which related to their immediate concerns – public speaking was an example. However, within the adult education dialectic of experience and development, it would be wrong simply to stop with the demand for public speaking. This he conceived as simply *one part* of 'a training in speaking and writing which is specially directed to equipping members of working-class movements for the discharge of public responsibilities'.[188]

Williams's early courses in public expression, such as those based on the Hastings Trade Council, were aimed at developing students' initial demands and the students themselves. They began with exercises in preparing arguments and reports which were then used in mock debates before looking at voice production, elocution and style. The class then moved on from speaking to writing and the preparation of letters to newspapers and short articles for trade union journals. This then led on to elementary logic, testing arguments in advertisements, newspaper articles and books, using Thouless' *Straight and Crooked Thinking* and Stebbing's *Thinking to Some Purpose*. Williams then addressed 'the essentially different kind of analysis which derives from literary criticism and which is concerned with the valuing of tone, feeling and sensibility.'[189] This section of the course was based on exercises from *Reading and Criticism* or Biaggini. And finally came methods of study. Throughout such a twenty-four week course – the first experiment was in Battle in the academic year 1951–52 – Williams sought to relate to the students' experience, using trade union documents and discovery methods – as in the class in Hastings which explored local employment. He also used his own novel methods such as getting students to read a book backwards 'an eccentric but penetrating device'.[190]

Williams had thus moved far beyond courses in public speaking: 'to teach expression', he asserted, 'is to teach the use of English in speech and writing.'[191] Moreover he was able to press home in these classes his interest in the analysis and organisation of cultural production and from them stemmed the approach and ideas in his 1962 book *Communications*. The courses themselves were noted for both bringing in new students and funnelling them into longer tutorial classes.[192]

As special courses for trade unionists began to develop in Oxford, based upon a study of the industrial relations of particular industries and their economic background, Williams took a keen interest and attended conferences devoted to developing the new trade union education. He argued that building a training in study skills into the subject matter of the course was more important than ever here, given the restricted educational background of the students. So far, so uncontroversial. But Williams's second suggestion cuts more against the grain of developments in the 1950s. He argued that 'education organisations must be prepared to offer courses in the use of English as an ordinary liberal study for trade unionists'.[193]

Whether or not such courses would have met the needs and interests of trade unionists is a contentious issue but one which was never fully tested. Williams clearly saw a distinction between 'the business of the unions to train their members as union members and the business of the adult education bodies to educate trade unionists and others in the most general way'.[194] But increasingly this distinction was blurred: the adult education bodies increasingly educated trade union representatives as trade unionists, just as the trade unions did. The broader education of trade unionists was neglected as liberalism waned and skills training waxed, and it did not include use of English courses on the lines Williams advocated. Even the expression component, organically built into the course, whilst it *was* developed, remained very much in the mould of industrial relations practicality. Ironically, when Williams started these courses he was criticised for not 'teaching a subject'. By the end of the 1950s, his approach was perceived as too liberal and broad for working-class activists.[195]

Valediction

Pickstock's testimonial to Williams on his departure from Oxford was a glowing one:

> *Williams is more inspiring as a teacher and as a person than he is as a writer. To say that he was successful as a tutor is understating the case. Amongst his colleagues both his thought and teaching has great influence.*[196]

This judgment is echoed today by his former colleagues who recall a patient, careful tutor with a keen understanding of the difficulties of learning. He was popular with students, even if they occasionally found him an intimidating figure, always 'happy to read a play by a car assembly worker or to help an amateur group making a film'.[197] Some felt that he was better teaching with a small group than lecturing to a large audience: 'in fact he was the archetypal adult tutor. His style was modest and he was anxious to draw out of the students rather than perform in front of them'.[198] Many recall how 'it became legendary in Delegacy circles that he opened his class in silence and would not pick up his own discourse until the students had broken that silence with a bunch of their own comments'.[199] He would in a class often 'wait for five or ten minutes in absolute silence until a student was brave enough to offer a comment',[200] a technique, it is claimed, that Leavis had used. He insisted on 'the virtues of unprompted response and strongly deprecated goggle-eyed admiration of and dependence upon the tutor by the student'.[201] His interest in the methods of adult education teaching and his constant involvement in 'exchanges of ideas over aims, methods and all the other adult education shop topics'[202] are often recalled, as well as 'his arguments about "the text, the whole text and nothing but the text" and his utter dismissal of such irrelevancies as literary history and biography'.[203]

However, Williams's teaching technique, determinedly student-centred and oriented towards the text in his first decade as a tutor, appears to have undergone some change from the mid-1950s. He became more insistent upon note-taking and written work and began to lecture more. His sometimes more detailed syllabuses now disclose formal lectures and discussion on, for example, the history of the novel which, as Pound notes, could be seen as a regression to the survey approach discarded in the 1940s.[204] Critical works are recommended more often and when, in one class at Brighton, the large numbers of students meant Williams had 'to abandon my ordinary tutorial method and to adopt the method of formal lectures followed by discussions' he reported in terms unlike his normal sober comments: 'The success of the class in these terms was really extraordinary and it has been by far the most stimulating adult education work I have done'.[205]

Williams had now been teaching adults for a decade and consciously, or subconsciously, may have felt the need for more variety of method. A tendency to talk more as a tutor gains experience is not uncommon, and Williams, by this stage, was well-published and starting to become well-known. Some of his classes were attracting large numbers – sometimes too large for the seminar discussion – whilst some of these changes may be explained by external factors.[206] Williams 'genuinely believed in the equality of student and tutor even if the evidence for it was less than totally convincing' but '. . . in fact, of course, he had so much to say himself that practice and theory did not always meet'.[207] However, it seems best to view Williams in his last period at the Delegacy as lecturing *more*, rather than lecturing to the exclusion of discussion and discarding practical criticism in favour of the survey. A new tutor placed under his guidance as mentor in 1958 recalls: 'The first class I attended he distributed a piece of prose, said nothing and waited silently. After thirty minutes silence the class erupted into a raging discussion. It was amazing . . .'.[208]

What made Williams the adult education tutor *par excellence* was his deep and abiding understanding that adult education was for its students, not for its professionals. It induced in him a combination of respect for rigour regarding content and disrespect for established and often ossified forms which came between the student and learning. Having established mastery over the orthodox literature curriculum, he was not content to teach this in orthodox ways and sought to transform literature teaching and to develop its techniques for use in related areas. He did this by focusing on the method which would enable him to connect with his students and make knowledge and skills accessible to them.

For Williams it was always the student, the student and again the student. And he saw a need to go beyond the formality of the classroom to connect with the student as a human being in a specific situation. Williams reacted against much of what he saw passing for education, which failed to relate to the lives of the students and this, at times, drove him to place too great an emphasis in educational terms on the lived experience of the student. As he stated, years later, this had to be emphasised in the conditions of adult education in the 1940s but it had its limitations: 'Experience becomes a forbidden word whereas what we ought to say about it is that it is a limited word, for there are many kinds of knowledge it will never give us in any of its ordinary senses'.[209] His practice demonstrated that he did not cut with the grain in the classroom whilst cutting against it in writing or discussion but that he fought through his thinking in all the aspects of his life as a tutor. What a man as determined and talented as Williams did, and did not, achieve here, speaks less of his abilities than the limits of the possibilities in post-war adult education Britain.

Williams exercised a strong influence through his teaching, writing and personality on the development of the curriculum and pedagogy of adult education in this period. But he did this, at least in the literature field, as one of a group of dedicated and innovating literature tutors. This was particularly true of the move towards student-centred/text-based practical criticism which did much to realise the aspiration of adult education for self-activity and exchange in contrast to the more passive lecture-discussion of the historical survey. The impetus here came from *inside* the university, although in the 1940s the influence of Leavis on internal courses was far from dominant. In the early period Williams was one of a group of equals experimenting, in slightly different ways, within the practical criticism problematic. Even from the mid-1950s, as Williams became more of a public figure:

> We were all, Raymond included, in the Cambridge tradition ...
> practical criticism was our preferred approach. I don't think any of
> us saw ourselves as Raymond's disciples. Remember that Richard
> Hoggart was quite as prominent an influence on the extra-mural scene
> as he was.[210]

Williams's distinction here was the purism and introversion of his 'head down on the text' approach. The mainstream practitioners of practical criticism in adult education often found themselves pressing up against history and sociology – and wondered whether or not the frontiers between these subjects and literature were arbitrary.[211] Williams, in his teaching in these years, was sure where the borders lay. His broader distinction lay in the reach of his work; the boldness of his experiments; the pains he took to pursue a working-class audience; and the way in which his courses on Culture, Film and Public Expression burst the bounds of the normal novel, poetry, drama, perspective of literature provision. Williams refused to stay within the confines of the academic literary critic although this, as we have noted, should not be exaggerated.

It is in danger of retrospective inflation precisely because Williams's ultimate distinction lay in the fact that his classes bore such fruit in his books. But, again, it must be remembered that others, such as Tony McLean and Clifford Collins, were involved in the Oxford Delegacy in the development of what came to be known as Cultural Studies – although Williams was more persistent and he published. The powerful influence of other tutors such as Hoggart is widely acknowledged. Here, the innovatory process flowed the other way: it was the experiments in adult education which influenced the internal curriculum – with the initial breakthrough – marked by the creation of the Centre for Contemporary Cultural Studies at Birmingham University, first under Hoggart then later Stuart Hall – leading to the growth of cultural studies, media studies and communications courses.

The impact of *Culture and Society* was far greater than that of *Reading and Criticism* but there can be little doubt that the earlier innovations, of which Williams was an important part, played a vital role in improving the quality of adult education, ensuring that the proper critical study of literature took place in adult classes, that the terrain traversed was properly reduced and that greater attention was paid to contemporary literature. But there were limits to the march of practical criticism; in Oxford in 1959 some decline was noted in its progress.[212] And there were limits to the radicalism of adult education literature and its extension. Some tutors were concerned not to stray too far into the bosom of the *avant garde* or popular culture. Brecht, Sartre, The 'Angry Young Men' and Beckett all figured in classes in this period but some thankfully observed: 'There still seems hope that we will escape the Beat Generation'.[213]

In literature, Williams himself stayed broadly within the framework of academic orthodoxy and the Leavis *Great Tradition* – Dickens, Eliot, Hardy, Lawrence – even if he proposed a re-evaluation. His approach to film was conventional and, as *The Long Revolution* demonstrates, he had little time for rock and roll. His pioneering work in classes on culture, film and public expression was on a very small scale and met with limited results in adult education with the seeds sown flourishing inside higher education. The attempt to provide an alternative curriculum *for workers* in all these areas produced no significant strand of radical working-class adult education, then or later. To take one example, the workers' cinema movement of the pre-war period received no real fillip from adult education in the post-war years.[214] The network of theatre groups, sports clubs, left book clubs received no new impetus from connections with conventional adult education and withered in the new prosperity.[215] Williams's inheritance was not organisational but lay ultimately in the potency of his thought and the inspiration of his example as a tutor teacher.

The Moment of Culture

> *... that none*
> *However destitute be left to droop*
> *By timely culture unsustained.*
>   Wordsworth: The Excursion

The new left

Williams's long retreat began to break up from 1956. He had had occasional contacts with Communist Party members after he moved to Hastings in 1952, particularly with the Party's Historians Group – and he had canvassed for Labour in the 1955 General Election. Whilst he was insulated from wider political activity and discussion his 'exceptional isolation'[216] in the years since 1948 should not be exaggerated. It was isolation from active political involvement but Williams was heavily committed in adult education. He was also, for example, involved in collaborating with F.W. Bateson, who also taught adult education classes at Oxford, in the journal *Essays in Criticism*, which was committed to publishing Marxist as well as more mainstream analysis. It was in the pages of this journal that the 'Idea of Culture' was published in 1953.[217] In the next two years Williams worked at developing this into what became *Culture and Society*.

The completion of that book in 1956 appears to have liberated Williams. E.P. Thompson saw him in 1961 as 'one of the very few intellectuals in this country who was not broken in some degree during that decade; and who maintained his independence from the attractive poles of cold war ideology'.[218] We can sense Williams's tenacity in the credo of Harry Price in *Border Country*:

> *'you set yourself a job, you finish it . . . . Only once turn aside from what you've set yourself, once keep back just a bit of your strength, then whatever happens, succeeding or whatever it is, whatever the others say, still it don't matter what you get, you're finished with yourself'.*[219]

But this resistance was purchased at a price. Again there is surely an echo of Williams's feelings in these years in Peter Owen working on his thesis in *Second Generation*:

> *He put down the pile of paper. He could not bear failure at any price. This was a thing he had said he could do and he would do it. You have to beat the system before you're in any position to reject it. Otherwise what? Just the ordinary griping of the failed. The griping that filled England.*[220]

By mid-decade, however, many of the issues Williams had pursued in isolation since 1945 were becoming part of the agenda of public concern. The increase in real wages, home ownership, cars and television sets – and two successive Conservative election victories – prompted discussion of social changes. The decline of working-class community, the burgeoning of mass popular commercial culture – the role of the new broadcasting media and the advertisement industry in its propagation – *embourgeoisment* and class convergence – the end of solidarity, the end of ideology – these were just some of the themes now debated by a wider audience than met in adult education classes. As Williams later noted: 'From 1956 to 1962 there was an intense development of ideas in the field of culture and communication and by the time of the Pilkington Report this had reached the level of open and conventional politics'.[221]

The ice was also breaking in that the completion of *Culture and Society* coincided with Suez, Khrushchev's revelations at the twentieth Congress of the CPSU, their impact on the British Communist Party and the thaw in the Cold War. In 1957 Williams established contact with a small group of young socialists centred on the university which began to publish *Universities and Left Review*. Williams found 'an immediate affinity with my own kind of cultural and literary work'.[222] The ULR group opposed to Stalinism and the Gaitskell Labour Party were involved in CND and the organisation of the Aldermaston marches and took a keen interest in popular and folk music, the new drama of Osborne and Wesker and the new novels of Amis, Braine and Sillitoe as well as a fuzzy interest in working-class culture which became more focused with the publication of Hoggart's *Uses of Literacy* in 1957. Raphael Samuel recalls that Williams sent *ULR* an article just before the first issue and *ULR 2* carried it as part of a symposium with work from Hoggart on working-class community.[223]

Contacts between the ULR group and a group largely composed of former CP members, such as E.P. Thompson, John Saville, Doris Lessing and Christopher Hill which published ten issues of the *New Reasoner* from 1957 led, in 1959, to the establishment of *New Left Review*. Williams was a member of the editorial board from its inception to the change of personnel and direction in 1962 which produced the present *New Left Review*. He saw in the emergence of the New Left and its new emphasis – conditioned by the new prosperity, the abating of overt class struggle, the social stability – on *cultural* struggle to transform the values and meanings generated by capitalist society, the opportunity to practise on the political plane the ideas he had been developing since 1948. Williams wrote regularly for both *ULR* and *NLR* and spoke at the New Left Clubs which were springing up over the country.[224]

The forcing ground for the new ideas was the contradiction between increasing material affluence and continuing cultural impoverishment. In as much as development was occurring, the new commercial consumerism was seen as endangering both high culture and working-class culture. The demand was for the state, in response, to become far more a cultural welfare state, regulating the tendencies to commodification, redistributing cultural benefits, building on the basis of the development of existing institutions such as the Arts Council, the BBC, the 1944 Education Act, a new cultural prosperity open to all sections of society. This would require an extension of public ownership and greater regulation of the media and the advertising industry. These ideas gripped a wider constituency than those grouped around the journals and clubs.

The New Left of the years 1956–61 of which Williams was a central figure, 'our best man',[225] was a small current. At its height there were some forty local clubs in existence. It had at its heart a socialist humanism and a moral critique of British society. It was essentially a group of writers, academics and thinkers with a limited youth base and limited links with the working-class movement – to some degree through adult education tutors such as Ken Alexander, Michael Barratt Brown and John Hughes. *Culture and Society* and *The Long Revolution* had a great impact on the New Left although their resonance was far wider. Whilst Williams was to argue later that 'we overestimated the possibilities of action by cultural change on the left' it was in Richard Johnson's phrase 'the moment of culture'.[226]

The achievement of Raymond Williams

The central problem for Williams lay in his dissatisfaction with the two major positions he saw as available to those seeking to develop the study of culture. On the one hand, he saw the tradition of Eliot and Leavis as ultimately looking backwards towards a mythical organic society. In the embattled present the emphasis was on an educated minority, producing and preserving great works of art and a quality of response to life against the disintegrative pressures of a polluting, commercial culture. On the other hand he saw a Stalinised Marxism which gave little autonomy or significance to culture but, rather, reduced it to false consciousness and ideology, referred it crudely to society's economic base and saw little role for cultural struggle this side of a revolution. The tendency on both sides was to see culture as primarily artefacts, great novels, buildings, works of philosophy – Arnold's 'the best that has been thought and said in the world'. Williams saw both these orthodoxies as militating against democracy and socialism, as constraining popular education and designating and affirming the subordinate and inferior role of the working class. In these perspectives this class had produced few great cultural artefacts compared with the ruling class, was crippled by innate insensitivity and inferiority – or alternatively irredeemably corrupted by bourgeois ideology – and, in both cases, consigned to an inactive consumerist role.

Struggling with this problem, he looked back to his early life and at the students he was now teaching, many of them excluded at an early age from any formal systematic induction into orthodox culture. He saw the difficulties they experienced in attempting to compensate for this but he also saw the extent to which they had built their own cultural universe in the collective democratic organisations of the labour movement. From his own experience of collectivism and solidarity Williams rejected the existing orthodoxies. Against them he asserted 'a culture is not only a body of intellectual and imaginative work, it is also and essentially a whole way of life'.[227] The emphasis on great paintings and great philosophy was far too limited a conception of culture which could only inflate the achievement of a small number of artists and thinkers and the ruling class and demean and disable the working class and the majority of ordinary people.

Breaking through the problems confronted, for example, by Edward Thompson earlier, as to whether the development of working-class culture involved an extension of élite culture or a deepening of popular culture Williams asserted:

> *working class culture . . . is not proletarian art or council houses or a particular use of language; it is rather the basic collective idea, and the*

> institutions, manners, habits of thought and intentions which proceed
> from this. Bourgeois culture similarly is the basic individualist idea
> and the institutions, manners, habits of thought and intentions which
> proceed from that.[228]

The working class was not, as many in the 1950s argued, worked
out, disappearing or converging with the middle class – if one looked at
matters in this light. All human beings – and this was Williams's affirming
experience as an educator – not just the 'cultured' élite generate and explore
meaning in all human practices and institutions. In Williams's phrase:
'culture is ordinary'. It is what ordinary people think, feel and do. It is not
just part of yesterday but very much part of today. Art and politics are not
separate from each other or from everyday life. Moreover – and Williams
was again clearly speaking from his experience of adult education:

> If it is at all true that the creation of meanings is an activity which
> engages all men then one is bound to be shocked by any society which
> in its most explicit culture either suppresses the meanings and values of
> whole groups, or which fails to extend to these groups the possibility of
> articulating and communicating these meanings.[229]

This suppression and failure to extend required cultural struggle against
the values and institutions of capitalist society to defeat the deadening
meanings and values it generated. The institutions of the labour movement,
the trade unions, the co-operatives, the Labour Party were seen by Williams
as not only 'a great creative achievement of the working people' but also
'the right basis for the whole organisation of any good society of the
future'.[230] Traditional popular culture, Williams thought, 'is small in
quantity and narrow in range. It exacts respect but is in no sense
an alternative culture'.[231] However, Williams was not as pessimistic
as many about the development of commercial culture in the twentieth
century. Contemporary students of popular culture he felt 'have tended
to concentrate on what is bad and to neglect what is good ... If the
readers of bad newspapers have increased in number, so have the users of
public libraries, so have students of all kinds of formal and informal adult
education'.[232]

Nonetheless, one had to avoid populism as well as élitism. If the extension
of existing high culture did not constitute the way forward, 'the basic
collective idea' was only the basis for the forging of a new common
culture. The struggle for a common culture which Williams saw as the
objective of his educational endeavours would require the struggle 'to
create a society whose values are at once commonly created and criticised
and where the discussions and exclusions of class may be replaced by the
reality of common and equal membership. That is still the idea of a common
culture'.[233]

In *Culture and Society* Williams developed these ideas through a
reconstruction of a long line of dissenting social and moral thinkers
of the right and left from Burke and Cobbett, Arnold and Ruskin to

Lawrence, Tawney, Leavis and Orwell whom had in their work soug[ht to] interpret responses of thought and feeling to the development of capit[al] as a human order from the 1800s, yet whom he saw as largely appropriated to buttress reactionary positions. In this context he examined the changing meanings of five key words *industry, democracy, class, art* and *culture*. The book was and remains a major achievement in its reconstitution of a lost or suppressed tradition of opposition to the organisation of society since the industrial revolution.

In *The Long Revolution* (1961) Williams laid out his argument in more extended form, distinguishing within the idea of culture the 'lived', the 'recorded' and the 'selective' – 'the whole way of life', 'the expression of that life' and 'high culture'. The book examines the means of expression in the development of mass education, the popular press, the novel and the reading public. Williams describes his idea of a truly democratic society characterised by open communication and participation by all in decision making.

> *If man is essentially a learning, creating and communicating being the only social organisation adequate to his nature is a participating democracy, in which all of us, as unique individuals, learn, communicate and control. Any lesser restrictive system is simply wasteful of our true resources; in wasting individuals by shutting them out from effective participation, it is damaging our true common process.*[234]

Williams notes the achievement of the political revolution which ushered in Parliamentary democracy and the industrial revolution which provided a new basis for economic progress. There still remains, however, the third phase, the cultural revolution which will extend the active process of learning beyond an educated élite to all citizens and make it an intrinsic part of social existence. This will be just as important as the development of scientific industry and democracy.

The two interlinked books treat cultural activity as a primary activity. There is still no concession to the base-superstructure distinction in Marxism, to economic determinism. In *The Long Revolution* what Williams terms the system of decision, the system of communication and learning, the system of maintenance and nurture cannot be separated out and one does not determine the others. Williams also deployed in this book the concept of 'structure of feeling' to get at the culture of a period: 'it is the particular living result of all the elements in the general organisation'[235] and each generation will have its own structure of feeling. Whilst this concept is not without its problems Williams applies it with great insight to an analysis of Britain in the 1840s and the 1960s.

The Long Revolution was an inspirational book and it is difficult now to re-experience its powerful impact in the early 1960s. To the idea of culture as a *way of life* and the struggle for a *common culture* Williams now added the central idea of a *learning community*, the cultural empowerment of the majority of the population, the excluded and disinherited who through the third phase of revolution would achieve enfranchisement in the cultural powers of meaning generation. The Learning Community reflected his experience of the democratic educational participation of the WEA but its realisation would close the existing gap between education and life. These three central, intertwined ideas represented a freshened restatement of the concerns of radical adult education and a programme to which existing adult education could contribute.

In *Communications* (1962) Williams extended the critique of the organisation of the press and radio he had developed in his classes and repeated the view that a cultural revolution, proceeding through gradual institutional reforms, would qualitatively deepen democracy and produce a learning society. Just as *Culture and Society* bore the marks of practical criticism, so in *Communications* Williams used this technique to examine the trivialisation practised by the advertisement-dominated mass media and their potential transformation as positive education agencies if integrated in a new system of popular education. The book discussed both the teaching of communications and the kind of reforms a Labour Government might introduce centred on public ownership but involving independent producers.

His two novels *Border Country* (1960) and *Second Generation* (1964) were also the product of this period and they imaginatively work through many of the characteristic concerns of Williams's work. *Border Country* traces the passage of Mathew Price from the Black Mountains in the border country between England and Wales to university lecturer in London and the developing connection of his home village with the outside world. The complex dualities of intellect and emotion, mobility and loyalty, past and present, individual and collective, are signified by the fact that Mathew is known as Will in Glynmawr, only assuming his proper name on departure, and by the triangular relationship of Mathew, his father Harry and Morgan Prosser. In the General Strike, Morgan Prosser, more militant and conscious than Harry yet lacking his anchored commitment, powerful character and attachment to the community, loses his faith in socialism at the same time as he is able to lay the basis for his own business. Both Harry and Mathew refuse to follow Morgan's path out of the working class. Through a process of return, climaxing with the death of his father, Mathew gains some understanding of the community from which he is now irrevocably separated and its continuity, as well as a commitment to its future.

In *Second Generation* Peter Owen is the son of parents uprooted from their Welsh working-class community. His father Harold, a shop steward in an Oxford car factory, operates within the new privatised working class of the 1950s whilst his mother Kate is active in the Labour Party. The parents reflect the tensions within the labour movement between radicalism and accommodation, socialism and 'bread and butter' trade unionism, intellectuals and workers. The mechanical, empty and troubled routinism of commitment of Harold and Kate which erupts with Kate's affair with a university lecturer is contrasted with the Lawrentian connection and wholeness of the other couple Gwyn and Myra. Both factory and university are portrayed as mechanical and cut off from real life, the city counterposed to Brynllwyd, the village. Peter struggles to make connections between the academic life and the world of work, community and atomisation, learning and socialist practice. The novel vividly embodies the emptying and insensitivity life dedicated to struggle can induce. In *Culture and Society* Williams wrote that whilst the clenched fist is a necessary symbol for the working class 'the clenching ought never to be such that the hand cannot open and the fingers extend to discover and give a shape to the new forming reality'.[236] These two novels explore the tension between opposition and transformation in society, between living vividly now and struggling for a better quality of living then. They embody in movement Williams's ideas and are an essential part of his work.

His output between 1958 and 1961 made Williams a well-known and respected social thinker. Despite the brilliance of its arguments and insights there are a number of important problems with Williams's approach. How does culture as a corpus of intellectual and imaginative work relate to culture as a whole way of life? What are our criteria for discrimination? What should be the principles of aesthetic judgment? Eliot or Leavis were clear on what was and what was not culture but Williams's broad anthropological approach made the drawing of lines difficult. There was in his work little account of nationalism or Britain's imperial past and multicultural future. And, in practice, the tension between culture as a way of life and culture as intellectual and imaginative work meant, because the working class had produced so little in the latter sphere, the creation of a common culture often seemed, for Williams and the New Left, to involve simply the transmission of the received body of intellectual and imaginative work to working-class people. This was essentially the Leavis project. This also represented a return to the classical conception of Marx or Lenin that good historical culture transcends class.

Williams's work was justly celebrated but also criticised from right and left whilst earning the respect of many of its critics. Anthony Hartley and Richard Wollheim criticised *Culture and Society* on traditional grounds,[237] whilst Victor Kiernan objected to the divorce of the work of the writers studied from its essential economic and social background and E.P. Thompson saw its method as offering 'a procession of disembodied voices – Burke, Carlyle, Mill, Arnold – their meanings wrested out of their whole social context'.[238] In an extended review of *The Long Revolution* Thompson noted the absence of any real emphasis on class struggle: the book operated on a communications rather than a conflict model and he suggested the replacement of 'culture as a way of life' with 'culture as a way of *struggle*'.[239]

The two books were clearly some distance from the Marxist tradition they critically engaged. Williams remarked dismissively about the debates in the Communist Party about Caudwell's work 'This is a quarrel which one who is not a Marxist will not attempt to resolve'.[240] But would the working class be capable of a peaceful, incremental, organic extension of values and democracy within existing society? Would capitalism allow the realisation of the ideal of a common culture and a learning community? Later criticism from the left argued, with some justification, that Williams's gradualism, *The Long Revolution*, the 'slow reach for control' of *Culture and Society* and the utopian nature of his programmes for reform, divorced from political agency, ignored power in capitalist society and the nature of the state, 'consecrated the reformism of the labour movement' and gave too high a profile to prefigurative cultural struggle in a capitalist society as against the prior economic and political struggle.[241]

Williams accepted much of this and these criticisms became part of his own move towards a revitalised humanist Marxism – beginning by the early 1960s, accelerating in the period after 1968. Starting from the time of his involvement with the New Left Williams was to begin to discover Gramsci and Goldmann, 'Marxist thinking which was different, in some respects radically different, from what I and most people in Britain knew as Marxism'.[242] By the 1970s Williams had at least attempted to integrate culturalism and materialism.

> *I believe in the necessary economic struggle of the organised working class. I believe that this is still the most creative activity in our society. But I know that there is a profoundly necessary job to do in relation to the processes of cultural hegemony itself. I believe that the system of meanings and values which a capitalist society has generated has to be defeated in general and in detail by the most sustained kinds of intellectual and educational work. This is a cultural process which I called the 'long revolution' and in calling it the 'long revolution' I meant that it was a genuine struggle which was part of the necessary battles for democracy and for economic victory for the organised working class.[243]*

Despite this development and reintegration in his work there is no need to revise the verdict delivered in 1961 on the importance of Williams's intellectual achievement in the period 1946–61:

> *With a compromised tradition at his back and with a broken vocabulary in his hand he did the only thing that was left to him: he took over the vocabulary of his opponents, followed them into the heart of their own arguments and fought them to a standstill in their own terms. He held the roads open for the young and now they are moving down them once again.[244]*

Williams and Adult Education

> *Dr Macelwee hovered over the class a persistent ghost. He was the previous tutor. He had come up through the old tough days of the WEA and had a steadfast commitment to working class culture and the critical analysis of newspaper advertisements. The middle class*

housewives found him marvellous. Now he had been translated to higher things.

(Malcolm Bradbury: The Adult Education Class)

Moving on

Culture and Society strongly reflected the social democratic ethos of the liberal adult education from which it emerged. It was very favourably received, *Adult Education* remarking that the publisher's blurb would not be far wrong in claiming that 'it may prove to be one of the seminal books of our time'.[245] It was noted that the book reflected 'a good deal of the work which has been undertaken by numerous WEA classes in literature'[246] and demonstrated the enduring potency of education for social purpose, although some of Williams's colleagues registered reservations: '. . . to believe that a truly popular culture will be a good one requires an act of faith'.[247]

The moment of culture crystallised around the publication of the *Uses of Literacy* and *Culture and Society* was also affecting the extra-mural world and the WEA. Again 1956 seems to have been a watershed and in that year there began a discussion in *The Highway* – which was stimulated by the publication of the two books – on the role of the mass media and advertising, popular culture, the condition of the working class in the 1950s and the prospects for cultural change. Williams contributed an article on culture and wrote on the media and educational reform.[248] This new emphasis was also reflected in *Adult Education*[249] and it was taken up in classes. In 1959–60 Williams was organising weekend schools in Oxford on 'Culture and The Worker' with speakers such as Stuart Hall discussing the press and its attitudes to trade unions, Gerry Bowen Thomas discussing the present state of the working class and Williams himself addressing questions of popular culture.[250]

Williams's long service in the Sussex frontier outpost had led to his move to Oxford in 1960 and the claims of fame were now pressing. Williams was now a public figure. He was a witness at the Lady Chatterley trial, his speech at an NUT conference on popular culture led to Penguin commissioning *Communications* and he was involved in producing evidence for the Pilkington Committee reviewing the development of television. In 1961 he was elected Fellow of Jesus College, Cambridge and accepted a Lectureship in English. It seems as if he was somewhat weary of his long stint in adult education and somewhat disillusioned at the way it was progressing. Although at the time of his departure he characteristically reaffirmed its value and its future, Williams was a passionate advocate of adult education who had reservations about *this* adult education, about its lack of ambition; its deference to the university and willingness to assimilate to its limitations; its bureaucracy; and its appeasement of the demand to train for jobs rather than educate for social emancipation.[251]

Williams's experience in adult education had been good but not an unalloyed good. His strong support for adult education and his hopes for change produced a certain critical reticence and understatement: the job had 'seemed absolutely right' but 'it was not to turn out so'.[252] Overall adult education seemed to have expanded an existing élite rather than contributed towards the ending of élites. Moving to Oxford in 1960 Williams seems to have been better placed to consider the way the wind was blowing. He had served his time loyally and well. Even the sober-sided officialese of the annual report referred to his 'notable contribution to the Delegacy's work since he was appointed Staff Tutor in 1946'[253] and at a gathering of tutors to mark his translation to Cambridge he was placed in the lineage of Arnold and Tawney.[254] Cambridge would offer more time and more scope for his thinking and writing, without many of the burdens of adult education. Williams felt it was time for a change and the pull to stay was insufficient.

Williams on adult education

Williams had entered adult education so as to make his passage from the working class only partial; so that he could help those who, unlike himself, had not negotiated the ladder of individual attainment successfully; and so that he could play a role in replacing the ladder which individualised, divided, inferiorised and disoriented the workers and forging means for raising, not a small number of individuals, but the whole class. What deeply disturbed him was the fashion in which the individual ladder was used against those who were left behind and the class as a whole, the sense that as Peter Owen in *Second Generation* puts it 'oppressed by an enemy a people had conceived its own liberation as training its sons for the enemy service'. Williams's general answers – an expanded education, a comprehensive education, an end to the private sector, a common and transformed curriculum – were not to resolve these problems, which were rooted in a class society. But they haunt his thoughts and his own writings on the organisation and philosophy of adult education which were fragmentary and scattered down the years.

His voice is first heard in relation to the controversy over whether adult education should reflect the standards of internal university education. Williams utilised the technique later developed in *Keywords*: 'this very discussion can be hindered by failure to understand the complexities of the word that we take as our title'.[255] Internal university education, he argued, was closed to the majority of people by the selection of 'the ladder' which allowed only a small minority to clamber up to the apex of the educational pyramid. University adult education, in contrast, was formally open but the insensitive application of standards would impose the internal nets of selection, exclusion and hierarchy externally. How could one capture statically the quality of living educational growth? Standards was a 'bullying word' and the practice of standards would impose an unnecessary sieve on the adult education involvement of workers. Williams thus observed the degree to which adult education was becoming more and more an alternative ladder, another individual route in, not an alternative for those who had to, or wished to, stay out together.

As Williams's most fertile period in terms of output began, he continually refers to education in a way which is of burning relevance thirty years later: 'I cannot accept that education is a training for jobs or for making useful citizens (that is fitting into this system) . . .' '. . . I ask for a common education that will give our society its cohesion and prevent it disintegrating into a series of specialist departments – the nation becomes a firm'.[256]

An extended piece written in 1959 illustrates Williams's ambivalence towards the development of adult education in the post-war period. He sees the expansion of adult education as an 'absolute necessity of an expanding culture'. He accepts the development of adult education for the already-educated as an intrinsic part of a growing continuing education. But the working class must not be neglected and he sees new developments in trade union education as 'an exciting growth point', because of its potential: 'The miners came to Oxford to study the coal industry and to join in an equal discussion with its leading officials but they also join in excitedly on discussions of language and social class, or contemporary literature and politics'. In this context he remarked the discussion between the NCLC, the WEA and the TUC: 'the current arguments about the organisation of workers' education which although given little publicity, are of fundamental importance'. But he also criticised the introversion, bureaucracy and lack of integrating and mobilising vision in adult education, displaying a flash of the frustrations of fourteen years, 'a large part of what passes for adult education theory is an extraordinary combination of sectarianism, special pleading, mythmaking and mortmain'.[257]

Two years later Williams again affirmed the importance of the WEA and its integration in his own work: 'I've often defined my own social purpose as the creation of an educated and participating democracy. The WEA taught me much in defining these terms'. The tradition of adult education was 'one of the best and deepest traditions in Britain'. Despite social and educational change the continuation of class society meant the 'historic mission is as urgent and central today as it was in the 1900s'.[258]

Yet based on his experience of what was already developing in the field he held out warnings to adult educators, prophetic warnings, on insularity, on lack of imagination and on political challenges which were appearing and which could only intensify. Already, at a conference in 1961, Williams quoted from a Conservative Minister who could not see 'why adult education should need a lot more public money for its development. Given that it was a good product people had sufficient free money to buy it if there was adequate salesmanship for it'.[259] Williams saw the threat of market economics and philistinism as embodied in 'the industrial trainers'. Adult educators had to confront this threat. Adult education was not relevant to industrial training – it was essentially part of public education. Adult education, he emphasised, was not relevant 'to expanding productivity nor to increasing the efficiency of the society in direct terms'.[260] Its objective was the extension of democracy and the deepening of the quality of active participation in society. If adult education was lulled and gulled, 'if adult education bases itself on the argument of an industrial trainer then, quite frankly, better ways will be found of doing it.

If you want to increase skills you do not run WEA classes, you get down to some training on the bench'.261

Adult education could only go forward if it stopped looking to its own small corner and sought to engage with the majority, not the earnest minority: to do this it was essential to look to the media – particularly television – and their decisive role in moulding consciousness in modern society. It was, moreover, essential to reject a paternalist, civilising approach towards adult education, the working class must gain greater access but on *its own terms*: for the first time in history working people were in a position where they could afford not to be saved.262

Through the 1960s Williams continued to think about adult education. He saw in the probable development of *éducation permanente* the impetus towards and, insofar as it developed, the germ of a learning society and a common culture. Williams supported the idea of the Open University and thought it could be combined with a reshaping of adult education, fusing 'a connection between education by television, radio and correspondence courses and the kind of tutorial class education which had been so well developed by the WEA'. However Jenny Lee, the Minister responsible, was determined to steer clear of 'the old types of adult education' and he felt the Open University lost out in terms of student involvement and democracy – and of course adult education failed to grasp the opportunities he had insisted were there in 1961.263

In thinking about the student revolt of 1968 he emphasised the need for democracy in education and the need to start from the students' experience. From the Correspondence Societies onwards, he explained, powerholders had sought to use adult education as a method of controlling the working class through finance and the authority of the teacher. This could only be resisted by insisting on democratic control by the students. Williams had encountered difficulties here in his adult education practice but he had struggled to enter the students' world, accepted 'the challenge to act as a man beyond a system of teaching' and had, often enough, seen a genuine participation by the students in his classes in the definition of educational ends and means. Against the excesses of 1968, however, 'the sillier rhetoric', he counselled that 'what teachers have learnt will also be relevant and will have to be part of any real reform . . . the teacher who pretends he is not a teacher (of course also with very much to learn) is a pathetic and irrelevant figure'. Once again there is the insistent emphasis on adult education as the precursor of a more democratic world 'in which the whole society is seen as a learning process'.264

Williams never fully developed the point he touches on here: adult education as a form of social control. Yet, of course, the involvement of the university and the WEA in this field was informed by very much the same impulses as Matthew Arnold's approach to culture criticised in *Culture and Society*. Arnold saw education, based on 'the best which has been thought and said in the world', as the means of 'getting us out of our present difficulties' and ensuring that what he termed the 'playful giant' of the working class did not stray on to the path of anarchy. In an age of revolution, education, for Arnold, was the antidote. *Culture and Anarchy* was written in response to riots in Hyde Park to which Arnold's answer was to flog the rank and file, execute the ringleaders and disseminate high culture as balm, civilisation and social cement.

Nonetheless when he later came to reassess the situation Williams stated 'Today, when I read of the Ruskin strike and the foundation of Plebs, I think that the opponents of the WEA conception were right'.[265] But this was far from a simple matter. The Plebs League–NCLC tradition was, he thought, not without its disadvantages. Independent working-class education in this mould will always 'run the risk of becoming subservient to particular party lines in particular periods and genuinely losing some of its educational characteristics'.[266] Workers often preferred a more open orientation to a propaganda ethos. Moreover within university adult education there had not been a simple topdown control but a continuing tension between the universities and working class students. The workers were often able to utilise the WEA to achieve the kind of education they wanted but pressure from the universities to 'incorporate the movement', to ensure that the workers received what the universities thought was good for them, was unrelenting. Williams felt that the battle was still being contested when he entered adult education.

But he argues the universities won in the end.

> *Over the years there, in the end, occurred a pretty successful conversion of the WEA into something that could be indifferently called Further Education: any other emphasis was deflected except in certain specialised areas of trade union education. That only became clear to me when I moved to Oxford in 1961 ... a plan was unfolded – it was quite explicit – to create a residential college in Wellington Square whose focus would be on refresher courses for young graduates who had gone into industrial management and so on. This was suddenly no longer the mixed situation I had lived in for fourteen years. When they moved to institutionalise these dreadful refresher courses for managers then of course adult education ceased to have enough meaning.*[267]

Williams adds 'It was at this point that I knew that I wanted to move on'.[268] This is rather subjective. In 1961 it was becoming difficult to characterise university adult education and the WEA in any general meaningful sense as working-class organisations. But there were certain kinds of work, in certain places, some of them still growing, where it was possible to develop working class education. The important truth in what Williams says is that by 1961 this occurred only in relatively well-demarcated enclaves: the middle class, the industrial trainers, the 'dreadful refresher courses' were growing stronger and, of course, came to be a permanent and ever more striking part of university adult education.

By the early 1960s many of those who, like Williams, had joined up after the war to make adult education a radical alternative to the individual ladder of the orthodox educational system, were undergoing various degrees of concern and disappointment. Adult education was now more a part of the wider orthodoxy and some were looking for their demob papers. There were now more ladders out of the working class than there had been in 1945 – adult education was one of them – but there were just as many talented individuals branded second-rate and left behind. Adult education had not qualitatively changed that situation for the better.

Williams today

Williams's work, his teaching and his writing, was a uniquely valuable contribution to adult education and social thought. We should appreciate it without inflation or romanticism. His distinctive contribution was largely an independent and individual one rather than made as part of a wider movement. As we have seen, his work in his classes had limitations in terms of size and reach. His writing was often dense and impenetrable and it is fair to ask why at least some of it was not made more accessible to the workers Williams wanted to reach. It has still inspired thousands in the last thirty years and it will hopefully inspire more in the coming decades. But we have to keep in view the mass radical adult education Williams wanted to see – and our distance from it. As Alan Sinfield remarks:

> *Human freedom has gained immeasurably from the books of Raymond Williams but, revisiting Pandy, I met Mrs Smith the retired postmistress who remembers him as a boy; she told me she has never read one of them.*[269]

Williams was never part of the adult education establishment and within the field his work was subversive in cutting against the trend of developments in the 1950s and 1960s. He himself left adult education in some disillusion at the height of his powers. Hoggart too left. And so did Thompson later and Hodgkin earlier. The reasons for this illuminate the limitations of British adult education.

In 1959 *Adult Education* quite rightly pronounced Williams's work 'a challenge'.[270] The challenge, if we read what Williams wrote and study what he did, was to produce an expanded and revitalised adult education as a radical cultural practice rooted in the organised collective efforts of the working class. To what degree, through sustained organisational, intellectual and educational work, have we made adult education intrinsic to the lives and concerns of the majority as a contribution towards 'the long revolution', 'the learning society', 'the common culture'? How have we answered Williams's challenge?

The answer must be, 'very inadequately'. The highpoint of the changes Williams and the New Left wished to encourage was probably the Robbins expansion and the creation of the Open University. State culturalism foundered with the 1966 Wilson Government. We are now faced with a government positively and vociferously pledged to the unleashing of a rampant commercialism and Victorian values. The *market* and *sponsorship* of the arts and education are today's keywords. 'Cost effectiveness'; 'value for money'; 'entrepreneurial'; 'contracts'; infiltrate educational discourse. Children are being 'tested' at seven years of age. The Arts Council is being wrecked and broadcasting is being handed over to the press magnates. The political attack, the beginnings of which Williams noted, has been skilful and successful; the opposition to it has been cautious and limited.

All over education the common culture which is being seeded is the enterprise culture. Within adult education itself radical work with the working class constitutes small islands, scarcely a minor archipelago, far from a movement. It is difficult in 1991 to see how the WEA can, in any sense except the vicarious, be termed a workers' organisation. In the universities you can hardly move without tripping over one of these 'dreadful refresher courses'. Williams's thought is even more subversive to tendencies in education generally and in adult education in particular today than it was in 1961. It is also more relevant and therefore more valuable. It must be used to help us in our present difficulties, but it can only do that if we avoid canonisation and hagiography.

Notes and References
1. S. Heath and C. McCabe, 'Obituary – Raymond Williams 1921–1988', *Critical Quarterly*, 30, 1988, p 3.
2. R. Williams, *Politics and Letters: Interviews with New Left Review*, Verso, 1979, p 97.
3. R. Williams, 'The new British left', *Partisan Review*, 27, 1960, p 342.
4. R. Williams, 'Introduction', *Communications*, Harmondsworth: Penguin Books, 2nd ed., 1966, p 2.
5. R. Williams, 'Figures and shadows', *The Highway*, February 1954; R. Williams, 'Standards', *The Highway*, December 1954.
6. R. Williams, 'Adult education and social change' in WEA South-Eastern District, *Adult Education and Social Change: Lectures and reminiscences in honour of Tony McLean*, n.d. probably 1983, p 18.
7. Williams, 1983, p 24.
8. R. Blackburn, 'Introduction' to R. Williams, *Resources of Hope*, Verso, 1989, p ix.
9. Heath and McCabe, p 3.
10. M. Joannou, 'Raymond Williams 1921–1988', *WEA News*, 35, 1988, p 10.
11. D. Tatton, 'Raymond Williams, the WEA and "Towards 2003"', *Workers Education*, 2, 1988, pp 27–30.
12. A. O'Connor, *Raymond Williams: Writing, culture, politics*, Oxford: Blackwell, 1989, pp 8–10.
13. Williams, 1979, particularly pp 78–83.
14. R. Williams, *An Open Letter to WEA Tutors*, WEA, n.d. probably 1961.
15. University of Oxford Archives, DES/F/10/3; University of Oxford Delegacy for Extra-Mural Studies, *Report 1946–47*, p 8; Williams, 1979, pp 64, 78.
16. Oxford University DES/MP/I/I Delegacy Committee Papers; Williams, 1979, p 78; T. McLean, 'Working with the South Eastern District of the WEA – Some Reminiscences, 1945–1956' in WEA SE District *Adult Education and Social Change*, 1983, pp 35–42.
17. R. Fieldhouse, *Adult Education and the Cold War: Liberal values under siege 1946–51*, Leeds Studies in Adult and Continuing Education, University of Leeds, 1985, particularly chapter 3; McLean, 1983.

316   *Border Country*

18. University of Oxford, *Report of the Committee on Extra-Mural Studies*, Oxford University, 1970, p 40.
19. T. Hodgkin, 'Adult education and social change', *Adult Education*, XXIII, 1950; T. Hodgkin, 'Objectivity, ideologies and the present political situation', *The Highway*, January 1951.
20. Williams, 1979, p 80.
21. R. Bellamy, *correspondence with author*.
22. R. Williams, 'The uses of cultural theory', *New Left Review*, 158, 1986, p 25.
23. R. Williams, 'Culture and revolution: a comment' in T. Eagleton and B. Wicker, eds, *From Culture to Revolution: The Slant Symposium*, Sheed and Ward, 1968.
24. Williams, 1979, p 67.
25. Lalage Bown, 'Review of R. Fieldhouse *Adult Education and the Cold War* ...', *Studies in the Education of Adults*, 18, pp 130–3; Lalage Bown, *correspondence with author*; S. Coltham quoted in Fieldhouse, 1985, p 33.
26. UCAE, *The Universities in Adult Education: A statement of principles*, UCAE, 1948.
27. For the background here see J. Blyth, *English University Adult Education 1908–58*, Manchester University Press, 1983; T. Kelly, *A History of Adult Education in Britain*, Liverpool University Press, 3rd ed., 1992.
28. S. Raybould, *University Extra Mural Education in England 1945–62: A study in finance and policy*, Michael Joseph, 1964, p 74.
29. A. Allaway, *Thought and Action in Extra-Mural Work, Leicester 1946–1966*, Leicester University, 1967, p 37.
30. Williams, 1979, pp 80, 81.
31. *See* J. McIlroy and B. Spencer, *University Adult Education in Crisis*, Leeds Studies in Adult and Continuing Education, University of Leeds, 1988, for a brief outline.
32. J. McIlroy, 'The demise of the National Council of Labour Colleges'; J. McIlroy, 'The triumph of technical training', both in B. Simon, ed., *The Search for Enlightenment: The working class and adult education in the twentieth century*, Lawrence and Wishart, 1990; 2nd ed., NIACE, 1992.
33. S. Raybould, *The English Universities and Adult Education*, WEA, 1951, p xv; Raybould, 1964, p 112.
34. Raybould, 1964, p 33.
35. Raybould, 1964, p 39.
36. University of Oxford Delegacy for Extra-Mural Studies, *Annual Reports*.
37. Raybould, 1951, p 1.
38. Raybould, 1951, p xvi.
39. Quoted in UCAE *Annual Report 1975–76*, p 4.
40. Raybould, 1964, pp 156–7.
41. McIlroy and Spencer, 1988, p 12.
42. O'Connor, 1989, p 8.
43. Williams, 1979, p 43. The comment comes from Williams's interrogators from the editorial board of *New Left Review*.
44. R. Ruddock, '170 tutors', *Adult Education*, XXXV, 1963, p 318.
45. University of Oxford Tutorial Classes Committee, *Reports*, 1947–48; 1948–49.
46. Oxford TCC *Reports*, 1948–49; 1957–58.
47. Oxford TCC *Reports*.

48. Oxford TCC *Reports*, 1947–48.
49. Williams, 1979, p 78.
50. Oxford TCC *Reports*.
51. M. Mortimer, 'Impressions of adult education', *Adult Education*, XVIII, p 181.
52. J. Sewell, 'Let's get this straight', *The Highway*, January 1948, p 55.
53. O'Connor, 1989, p 8.
54. C. Joad, 'I pontificate', *The Tutors Bulletin of Adult Education*, April 1952, p 5.
55. M. Checksfield, 'Joad's pontification', *The Tutors Bulletin of Adult Education*, June 1952, p 30. The question of Williams and feminism, 'the problems of women and the family' and their absence from Williams's work in this period are briefly raised in Williams, 1979, pp 148–9. Williams claims 'It was not however that I wasn't thinking about them'. See also J. Swindells, L. Jardine, *What's Left? Women in culture and the Labour Movement*, Routledge, 1989; M. Beard, *London Review of Books*, 20, October 1989. For an unconvincing (and unnecessary) suggestion that Williams's categories of thought were linked to the characteristic concerns of feminist writing see R. Blackburn, 'In defence of Raymond Williams', *London Review of Books*, 9 March 1990.
56. J.R. Williams, '*Review of Drama From Ibsen to Eliot*', *The Tutors Bulletin of Adult Education*, June 1953, p 19.
57. L. Butcher, 'Education in home-making', *Adult Education*, XXVII, 1955, pp 252–6.
58. Williams, 1979, p 81.
59. Williams, 1979, p 81.
60. Fieldhouse, 1985, p 35.
61. Fieldhouse, 1985, ch 2.
62. H.J. Fyrth, *correspondence with author*.
63. M. Ward, 'Michael Carritt', *The Guardian*, 13 February 1990. Williams himself was reticent about his role in these events – see Williams, 1979, pp 80–81; but see, also, the comments in Williams, 1983. Carritt was a former official of the Communist Party – see J. Saville, 'A Red in the Raj', *The Guardian*, 5 February 1990.
64. Williams, 1979, p 39ff.
65. Williams, 1979, p 91.
66. Williams, 1979, p 63.
67. Williams, 1979, pp 65–77; O'Connor, 1989, pp 10–13.
68. M. Pope (Williams) 'The state and popular culture: a note', *Politics and Letters*, 1, 1948, pp 72–3.
69. See, for example, the favourable review of *Politics and Letters* by H.P., *The Highway*, November 1947, p 23. But also a dismissive review of Williams's piece 'Writers today' in the Spring 1947 issue of *The Critic*, *The Tutors Bulletin of Adult Education*, July 1947, p 15.
70. Williams, 1979, p 71.
71. Williams, 1979, p 77.
72. Williams, 1979, p 77.
73. J. Vickers, *correspondence with author*.
74. Fyrth, *correspondence*.
75. Fieldhouse, 1985, p 27 for East Sussex.
76. A. Woolford, *correspondence with author*.
77. Fyrth, *correspondence*.

78. Woolford, *correspondence*.
79. Woolford, *correspondence*.
80. Williams, 1979, p 93.
81. Fyrth, *correspondence*.
82. F. Pickstock, conversation with author.
83. C. Scrimgeour, *correspondence with author*.
84. R. Williams, 'Notes on British Marxism since the war', *New Left Review*, 100, 1977, p 88.
85. Williams, 1983, p 17.
86. Williams, 1983, p 12.
87. Oxford University Delegacy for Extra-Mural Studies, *Reports*; Oxford University TCC *Reports*, T. McLean, 1983.
88. WEA SE District 1983; *correspondence*, Fyrth, Woolford; R. Williams, *Culture and Society*, Chatto and Windus, 1958, p 11; H.J. Fyrth, 'Henry Collins', *Bulletin of the Society for the Study of Labour History*, 20, 1970, pp 9, 10.
89. J. Levitt, *correspondence with author*; W.P. Baker, F. Jacques, correspondence with H.P. Smith, 13, 18 July 1946.
90. F. Bayliss, A. Marsh, G. Bowen-Thomas, G. Stuttard, *correspondence with author*.
91. Scrimgeour, *correspondence*.
92. Woolford, *correspondence*.
93. Oxford University Delegacy for Extra-Mural Studies, *Report*, 1949–50, p 7.
94. Oxford University TCC *Reports*, 1946–58.
95. Oxford University TCC *Report*, 1954, p 9.
96. Oxford University TCC *Report*, 1950, p 8.
97. D. Hewitt, *correspondence with author*.
98. Woolford, *correspondence*.
99. Marsh, *correspondence*.
100. Scrimgeour, *correspondence*.
101. Williams, 1979, p 106.
102. Woolford, *correspondence*.
103. Woolford, *correspondence*.
104. Scrimgeour, *correspondence*.
105. Marsh, *correspondence*.
106. Marsh, *correspondence*.
107. O'Connor, 1989, p 120.
108. Williams, 1979, p 132.
109. R. Williams, *Second Generation*, Chatto and Windus, 1964, p 96.
110. E.P. Thompson, *The Making of The English Working Class*, Harmondsworth: Penguin Books, 1968, p 14.
111. Williams, *Open Letter*, 1961.
112. Williams, 1962, p 21.
113. D. Hewitt, 'Why teach literature in adult education?', *Critical Quarterly*, 11, 1959, pp 53–6.
114. M. Bradbury, 'The adult education class' in M. Bradbury, *Who Do You Think You Are?* Secker and Warburg, 1976.
115. TCC *Report*, 1954–55, Literature Cuckfield.
116. A. Hudson, 'Literature and adult students', *The Highway*, February 1946, p 60.
117. D. Bland, 'Written work in the literature class', *The Highway*, September 1948.

118. E. Shackleton, 'Written work in the literature class', *The Highway*, December 1948; H. Peschmann, 'Literature and written work: a reply to D.S. Bland', *The Highway*, January 1949.
119. J. Carr, 'A novel for written work', *Adult Education*, XXXVI, 1964, p 257.
120. Scrimgeour, *correspondence*; Williams, 1979, p 82.
121. E. Birkhead, 'The position of staff tutors in extra-mural departments', *Adult Education*, XXXI, 1958, p 132.
122. R. Hoggart, 'Some questions on the work of full-time tutors in university extra-mural departments', *The Tutors Bulletin of Adult Education*, July 1952, p 24.
123. D. Caradog Jones, 'The forthcoming year', *The Tutors Bulletin of Adult Education*, Spring 1951, p 3.
124. Hewitt, 1959, p 54.
125. Williams, *Open Letter*, 1961.
126. Williams, *Communications*, 1966, p 9.
127. Woolford, *correspondence*.
128. Williams, 1983, p 10.
129. Williams, 1983, pp 10–11.
130. P. Scott, 'Man of the border country', *Times Higher Educational Supplement*, 15 March 1985.
131. R. Williams, 'Some experiments in literature teaching', *Rewley House Papers*, 2, 1949, p 9.
132. Williams, 1949, p 9.
133. Williams, 1949, p 14.
134. Williams, 1979, pp 80–81.
135. Marsh, *correspondence*.
136. Williams, 1949, p 9.
137. Williams, 1983, p 22.
138. Williams, 1983, pp 11–12.
139. Williams, 1949, p 11.
140. Williams, 1949, p 10.
141. Williams, 1949, p 10.
142. R. Hoggart, 'Some notes on extra-mural teaching', *Adult Education*, XXXIII, 1960, p 178.
143. D. Thompson, *Reading and Discrimination*, Chatto and Windus, 1934, p 4.
144. Williams, 1949, p 13.
145. Williams, 1949, p 13.
146. Oxford University TCC *Reports*, 1947–48.
147. F.R. Leavis and D. Thompson, *Culture and Environment*, Chatto and Windus, 1933, p vii.
148. T. Pound, *Developments in Teaching Literature to Adults in the Immediate Post-war Period*, University of Keele, MA thesis, 1982.
149. D. Butts, 'The development of literature teaching in the Oxford Tutorial Classes', *Rewley House Papers*, 3, 1959, p 17.
150. Pound, 1982, p 4. This thesis provides an excellent analysis of the development of practical criticism.
151. Williams, 1949, p 15.
152. C. Collins, 'Literary criticism in adult education', *The Tutors Bulletin of Adult Education*, November 1946.
153. Williams, *Culture and Society*, p 11.
154. Oxford University TCC *Reports*, 1946–47, 1947–48. Williams 1979,

apparently erroneously, dates the first of these courses as 1949, see p 13
and again at p 97. Other tutors such as Tony McLean were also involved
in similar courses. See the tribute '. . . so strange was this to the universities
that they said "My God, here is a new subject called Cultural Studies".
Tony McLean was one of the best of those who had been teaching Cultural
Studies for years before the birth of this new subject', Williams, 1983,
p 17.

155. Williams, 1979, p 133.
156. Williams, 1979, p 97; R. Williams 'The idea of culture', *Essays in Criticism*,
    1, 1953, pp 239–66.
157. Butts, 1959, p 16.
158. E.P. Thompson, 'The condition of the arts', *The Highway*, April 1949,
    p 138.
159. E.P. Thompson, 'A cultural policy', *The Tutors Bulletin of Adult Education*,
    Summer 1950, pp 7–12.
160. Thomas Hodgkin, Professor Raybould and Lady Shena Simon were the series
    editors.
161. R. Williams, 'A note on Mr Hoggart's appendices', *Adult Education*,
    XXI, 1948, p 96. Although they did not meet until 1959–60 Hoggart and
    Williams were thus aware of each other's work at an early stage.
162. Williams, 1948, p 96.
163. C. Lee, 'Review of *Reading and Criticism*', *Adult Education*, XXIII, 1950,
    p 235.
164. T.W. Thomas, 'Practical criticism and the literature class', *Adult Education*,
    XXIV, 1951, p 20.
165. H. Sherwood, 'Review', *The Tutors Bulletin of Adult Education*, Autumn,
    1950, pp 16, 17.
166. Thomas, 1951, p 20.
167. Thomas, 1951, p 27.
168. R. Williams, *Drama From Ibsen to Eliot*, Chatto and Windus, 1952,
    p 14.
169. Williams, 1952, p 111.
170. Williams, 1979, p 196.
171. Williams, 1952, p 32.
172. D. Hewitt, 'The literary critic and the historian', *The Tutors Bulletin of
    Adult Education*, October 1952, pp 10, 11.
173. J.R. Williams, 'Review of *Drama From Ibsen to Eliot*', *The Tutors Bulletin
    of Adult Education*, June 1953, p 20.
174. R. Williams, 'Letter', *The Tutors Bulletin of Adult Education*, Autumn,
    1953.
175. R. Williams, 'Text and context', *The Tutors Bulletin of Adult Education*,
    December 1953, p 19.
176. Williams, 1953, p 21.
177. R. Williams, 'Literature in relation to history: 1850–75', *Rewley House
    Papers*, 3, 1949–50, p 41.
178. W. Simpson, 'Documentary theatre', *The Highway*, March 1947; G. Taylor,
    'Drama as literature', *The Tutors Bulletin of Adult Education*, April 1952;
    J.R. Williams, 'The art of the theatre', *The Highway*, February 1955;
    H.A. Jones, 'Music and drama in adult education', *Adult Education*,
    XXVII, 1955.
179. Oxford University TCC *Reports*, 1950–51.
180. Williams, 1979, p 39.

181. R. Manvell, 'Film appreciation in adult education', *Adult Education*, XVIII, 1945, pp 16–21; M. Reeves, 'The film societies and adult education', *Adult Education*, XXI, 1949, pp 175–8; J.R. Williams, 'Film and the cinema', *The Highway*, December 1946.
182. Manvell, 1945, p 21.
183. R. Williams, 'Film as a tutorial subject', *Rewley House Papers*, 3, 1953, p 35.
184. Butts, 1959, pp 15–16.
185. O'Connor, 1989, p 9; Butts, 1959, p 15.
186. Butts, 1959, p 15.
187. Marsh, *correspondence*.
188. Williams, 1952, p 248.
189. Williams, 1952, p 250.
190. Williams, 1952, p 251.
191. R. Williams, 'Public expression', unpublished paper for conference on teaching methods in trade union education, probably 1956.
192. Oxford University TCC *Report*, 1954, p 9; Woolford, *correspondence*.
193. Williams, 1956, p 2.
194. Williams, 1956, p 2.
195. D. Butts, 'Public expression', *Adult Education*, XXXII, 1960, p 133.
196. F. Pickstock to W.E. Styler, quoted in T. Pound, 1982, p 97.
197. Joannou, 1988.
198. Lalage Bown, *correspondence*.
199. Scrimgeour, *correspondence*.
200. Stuttard, *correspondence*.
201. Woolford, *correspondence*.
202. Levitt, *correspondence*.
203. Woolford, *correspondence*.
204. Pound, 1982, p 96.
205. Oxford University TCC *Reports*, 1956–57, Literature Brighton.
206. Pound suggests an HMI inspection in 1955–56 may have played some role.
207. Woolford, *correspondence*.
208. Bowen Thomas, *correspondence*.
209. Williams, 1979, p 172.
210. Levitt, *correspondence*.
211. Hewitt, 1959, p 55.
212. Butts, 1959, p 17.
213. Hewitt, 1959, p 56.
214. B. Hogenkamp, *Deadly Parallels: Film and the Left in Britain 1929–1939*, Lawrence and Wishart, 1986.
215. S. Jones, *The British Labour Movement and Film 1918–1939*, Routledge, 1987.
216. The description is Williams's, in R. Williams, *Marxism and Literature*, Oxford University Press, 1977, p 2.
217. Williams, 'The Idea of Culture', 1953.
218. E.P. Thompson, 'The Long Revolution', *New Left Review*, 9, 1961, p 27.
219. Williams, 1960, p 240.
220. Williams, 1964, p 137.
221. Williams, *Communications*, 2nd edition, 1966, p 10.
222. Williams, 1977, p 3.
223. 'Conference Scrapbook', in Oxford University Socialist Discussion Group,

Out of Apathy: Voices of the New Left 30 years on, Verso, 1989, p 136.
Williams describes the first contact as an invitation to speak at the ULR
club in London – Williams, 1979, p 361.

224. See, for example, R. Williams, 'The Uses of Literacy: Working Class Culture'
Universities and Left Review 2, 1957; R. Williams 'The press the people
want', *Universities and Left Review* 5, 1958; R. Williams, 'Freedom and
ownership in the arts', *New Left Review*, 5, 1960.

225. Thompson, 1961, p 24.

226. Williams, 1979, p 364; R. Johnson, 'Thompson, Genovese and socialist
humanist history', *History Workshop Journal*, 6, Autumn 1978, sees an
emphasis on cultural issues and human agency at the expense of important
structural and economic changes within capitalism and the working class
characterising the New Left in this period. The term and characterisation
have been contested by Edward Thompson who points to the different
concerns and approaches of figures such as himself, Williams, Hoggart
and Stuart Hall in this period; E.P. Thompson, 'The politics of theory',
in R. Samuel, ed., *People's History and Socialist Theory*, Routledge, 1981,
pp 396–408.

227. Williams, 1961, p 312.

228. Williams, 1958, pp 313–14.

229. Williams, 1968, in T. Eagleton, B. Whicker, 1968, p 29.

230. R. Williams, *The Long Revolution*, Chatto and Windus, 1961, p 328.

231. Williams, 1958, p 307.

232. Williams, 1958, p 231.

233. R. Williams, 'Culture and Revolution: A response' in T. Eagleton, B. Wicker,
1968, p 308.

234. Williams, *The Long Revolution*, p 118.

235. Williams, *The Long Revolution*, p 64.

236. Williams, *Culture and Society*, p 333.

237. A. Hartley, 'The loaf and the leaven', *Manchester Guardian*, 7 October 1958;
R. Wollheim, *Socialism and The Intellectuals*, Fabian Society, 1961.

238. V. Kiernan, 'Culture and Society', *New Reasoner*, 9, 1959, pp 74–83;
Thompson, 1961, pp 24–5.

239. Thompson, 1961, p 33.

240. Williams, *Culture and Society*, p 269.

241. T. Eagleton, *Criticism and Ideology*, Verso, 1976; A. Barnett, 'Raymond
Williams and Marxism', *New Left Review*, 99, 1976, pp 47–66.

242. Williams, 1977, p 3.

243. R. Williams, 'You're a Marxist, aren't you?' in B. Parekh, ed., *The Concept
of Socialism*, Croom Helm, 1975, p 241.

244. Thompson, 1961, p 27.

245. 'Review of *Culture and Society*' in *Adult Education*, XXXII, 1959, p 73.

246. D. Hewitt, 'Review of *Culture and Society*', *The Highway*, February 1959,
pp 10, 11.

247. Hewitt, 'Review', p 11.

248. R. Williams, 'A kind of Gresham's Law', *The Highway*, February 1958;
R. Williams, 'The press and popular education', *The Highway*, April 1959;
See also D. McCrae 'Mass culture', *The Highway*, April 1956; M. Cole,
'Mass culture', *The Highway*, November 1956; W. Whiteley, 'Working class
literacy', *The Highway*, March 1958; The Editor, 'The arts and society
and the WEA', *The Highway*, December 1958; W. Whiteley, 'The Uses of
Literacy', *The Highway*, April 1959.

249. See, for example, B. Groombridge, 'Adult education and the Admass', *Adult Education*, XXX, 1957, pp 42–7; B. Groombridge, 'Democratic communication', *Adult Education*, XXXIII, 1960, pp 31–4.
250. See the report in *Adult Education*, XXXIII, 1960, pp 35–6.
251. Compare the tone and comments of Williams, 1979, pp 78–83 with the powerfully affirmative *Open Letter* of 1961.
252. Williams, 1979, p 67.
253. University of Oxford Delegacy for Extra-Mural Studies, *Report*, 1960–61, p 5.
254. Scrimgeour, *correspondence*.
255. R. Williams, 'Standards', *The Highway*, December 1954, p 46; R. Williams, 'Figures and shadows', *The Highway*, February 1954.
256. R. Williams, 'Culture is ordinary' in N. McKenzie, ed., *Conviction*, McGibbon and Kee, 1958, p 85.
257. R. Williams, 'Going on learning', *New Statesman*, 30 May 1959, pp 750–1.
258. Williams, *Open Letter*, 1961.
259. R. Williams, 'The common good', *Adult Education*, XXXIV, 1961, p 192.
260. Williams, 'The common good', p 195.
261. Williams, 'The common good', pp 196–7.
262. R. Williams, 'Introduction' to *Communications*, 2nd edition, Penguin Books, 1966.
263. Williams, 1979, p 274.
264. R. Williams, 'Different sides of the wall', *The Guardian*, 26 September 1968.
265. Williams, 1979, p 79.
266. Williams, 1979, p 79.
267. Williams, 1979, p 81.
268. Williams, 1979, p 81.
269. A. Sinfield, *Literature, Politics and Culture in Postwar Britain*, Blackwell, 1989, p 268.
270. *Adult Education*, XXXII, 1959, p 73.

Excavating the Future: Towards 2000

Sallie Westwood

'*The world without an alternative needs self-criticism as a condition of survival and decency. But it does not make the life of criticism easy.*'[1]

Bauman, writing in another decade, the nineties, reinforces one of the major driving forces of Williams's writing, the necessity to scrutinise all ideas and premises, however difficult personally and politically. The emphasis upon critique was so clearly evident in the volume of his essays entitled *Towards 2000*, which is the main focus of the present chapter.[2] It is important in a collection such as this that some attention is given to this text. The materials brought together in this volume have largely focused on the past and on a task of recovery from within Williams's own biography. In this task we wish to claim a space for him within adult education and demand that this space does not go unheeded, as it has tended to do, within the accounts of his life and work. It is also the case that Williams wrote about the past. But while properly concerned with cultures and histories, Williams also sought to make sense of his present through a view of the future expressed in *Towards 2000*. The book was published in 1983, four years into Thatcherism, the year following the defeat of the health workers and prior to the miners' strike. It was, as now, a time of recession, unemployment, restructuring and cuts in public expenditure, offering clear signs that 'the forward march of labour' was, indeed, halted. *Towards 2000* was a political intervention in an ongoing debate in which Raymond Williams was a central figure. This chapter does not seek to re-create that moment but to offer a review of the book and some considerations of its main concerns, in part as a reminder, if we need one, of the importance of Williams's voice today. So, what of the future that is now our present?

Characteristically, Williams begins by looking back – to the sixties and the final essay of *The Long Revolution*, published in 1959. *Towards 2000* uses this final essay, 'Britain in the sixties', as a way of debating the future in relation to the familiar themes of Williams's writing – class, culture and community, issues of democratisation, the nation and the socialist agenda. The essay weaves these together around a discussion of the changing nature of the economy, the limitations of representative democracy, the nature of classes in Britain economically and culturally, and changes within the media fields. This essay, written as the sixties dawned, is, overall, an optimistic account of change. One in which the increased prosperity of Britain and the growth of public sector employment is underlined. But it is, more importantly, about what kind of society we inhabit and the ways in which capitalism undermines community and society, offering consumption against community and the market rather than society. Themes, of course, which were underscored during the early Thatcher period. In an analysis of what we would now call hegemonic relations, Williams considers the ways in which capitalism has subordinated the radical impulse of the trade unions and the Labour Party via incorporation.

This has, of course, a direct bearing upon Williams's concerns with democracy and the lack of democratic forms in our everyday lives, '. . . we do not get enough practice in the workings of democracy' (39), borne out in the lack of democratisation within both working and community lives. We are not encouraged to engage in forms of participatory democracy but are offered a pale shadow, representative democracy, and, as the current debates around Maastricht confirm, even a referendum is beyond the UK model. None of this is a surprise, because at this juncture Williams seemed to subscribe to a view of democracy within capitalism which left it at the mercy of capitalist forces. This was true also of the changing nature of class relations defined by capitalism; there could be no classlessness without the social ownership of capital. 'Most of us are servants' (53) was Williams's view, although he clearly recognised that this was framed and made specific within the sale of labour power on the market. The 1959 Labour defeat was much debated at the time in relation to the collapse of traditional working-class communities and loyalties to Labour, a not unfamiliar debate today. Williams was aware of the migrations of populations and the existence of the new housing estates with their 'privatised workers', but he was wise enough to know also that somewhere there had to be a viable and relevant programme to command the loyalty and support of voters and he is clear that '. . . just at this point Labour seems to have very little to offer' (59). The failure of imagination within the Labour Party meets a failure of social analysis which suggests that there are 'telly-glued masses'. For Williams the masses '. . . do not exist; they are the bad fiction of our second-rate social analysts' (59).

Instead, Williams returns to the basic Marxist point that people have to have more control over their lives. This is interrupted for Williams by the powerful theme of community, which, for Williams, is the only route towards a more egalitarian society in which the differentials between classes can be eroded and a sense of society and togetherness generated. The romanticisation and concretisation of community in Raymond Williams's work is well known, as is his rather arch appraisal of popular culture, when it is not being romanticised in relation to community. So, as far as he can see, as we moved into the sixties there was plenty of scope for the development of cultural forms and a democratisation of culture but there was also plenty of 'bad' art, literature and cultural products with which we were burdened. For Williams too much was still left to the market, while the BBC needed to be more accountable to 'responsible choice' and the press was concentrated in too few hands and not subject to enough scrutiny. There was a clear need for 'public assurance' to stimulate and encourage 'healthy cultural growth'. Williams was not discouraged by the discussions of 'massification' but trusted to the resistances of ordinary people and the numbers of creative innovators who would continue to be part of the long revolution, and would maintain its impetus.

In his re-assessment of his *Long Revolution* essay, which forms the second part of *Towards 2000*, Williams turns first to economic relations and the debates around the notion of the 'post-industrial' society. The discussions have, of course, moved on into the delineation of post-Fordism and the cultural and social concomitants of postmodernity. Williams nods in this direction in so far as he is aware that it is not simply productive processes that are changing but the relations of production, the way people work, working relations and the relationship between work and non-work. He is conscious that definitions of employment do not account for work, especially the reproductive work of women via domestic labour and servicing of the household. But he did not comment on the way in which employment has always been and continues to be both gendered and racialised. Equally, we now understand that the fall in the manufacturing base and heavy industry sectors in Britain has been met with increasing service sector employment; most of this work is casualised, poorly paid, racialised and feminised. It is also, as the decline in union membership shows, difficult to organise and promote collectivity, which has major implications for the democratisation of the workplace that Williams was so keen to support.

More importantly, in relation to Williams's analysis his critique of the market as an organising principle for capitalism and his call for control of production as the basis for more egalitarian and democratic work and social relations has been overtaken by the reification of the market and the growing power of state intervention in relation to the restructuring of the Thatcher years. For the last 10 years the vexed and complex question of progress within scarcity has been set aside and, further, referred to the market. Williams foreshadows this when he notes: 'The world is not only as tough as the capitalists keep telling us; it is very much tougher' (100). But he sees in the changes in work a new opportunity for 'sharing' through a political intervention. The political intervention that we have lived through in the eighties was not the one promoted by Raymond Williams, although the language of 'toughness' has been very much in evidence. The market and with it the consumer has been foregrounded, while the disparities in wealth, income and shares of the social product have been massively increased. Unemployment has grown and continues to divide Britain in relation to fundamental democratic rights. As I write news of the threatened final closures of the pits and the end of the era of coal mining in Britain is evidenced.

The relationship between economic power, or lack of power, and the democratic impulse is a major preoccupation for Williams and he moves from the economy to a critique of bourgeois democracy, uncovering in the process and thereby demystifying the role of the monarchy and the

House of Lords in Britain. For Williams what is required is an 'educated and participatory democracy' (102); 'learning democracy' is about being involved in democratic institutions and decision-making arenas which within representative democracy we lack. In fact, only one part of the process of democracy is at work, the election of Members of Parliament. It is quite clear that the House of Lords is undemocratic and should be replaced by a second chamber related to the electoral process. Williams demystifies the notion of representation, showing how slippery it is. Who is represented by whom and in relation to what?, are questions that are essential. He correctly points out that even general elections in Britain are not tied to a specific time-scale but within a five-year period the government can decide on the election date. It is all highly problematic, which is not to decry the importance of liberal democracy but to suggest that it has the potential to be a lot better. It is also vital that socialism understands the democratic impulse. Williams is mindful of the anti-democratic impulse within vanguardism and the Leninist programme: 'It is my belief that the only kind of socialism that now stands any chance of being established, in the old industrial bourgeois-democratic societies, is one centrally based on new kinds of communal, co-operative and collective institutions' (123). How, one wonders, would Williams have viewed the 'new Europe'? With a mixture of optimism and dread, one may suspect. Williams opts for 'scales of relevant community' as a basis for greater democratisation and the bedrock of a more communal and co-operative world. This is in part to guard against the growing authoritarianism of the social order, of which he was so clearly aware. But in setting up this opposition Williams did not foresee that communalism is as contradictory as representation and that Europe's history is rife with this contradiction, now foregrounded for the nineties. It was certainly not that Williams was unaware of nationalisms, which he examines later in the book and to which we will return.

Instead, Williams develops his analysis of the importance of new technologies and their impact on the forms of mass media and cultures more widely. He provides a critique of the technologically determinist view of the 'paperless office' while recognising the impact of new technologies, especially in the print media. The basic point is that there is no technology without the social, political and economic relations that surround it. Thus Murdoch had to go to war with the printers, their history and craft in order to use the new technologies for his newspapers. In a different political climate, in Germany, this was less confrontational but the death of a whole work culture and the skills and history that surround it was no less painful. Williams points to the ways in which we are sold the idea of a technological juggernaut over-riding collective and individual concerns and how this culminates in a form of 'cultural pessimism' with its roots in the misunderstood opposition between minority and mass cultures and an exaggerated power given to money as a means of securing outcomes. We have to ask, why these particular outcomes? Political agendas are always in play. As Williams writes: 'The moment of any new technology is a moment of choice' (140). Thus, the new cable television could in fact be a public service; it is not a foregone conclusion that it will be developed and financed with private capital, as it has been. The new forms of television open up possibilities for independent film and video makers. More channels need not mean, to quote the Bruce Springsteen song, '57 channels and nothing on . . .'. Williams saw clearly the merit of the coming together of public and private in the world of television and that the BBC monopoly needed to be set alongside a more direct channel with a wider input and variety of ideas than those coming from the programme controllers of the extant channels.

Williams linked this optimistic view to the importance of information within civil society and the ways in which the variety of media forms can be used to strengthen the voluntary sector and thereby civic culture, alongside the educative role of television and radio already explored by the Open University. The potential and the need for information flows and new forms of expression to strengthen democracy was vital to the extension of democratic modes and the support and encouragement of diversity. Because these technologies are vital and vibrant this is no time to leave their control, uses and extension to simple technologically determinist arguments or cultural pessimism. The issues need to be confronted and a discussion on the availability, control and extension of these technologies needs to begin. Williams would find much of interest in the debates that have surrounded the Broadcasting Bill and the moves away from BBC monopoly towards an extension of diversity in the provision of television, while the world of Sky would have presented some of the difficulties to which Williams alludes.

'Class, politics and socialism', the third chapter in the re-consideration of *The Long Revolution*, returns to the issues that surround the Labour Party, socialism and the working class. Williams is very clear that despite the acknowledged shifts in the composition of the working class a socialist impulse was not generalised, and that instead of looking for the reasons for the shift away from Labour since 1951 we need to consider the implications of Labour's attempt to build a broad-based, radical party. As he suggests, the two-party system has always polarised a multiplicity of political views that have not gone away but were, between 1918 and 1951, more closely tied to class than is presently the case. Thus, to try to unravel the electoral failure of the Labour Party in relation to a specific shift within a small time-scale is to misunderstand the long-time ambiguities of Labour support. In 1993, following another Labour defeat, it is a timely reminder and a very sobering account of the onward march of Labour halted. The focus has by now shifted away from the unitary view of the working class and the working class as subject. The introduction of both 'race' and gender have provided axes of fractionalisation within the working classes and encouraged a multiple account which increases with complexity as regionalism, age, work experience, or the lack of it, come to be part of the sustained attempt to grapple with current notions of class. Williams suggests some of the problems as he turns to consider the very notion of class. He does this initially via the work of Erik Olin Wright,[3] who introduced the notion of contradictory class locations and then sought to show the extent of the contradictions empirically by including supervisory staff within the definition and those who were state sector workers. But, as Williams points out, while this may provide a class map it cannot provide a language for discussing the politics of the changing 'geography' of class. Rather, he suggests: '. . . the received definitions of class, as they bear on politics in the widest or simply in the electoral sense, have at best some general indicative value, of a complex kind, and at worst the effect of confusion and displacement . . .' (160).

Williams begins with what he considers to be the hardest question: what are the real relations between the labour movement and socialism? It is an immensely complex question, confused first by the notion of the labour 'movement', which grew from economic concerns, developed a political wing through the Labour Party, and has been living with the contradictions ever since. Equally, there are the problems surrounding the definition of 'interests' and in what ways the labour movement can be said to express national or general interests. Williams returns to the point that capitalism is 'inherently hostile to the general interest' (163). Although labour movement struggles are often organised around particularist interests there are moments when there is the possibility of particularist interests coming together for the general interest against capitalism and this is the moment of possibility for socialism. It is not a once and for all moment but one that is 'lost and found again' (163) over and over, one that requires development and nurturance. But the overriding problem, and Williams deems this a failure within society and the labour movement, is the lack of 'any accepted concept of the general interest' (165). Instead, we are offered the mystifying notion of the 'nation' or the 'needs' of the economy, which are, in fact, tied to particular interests.

The difficulty for the relationship between socialism and the labour movement is that both are tied to a collectivism organised around the identities of people, men and women, as workers. Yet it is clear that there is a multiplicity of forms of collective and communal practice that are beyond employment, kin relations, locality and ethnicity (somewhat neglected by Williams). At the same time, it is in precisely those communities where trade unionism and community relations come together, like the mining communities, that the radical impulse is strong. Williams is crucially aware that the moment for building socialism on the basis of the male (white) worker is past and that newer forms of organising located outside the production process are what mark the current period. He notes: 'All significant social movements of the last thirty years have started outside the organised class interests and institutions. The peace movement, the ecology movement, the women's movement, solidarity with the third world, human rights agencies, campaigns against poverty and homelessness, campaigns against cultural poverty and distortion: all have this character, that they sprang from needs and perceptions which the interest-based organisations had no room or time for, or which they had simply failed to notice' (172). Williams is equally clear that it is these movements that are '. . . our major positive resource' (173), for without them and a re-visioned socialist agenda 'socialism will be left stranded as a theory and a sect' (173). Williams could see what we have indeed witnessed, the break-up and decline of the old working-class communities and the incorporation of the labour movement. In fact, it has been swifter than expected due to restructuring, and it is the economic crisis and legislation which have increasingly sidelined the labour movement, rather than incorporation.

For Williams these are painful acknowledgements, felt more keenly as I write in a week when 30,000 miners have been declared redundant and the remnants of the mining industry scrapped in the face of a privatised electricity network that has 'dashed for gas'. Williams faced the issue and called for a re-visioned socialism able to articulate the collective impulse in new ways in relation to the new social movements, a politics he might have characterised as no longer of class in the old sense, but of caring, shared concerns that could be crafted into a general interest. It is especially interesting to consider this now with the eighties over and the suggestion that the nineties will usher in a more caring and gentle decade. The evidence so far seems to contradict this.

The Analysis Extended

The latter part of the analysis moves beyond a reconsideration of the *Long Revolution* debates, starting with what has become already a major preoccupation of the nineties, the nation and nationalism. Williams did not live to see the resurgence of nationalisms throughout Europe in the wake of the break up of the old Soviet empire, but the Scottish, Welsh and Irish challenges to the notion of a 'united kingdom' have a long history and were much in evidence as he wrote, alongside the last gasp of British jingoism and fervent nationalism which saw its expression in the Falklands War.

He begins with what we now see as among the defining features of postmodernity – hybridisation and the urbanscape in which elements of national cultures can be consumed, from food to music and fabrics, across the globe. While this is happening and diasporic populations re-create and embellish cultural forms throughout the world, there is, simultaneously, a resurgence of nationalism at just the moment when extant national identities are fractured. For Williams the contradictions of this are expressed in the call to universalisms and internationalisms which hold as many contradictions as the idea of the nation. Socialism has raised the proletariat to the status of a universal and yet people's lives are given texture by the local and the familiar. Thus, Williams puts on the agenda what we now characterise as the relationship between the global and the local. The nation-state is placed, historically, between the local and the global, using locale and heritage within an administrative framework generated and supported by the ruling class. For Williams 'the building of states, at whatever level, is intrinsically a ruling-class operation' (181). He points to the ways in which 'the family' and 'the nation' are seen to elide and notes that the sense of bonding and belonging is manufactured in relation to the nation, especially in times of war. The problem for radicals who have provided a critique of nationalism is that it is recast as an opposition to 'the nation' in the 'old' nation-states, whereas in opposition to colonialisms nationalism has been the major player in welding a revolutionary movement.

Against this, capitalism has overridden localities and has shown itself capable of forging together nationalistic and patriotic sentiments that assist capitalism over any specific population. Capitalism does not respect traditions or communities and, as is now so clearly apparent, operates on a global scale, moving not only finance and plant around the world, but peoples too. In the process ways of life are disrupted, community ties severed and the fate of areas decided. 'It is an outrage that this has happened and been allowed to happen' (187). The internationalisation of capital has produced a massive growth in consumption and the notion of the consumer as 'sovereign', but as an identity it is '. . . at best a radically reduced identity, at worst mean and greedy' (188). For Williams it is a form of consumption that he characterised as 'mobile privatisation', in which consumption within the market or the shopping mall is brought back home for private enhancement and pleasure, thus denuding conviviality, collectivity and the sense of the social. Yet he consistently recognises the importance of community and familial ties in providing a social world. The problem is that the world of the market and the world of the home or the community are juxtaposed and interpenetrated in ways organised by capitalism.

Given the ability of capitalism to organise a world system, Williams asks why we should bother with nation-states, and his answer relates to the importance of ordering the world into markets and ensuring, via the military and state apparatuses, that the system has a degree of stability. Thus, 'it is a conscious programme to regulate and contain what would otherwise be intolerable divisions and confusions' (192). Yet this regulation, the disciplining of populations, requires more than the power of state forces; it needs forms of legitimation and the generation of common bonds, whether real or imagined. Williams elaborates this in relation to the commonly held view of the British as 'this island race', with a linear history and a degree of homogeneity. This is maintained only by ignorance and, moreover, 'what is from time to time projected as an "island race" is in reality a long process of successive conquests and repressions but also of successive supersessions and relative integrations' (194). Britain has always been varied and diverse, even though attempts have been made to write out and suppress Irish, Welsh and Scottish identities made more complex by the settled Jewish, South Asian, African and Caribbean populations. Williams berates the upper class for their powerful fiction of 'the true-born Englishman' and the imperial 'British' who have hegemonised the discussion of identities. For Williams, racism, though ever-present and virulent, cannot tell the whole story of the complexities posed by Britain and its relations with the world. It is not enough to say that black people are British, because 'to reduce social identity to formal legal definitions, at the level of the state, is to collude with the alienated superficialities of "the nation" which are limited functional terms of the modern ruling class'. But the counter from socialists is often couched in universalistic terms, which also carries problems for Williams, who cites his own background as an important part of his view of social identities as 'lived relations', what he terms the 'practical formation of social identity', whether derived from the now disappearing settled communities or being re-forged within conditions of dislocation and displacement. He sees in these attempts to build community a real hope that is tied to the desire for greater devolution and a fracturing of the market-led notion of identity tied to consumption. The regional and the local offer 'real' places and spaces in which to exercise power and develop a sense of the social, giving rise to diversities which contribute to what Williams calls 'variable societies'. Socialism, too, has to be multiple and alive to the possibilities of diversity, generating a 'variable socialism'. 'We have to begin again with people and build new political forms' (199). In so many senses the discussion offered by Williams presents, in my reading of his text, a critique of the universalisms of the Enlightenment project and a re-visioned socialism in which difference is highlighted and the politics of identities, as we now know it, is foregrounded. But, in other ways, Williams remains tied to a populist vision of 'the people' and, of course, to community as the mainstay of the socialist vision.

Williams's narrative moves back to the world stage and deconstructs the categories, generated in the West, by which the world has come to be known – East/West, North/South – arguing, especially in relation to the South, that the homogenisation present in these terms is inappropriate and ideological due to the diverse economies that are subsumed within this category. The response from the West is to use aid in relation to development models generated and sustained in the West, but this does little to counter the unequal terms of trade which are the mainstay of North/South relations. This is tied to a conception of the world, including the peoples of the world, as consumable resources to be used in the interests of 'growth'. It is a vision of the world which needs radical change in the light of both socialist and ecological arguments that make clear the damage inflicted by capitalist exploitation. Williams emphasises that the most far-reaching changes are required in the 'old' economies: '. . . not only in major shifts towards conservation . . . but also in their deep assumption that the rest of the world is an effectively vacant lot from which they extract raw materials' (216).

Williams calls for a radical revision of the socialist agenda to overcome the East/West, North/South opposition and to offer a future to the world as a whole. But he acknowledges the difficulties of this and the importance of the struggle within the West to shift the agenda. He did not live to see the movements for democracy in the 'East', nor the break-up of the old Soviet empire and the speed with which capitalist values were imported, encouraged by a new version of aid in the form of banking and market expertise. The instability generated by the Cold War has been overtaken by a new world 'disorder' in which economic chaos and nationalistic militancy are the main players.

The instability of the world and the threat of war, as he saw it at the beginning of the eighties, is addressed in the penultimate chapter of *Towards 2000*. It is not just that wars have marked human existence; the modern era has 'industrialised' war and produced weapons of annihilation not seen before. The nuclear programme, Williams emphasises, is the apex of the military-industrial complex but it is not the only war machine. Wars and stock-piling of conventional weapons also mark states around the world not in the superpower league. The Orwellian nightmare of three super-states locked in a permanent war needs to be tempered by the importance of 'secondary' states on the political map. Equally, the armaments race also includes problems for the military-industrial complex. The cost is enormous and the contradictions between the political leaders and the military are evident. However, the problems serve to heighten the seriousness of the issue and it is a crucial area for struggle, especially at the time Williams was writing, in relation to a Europe conceived within the miliary map as a 'theatre of war' in relation to limited nuclear capabilities. Williams would have cheered the end of the Cold War and the removal of Cruise missiles from Greenham and he would have been heartened by the popular support, especially among young people in Europe, for the peace campaign. But he could not easily have seen the world as a safer place for the end of the East/West divide. The ferocity of the nationalist wars which have erupted in the new Europe shows clearly that Europe is indeed a 'theatre of war' and that the culture and politics of violence pre-dates and survives the Cold War.

Resources for a Journey of Hope

Williams wishes to plot futures, in relation to resources rather than strategies,[4] as an antidote to what he sees as the growing importance of 'the new hard line on the future: a new politics of strategic advantage' (243). The concern here is with rational planning by a minority bound to specific interests within conditions of deepening crises. The politics of this moment Williams calls 'Plan X politics', in which technicism, efficiency and rationality are key players and in which the well-being of the majority is not necessarily a priority. Instead, this is a politics, deeply pessimistic, which is '. . . sharp politics and high-risk politics. It is easily presented as a version of masculinity. Plan X is a mode of assessing odds and of determining a game plan' (246).

   Contrary to this version of the future and its control is the lived politics of the new social movements and the growing impact of professional knowledge in relation to ecology. These are, as yet, separate spheres but they have come together within the peace movement and the green movement. This does generate a new politics as, similarly, the feminist movement has done, but both are often operating at the local level in diverse settings and via a wide range of groups. The danger is that this politics and those active within it will give up on extant institutions and other cultural forms which, argues Williams, are also in the process of change and flux. Thus, while it has been the case that in looking to the political parties the new social movements have had enormous problems of legitimacy or incorporation, 'it need not stay like this' (251) argues Williams. However, it requires not simply argument but a direct challenge to the extant institutions of social and political life. It has to go further than putting the issues on the agenda or marking them out for election periods. To some extent this is precisely what the feminist and anti-racist struggles of the eighties did, finding more sympathy and support within local government than at Westminster. What began as a challenge was, however, incorporated within state strategies in relation to equal opportunities, multi-culturalism and some anti-racist work. The best expression of this, with all its faults, was the GLC, abolished, of course, along with the Inner London Education Authority.

For Williams the place to begin is with the economy, for while there is a real mobilisation around the ecological, peace and feminist issues the underlying relations of production and exchange remain, giving rise to high levels of unemployment, crisis-ridden infrastructure and threats to workers. For it is workers who already carry the marks of the ecological crisis and of sexism and, I would wish to emphasise, racism. Williams outlines a minimalist way forward in relation to economic and international issues, the move beyond a market economy, ecologically-based production, and new forms of monetary institutions. To develop these new forms the trade unions have to come into play but in ways that take account of new constituencies and the changes underway in all the industrial economies. There needs to be an alliance between trade unions and professional expertise and a move beyond industry-based organising.

Williams is clear that however tempting it might be to look backwards it is no answer to what have to be profound changes, in both the forces and relations of production. Change must begin with the annexation of the view of the natural world and people as raw materials, which, he argues, is more pernicious now than ever before because it has entered the psyche and relationships. Williams uses the critique from feminisms of women treated as sex objects to make the point that at the deepest level individuals are turned into raw materials for work and for pleasure. Equally, there is some important intellectual work to be done, especially around the concept of 'mode of production' which has guided Marxist analysis and proved crucial to the development of a critique of capitalism. And yet its time is up, because it adheres too closely to an emphasis on production itself rather than its effects on the habitat and on people and social relations. Thus Williams argues for a new orientation away from 'raw materials' and production and towards 'livelihood', 'the direct and practical ways of life' (267). And Williams underlines this view by suggesting that it coincides with the major shifts in the world economies. These shifts signal a period of retrenchment and hard times following the prosperity of the post-war era. 'It is reasonable to see many dangers in the years towards 2000, but it is also reasonable to see many grounds for hope' (267). Given the bewildering and difficult times of the eighties, Williams insists on the capacities for change within everyday lives and everyday people. The first step is to believe that nothing is inevitable, which returns us to Plan X politics. 'Once the inevitabilities are challenged, we begin gathering our resources for a journey of hope' (268). To read Williams now, in 1993, when the difficulties of the eighties have deepened and the bewilderment amplified is, indeed, cheering. It is a reminder of struggles past and present and of a deep conviction that we are not powerless but that collectivity is empowering and is the first weapon. There is no simple programme or slogan on offer but the book is underscored by a vision of a better world fuelled by hope located with active, critical people and communities. Williams's call to critique, echoed by Bauman, is crucial to the nineties, already denuded by the pacifications and authoritarianism of the eighties. *Towards 2000* brings together familiar themes from Williams's writings, with a politics, by this stage of his life, deeply but not uncritically rooted in Marxism, committed to the extension of democratic forms as the bedrock of the socialist project. Williams, although his mode of address often belied it, displaying the ongoing tension between his Leavisite and Marxist impulses, had a deeply populist impulse expressed in his references to the people and community and this was rooted in his life-experience and his own biography. As Eagleton[5] suggests he lived the personal as the political long before it became a central premise of feminist politics. But he was not unaware of the fractures within these 'imagined communities' of 'the people' and 'community'.

In terms of practical politics Williams supported the move into Europe, suggesting that it offered the possibility of new alliances, although he was acutely aware that 'we will still need a proper left movement in the heartland of England'.[6] The interviews with *New Left Review*, from which this comment comes, also articulate support for proportional representation and a reiteration of the view that within the prevailing crises that will mark the eighties: 'the objective conditions are now increasing for the Left to break out of its marginal situation in England'.[7] Well, it did not happen, but it is indicative of the optimism of Williams that he suggested it might. The interviews, the most accessible Raymond Williams, show us not only Williams the scholar, the polemic alert to critique and questioning, but the Williams of politics and the heart more usually hidden in the presentation of the austere don, or so he seemed to me. Instead, Williams expresses his anger at the waste and objectification of people within capitalism and the anger is located with his hope and faith in ordinary lives and their creative capacity. It might be called a romance – the romance of populism, community and cultures gone before, but we all tell ourselves stories, narratives to get by on, to dream on and act on, and Williams's great romance is worth telling and telling again. The resonances with popular adult education will be clear. It is a practice built on faith, hope and too often the charity of the activists. But it is not only this that makes Williams a key figure for adult educators; it is his insistence on the maintenance of a critical edge and academic rigour as sources of empowerment.

Williams, a major left intellectual and key contributor to left politics and scholarship,[8] sought community and sharing from a position where he always carried a sense of discomfort. From Border Country to Cambridge, intellectually and, it would seem, emotionally he felt the marginalisation of the left and left culture more keenly in relation to his own biography. How, one hopes, he would have been cheered by the current emphasis upon the dissolution between the opposition of centre and periphery or margin.

Williams certainly grasped the significance of the new social movements and what this meant for the socialist agenda and he was conscious of the changing landscape of British lives in relation to racism and diasporic politics but he did not place this centre-stage in the way that we are now able to do. Equally, he would have had some sympathy with Bauman's view: 'We, the residents of the postmodern habitat, live in a territory that admits of no clear options and no strategies that can ever be imagined to be uncontroversially correct. We are better aware that ever before just how slippery are all the roads once pursued with single-minded determination.'[9]

Williams prefigures this in *Towards 2000*, offering forward glimpses of the current debates surrounding the politics of identities, issues around consumption and citizenship, socialism and democracy and the bifurcation of individuality and collectivity. It is a terrain that is central to the politics of adult education and in which the work of Williams is foregrounded. For many of us it is part of the 'resources for a journey of hope' that constitute one part of the route towards 2000.

Notes and References

1. Z. Bauman, *Intimations of Postmodernity*, Routledge, 1992.
2. R. Williams, *Towards 2000*, Chatto and Windus, 1983, to which page numbers in the text refer.
3. E. Olin Wright, *Class, Crisis and the State*, New Left Books, 1978.
4. F. Mulhern, 'Towards 2000', *New Left Review*, 148, 1986.
5. T. Eagleton, 'The resources of hope', *New Left Review*, 168, 1988.
6. R. Williams, *Politics and Letters: Interviews with New Left Review*, New Left Books, 1979.
7. *ibid.*, p 383.
8. R. Blackburn, 'Williams and the New Left', *New Left Review*, 168, 1988. See also Eagleton, *op. cit.*
9. Bauman, *op. cit.*, p 185.

Index

Page numbers in italic type refer to notes to the text; page numbers in bold type indicate authorship.

Thouless, R.H.   176, 183, 296
Tikhonov, N.   42
Tillyard, E.M.   12, *24*
Toller, Ernst   187
Townsend, Peter   130
Toynbee, P.   78
Trollope, A.   148

Universities Council for Adult
 Education   285
'Unwin and Stevens' *see* Stevens, G.

Valery, Paul   187
Virgil   187

Wain, J.   107
Walter, John   86–7
Warner, Rex   50, 266
Wells, H.G.   79
Werth, Alexander   47
Wesker, Arnold   130, 302
Wesley, John   217
West, Alick   266
Westwood, Sallie   268; 'Introduction'
 1–2; 'Excavating the Future:
 Towards 2000'   324–36
Williams, Joy   11–12
Williams, J.R.   Review of *Drama
 from Ibsen to Eliot* 193–5; 293
Williams, Raymond   *Context*, adult
 education after the Second World
 War, 3–7, and the working class,
 13–17; intellectual influences, 7–13,
 conditions of intellectual production,
 280–7; RW in adult education,
 269–79; as a teacher, 287–97,
 297–300; achievements, 300–8;
 moving on, 308–14; RW today
 17–19, 314–15; *Towards 2000*,
 324–36

Works noted
Border Country, 269, 271, 301, 306
Communications, 19, 265, 275, 285,
 296, 306, 309
The Critic (ed.), 1, 26–8, 33, 38–40,
 277–8
Culture and Society, 1, 3, 4, 5, 9,
 12, 13, 18, 19, 28, 29, 98, 111,
 129, 133, 203, 204, 252, 265,
 266, 269, 274, 282, 285, 286,
 290, 294, 300, 301, 302, 303,
 304–5, 306, 307, 308, 309, 312

Drama from Ibsen to Eliot, 10;
 reviewed 193–5; Correspondence
 196–8; 292–4
Drama in Performance, 3, 4, 11,
 191
Keywords, 5, 203, 204, 269, 310
The Long Revolution, 1, 3, 9, 10,
 19, 29, 265, 267, 269, 282, 285,
 290, 294, 300, 303, 305–6, 307,
 308, 324, 326, 328, 330
Loyalties, 267
Marxism and Literature, 3, 266, 294
People of the Black Mountains, 268
Politics and Letters (ed.), 1, 8, 26–8,
 31–3, 34–7, 38, 40, **41–53, 54–6,**
 178, 250–4, 265, 277–8
Preface to Film, 10, 295
Reading and Criticism, 1, 3, 7,
 152–8, 159–65, 175, 183, 193,
 275, 289, 292, 296, 300
Second Generation, 269, 301,
 306–7, 310
Towards 2000, 2, 267, 324–36
The Volunteers, 269

Extracts from RW's writing
 on concerns, 26–131; on teaching
 and learning, 132–202; on adult
 education, 203–64
Sources other than above:
Adult Education, **143–5, 226–32**
Conviction, **89–102**
Critical Quarterly, **103–5**
Essays in Criticism, **56–7, 78–83,**
 106–10
The Guardian, **233–4, 237, 242–6**
The Highway, **84–8, 121–6, 181–4,**
 207–10, 211–14, 215–17
The Listener, **247–9**
New Left Review, **111–20, 250–4**
The New Statesman, **218–21, 235–6**
Partisan Review, **127–31**
Rewley House Papers, **146–51,**
 166–73, 185–92
Tribune, **238–41**
The Tutors' Bulletin, **196–7**
The Use of English, **174–80**

Wilson, Colin   5, 28; review of *The
 Outsider* 78–83
Wilson, Harold   55, 314
Winkler, R.O.   27, 29, 33
Winnington, R.   177
Wisdom, John   33